AF352577

AFFECTIVE GEOGRAPHIES

Cervantes, Emotion, and the Literary Mediterranean

Affective Geographies

Cervantes, Emotion, and the Literary Mediterranean

PAUL MICHAEL JOHNSON

UNIVERSITY OF TORONTO PRESS
Toronto Buffalo London

ISBN 978-1-4875-0751-0 (cloth)   ISBN 978-1-4875-3640-4 (EPUB)
                                 ISBN 978-1-4875-3639-8 (PDF)

Toronto Iberic

Library and Archives Canada Cataloguing in Publication

Title: Affective geographies : Cervantes, emotion, and the literary
    Mediterranean / Paul Michael Johnson.
Names: Johnson, Paul Michael, 1982– author.
Series: Toronto Iberic ; 55.
Description: Series statement: Toronto Iberic ; 55 | Includes bibliographical
    references and index.
Identifiers: Canadiana (print) 20200311077 | Canadiana (ebook) 20200311107 |
    ISBN 9781487507510 (cloth) | ISBN 9781487536404 (EPUB) |
    ISBN 9781487536398 (PDF)
Subjects: LCSH: Cervantes Saavedra, Miguel de, 1547–1616 – Criticism and
    interpretation. | LCSH: Emotions in literature. | LCSH: Mediterranean
    Region – In literature.
Classification: LCC PQ6358.M42 J64 2020 | DDC 863/.3–dc23

University of Toronto Press acknowledges the financial assistance to its
publishing program of the Canada Council for the Arts and the Ontario Arts
Council, an agency of the Government of Ontario.

To my family, who taught me about passion

Remember, Paul, it is passion that makes the world go round. [...] In the absence of passion the world would still be void and without form. Think of Don Quixote. Don Quixote is not about a man sitting in a rocking chair bemoaning the dullness of La Mancha. It is about a man who claps a basin on his head and clambers onto the back of his faithful old plough-horse and sallies forth to do great deeds.

J.M. Coetzee, *Slow Man*

Contents

Part Three: Other Ports of Call

Illustrations

Acknowledgments

The gulf between reason and emotion is not always as vast as conventional wisdom would have it. For Cervantes, as this book sets out to show, the two often go hand in hand. Its writing would likewise have been impossible without both the intellectual and the moral support, the simultaneously academic and affective sustenance with which a great many people have furnished me over the last several years. Early on, Luis Avilés modelled how to combine critical theory with rigorous, text-centred interpretation and provided steady, yet never heavy-handed, guidance on the ideas out of which this book has grown. Since then he has continued to be an unwavering mentor, sympathetic interlocutor, and dear friend. I owe a similar debt to Steve Hutchinson and Santiago Morales-Rivera, who have served not only as exemplars of discerning scholarship but as incredibly generous champions of my work. My good fortune in knowing Steve is such that I cannot imagine my career in early modern Spanish literature and *cervantismo*, nor the fields at large, without his care, critical vision, and the characteristic grace with which he leavens the sophistication of his work with mirth and levity. I also wish to acknowledge at the outset Diana de Armas Wilson and María Antonia Garcés, whose affection and kind-hearted devotion to my success have been an unexpected and humbling windfall of my early career. The privilege of being their travel companion and co-panelist at several conferences – from Colombia and Malta to Colorado and California – has allowed me not only to rehearse parts of the book and learn from their immense erudition but to make memories I will forever cherish.

This book has profited from a veritable sea of expert advice. Deserving of special mention are Susan Byrne and Michael Armstrong-Roche, who showed the utmost generosity by reading and commenting on a draft of the manuscript in its entirety. While any and all errors and infelicities remain my own, the final product is better thanks to their scrupulous feedback. I would also like to recognize Adrienne Martín and Cory Reed for their charitable and constructive scrutiny of parts of my work. Numerous other scholars have graciously offered their expertise and been extraordinarily supportive of my project, in some cases long before it had coalesced into something deserving of the name. Among them I thank Jim Amelang for his selfless goodwill, hospitality, and historical acumen; Mercedes Alcalá-Galán and her infectious élan for literature and for *Persiles y Sigismunda* in particular; Manuel Piqueras and Blanca Santos for their enduring warmth, friendship, and philological insights; Sanda Munjic for sharing her knowledge of early modern emotion early on; and Sonia Velázquez for her neighbourly spirit and theoretical prowess. Many of the revelations I had for this book would not have struck me were it not for the opportunity to pursue various other projects alongside it. For this I thank Mercedes García-Arenal, Barbara Fuchs, Fernando Rodríguez Mediano, Ignacio Panizo, and George Peale.

Many other scholars in the field offered me worthy insights, seasoned advice, encouragement, or amiable encounters that served as welcome interludes to the largely solitary labour of writing. These include Antonio Barnés, Ted Bergman, John Beusterien, Hall Bjørnstad, David Boruchoff, Brian Brewer, Elena Carrera, Bill Clamurro, Eli Cohen, Marsha Collins, Randi Lise Davenport, Fred de Armas, Julia Domínguez, Esther Fernández, Charles Ganelin, Gaspar Garrote, David González Ramírez, Or Hasson, Ivette Hernández-Torres, Daniel Hershenzon, Stephen Hessel, Jesús David Jerez-Gómez, Nick Jones, Ana Laguna, Ignacio López Alemany, José Manuel Lucía Megías, Carolyn Nadeau, Ignacio Navarrete, Eduardo Olid Guerrero, Ángel Pérez Martínez, Mary Quinn, Adrián Sáez, Rachel Schmidt, Ryan Schmitz, Víctor Sierra Matute, Felipe Valencia, and Sherry Velasco. I gratefully acknowledge the suggestions offered by the anonymous readers of the manuscript, as well as the editorial board and editors at University of Toronto Press. Special thanks are due to Barbara Porter and Angela Wingfield for their diligence and painstaking attention to detail, and to Suzanne Rancourt for the enthusiasm, efficiency, and professionalism with which she shepherded the manuscript through to the final product. I am also grateful for the incisive questions I received from the attendees at various conferences and speaking engagements, as well as for the many other individuals who, though I may have failed to name them here, have made a worthwhile impact on the pages that follow.

Closer to home, I express my sincere gratitude for those faculty and staff colleagues at DePauw University who, though too numerous to list them all here, helped to foster a convivial, mutually sustaining, and intellectually stimulating community. I would especially like to thank CJ Gomolka, who not only offered feedback on parts of the manuscript but, as a fellow junior colleague and friend, has been a perpetual source of comfort and release, commiseration and motivation, particularly when it felt like I was tacking into the wind. Support and assistance of various other kinds came from Tamara Beauboeuf, Dave Berque, Istvan Csicsery-Ronay, Angela Flury, Anne Harris, Matt Hertenstein, Carrie Klaus, Glen Kuecker, María Luque, Heidi Albin Menzel, Sherry Mou, Keith Nightenhelser, and Alex Puga. The trust and corresponding leeway bestowed on me by the Department of Modern Languages and the World Literature Program to schedule and develop my courses opened windows of both inspiration and time to advance my writing. My students also deserve credit for sharing their insightful observations and for challenging me to render accessible my scholarship and to link Cervantes, the classroom, and contemporary concerns. Melinda Franke, a former research assistant and future colleague, merits unique mention in this regard.

Various forms of institutional support, at home and abroad, were instrumental in bringing this project to fruition. Long stints at the Biblioteca Nacional de España, the Archivo Histórico Nacional, and the Biblioteca d'Humanitats "Joan Reglà" at the Universitat de València were made possible by the Fulbright Program and a pre-sabbatical leave. I thank the many staff members who cordially helped me to navigate the collections of these institutions. DePauw's Fisher Course Reassignment afforded me additional time away from teaching to forge ahead in my research and revisions, and the robust faculty and professional development funds from the Office of Academic Affairs underwrote extensive conference travel and offset other costs associated with this book. Beth Wilkerson, geographic information systems specialist at DePauw, patiently worked with me to produce the Mediterranean map featured in the book. The images reproduced here appear courtesy of the Vatican Library, the Biblioteca Nacional de España, the Real Academia de Bellas Artes de San Fernando, the Archivo General de Simancas, the Metropolitan Museum of New York, and the Cervantes Project at Texas A&M University, directed by Eduardo Urbina, to whom I am most grateful for the ongoing support. Portions of chapters 3 and 6 appeared previously in the journal *eHumanista*, and I thank the editor, Antonio Cortijo Ocaña, for permission to reproduce them here. A special note of appreciation is due to Javier Moscoso at the Spanish National Research Council and other members of Historia y filosofía de la experiencia (HIST-EX), who kindly welcomed me into their interdisciplinary research group, sponsored by Spain's Ministerio de Ciencia e Innovación (FFI2016-78285-R).

Inspiration of a less tangible though no less vital sort has come from multiple shores. Since graduate school Sam Jaffee has been an anchor of pedagogical, conversational, and gastronomic camaraderie, as well as a font of unparalleled wit. Pete Molfese has been a trusty mainstay, the friend I could call with any problem whatsoever, and I am also grateful for the fraternal constancy of Yusaku Kawai and Dan Reck. I will always treasure the foundational lessons on Spanish that Barbara Siegfried inculcated in me at Clinton Central, as well as the persistent care, communion, and Catalan culinary nourishment that Gloria Coral offered me in Horta. The ongoing tutelage of Linda Elman, a true Golden Age lodestar, and Art Evans, a confrere extraordinaire and *conseiller sans pareil*, has redounded much to my benefit. At Middlebury College in Spain, Paco Layna, an endless source of wisdom and liberality, awakened my love for *Don Quijote* and encouraged me to edge forward in my studies. And the late Bob Hershberger, quixotic in the absolute best sense of the term, led a life of plenitude in service to others and led me to discover my own calling. As my professor, mentor, colleague, and friend, he showed me the ropes of the profession while urging me with calm assurance to chart my own course. To paraphrase Machado, one of Bob's favourite poets, and because as a watersports enthusiast he was amenable to nautical metaphor, he taught me that "there is no road, only a ship's wake on the sea." In his absence, I find solace in knowing his wake is still visible in every page of this book.

Finally, I want to recognize the loving, steadfast, and unconditional backing I have received from four generations of family, without which I would not know how to steer, let alone stay the course. As my first mate and first reader, Sujung has nurtured me and this project in manifold and inexpressible ways. She has been the wind in my sails, and now so is our beloved daughter, Reina. With my deepest admiration and affection I dedicate this book to them; the Kim family in Korea; my nephews, Ethan and Eli; my sister, Addy; my parents, Lee and Kathy; and my grandparents, Clair, Phyllis, Chuck, and Audrey.

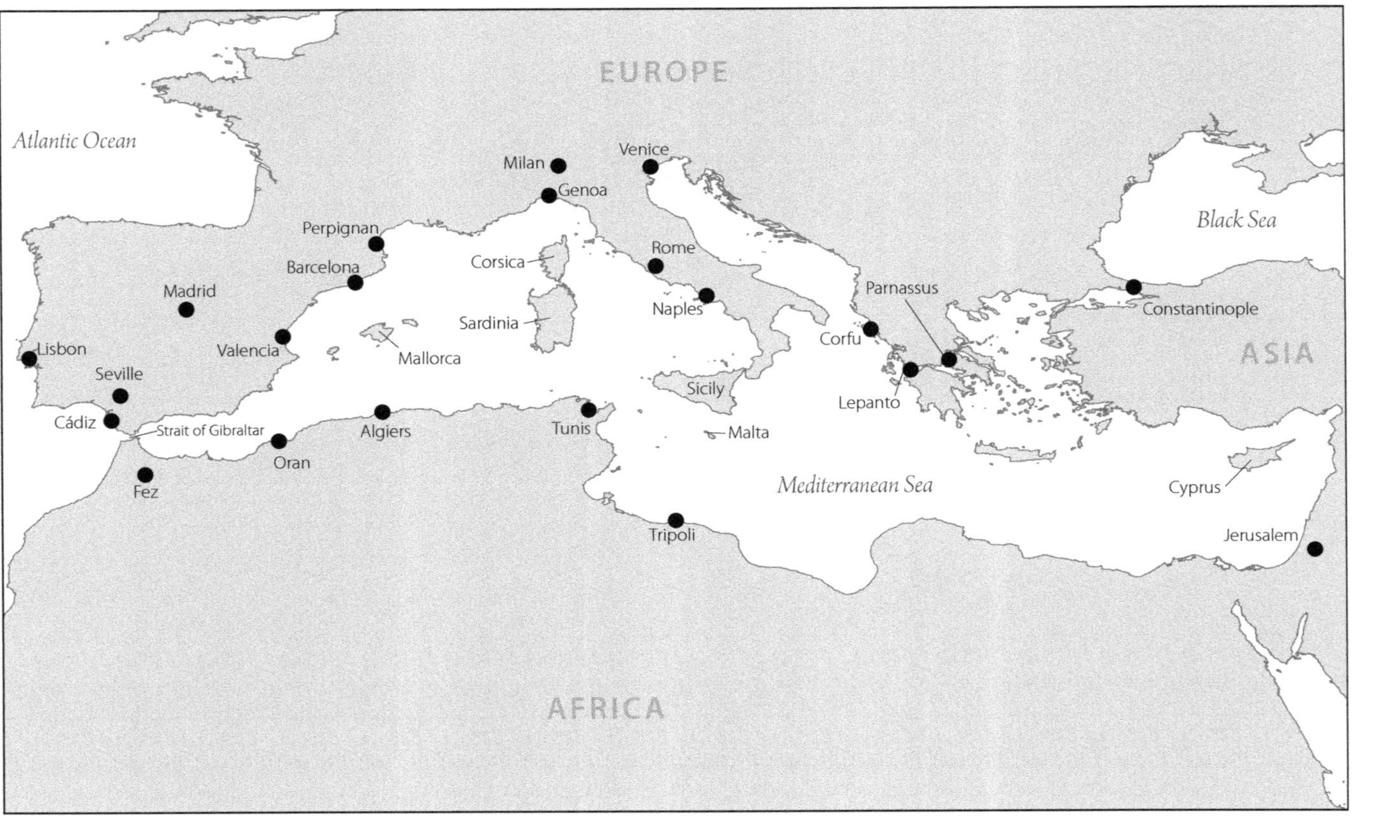

Cervantes's Mediterranean

[I]f he had concerned himself only with my thoughts, my sighs, my tears, my virtuous desires and my brave deeds, [my historian] could have had a volume larger than, or just as large as, the collected works of El Tostado.

[E]n sólo manifestar mis pensamientos, mis sospiros, mis lágrimas, mis buenos deseos y mis acometimientos [mi historiador] pudiera hacer un volumen mayor, o tan grande que el que pueden hacer todas las obras del Tostado.

Don Quijote, *Don Quijote*

[T]ears filled my eyes, and I began to lament, and if the author of our history didn't put that in, you can be sure he left out something good.

[A]cudiéronme lágrimas a los ojos y hice una lamentación, que si no la puso el autor de nuestra historia, puede hacer cuenta que no puso cosa buena.

Sancho, *Don Quijote*

The pen will go dry if I continue with my emotions.

Abdallah bin Aisha, early modern Mediterranean traveller

PART ONE

Casting Off

Chapter One

Introduction

The Mediterranean is not merely history.
The Mediterranean is not merely geography.

Predrag Matvejević

Miguel de Cervantes opens his *Ocho comedias y ocho entremeses nuevos, nunca representados* (Eight comedies and eight new interludes, never before performed) of the year 1615 with a bold assertion. After alerting the reader in a kind of self-conscious *captatio benevolentiae* to his imminent audacity – "here begins my leaving the limits of modesty" (aquí entra el salir yo de los límites de mi llaneza) – he declares that he "was the first to represent the hidden thoughts and feelings of the soul" (fui el primero que representase las imaginaciones y los pensamientos escondidos del alma) on the stage.[1] Mobilizing a metaphor of interiority and invisibility, his prologue performs the feat he claims to have accomplished in his drama: by departing from the restrictions of self-imposed decorum, Cervantes shows how his theatrical works departed from the restrictions of aesthetic convention to make visible what had hitherto remained hidden. In other words, it is only by revealing the truth of his internal thoughts and feelings that the author is able to reveal to the reader an analogous truth about his art. As in the manner of actors stepping onto and exiting the stage, such a performative act implies the simultaneous necessity of entering and leaving ("entra el salir") – entering a public space where one is subject to external scrutiny, while leaving an internal space of private subjectivity. These movements from soul to stage likewise suggest the crossing and transgressing of borders, not just those of early modern dramatic traditions such as the schism of plot or action versus morality or conceptualism, but also the frontiers between body and soul or soul and mind, and especially those that have more generally governed the distinction between thoughts and feelings or reason and emotion ("the hidden thoughts and feelings of the soul").

This book is impelled by similar movements and border crossings, namely those that engage Cervantes's texts through two principal itineraries. First, in the context of what Fernand Braudel called the Mediterranean "world," or an expansive maritime perspective in which, beyond regional, national, and ideological boundaries, the Mediterranean Sea may be regarded not as yet another barrier but as an analytical point of departure or *medium* for exploring issues of difference and interconnectedness. Second, the book ventures to read Cervantes through the lens of affectivity, or the diverse forms of emotional expression through which early modern individuals sought to communicate, represent, and make sense of the Mediterranean experience. Emotion and the Sea do not constitute merely topical approaches to be considered in isolation, however, nor is their relationship to one another and to Cervantes's works thematically arbitrary. As the examples in the following pages underscore, they are mutually germane, even interdependent. For Cervantes, to represent a Mediterranean experience is to speak always already of an affective experience.

Most large-scale approaches to the Mediterranean, in contrast, have hinged on geography, climate, or economics as the organizing principle of the region. From Braudel's famous *La Méditerranée et le monde méditerranéen à l'époque de Philippe II* (1949) to Peregrine Horden and Nicholas Purcell's *The Corrupting Sea* (2000), a privileging of geologic time has often dominated at the expense of the human experience of the individual, to say nothing of individual emotional expression. Essential though their impact has been, such paradigms tend to consign literature and other forms of cultural production to the austerity of the economic machine, to the inexorable geographical logics of the longue durée.[2] The recently renewed interest in the interdisciplinary field of Mediterranean Studies underlines the urgent need to account for the place of these forms in the Mediterranean experience,[3] for fictional, musical, and visual works of art not only articulated the affective experience of Mediterranean life and informed the popular conceptions of the region in the early modern imaginary but also powerfully condition the concept and connotations of "Mediterranean" held today. *Affective Geographies* takes as its point of departure the premise that literature, in particular, may be as influential in constructing the Mediterranean as are its geomorphological, climatic, or economic features. As the writer with what is likely the most extensive Mediterranean experience of his era – whether by choice or by force – Cervantes is exceptionally well suited for the critical task of recovering the literary Mediterranean.

The following chapters will therefore consider Cervantes's texts through and alongside the affective structures that inscribe the Mediterranean as a space of conflict, commerce, expansion, and empire. In this schema, emotion itself becomes a medium of exchange, a kind of common currency or lingua franca whose circulation offers subjective and political possibilities outside the normative contours of this space. As a literary device that to a large degree resists conventional mimetic representation, affect is particularly agile at calling forth and reconfiguring the political structures of what Braudel called the Mediterranean "world economy."[4] Mediterranean individuals are not simply *Homo economicus*, instruments of mercantile exchange in this economy, but, as Cervantes reminds us, they inhabit what human geographers have called "felt worlds."[5] We might say that Cervantes's works are traversed by an *affective economy*, one that casts emotions as an alternative commodity to be constantly shared, circulated, plundered, recovered, and revalued. Cervantes's writing thus becomes a fertile "geopoetic" locus for mediating between the macro (Mediterranean framework) and the micro (emotional subjectivity), realms that have traditionally remained sequestered and even antithetical. That such a convergence emerges in literature prompts a vital set of queries: What would it mean to be a Mediterranean author? How might one delineate the contours of a specifically literary Mediterranean, and how would they transpose or realign those drawn by predominantly historical modes? And, most importantly, what potential purchase, to echo Braudel, could a Mediterranean world literature proffer to Cervantes, early modern Hispanism, and beyond?

"When I think of the individual," Braudel famously mused, "I am always inclined to see him imprisoned within a destiny in which he himself has little hand, fixed in a landscape in which the infinite perspectives of the long term stretch into the distance both behind him and before."[6] To focus on a single author, as the present study does, is not to suggest that Cervantes alone holds the key to answering the questions just posed. It is instead an attempt to theorize a literary Mediterranean from the bottom up and thus to problematize the Braudelian model in at least two principal ways. First, by studying modes in which the microliterary informs, reflects, and refracts the macrohistorical landscape, this monograph juxtaposes by design the individual and the collective. On the one hand, emotions stand as one of the most individual phenomena imaginable, a fact demonstrated by their conventional dismissal in literary studies as "fallacious" and overly "subjective." On the other hand, they can transcend the individual and internal realm to become a source of group unity or division, of emotional transmission or contagion, or of strategies of othering, in which differential structures of power are brought to bear on a collective psyche. A focus on the micro level of emotions allows one to attend not only to the individual but also to *individual difference*: to the emotional bodies at once most affected and neglected by sweeping stereotypical – and, at times, historiographical – generalizations. Paradigmatically, as an individual author Cervantes furnishes insights into this dialectic that might otherwise recede in the universalizing pretensions of a study about a collective group of Mediterranean writers.

Second, by grounding its analysis in Cervantes, *Affective Geographies* intends to stake a claim for literature's own longue durée. Harold Bloom aptly deploys a nautical metaphor to assert that *Don Quijote* "contains within itself all the novels that have followed in its sublime wake."[7] Similarly, as "the man who invented fiction," as William Egginton describes him in his recent book of the same name, Cervantes has exercised an immense and enduring influence on writers ever since. Egginton goes on to affirm that Cervantes, as "a keystone of Western intellectual culture," "influenced thinkers whose writings would later lay the foundations for developments in politics, economics, and science."[8] In addition to their impact on the literary field itself, then, Cervantes's works boast more than a four-hundred-year history of affecting the hearts and minds of readers, of shaping what Derek Attridge calls an "idioculture," or the wide body of cultural codes at the disposal of an individual human subject.[9] By exploring how a literary text not only reflects the historical conditions in which it was engendered but also plays a part in generating these very conditions, I propose that Cervantes's works ramify beyond the literary proper to affect the broader popular and psychological imaginary, altering the long-term cultural landscape as well. When observed on a large scale, literary and historical texts themselves tend to bear out Aristotle's well-known declaration in the *Poetics* that fiction is more universally impactful than the particularities of history.[10] That readers have returned time and again across the centuries to a text like *Don Quijote* suggests that the duration of its impact is particularly long, spawning a wealth of cultural conceptions, associations, models, and motifs. Of course, fictional literature may not only represent Aristotelian general truths but also be complicit in inscribing and reinforcing stereotypes and clichés, and that is doubtless why seventeenth-century Spaniards were mortified that an irreverent, comical, and highly unorthodox bestseller about an aging madman might malign their international reputation.[11] But literature can also serve to unsettle, contest, and realign popular misconceptions. Part of the longue durée of Cervantes's writing is its potential to defy a series of discourses about the Mediterranean that we have inherited today, most notably that its peoples are naturally or intrinsically "impassioned." In some sense, literary characters like Don Quijote and Sancho can therefore affect the longue durée of history to an even greater extent than certain historical figures can, perhaps even rivalling the influence of the geological events codified by Braudel. Such an admittedly bold statement is designed to chisel out a modest yet arable terrain for literature among the bedrock of Mediterranean frameworks that, regardless of whether they conform to Braudel's model of geological time or total history, have been shaped almost exclusively by historiography.

Literature constituted an especially powerful vehicle for encountering emotion in early modernity, and the reception and circulation of Cervantes's works – which attest to the deep and deeply variable emotional topographies of life in, around, and across the Mare Nostrum – supposed an emotional transaction with his early modern readers and spectators. Yet, in like fashion, until recently affect has been largely absent in literary and cultural studies, all but cordoned off from serious criticism. This inattention could be attributed to the supposed ambiguity and subjectivity attending any expression of emotion; its conventional opposition and inferiority to modern philosophical rationalism; the difficulty in localizing the source of emotions and the lack of a universal vocabulary for describing them; their dismissal by the New Criticism's "affective fallacy" that cast them into the critical dustbin of readerly whims; or, ironically, to the truism that literature is, ipso facto, "about feelings."[12] And this is in spite of the fact that the very foundation of our discipline derives from "a love of words," as the latest efforts to reinvigorate philology have reminded us.[13] In effect, emotion has traditionally comprised an intractable critical lacuna for a number of fields in the humanities and social sciences, including history, anthropology, cultural studies, and critical theory. What has been coined the "affective turn" in these disciplines – along with corresponding scholarly momentum on emotion in neuroscience and psychology – stands as a compelling invitation to investigate these issues in what yet remains their relative neglect in early modern Hispanism.[14]

This dearth of scholarship, coupled with conventional understandings and *idées reçues* of early modernity, might lead one to believe that feelings in early modern Europe were a rarefied commodity. After all, the inductive reasoning, educational reform, scientific observation, and classical erudition that flourished as hallmarks of the Renaissance not only had little to do with something as seemingly trite as feelings but also in some ways explicitly rejected their influence on human behaviour, fortifying the timeworn contrast of a hopelessly impassioned, irrational Middle Ages.[15] Yet if the Renaissance laid the rational groundwork for the Enlightenment, it could be said to have made a cognate impact on the emotive aura of Romanticism. Like all historical periods, the early modern era is fraught with contradictions, and thus it harbours movements and individuals keen to dispel emotions from everyday life yet vitally dependent on them for the aesthetic projects that ushered in Spain's Golden Age. A defining adage of the epoch is that the most sublime art and literature emerged precisely when Spain was grappling with the bleak prospect of imperial decline.[16] The country's social turmoil and material inequalities that galvanized, for instance, the highly original genre of the picaresque are in many ways indissociable from the literary form itself.[17] When the frame is expanded to the Mediterranean, one can not only discern similar traces but also identify competing means of coming to terms with the emotional challenges engendered by interimperial strife. There were, on the one hand, those who would stoically attempt to abstain from the world and banish the emotional affliction of a conflictive age, and, on the other, those who would seek to channel it into creative arts or even harness it for moral philosophy.

Underlying the former approach was a stark oppositional hierarchy that privileged reason over emotion, an ideology evident in a number of ways: a burgeoning neo-Stoicism that advocated the repression of emotion; a Neoplatonism that censured base desires, sensory appetites, and passions of the soul; a Counter-reformational fervour that reinforced the relationship between these passions and sinful vices; the behaviour manuals that prescribed the dissimulation of emotions in newly forming social spaces such as the royal court; and a more general curbing of emotional expression as part of what Norbert Elias called "the civilizing process." That some of the most pernicious and mortal sins corresponded with emotional states – including acedia, pride, wrath, and envy – was not fortuitous. Yet even the most emotive poets of early modern Spain advocated for banishing sentiment from everyday life. Garcilaso de la Vega's prosody portrays love as an arduous tribulation whose inevitable end is dissatisfaction and discord,[18] and Diego Hurtado de Mendoza and Juan Boscán extol the wisdom of living a tranquil life "without ever hearing the sound of the passions."[19] One of the first aphorisms of Baltasar Gracián's *Oráculo manual* of 1647, an early modern version of a self-help guide for personal and professional success commonly translated as *The Art of Worldly Wisdom*, similarly counsels the reader to cultivate "mastery over yourself and your affects."[20]

The neo-Stoic movement, in particular, which exerted an ideological influence across much of Europe, had reached a fever pitch in the Iberian Peninsula towards the end of the sixteenth century and in the first few decades of the seventeenth century – coinciding almost entirely with Cervantes's literary career. It was Justus Lipsius's 1584 treatise *De constantia* that sowed a swift revival of classical Stoic texts, especially those of Epictetus and Seneca, and in Spain had an impact on Francisco Sánchez de las Brozas, Gonzalo Correas, and Francisco de Quevedo. Based on Hellenistic Stoicism's fundamental principle of *apatheia* – or the purgation of emotions – and an exclusive recognition of *logos* or universal reason as the key to a virtuous life, neo-Stoicism gathered a new generation of devotees who would attempt to syncretize these values with Christian doctrine in order to prescribe a moral system for early modern Europe. Quevedo provides an instructively colourful, if extreme, example of the popularity of the paradigm. Exhibiting a fervent curiosity for neo-Stoicism early on, he exchanged letters with Lipsius himself and incorporated the Belgian humanist's ideas into his doctrinal writing with such zeal that Stoic principles pervade all of Quevedo's moral and philosophical treatises.[21] His 1635 translation of Epictetus's *Encheiridion* – a touchstone of Stoic philosophy – further solidified his place as one of the most prominent disciples of the neo-Stoic movement.[22] According to the creative imagining of one scholar, for Quevedo the elimination of all passions was not simply a seductive hypothesis that he openly espoused, however, but a way of life that he actively pursued, as though in neo-Stoicism he had discovered a slightly perverse yet religiously endorsed justification of his own infamous misanthropy.[23]

Yet we should not be ensnared by misconceptions that have collectively imposed on premoderns an impoverished emotional life, deprived them of interiority, or rendered selfhood one-dimensional. Two of the most enduring commonplaces among early modern critics are those of "Renaissance self-fashioning," projecting an ideal image in place of one's true status, and, particularly with the rise of court society and the Baroque, of everyone becoming an actor performing a role.[24] Pivotal though these familiar tropes have been in advancing the study of early modernity, they have also tended to reduce things like individual feelings to an overly restrictive, totalizing system of performativity. Combined with other influential paradigms such as Elias's civilizing process or Philippe Ariès's socio-historical notion of weak affective bonding between families and children, it is not surprising that our critical understanding of early modern interiority has remained limited and, at times, distorted. The recent emergence of the history of emotion as a field of scholarly inquiry has begun to redress these essentialisms, and we now know that feelings were an omnipresent reality of all corners of premodern everyday life, from individual selves to social and familial spaces and political and religious institutions. A resurgence in the late Renaissance of the pseudo-science of physiognomy was predicated on the belief that one's outward appearance, gestures, and emotional temperament betrayed more fundamental internal qualities.[25] In a similar fashion, early medicine theorized the relationship between the affects and physiological health, with physicians like Cristóbal de Vega earning Spain the reputation of being "the cradle of psychiatry."[26] Melancholy, that grand affliction that inspired poetic and artistic genius, seemingly beset an entire generation as Spain began to contemplate the waning of its empire and gaze at the navel of national decadence.[27] Rituals of pious devotion, public spectacles, processions, and assorted *ars moriendi* required affective labour such as copious weeping, which gave rise to its own body of literature and to rented penitents whose hypocritical tears wetted the streets of Madrid during Holy Week processions.[28] As I have demonstrated elsewhere, even the Inquisition, with its cold, calculated directive to prosecute heretics, found itself increasingly relying on minute emotional cues like sighs and tears in order to certify the sincerity of confessions.[29] Emotions could also be therapeutic, though, since those roused by travel were prescribed as a cure for miscellaneous ailments, thus suggesting yet another intimate way in which affect intersects with the Mediterranean mobility that is the other underlying theme of this book.[30]

Emotion likewise suffused the many creative, artistic, and philosophical strands of the European Renaissance and Baroque, enriching their development and the periods as a whole. It goes without saying that compelling fiction requires emotion – for suspense, intrigue, identification, conflict, climaxes, and all manner of elements appealing to the reader, even if the control of the passions has long been bound up with literature.[31] A central point of contention in the *paragones* was the question of which art most naturally represented the passions of the soul.[32] In painting, as early as the fifteenth century Alberti wrote on the importance of the affects to visual representations that both reflected nature and avoided monotony, proposing that painterly subjects that failed to represent the passions of the soul were "doubly dead."[33] The Cinquecento painter Lorenzo Lotto, "sensitive to the varying states of the human soul," elevated the art of portraiture by representing his subjects with a psychological depth that invited the viewer to contemplate their emotional interiority, hence establishing him as an eminently modern artist and paving the way for the *maniera moderna* of Mannerism.[34] Even Lotto's rough sketches evince a concern for depicting this interiority (fig. 1.1), in a way that calls to mind Charles Le Brun's more famous study of emotional expression in the late seventeenth century.

Figure 1.1. Lorenzo Lotto, *Head of a Bearded Man* (1516–17). Black chalk on paper. Metropolitan Museum of Art, New York.

In Spain, Vicente Carducho and Antonio Palomino expounded on the painterly techniques required to bring into relief these affective dimensions of portraiture, describing at length various gestures, poses, and facial expressions and their corresponding emotions.[35] Analogous developments took place in the theatre. Lope de Vega, in his *Arte nuevo de hacer comedias* (*The New Art of Writing Plays*), mused on which styles of verse were best suited for evoking distinct emotions in the audience.[36] More fundamentally, in 1559 the Italian poetic theorist Antonio Minturno had appended a third element to Horace's classic formula to propose that fiction should not only instruct (*docere*) and delight (*delectare*) but also move the reader or spectator emotionally (*movere*).[37] His prescription coincided with the gradual professionalization of actors, whose fashioning of a theatrical *techne* chiefly depended on emotion.[38] By transcending the model of natural *imitatio* and transforming themselves into their characters through increasingly realistic emotional portrayals, actors endeavoured to make their performance appear "true" to theatre-goers.[39] Testament to the success of their enterprise were the many complaints and anxieties of moralists opposed to the *comedia*, who fretted about the corrupting potential of theatrical affects on spectators.[40]

Finally, in the realm of philosophy, ample alternatives to neo-Stoicism were available. The Valencian humanist Juan Luis Vives, who has been called the father of modern psychology, went so far as to claim in his *De anima et vita* of 1538 that the study of the "affections" of the soul constituted "the supreme task of philosophical inquiry," since they were "the foundation of all moral training, both private and public."[41] Even if classical and medieval thinkers like Cicero and Aquinas had devised distinct taxonomies for cataloguing the passions, the classificatory fervour of early modernity ensured that by the mid-seventeenth century further schemes had proliferated into a vertiginous and characteristically Baroque cluster of competing lists.[42] Hobbes mentions about thirty different passions in the *Leviathan* (1651), Spinoza tallies at least forty affects in his *Ethics* (1675), while the comparably restrained philosophical psychology of Descartes in *Passions of the Soul* (1649) recognized six "primitive" feelings, even if their admixture could give rise to many more.[43] Other philosophers, including Spain's own Oliva Sabuco, went to great pains to develop similar catalogues, writing at length and in perceptive psychological depth about sundry passions. Much of this labour aligned with the more general Baroque fascination with language and phenomena that seemed to confound rational faculties. In fact, by the late Renaissance a new-found estimation of the affections of the heart, sparked by a revival of interest in Augustine's *Confessions*, had managed to loosen reason's grip on moral philosophy to the point that "the passions could now be regarded as resources for life rather than threats to virtue," while reason itself, "so long glorified, was now in some quarters suspect."[44]

The complex yet necessarily brief picture of the early modern role of emotion I have just outlined – caught in a dialectic of repression and innovation – reflects in some sense the reasons for its neglect among the vast annals of scholarship on Cervantes. On the one hand, Cervantine affectivity has been befogged by a veil of clichés, received notions, and unquestioned essentialisms regarding the Renaissance and literary art at large.[45] On the other, it may well be that the very tendency to read Cervantes as an anomaly or visionary among fellow writers of fiction has destined Cervantists to give short shrift to one of the most vital elements of literary aesthetics. Perhaps one of the ironic legacies of Hispanism's noble quest to elevate *Don Quijote* to the canonical echelons of world literature – to establish its novelty as the first novel, so to speak – is a certain critical inclination to ascribe to it an overly iconoclastic function, an unceasing impulse to pinpoint the genesis and epicentre of a fundamental paradigm shift in Madrid, year 1605. In this drive to showcase singularity, literary emotions have taken a back seat to those elements that break with prior literature altogether.

Nevertheless, my purpose is not merely to fill a critical void, however gaping it may continue to be. Attending to a broadly comparative and multidisciplinary landscape, *Affective Geographies* argues that Cervantes's engagement with affect is not only fundamental but fundamentally different. Steven Hutchinson, the Cervantes scholar who has most persistently studied the problem of emotion, makes a similar assessment.[46] Noting that "the problematic of literature and emotion has yet to be thought out," he posits that "[c]ertain 'places' are more privileged than others as vantage points [...] and Cervantes' writings offer one such vantage point because they have so much to say about emotion."[47] I would add that the reverse is also true: emotion has much to say about Cervantes's writings, opening new, sometimes radically different, and yet historically responsive vistas on age-old questions and critical debates – as the present study will explore, for instance, the question of humour in *Don Quijote* or verisimilitude in *Los trabajos de Persiles y Sigismunda* (*The Trials of Persiles and Sigismunda*). The Cervantine corpus's deep enmeshment with political and historical issues – recently illuminated in studies by Anthony J. Cascardi and Susan Byrne, respectively[48] – coupled with its diversity of genre, characters, and narrative styles, reinforces Cervantes's texts as especially fruitful for exploring affect and the contours of the social spaces that shape its expression.[49] Among these spaces are a number of historical projects unique to the early modern Mediterranean, such as those of maritime commerce and exchange, imperial conflict and expansion, captivity and the slave trade, interreligious encounter, and the Inquisition.

These affective geographies are textual as well as topographical. To recognize the centrality of emotion in Cervantes's works is not to suggest that his characters exhibit a degree of psychological inwardness like those of the modern realist novel, for example, but to appreciate that they perform an even more complex function.[50] Although at times affects disclose a meaningful relationship to the world outside, they are just as frequently sites of signification in their own right, building suspense, shifting meaning, measuring conflict, mapping onto characters, and rising and falling with the changing landscape of individual works and passages. Cervantine emotions are waypoints for navigating the text yet, like the Mediterranean itself, can just as easily produce unexpected encounters or even throw the reader off course. By sweeping us into emotional eddies and implicating us in their resolution, they disturb the work-world dichotomy by pulling on the needle of our own affective compass until we arrive at the shore of the last page. And yet since the emotions of Mediterranean experience are often difficult to resolve, even after folding the sails or closing the book we may well find ourselves still affected by their lingering intensity.

Emotion in Cervantes's texts does not mean merely emotional affliction, however. It can also intersect with humour, parody, and the burlesque, as I will demonstrate in chapter 4 by recuperating the early modern understanding of laughter as a passion. May it suffice to recall here the meta-literary allusions in *Don Quijote* to chivalric romance and its central theme of courtly love, parodied by the protagonist's affection for Dulcinea and by related tropes of the *princesse lointaine, dame jamais vue*, and "amor de oídas."[51] The text's vacillation on how many times the devoted knight laid eyes on Dulcinea, if at all, along with the litany of less-than-sublime characteristics of Aldonza Lorenzo, renders the satire all the more comical yet no less significant. In fact, one could hardly conjure a more incisive parody for courtly love than a madman enamoured of a plebeian woman who might or might not even exist. Unfounded, unrequited, and unconsummate, this love is expressed not by *eros* or impassioned desire but by the enactment of performative rituals culled directly from the books of chivalry. Cervantes's parody of courtly love points up his willingness to usurp revered models of literary sentiment in his own quest to experiment with novel emotions. His fabrication of love as a critical cog of the larger satirical machine that is *Don Quijote* likewise indicates that emotions will command a crucial stake in the author's development of new literary forms and hybrid genres like the novel.[52]

As suggested in the opening epigraphs, even the characters appear to be conscious of their emotions and emotional representation within the narrative, with Don Quijote boasting of the affective wellspring he carries inside, and Sancho demanding his own affects be accorded due recognition. The contrast between the parochial reality of Alonso Quijano's nameless village, languishing in the dry expanse of La Mancha, and the exuberant fictional worlds of the books he incessantly reads could not be starker. It is this contrast that inspires the aging hidalgo, in a flight of fancy and a fit of madness, to adopt the *nom de guerre* of Don Quijote and to sally forth to re-enact the chivalric scenes and deeds of his literary obsession. But his quest for unfamiliar geographical frontiers is as much about seeking out new emotional worlds as it is about discovering physical adventures or feats of prowess. His emotions are at once an integral part of his madness and yet, as I have shown elsewhere with the particular case of shame, also escape it and delineate its contours.[53] Throughout the course of his wanderings Don Quijote experiences an entire gamut of emotions, from the exhilaration and élan of the journey itself to the disappointment, shame, pride, longing, jealousy, rage, sadness, and dejection that accompany his perennial defeats, momentary triumphs, and everything in between. Towards the end of the novel, this long and winding emotional trajectory culminates in Barcelona, where, with his small, landlocked village at his back, the knight errant marvels at the sight of the Mediterranean Sea for the first time, no doubt imagining what further adventures await beyond the vast maritime horizon.

Yet even the arid Iberian interior from which many of Cervantes's characters hail forms part of the larger Mediterranean region, as thinkers from Isidore of Seville to Braudel have long established. Limited to neither the Sea proper nor its extensive coastlines, Braudel's Mediterranean "world" circumscribes vast areas of Europe, North Africa, and the Near East.[54] In the early modern period it was a far-ranging network of nodes and flows, a "liquid continent" of unity and exchange in which multi- and transnational actors, including captives and corsairs, pirates and privateers, merchants and mercenaries, and renegades and ransomers, all experienced its fortunes or misfortunes. That the Mediterranean served as a geographical *medium* for these encounters evokes its etymology as a "middle land." It comprises a limitless trove of not only cultural contact zones but also, adapting Mary Louise Pratt's well-known terminology, what might be called emotional contact zones.[55] These traverse all manner of spaces, from the ennui of a sleepy rural village to the wonder of a cosmopolitan city, from the intimacy of a private room to the commons of the public square, or from regional enclaves to nation states and the Mediterranean basin writ large. Emotions modulate according to the distinct topographies of their social environs and further morph as they are differentially exchanged across these zones, pervading and often fuelling the kinds of transcultural and transreligious encounters that deeply concerned Cervantes. Affect is indissociable from these Cervantine encounters with the "other." Here an emotion might just as easily serve to underscore difference as to signal a shared path towards reconciliation or unity. It is wholly neither symptom nor cure.

Even as Spain's Philip II increasingly turned away from the Mediterranean and towards the Atlantic (as argued, at least, by Braudel),[56] Cervantes remained firmly entrenched in the region, as if to heed the mythical motto of *non plus ultra* inscribed on the Pillars of Hercules. His request for a transfer to the New World was denied, and so he continued to inhabit the Mediterranean, where, like an early modern Odysseus, his experience was both vast and diverse. He escaped to Italy in order to avoid legal troubles, served as a spy for Philip II in Oran, and was captured by pirates and held for ransom for five years in Algiers. As a soldier in the company of Diego de Urbina, Cervantes engaged Ottoman forces at Tunis, Corfu, and La Goulette and lost the use of his left hand in the storied Battle of Lepanto, the climax of Braudel's book and what the French historian considered "the most spectacular military event in the Mediterranean during the entire sixteenth century."[57] A rash of recent biographies have further pursued the claim that Cervantes possessed a *converso* background (that of a Spanish Jew forced to convert to Catholicism), thus aligning him, albeit with scant historical evidence, with those communities most affected by Iberian blood purity statutes and which constituted an immense Mediterranean diaspora.[58] What remains clear is that Cervantes's biographical involvement with the Mediterranean greatly affected his fictional output, as the character of Don Lope intimates in *Los baños de Argel* (*The Bagnios of Algiers*): "Not from the imagination / this treatment was taken, / but the truth forged it / very far from fiction" (No de la imaginación / este trato se sacó, / que la verdad le fraguó / bien lejos de la ficción).[59]

Cervantes's body and his body of work bear the marks of his Mediterranean experience. María Antonia Garcés has probed the deep influence that the author's North African captivity exerted on his psyche, arguing in her ground-breaking book *Cervantes in Algiers* that his revisiting of this experience through literary writing allowed him to work through the profound emotional trauma of his imprisonment.[60] Here

I will be interested to explore the Mediterranean where its presence is less apparent or biographically inflected, for even as he veers into remoter domains, Cervantes always keeps one foot in the Sea, never managing to fully jettison the region from his writing.[61] Although it may be most noticeable in his Algerian captivity plays and narratives like "La historia del cautivo" ("The Captive's Tale"), the Mediterranean intervenes in all of Cervantes's texts – from the Cyprus and Sicily of *El amante liberal* (*The Generous Lover*) to the Rome of *Persiles y Sigismunda*, the Constantinople of *La gran sultana* (*The Great Sultana*), or the Oran of *El gallardo español* (The gallant Spaniard). The *Viaje del Parnaso* (*Journey to Parnassus*) recounts in imaginative verse the travails of Spanish poets in a boat around Greece. Even the pastoral *Galatea* exchanges its *locus amoenus* for the Mediterranean, corsairs, and coastal raiding parties in the intermittent tale of Timbrio, Silerio, Nísida, and Blanca. The Sea is most obvious in those texts that represent explicitly maritime crossings (of which there are several in the Cervantine canon), but it still pulls on the many characters who inhabit the Iberian hinterland. In fact, due to its unique history and location, Spain has been deemed a "Mediterranean in microcosm,"[62] and one should not forget that Philip II was the anchor of Braudel's path-breaking study, even if the monarch was overshadowed by the author's concern to avoid an *histoire événementielle* that would privilege kings and other individuals. In sum, as Hutchinson and Antonio Cortijo Ocaña underscore, "quite probably, no other author or treatise writer of the epoch has better understood the Mediterranean of their time – or known how to represent it in the novel and theatre – than Cervantes."[63] The omnipresence of the Mediterranean in Cervantes's experience and oeuvre represents a peerless critical opportunity not only for early modern Hispanism but also for the burgeoning field of Mediterranean Studies. For the same reasons, Cervantes holds an uncommon potential to illuminate the specifically literary stakes of the Mediterranean and its scholarship and, therefore, to contest the premise – implicit in almost all large-scale approaches to the field – that only those of a historiographical nature are valid for grasping a sense of what the Mediterranean means as a whole.

A Spanish map from 1621, reproduced in figure 1.2, reminds us just how contiguous the opposite shores of the Mediterranean could feel, both in reality and the early modern imaginary. Although its cartographic details are obviously skewed and not drawn to scale, the map's continental proximity is not entirely a figment, because mutual visibility always served as a lodestar for Mediterranean navigation and there are relatively few areas of the Sea from which one cannot glimpse land.[64] This particular image affords viewers the sensation of peering

Figure 1.2. Anonymous, *Galeras en el Mediterráneo oriental para la lucha contra los corsarios de Argel* (1621). Watercolour on paper. España: Ministerio de Educación, Archivo General de Simancas, MPD, 64, 024.

out from a promontory in North Africa, reconnoitring the fortified cities of Oran, Mostaganem, and Algiers, and, across the sea on the Iberian coast, those of Cartagena, Alicante, Denia, and Tarragona, along with the Balearic Islands in between. Several galleys also pepper the waters, a feature that betrays the map's apparent purpose of buttressing a proposal for Spain to invade Algiers, whose outsized jetty and ramparts reflect the metropolitan port's early modern strategic importance as a hub of Ottoman piracy.[65] What is interesting is how, thanks to the artistic ornamentation of the natural landscape, urban skylines, and the telescoping, three-dimensional quality of the picture plane, the spectator's vantage point is effectively projected to the "other side" of the Mediterranean. In spite of the map's original intent, surveying the Spanish littoral from the Berber and Ottoman perspective draws the viewer into the unfamiliar, behind enemy lines, and augments the perception of geographical as well as symbolic contiguity. Cervantes's writing can be seen to foreshorten the Mediterranean in an analogous way, to place the reader in a similarly panoramic and anamorphic position, keeping reciprocal lines of sight open while taking stock of the dominant and familiar from foreign and sometimes marginalized vistas.

Like Cervantes, many other early modern individuals experienced Mediterranean mobility through various motives for travel, in some cases traversing astounding distances.[66] But those who reflected in writing on their sojourns, such as the first-person *rihla* of Arab travellers in Europe, tend to "[tell] more about the outer world they visited [...] than the inner world they experienced."[67] Eyewitness travel accounts of Europeans, while anticipating the ethnographic methodologies of later schools of anthropology, also lack the psychological inwardness one expects from later practitioners of travel writing.[68] Despite their dissimilar settings, authorial motivations, and ideological leanings, and whether they are penned by captive, cleric, tourist, or diplomat, what all these reports on foreign lands share is a sharp attention to either objective details or normative judgments that would be widely appreciated by their intended audience. The comparably sparing depictions of emotional experience in these early modern travel accounts thus suggest a parallel with modern scholarly studies of the Mediterranean, from Horden and Purcell's turn-of-the-century *Corrupting Sea* – a major portion of which is dedicated to physical, geographical, and environmental features – to Braudel's mid-century classic. Most of the limited studies on the presence of the Mediterranean in Cervantes's writing have likewise tended to focus on the relevance of geographical locales, historical references, and autobiographical gestures.[69] A survey of existing scholarship might give the mistaken impression that Cervantes was, like many of his fellow Mediterranean travellers, interested more in documenting the impartial immediacy of topographical features or the exoticism of local customs than in noting the internal experience of encountering them for the first time; in recording an exacting account of historical events than in exploring the diversity of subjective responses to them; in empiricism than in expression; in an ethnography of foreign cultures than in the feelings aroused by an exchange with their peoples – in short, that Cervantes's Mediterranean is rich in exposition yet scant on emotion. On the contrary, by granting the reader access to the affective dimensions of Mediterranean experience, his writing not only transcends the frontiers of emotional expression but also ramifies beyond the realm of the literary proper to alert us to those of regional, national, sexual, religious, and racial difference.[70] This is important because, even if human feelings appear universal in an abstract way, they are neither transcultural nor transhistorical. Emotions bear singular traces of the cross-Mediterranean practices of othering that are so common to Cervantes's epoch, and of the author's often heterodox representation of those who inhabited the "other side."

Cervantes's assertion to have been the first dramaturge to represent "the hidden thoughts and feelings of the soul" on stage confirms that he was deliberately invested in the affective dimensions of fiction. I want to suggest, however, that it is not in Cervantes's theatre that emotional interiority materializes most innovatively but in his prose. The novel and the novella were for him the ideal literary terrain for both a geographical and an emotional expansiveness. Limited to neither the dramatic constraints of unity of action nor the neoclassical remnants of the fear and pity of catharsis, these ground-breaking new genres allowed him to explore the untold horizons of the Mediterranean with formal as well as emotional abandon.[71] Psychologists and other students of the mind have turned to literature time and again to probe or illustrate their hypotheses, with Freud's use of *Hamlet* or the Oedipus myth as a prominent example.[72] But there are in fact compelling structural reasons for which prose narrative is uniquely well adapted to the expression of human emotions. This is chiefly because we experience the affectivity of everyday life as a kind of narrative as well, our moods and temperaments changing over the course of a given unit of time and fluctuating in response to any number of external events and stimuli. As John Dewey observed, emotion "attends the development of a plot; and a plot requires [...] a space, wherein to develop[,] and time in which to unfold," which suggests that long-form fiction like the novel, unfettered by formal precepts, is the ideal literary genre for expressing affectivity.[73] If fictional narrative is distinctively well suited to the lived experience of emotion, and if Cervantes is indeed a pioneer of the modern novel, then surely we have much to gain from broadening and deepening our understanding of affect in his prose.

The prescriptive models of which Cervantes could have availed himself for this literary-emotive labour are scarce because early poetic theorists, unlike their counterparts in music and painting, rarely expounded on "the fine details of pathetic composition."[74] El Pinciano, whom some regard to have been the single greatest influence on his writing,[75] commits a section of his *Philosophia antigua poética* (Ancient poetic philosophy) to a discussion about "afectos," "passiones," and "perturbaciones."[76] However, beyond reciting the taxonomical conventions of philosophers like Aquinas, El Pinciano adds little insight to the topic and even less to the ways in which emotions ought to function in prose fiction. Juan Huarte de San Juan, in contrast, dedicates extensive thought in his *Examen de ingenios para las ciencias* (*The Examination of Men's Wits*) to the question of affective physiology and psychology, and there is little doubt that Cervantes had this in mind while concocting his most famous character. Yet the recognition of the influence of Huarte's humoral theory has actually tended to produce the contrary effect of restricting critical understanding of Don Quijote's emotional behaviour to a binary choleric-melancholic paradigm, one that upon closer examination is wholly incompatible with the range, complexity, and dynamism of affect in the novel.[77] In point of fact yet further afield, scholars have argued that the modern novel owes its birth to factors less aesthetic than socio-historical, whether it was precisely the "multi-racial, multilingual, mixed Mediterranean"[78] or the "contested identity, violence, and expulsion"[79] of Cervantes's Spain that quickened the innovation of untried narrative forms.

The theatre nonetheless can shine a spotlight on the task of recovering the emotional richness of Cervantes's prose, particularly because despite his arch-rival Lope and the *comedia nueva* overshadowing his ill-fated bid at popular dramatic success, Cervantes continued to value the theatrical arts. This ongoing investment bestowed an acute theatrical influence on his manner of conceiving and expressing emotion in his novels and novellas.[80] In so far as each endeavours to foster an emotional exchange between characters and consumers of the work, dramatic and literary arts share a great deal in common, for though the novel lacks the visual immediacy and plasticity of the stage, it mobilizes performative praxis in order to endow its characters with a more or less realistic repertoire of bodily and gestural affects for the benefit of the reader's imagination.[81] An inherent difference is that, because a dramatic script can rely on actors to animate it and move the audience, emotions need not be fully developed in the text itself, whether in the dialogue or in the *didascalia*, whereas prose must contend with its non-performative medium from the outset. It is almost as though Cervantes's failure to secure a theatre company to perform the plays he would eventually publish as *Ocho comedias y ocho entremeses nuevos, nunca representados*, with their interest in staging "interior thoughts and feelings," suggests that they were already preordained for readers and not spectators. Such it is that critics like Cory A. Reed, channelling Bakhtin, can speak of the "novelization" of Cervantes's drama.[82] In complementary fashion, however, the author's use of an eminently visual language in his prose tends to displace the potency of textual words themselves onto a gestural, bodily, or material semiotics.[83]

What this entails in practice is that we must not only engage in a close affective reading of the text but also turn to additional mechanisms for bringing into relief the embodied, histrionic, and visual functions of affect, including the highly corporeal etymologies of early modern Spanish terms for emotions; classical and premodern treatises on painting, sculpture, music, and oratory; stage directions and actorly technique in the early modern theatre; and writings on mysticism and physiognomy. The images that appear throughout the present book likewise afford a more immediate means of deciphering what Frederick de Armas has called "writing for the eyes in the Spanish Golden Age."[84] But even if one were to exhaust the cumulative archive of images from illustrated editions of Cervantes's works, there would still be plenty of unrepresented moments that would require full reliance upon the text and the imagination for picturing.[85] Of course, the paucity of pictorial representations in most early editions meant that seventeenth-century readers had to lean on textual imagery and their own mental *phantasia* to an even greater extent. Perhaps this well-developed imagination is to blame for Don Quijote's mad penchant for seeing images from the romances of chivalry in everything around him. What I wish to underscore, at any rate, are the limitations of praxis that inhere in certain habits of reading, those that tend to obfuscate the aesthetic and political work of affect in the text. In the words of Sara Ahmed, affect is "sticky," adhering to myriad bodies, situations, and spaces.[86] It might also be called "slippery," as it just as often appears nebulous, unwieldy, and immeasurably vast or minute, maintaining a marked tendency to elide its own critical recognition. Especially since modernity has conditioned us to conceive of affect as a private quality of the self, this sometimes means in Cervantes's texts that emotions hide in the plain sight of public spectacles, communal rituals, and social bonds. At other times this obscuring effect obtains with the occlusion of affects in figures of ineffability (chapter 6), their apparent withdrawal into temporal interruptions of the narrative (chapter 5), or even their confluence with laughter (chapter 4). So too does the feeling of shame partake in this phenomenon, given its own will to concealment in the form of the blush, which was traditionally regarded as a natural mechanism for disguising a subject's moral deficiencies (chapter 3).

In order to grant these emotions clear visibility, *Affective Geographies* is divided into three parts of two chapters each. Part 1 ("Casting Off") serves to introduce the overarching themes of the Mediterranean and affectivity while proposing theoretical approaches to the problems they pose in literature. To do so, this section surveys textual examples from across the Cervantine body of work, including the author's poetry, prose, and drama. Part 2 ("Quixotic Passages") homes in on *Don Quijote* to understand how these themes operate in Cervantes's best-known text and that which is widely considered the first Western novel. Cervantes's other major prose works – the *Novelas ejemplares* (*Exemplary Novels*) and *Persiles y Sigismunda* – form the backdrop for exploring Mediterranean emotion in part 3 of the book ("Other Ports of Call").

In so far as it neither presents straightforward, easily digestible organizational schemas nor adheres to universally recognizable borders, affect finds a germane analogue in the Mediterranean itself. These mutually subjective bedfellows inform the following chapter of the book, "Connected (Hi)stories: The Cervantine, Literary, and Affective Mediterranean," which plots the broader stakes of a Cervantine Mediterranean, read through the optic of affectivity. The individual self-narratives recounted time and again by Cervantes's characters – marked without exception by emotional strife and affliction – are the lifeblood of his fiction. With their stories within a story, these emotional bodies open a kind of bidirectional *mise en abyme* through which their affects reverberate outwards to affect the Cervantine body of work as well as the body politic of the Mediterranean. This lays the groundwork for my consideration of the literary Mediterranean, whose long-term, generative function allows me to posit a number of constitutive traits of the Mediterranean literature for which a handful of other critics have begun to call. After surveying different historiographical methods of conceiving the Mediterranean, I suggest that Cervantine affectivity not only mobilizes the subjective richness of the region but also unsettles a number of Mediterranean stereotypes erected by vaguely emotional discourses.

Chapter 3 of the book, "Shadows of the Inquisition: Honour, Shame, and a Cervantine View of Mediterranean 'Values,'" reflects an even greater concern for what Ahmed has called the "cultural politics of emotion,"[87] or the ways in which literary affects underwrite and call forth the historical and political conditions of Cervantes's epoch. By examining the representation of popular and inquisitorial forms of punishment in the author's works, here I seek to recover shame as an emotional register of lived experience in the early modern Mediterranean, an affect that has hitherto remained overshadowed by the abundance of critical literature on honour, as well as by large-scale Mediterraneanizing studies. The identification of an inquisitorial discourse of shaming in the episodes of Don Quijote's encagement suggests the need, on the one hand, to re-evaluate what twentieth-century anthropology denominated the "values" of Mediterranean society and, on the other, to rehabilitate local (hi)stories that are all marked by blood: the blood of shame's blush, that shed through violent conflicts, and that governing the racial politics of blood purity.

Examining the oft-commented episode of Ricote, my chapter 4, "A Mediterranean (Tragi)comedy: Sancho, Ricote, and the Emotional Politics of Laughter," sets out to comprehend Cervantine humour. Here I argue for the need to recuperate the early modern understanding of laughter not as the response to a given stimulus but as an emotion in its own right. This historically grounded conceptual shift not only troubles the designation of *Don Quijote* as merely a "funny book" but also moderates the critical polarization of the so-called hard and soft approaches to the novel. After studying distinct modes of humour in the royal court, I show that the laughter shared by Sancho and the Moorish Ricote represents an omnidirectional emotional event that disrupts structures of power as it echoes across the Mediterranean.

Chapter 5 is entitled "Suspended Admiration: Wonder, Surprise, and Emotional Exemplarity in *La española inglesa*" and interrogates the irruption of what I call moments of "suspension" in the novellas. Marked by a number of terms such as *suspensión*, *confusión*, and *admiración*, these moments – related to the affect of surprise – interrupt the temporal flow of the narrative and thus open a space of reflection for the characters and reader alike. By studying the etymological, cultural, and corporeal registers of these terms, I identify their function not only as a fundamental tool for building an aesthetics of sentimental suspense but also as instantiations of Cervantes's emotional ethics in the Mediterranean context.

In chapter 6, "Aporias of Love: Articulating the Ineffable in *Los trabajos de Persiles y Sigismunda*," I respond to the critical discourse that regards Cervantes's last work as a love story governed by the laws of sentimentalism, by charting how the novel resists the very expression of love and desire. My scrutiny of tropes of aporia, ineffability, and materiality reveals that Cervantes avowedly exploited the inadequacies and limitations of poetic language in order to underscore the potency of intense affects, adding a dose of emotional realism to a text mired in debates about verisimilitude. This allows me to suggest, finally, that the novel's septentrional setting functions as an exoticized analogue of the Mediterranean that Cervantes knew so well.

My ultimate goal throughout these chapters is not to identify a singular, defining affect or, to appropriate Raymond Williams's term, a "structure of feeling" for the early modern Mediterranean[88] – as has incessantly and, I believe, erroneously been attempted with its designation as an "honour-shame culture." Although I do rescue shame as an oft-eclipsed emotion from the dominant discourse of honour in early modern Spanish literary criticism, I do not mean to suggest that shame constituted what Heidegger called a "mood" (*Stimmung*) or a psychological culture akin to Roger Bartra's seminal study of melancholy in sixteenth- and seventeenth-century Spain.[89] Rather, I am interested in recuperating the Mediterranean's affective micro-(hi)stories, or what Horden and Purcell have called the region's distinct "microecologies": the epiphenomenal conditions of certain enclaves within the Mare Nostrum that differentiate themselves from, yet contribute to, the unity of the space at large.[90] Cervantes's texts reflect many such microecologies, particularly when one recalls the life stories of individual characters populating each of his long novels. In this literary domain, focusing on the affective diversity, nuances, heterogeneity, and even seeming minutiae of the text tends, on the one hand, to foreclose on psychological essentialism and reductionism and, on the other, to disclose critical insights at both micro and macro levels.

One of the most persistent accessories to this kind of reductionism is critical language itself, a fact complicated by the lexical and semantic complexities of affect and, greater still, by the challenge of translation. Hence a note on terminology is in order here. At times creating a seeming gulf between the signifier and the signified, feelings count among the most difficult things to articulate in words. In some sense, designating an emotional state as one of "fear" or "sadness" is always already inadequate for conveying the complexity of what we truly *feel*.[91] Moreover, since emotions are culturally and historically mediated concepts, rarely can we expect a modern word to capture perfectly the nuances of their early modern meaning. Sometimes these differences are so vast as to require the creation of emotional neologisms to refer to the feelings of other cultures and time periods that lie wholly outside the conceptual range of even provisional language.[92] In sixteenth- and seventeenth-century Spain a surfeit of words – including *accidente, afecto, afección, apetito, desorden, estado de ánimo, imaginaciones, movimiento, perturbación, pasión, sentimiento, turbación,* and *turbamento* – could all perform the work of signifying what is generally meant by the term *emotion*. Its most direct Spanish equivalent, *emoción*, also existed but was scarce and would not enter the official lexicon until generations later,[93] even if the term *movimiento* – which shares its etymological affinity with *motion* – was common in early modern Spanish.[94] The word *pasión* was also widely used, having derived from the Latin *passio* and often connoting suffering, as its association with the passion of Christ suggests.[95] The other major term for designating the idea of emotion in English – *affect* – and for which there is a corresponding term in Spanish (*afecto*), is also the one whose early modern definition most accurately captures the same idea: "strictly speaking, it is a passion of the soul, which, redounding in the voice, alters it and causes a particular movement in the body, with which we move to compassion and mercy, anger and vengeance, sadness and happiness; a necessary and important thing for the orator."[96] In addition to the term's precision, the mention of its necessity to the public speaker derives from the influence of Aristotle's *Rhetoric*, whose extensive treatment of emotion is reflected in much of Cervantes's own emotional philosophy.

Since this Cervantine philosophy tends to conceive of affect not as a condition suffered by the subject but as an impetus to action, my use in the book of the term *passion* – which has even broader connotations in English – is limited, as is that of the somewhat more ambiguous *feeling* and *sentiment*. The words *affect* and *emotion* carry less connotational baggage, even if they have begun to acquire newly differentiated meanings since the so-called affective turn of the last few years. Despite the fact that there is little to no agreement on the nuances of their definitions – at least among literary scholars and cultural theorists – *emotion* is commonly taken to refer to a cognitive concept that is more readily quantifiable (especially in its plural form, *emotions*, with all their discrete variations) than affect, which for some scholars connotes a bodily, involuntary, or asignifying content and therefore tends more frequently to elide cognition and language. I acknowledge the value of such debates and often choose to employ the terms *affect* and *emotion* in a manner consistent with these provisional definitions. Nevertheless, for both practical and stylistic purposes – and following the lead of still other scholars who refer to the terms indistinguishably – I do not do so under the auspices of a rigid criterion.[97] Instead, whenever possible I provide in what follows both the original usage and an abundance of cultural and etymological contextualization for terms whose meanings run the most acute risk of becoming diluted in translation. I believe that this solution, though admittedly imperfect, allows for the greatest equilibrium between, on the one hand, the necessary recognition of lexical differentiation and terminological precision and, on the other, an analytical prose that is not overly laboured, redundant, or unwieldy. If anything, these deficiencies and debates incontrovertibly signal the need for further work on the problem of affect, to which the chapters that follow are devised as a fundamental yet incomplete contribution.

Chapter Two

Connected (Hi)stories: The Cervantine, Literary, and Affective Mediterranean

Cervantes does not forget the sea, he cannot forget the sea, he will never forget the sea.

Azorín

I have loved the Mediterranean with passion.

Fernand Braudel

Among the often-conflictive relations with other scholars that characterize his long career as one of the most illustrious and influential students of Cervantes over the last four centuries, Américo Castro reserved some of his most trenchant criticism for Fernand Braudel, the father of longue durée historiography and the author of the monumental *Mediterranean and the Mediterranean World in the Age of Philip II*. With its panoramic view of the geographical, meteorological, and economic conditions of the Mediterranean basin, Braudel's volume brought into relief the supra-individual structures that have shaped the development of this space across the centuries. In a sense, Castro's foundational *El pensamiento de Cervantes* (Cervantes's thought) is not all that different. Aspiring to similarly ambitious heights, it mapped the varied literary and philosophical influences on Cervantes's oeuvre and attempted to forge a systematic understanding of his modes of thinking. With these works, moreover, Braudel and Castro each managed to set the tone – one that was not always harmonious – for the debates that subsequently followed in their respective fields and beyond. Although the widely admired scope of Braudel's book would not be imitated by others for another half-century, it left an indelible mark on historiography, and Castro influenced an entire generation of Cervantes scholars, an impact that, especially in the North American academy, continues to be felt today.[1]

Yet, unlike Castro – as well as fellow members of the Annales school who preceded and followed him – Braudel was concerned with neither *mentalité* nor the cultural history of the internal experience of Mediterranean subjectivity. Predictably, perhaps, this is where Castro's rebuke is most pointed. Under the blunt, categorical title – "The Past Was How It Was: It Is Not Manufacturable" – of the foreword to *De la edad conflictiva* (On the conflictive age) Castro emphasizes that "[t]he economic perspective is contemplated and made functional from human situations." Even less subtle is his accusation that "whatever reflects people's thoughts or feelings [*el sentir de la gente*] gets in the way of economic-materialist historians, since in the end all of that is damaging to the ultimate goal of maintaining the human flock well enchained, silent, and submissively accepting the orders of its shepherds (as it occurs in all forms of dictatorship)."[2] Evoking the tense political climate of the 1960s and 1970s as well as his own personal circumstances of exile from the Franco regime, Castro denounced Braudel and those of his ilk for pulling the wool over our eyes through what he regarded, somewhat paradoxically, as a dictatorial liberty with historiographical interpretation. If this broader polemic is set aside, however, we are still left with a Braudelian model that, according to Castro and other critics, subsumes the particularities of Spanish everyday life to a grand economic system and therefore neglects human emotion and, far more troublingly, the racial politics of blood purity among Christians, Jews, and Muslims in which such feelings were frequently embedded.[3] Given that he fails to address these feelings in any depth, Castro's critique raises a paramount question: Is it even possible to comprehend something as seemingly individualized and subjective as human emotion within a broad Mediterranean framework like Braudel's?

As a whole, this book tenders an affirmative response to the question. In the following pages I demonstrate that, for Cervantes, emotions were an integral and inevitable component of the early modern Mediterranean; to narrate a Mediterranean experience was, perforce, to speak of an emotional experience. Such an idea is inherent in the book's title – bridging Castro (feeling) and Braudel (geography) – even if it is not my intention to reconcile the important differences that remain between these patriarchal figures. Rather, *Affective Geographies* suggests that in Cervantes's works an innate and potent relationship exists between affectivity and the spaces in which it is expressed. To that end, this chapter sets out to map the distinct themes of the book – Mediterranean, emotion, literature, Cervantes – each of which has remained largely neglected by and isolated from the rest. Taking a cue from what has long been regarded as a defining characteristic of the medieval and early modern Mediterranean – its connectivity – the present chapter performs this connectivity by foregrounding the intimate, and often complex, ways in which the Sea, affectivity, history, literature, and Cervantes are mutually constitutive, and how each theme reflects back on the others. Triangulating Cervantes, emotion, and the Mediterranean, in other words, allows us to peer across boundaries at once conceptual, disciplinary, geographical, and thalassographical. The organization of this chapter into corresponding subdivisions is thus intended to be provisional, as reciprocal incursions frequently take place across borders that, as in the Mediterranean itself, are always porous, shifting, and unstable. Examples from Cervantes's texts examined here arise in a similarly dynamic fashion: instead of focusing on a single work or instituting a more linear progression, I have opted in this chapter to evoke the fluid nature of the Mediterranean by following a multiplicity of different intratextual currents that come forth, circulate, and recede but perhaps never fully disappear from view. This approach also mirrors the diversity that I identify as a defining characteristic of the literary Mediterranean, because Cervantine affectivity, by skilfully adapting a common Renaissance trope, is marked above all by a concern for variety, which is consonant with the author's emotional philosophy that affects are neither inferior nor opposed to reason.

Crucially, however, in exploring this connectivity and diversity, I also intend to problematize it, for Cervantes's Mediterranean does not merely reproduce the so-called Romantic approach to the region, whose emphasis on connection and exchange risks losing sight of the ways in which imperial, sectarian, and racial violence have also traversed the Sea.[4] It directs us, rather, towards a more critical Mediterranean Studies. Read in the key of affect and the Sea, Cervantes's texts harbour the potential not only to broaden and deepen our understanding of "Mediterranean" but to contest a number of long-held assumptions, misconceptions, and stereotypes of the region, many of which have rested upon vaguely emotional discourses to reinforce the structures of racial and religious difference and cross-Mediterranean practices of othering. What I call *Cervantine affectivity* may help to clarify the murky and often troubling waters of a veritable sea of conventional discourses. Near the end of the chapter I chart how this destabilizing potential of Cervantes's texts, some four hundred years on, further signals literature's own longue durée. By juxtaposing history and literature throughout, my intention is not to displace the former but rather to shore up, so to speak, critical awareness of the equally vital role of the latter in constructing the Mediterranean, in the early modern period as today. Hence the title of this chapter pays subtle homage to Sanjay Subrahmanyam's model of "connected histories," which judiciously advises that "we cannot attempt a 'macro-history' of the problem without muddying our boots in the bogs of 'micro-history.'"[5] As suggested previously, a central proposition of this book is to interrogate the macro (Mediterranean framework) and the micro (emotions). A primary conduit for doing so in Cervantine narrative, however, is a plethora of micro-stories of individual characters that punctuate each of the author's novels and novellas, many of which are rooted in Mediterranean experiences of separation and loss, but also of unity and reconciliation. These "connected stories" will likewise serve as a unifying thread for this chapter and beyond.

The Historical Mediterranean

Castro's rebuke of Braudel reflects a broader debate as to how the Mediterranean should be delimited or characterized in its totality – or even if it ought to be at all. Scholars have generally approached this problem in one of two ways, both of which derive from what Horden and Purcell call a Romantic evaluation of the region.[6] The first represents a sustained focus on economic exchange as the foundation for a uniquely Mediterranean way of life. As a fluid network and entrepôt for this exchange, the Sea and its surrounding coasts became a central site not so much of production but of cabotage of goods and services, trade that was increasingly facilitated by advances in maritime and seafaring technologies, the establishment of international diplomatic relations, and the development of mercantile capitalism. The study of these interconnected economic nodes gave rise to the "interactionist" paradigm in Mediterranean historiography, in which "[r]edistribution, in its commonest image as trade, has been made the key to understanding not just the economy of the Mediterranean but everything else in the region as well."[7] The second major offshoot of the "Romantic" tradition of Mediterranean historiography concerns the region's topography and environment. In contrast to the relatively harsh climate of the Northern European authors who often wrote about it, for centuries the Mediterranean was trumpeted as a paradisiacal realm whose geographical and meteorological charms could not but beget certain psychological and behavioural effects on its inhabitants. The supposedly rarefied airs of Southern Europe continue to exert a potent force on the contemporary imagination, evoking vaguely exotic attributes of warm beaches, green mountains, clear skies, and other staples of the tourist trade.[8] Traditionally, the growth of the olive tree and the palm tree defined the geographical borders of the Mediterranean, and other natural features have served as organizing principles for drawing the region's boundaries and as the source of a strong environmental determinism in many scholarly studies, which will be considered in greater detail.

There are a number of additional problems that may crop up when one applies the Mediterranean as an analytical or geographical framework, as other scholars have noted since the publication of Braudel's study. I believe it is crucial to acknowledge some of the more egregious risks of uncritical "Mediterraneanizing." The first objection is that the concept of Mediterranean that has informed most recent studies of the region is ahistorical and therefore inappropriate for analysing early modernity. It is true that the broader, all-encompassing area of which Braudel speaks is largely a product of the nineteenth century, and, in this sense, it is a somewhat artificial category whose meaning is unstable.[9] Nevertheless, as Isidore of Seville notes in his *Etymologiae*, capacious notions of the Mediterranean and its relationship to surrounding lands had already emerged as early as the seventh century, exercising a potent influence on medieval and early modern thinkers, many of whom had never abandoned terra firma.[10] The Mediterranean is, in the well-known and respective terminologies of Benedict Anderson and Edward Said, an "imagined community" or an "imaginative geography," but it is one that sparked the imaginations of early modern individuals as well.[11] While it is important to recognize that *Mediterranean* is unfixed and in flux, one must not forget the same is true – and perhaps even more so – for national concepts and toponyms like *Spain*, as Patrick Geary has effectively shown in *The Myth of Nations*. The national literatures that prop up area studies and disciplinary boundaries are likewise (a)historical products, and the very meaning of *border* itself is, as Étienne Balibar reminds us, simultaneously overdetermined, polysemic, and heterogenous.[12] Of course, the critical deployment of a Mediterranean framework ought not to preclude the development of alternative transnational models, as yet other scholars have cautioned.[13]

A second and more serious concern with Mediterranean Studies is its tendency to either elide or reinforce unequal structures of power among the national, ethnic, racial, and religious entities that find themselves encircled by its purview. The disproportionately greater attention granted Southern Europe vis-à-vis North Africa and the Near East in much purportedly Mediterranean scholarship betrays the lingering Eurocentrism of otherwise earnest attempts at transcending outmoded paradigms.[14] At its worst, an exoticized Mediterraneanism can even reproduce the discourse and practices of orientalism, coloniality, and cultural imperialism.[15] The Mediterranean is far from uniform in terms of political and economic power, for, despite scholarly aspirations of a borderless region, it includes many centres, peripheries, and internal frontiers. To pretend otherwise would be to activate a homogenizing process whereby difference is subsumed under a felicitous organizational schema. As Simone Pinet penetratingly observes, this schema should already appear suspect due to its often constitutive reliance on economics, noting the perturbingly "celebratory tone in which terms such as 'exchange,' 'circulation,' 'production,' and 'connectivity' move about without others, such as 'exploitation,' 'subjection,' 'hegemony,' and 'politics.'"[16] Even if he naturally lacked the critical vocabulary of post-colonialism and other theoretical developments of the later twentieth century, I believe that this is in part what Castro had in mind when rejecting Braudel's methodology for its failure to capture the experience of racial and religious minorities like the conversos and Moriscos (respectively, Spanish Jews and Muslims forced to convert to Catholicism).

I also believe, however, that there is no need to throw the proverbial baby out with the seawater. My study holds no illusion of entirely avoiding the worthwhile critiques of Mediterranean Studies; after all, its primary focus remains a European author whose canonical status and nationality inevitably link him to the zenith of early modern imperial hegemony. This is so in spite of the possibility, however remote, that Cervantes's own ethnic and spiritual heritage might approximate him to the identities of some of the marginalized characters who, to a degree unrivalled by his contemporaries, populate his texts. A recognition of authorial positionality is imperative to stem the perils of Mediterraneanism, yet Cervantine affectivity may hold the key to opening an entirely new model for Mediterranean Studies, one that may well avoid the more pernicious of these perils. To evoke a Homeric and quintessentially Mediterranean metaphor, the field would seem to be caught between the Scylla of smoothing over often-conflictive cultural differences and the Charybdis of falling back on facile, ahistorical national models. It is as though one were faced with an inverse yet equally objectionable reductionism on both sides. Affectivity offers a passage through these twin perils by virtue of its own fluidity, mobility, and malleability, as well as, in Ahmed's words, its "stickiness,"[17] adhering to empire and nation, economy and ideology, centre and margin, the indigenous and the foreign, the collective and the subjective, and macro and micro. While literature can most certainly reify historical inequalities and those that inhere in some Mediterranean scholarship, it also harbours the potential to destabilize these discourses in ways that historiographical and anthropological approaches to the region have not.

Yet what is most conspicuously absent in Mediterranean Studies today is precisely literature. Long after the influential studies by Hayden White, Keith Jenkins, and other so-called postmodern historians registered the instability of purportedly historical, objective "truth," the wholesale exclusion of literature from Mediterranean Studies is perhaps even more puzzling today. The linguistic turn of the discipline of history pointed up the inescapable narrativity of historical writing, while suggesting that literature does not necessarily reflect the testimony of lived experience any more or less than ostensibly more objective documents do.[18] The slippages between history and fiction that emerge at any given spatio-temporal coordinates are magnified in the premodern Mediterranean, where merchant and cultural networks operated on an almost unprecedented scale and where "the boundary between 'literary' and 'nonliterary' texts is porous and in large measure artificial."[19] Perhaps this ambiguity explains the anxieties of Inquisitors "to force people to read good books and genuine histories,"[20] yet even official chronicles, as Richard Kagan has elucidated, were far from immune from the bias and spin of parties with a vested concern over their portrayal in the historical record.[21] As critics have long recognized, in any case, Cervantes's engagement with "genuine" historical events suggests that his Mediterranean can be read not only as literary history but as what Edward H. Friedman has called "periphrastic realism" or "metahistoriography."[22] Indeed, like the ambiguity that already inheres in the term *historia*, Cervantes revels in tugging at the fringes between fiction and history, "mixing truths with fabulous inventions" (mezclar verdades con fabulosos intentos), as he declares at the end of *El gallardo español*.[23] As Lucian did in his *Verae Historiae*, he casts *Don Quijote* as a chronicle of real events but, among other tricks, sharpens the ruse through the "historian" Cide Hamete Benengeli, the publication of the "real" part 1, and the titular character's resulting self-consciousness of his portrayal in part 2 of the novel. And in *Persiles y Sigismunda* Cervantes will pre-empt postmodern historians by proclaiming: "History, poetry, and painting resemble each other and indeed are so much alike that when you write history you're painting, and when you paint you're composing poetry" (La historia, la poesía y la pintura simbolizan entre sí y se parecen tanto que, cuando escribes historia, pintas y, cuando pintas, compones).[24]

Just as literature has inhabited, at best, the margins of Mediterranean Studies, so too has it struggled to gain a foothold in the burgeoning field of the history of emotion. Here a "disciplinary impasse" between history and literature has perpetuated a state of affairs in which "the more literary the text, the less likely it is to be regarded as a valuable source for the history of feeling."[25] As Sarah McNamer has recently argued, however, the "literariness of literature" should neither confound nor deter scholars of the field but, rather, signal the opportunity for "revealing another way that a historical source can operate: not only as documentary witness reflecting or representing what already exists in a given culture but as 'source' in the generative sense – as font, wellspring." "For literary texts have always served," she continues, "as affective scripts, capable of generating complex emotional effects in those who engage with them."[26] The need to recognize this generative function of literature is particularly acute in Mediterranean Studies and therefore signals yet another way in which a sustained analysis of affect in the region may yield critical, complementary insights for fields both historical and literary.

An example of such an opportunity can be found in scholarship on the emotion of fear, through which little agreement has been reached on its role in premodern cross-Mediterranean travel. At the heart of the dispute are steadfast pronouncements by historians who have either emphasized or downplayed the trepidation of life on the sea. Among the former camp, "the sea could only provoke fear, anxiety, and repulsion,"[27] and as such the sole motive for Mediterranean transit was the guarantee of material gain, the dread of maritime voyages being tempered only by the promise of profit.[28] In stark opposition are the assertions that, already by the mid-fifteenth century, "the allure of Mediterranean travel was no longer exclusively religious or commercial"[29] and that "Mediterranean man in the Middle Ages was an impassioned and persevering traveler."[30] What is one to make of these competing claims? Where is the critic to draw the line between rational fear and premodern wanderlust, between necessity and passion? Obviously these questions are laborious, and their answers depend as much on the availability of sources as on the hermeneutics of emotion. As a case study, fear thus underscores the challenges facing practitioners of the history of emotion and the manners in which fictional literature – by either frightening and dissuading readers from sea travel or romanticizing the adventure and magnifying its allure – has mediated the Mediterranean experience.

It is not surprising that fear surfaces with relative frequency in Cervantes's texts. In *Persiles y Sigismunda*, a remarkable number of shipwrecks, storms, naval skirmishes, near drownings, and other mishaps transpire at sea. For instance, while traversing the Northern Seas, the character of Mauricio abruptly interrupts a state of calm on board – "The sky, the sea, the wind, all of them together and each one by itself, were promising a very successful journey" (el cielo, la mar, el viento, todos juntos y cada uno de por sí, prometían felicísimo viaje) – by screaming out a sudden turn of fate: "We're definitely sinking! We're sinking without a doubt!" (¡Sin duda nos anegamos! ¡Anegámonos sin duda!) The reader's shock is carried across the chapter break, after which a "terrified sailor" confirms that the pilgrims' ship is sinking, forcing them to frantically abandon it while facing the fear of losing their lives: "all the terrified, frightened people rushed around looking for a way to save themselves" (todos, sobresaltados y temerosos, acudieron a buscar su remedio).[31] Similar expressions of fear on Cervantine high seas emerge in the author's novellas.[32] However, moments of thalassophobia or explicitly maritime anxiety are scarce in comparison with the trepidation that characters feel in other circumstances, for on the whole Cervantes favours the exploration of such emotions in scenes of interpersonal relations or when fear intersects with other feelings like love, jealousy, or shame.[33] What this means is that literary affects can arise in unexpected ways and with intensities that neither fully correspond with nor wholly deviate from what might be expected in a given historical situation, such as the critical stalemate on Mediterranean fear among historians. What is clear is that literature allowed readers to experience these affects from the relative safety of shore, to "travel" with neither mortal fear nor financial motive, and to experience Mediterranean mobility without moving from the armchair.

The Literary Mediterranean

Narrative transportation theory, a growing subfield of contemporary psychological research, has confirmed that being "lost in" or "carried away by" a story is not merely metaphorical but that fictional literature affords readers a host of potent effects on mood, sociability, and empathy. Through varied and extensive empirical studies, proponents of this theory have demonstrated that narrative not only emulates "reality" but also is responsible for constructing it, that literature not only represents a fictional world but also plays a role in altering the world of the reader. Emotions are the supreme vehicle for travelling through these different worlds.[34] This phenomenon was even more decisive centuries ago, when, in lieu of a psychotherapist or self-help handbooks, fictional narrative furnished readers a therapeutic outlet for exploring, experiencing, and understanding emotions. Before psychology, literature provided stories akin to emotional case studies, by which early modern individuals might either work through the conflict and commotion of Mediterranean experience or live out the affects proscribed by societal norms, or what the sociologist Arlie Hochschild long ago called "feeling rules."[35] Don Quijote is the apotheosis of narrative transportation theory, the meta-literary embodiment of the power of fiction. But perhaps the natural fixation within Cervantism on the madness of such processes has prevented an exploration of how readers themselves might more reasonably be moved by emotions in Cervantes's text.

Debates on its quantitative intensity notwithstanding, fear did not prevent the premodern circulation of people and ideas across increasingly vast distances, with soldiers, merchants, privateers, functionaries, administrators, and members of clerical orders traversing the Mediterranean for all manner of imperial and personal business. The image of the sedentary, isolated medieval village has become all but obsolete. Nevertheless, the percentage of individuals who left the confines of their regional community was still relatively low, and even fewer ventured across national and maritime borders. What this meant, once again, is that literature constituted a highly effective vehicle in its own right for encountering the Mediterranean. Whether in a private chamber such as Alonso Quijano's, a public square through communal storytelling, or on the stage of the favoured genre of theatre, fictional arts mediated the Mediterranean "experience" of many an early modern reader, listener, and spectator. Like the romances of chivalry it parodied, *Don Quijote* itself garnered an avid readership, becoming nothing short of an international bestseller soon after its publication in 1605 and 1615, and appearing in numerous editions and translations. Indeed, stories – and, since the advent of the printing press, books – formed yet another axis of the concomitant commercial revolution of Mediterranean trade, functioning as complex material instruments not only of economic exchange but also of transculturation. In their journey from one port to the next and one language to another, these stories were translated and quite often transformed.[36] Even if they remained rather expensive to possess and were overshadowed by more dominant goods like spices, glassware, or textiles, the circulation of books and manuscripts made a peerless contribution to the spread of ideas, images, motifs, characters, and styles across the Sea. One cannot deny the existence of a specifically literary economy of the Mediterranean.

As of late, the curious absence of literature in Mediterranean Studies has not gone entirely unnoticed. "Literary historians have arrived late to the Mediterranean, a fact which the observer of modern intellectual history might find baffling," as the medievalist Karla Mallette has recently recognized. Adding to this paradox, "[t]he sea would seem to be a natural field of play for literary historians: ripe with metaphorical possibility, a map with a trackless void at its centre, theory-ready. Yet we have not tried to formulate a theory of the Mediterranean."[37] Rather than plotting a prescriptive road map for such a theory, Mallette's short text serves as a clarion call to literary scholars to address this "void" and supplement the growing body of Mediterranean scholarship in other fields with our own uniquely philological, linguistic, and interpretative disciplinary tools. To do so, according to Mallette we must complement the "poetics of plurilingualism," which she identifies as a trademark of Mediterranean literature, with an equally broad professional commitment as scholars to work across multiple languages; she concludes that "the literary history we seek to understand would be better-served by scholarship with linguistic breadth in place of depth."[38] Her plea to enliven Mediterranean literary studies represents both a persuasive diagnostic of the field and a refreshingly candid affirmation of the polyglot nature of the medieval and early modern Mediterranean, which included speakers of Arabic, Greek, Latin, Romance, Turkish, Armenian, and Hebrew, to name just a few. She cites Petrarch – who infamously despised all Arabs – as proof that this characteristically Mediterranean linguistic hybridity cannot but attend the medieval literature of the region, even among the most self-avowedly monolingual authors.[39] Multilingualism flourishes in Cervantes's works as well – no fewer than fourteen different languages are mentioned in *Persiles y Sigismunda* alone. Fundamentally heteroglossic, his works incorporate other regional and foreign tongues into the text with zeal, most notably Arabic, whose spoken and written use had been criminalized by Spanish royal decree in 1566, resulting in the confiscation and burning of documents written in Arabic and Aljamía, a Castilian dialect in Arabic script, and further persecution of the Moriscos.[40] The rustic Sancho, in a powerful act of linguistic solidarity in *Don Quijote*, extemporaneously adopts the argot of the Moorish Ricote's travel companions, transcending cultural, religious, and communicational barriers while subtly critiquing the plight of the Morisco diaspora.[41] And, of course, the novel itself rests on a grand meta-linguistic irony: the narrator reports that, from chapter 10 on, it was written by the Muslim historian Cide Hamete Benengeli and translated from the Arabic by a young *morisco aljamiado*.[42] Prevalent though such plurilingual play may have been among premodern authors, few could boast such a robust and sustained engagement with other languages as Cervantes. If this is, as Mallette suggests, an essential trait of Mediterranean literature, then Cervantes epitomizes the Mediterranean author par excellence.

The Mediterranean lingua franca or Sabir, a pidgin that borrowed from Turkish, Greek, Arabic, Berber, and various Occitano-Romance languages and was spoken for centuries throughout the region, allowed travellers across this sea of languages to meet, as it were, on mutually intelligible grounds.[43] Yet spoken language was not the only means of intercultural communication available. In the early modern period as today, a great variety of gestures, facial expressions, bodily movements, physiognomic cues, rudimentary signals, contextual improvisation, and other protolinguistic signifiers all enabled individuals to transcend perceived language barriers for the purpose of transacting, or simply interacting, with linguistic others. Emotions carry out a crucial function in these kinds of exchange, as sighs, smiles, frowns, gasps, tears, blushes, and any number of expressive techniques or involuntary reactions transmit an emotional message, even those whose outward manifestation is not as immediately perceptible. This is not to say that affects are universal or infallible or that they can entirely replace strictly linguistic forms of communication; in the textual realm of literature, indeed, words are the sole medium of emotional expression. The point I wish to make is this: to fully grasp the affective work performed by the text, the critic must exercise careful attention to the nuances of language, to the sort of double translation it undergoes at the author's behest from protolinguistic signifier to literature. A comparative or trans-Mediterranean approach ought not by necessity preclude a critical awareness of these nuances that inhere in a given national language, for they can guide us to knowledge of how emotions were encoded, expressed, interpreted, exchanged, and valued, and even how they themselves constituted, at times, a lingua franca for individuals of otherwise vast cultural differences. In other words, though Mallette's call for "linguistic breadth" is well taken, first, as literary critics we must not forget the vitally non-linguistic forms that make Mediterranean communication truly broad, and, second, in striving for breadth, we need not sacrifice "depth." The Sea itself is both broad and deep, and our scholarship – inasmuch as practical and professional constraints allow – should be as well. Cervantes's writing exhibits a profound interest in these diverse forms of emotional communication, and this is another reason why a close reading of a single author can make an exceptionally valuable contribution to Mediterranean Studies.

The visual and corporeal grammar of affect in Cervantes's narrative fiction is manifest from his first long narrative, *La Galatea*. Here an attention to facial gestures initiates the reader in the ambivalent relationship between the eponymous character and Elicio, which will engender copious irruptions of sighs and tears throughout the pastoral work. Although Elicio attempts to dissimulate his love for her, "Galatea's discretion knew well, from the movements of his countenance, what Elicio was carrying in his soul; and those of her own face froze the enamoured shepherd's words on his mouth, leaving him with only the taste of that first movement" (La discreción de Galatea conocía bien, en los movimientos del rostro, lo que Elicio en el alma traía; y tal el suyo mostraba, que al enamorado pastor se le helaban las palabras en la boca, y quedábase solamente con el gusto de aquel primer movimiento).[44] The mutual scrutiny and visual appraisal that the characters perform on one another serve a hermeneutic function for interpreting their inner emotional states. Beyond the classical belief in physiognomy as the science of discerning another's soul and moral character, this passage evinces the priority given to minute sensory cues as markers of passion, especially in so far as they accord the careful observer a "taste" of potential love when the mouth is otherwise "frozen." The characters' discreet savvy in reading facial movements corresponds to the refined skill of the author in composing tableaux of such emotional interplay and sensorial richness.

Similar examples of penetrating interiority through bodily and facial legibility abound in the Cervantine corpus. Don Quijote himself professes to be fluent in the art of reading "the very true dispatches that carry the news of what happens there on the inside of the soul" (certísimos correos que traen las nuevas de lo que allá en lo interior del alma pasa), as he instructs Sancho to observe the semiotics of the entirety of Dulcinea's "exterior movements and affects" (acciones y movimientos) so that the enamoured knight can infer her feelings for him: "I will capture what she has hidden in the secret parts of her heart about that which concerns the fact of my love for her" (sacaré yo lo que ella tiene escondido en lo secreto de su corazón acerca de lo que al fecho de mis amores toca).[45] In addition to this comically exaggerated example, countless other personages manifest their facility with interpreting each other's emotions, usually by attending to subtle corporeal cues. The most patent case may be the one that increasingly ensues from the relationship between Don Quijote and Sancho themselves. This is how the latter, having recognized the knight's melancholic demeanour, is able to christen him, seemingly spontaneously, as the Knight of the Sorrowful Face (Caballero de la Triste Figura), or how, upon observing Don Quijote's ire, he can quickly deflect or pacify it by inventing a clever scapegoat for his own laughter.[46] A number of other characters also temper their laughter when they notice that Don Quijote has begun to blush, and sympathetically wish to spare him further humiliation.[47] These kinds of empathy, emotional acuity, and intuition would prove impossible without a characterological aesthetics concerned with developing affective depth and interiority in the first place, yet so often the visuality of narrative is, so to speak, overlooked, as critics of prose fiction have tended to take for granted the manners in which emotions make their presence both felt *and seen*.

The affective economy of Cervantes's Mediterranean places a particularly high premium on self-expressive communicability, on giving an account of one's emotional state. This is why so many characters are called upon to share the testimony of their life circumstances before an intra-diegetic audience, and why such stories within the story could be called the marrow of Cervantes's long novels (*La Galatea*, *Don Quijote*, and *Persiles y Sigismunda*). Such a "multiplicity of micronarratives" represents a radical departure from prevailing literary conventions and classical models.[48] And yet, almost without exception, this autobiographical narration cannot occur until other characters have noticed something irregular about either the outward appearance or the affective temperament of a newly introduced character and, as a result, entreat the stranger to treat them with said narration. These irregularities reveal something about the constitution and internal state of the character and thus stand as an invitation to share "the hidden thoughts and feelings of the soul,"[49] to cross the border between exteriority and interiority, the public and the private, through the act of self-narration. Sometimes the necessary irregularity relates to physical beauty or cultural signifiers like clothing, but, more often than not, characters take interest in others by observing subtle, non-linguistic indications of their emotional state – one marked almost inevitably by personal hardship or catastrophe. Their affliction – which, particularly for the numerous characters displaced from their origins, frequently involves trans-Mediterranean forces – conditions the possibility of the ensuing narrative and the personal stories recounted time and again across Cervantes's works. Emotions constitute the expressive precondition of the act of storytelling or writing itself.

Such is the case of Ricardo in *El amante liberal*, who languishes as a captive in Cyprus while believing his beloved Leonisa to be dead. He recounts the details of his misfortune to his friend Mahamut only after the latter has observed from afar the signs of woe in his behaviour; namely, his indulgence in a grief-stricken apostrophe to the crumbling walls of the former Christian fortification of Nicosia, "as if they could understand him: a condition peculiar to the afflicted" (como si ellas fueran capaces de entenderle; propia condición de afligidos).[50] Noticing that Ricardo appears lost in his "constant thoughts" (continuos pensamientos) and is "humbled into giving wretched signs of [his] misfortune" (rendido a dar miserables muestras de [su] desventura) and "signs of extraordinary feelings" (muestras de extraordinarios sentimientos), Mahamut implores him to divulge "what makes [him] so extremely sad" (qué es la causa que [le] trae tan demasiadamente triste).[51] His perceptive renegade friend has, true to the formula, interpreted these "signs" (muestras) or external cues as signifiers of a deeper emotional affliction, and requests that Ricardo explain its cause so that he may help to alleviate its burden. He describes his grief thus:

> "This is, Mahamut my brother, my sad story; this is the cause of my sighs and my tears; look now and consider whether it is enough to take them from the depths of my soul and engender them in the despondency of my wounded heart. Leonisa died, and with her my hope, and even though, when she was alive, that hope survived on a slender thread, still, still ..." And with this last "still" his tongue cleaved to the roof of his mouth so that he could not speak another word or stop the tears that, as they say, streamed down his cheeks so abundantly that they dampened the earth.

> "Éste es, ¡oh Mahamut hermano!, el triste suceso mío; ésta es la causa de mis suspiros y de mis lágrimas; mira tú ahora y considera si es bastante para sacarlos de lo profundo de mis entrañas y para engendrarlos en la sequedad de mi lastimado pecho. Leonisa murió, y con ella mi esperanza; que, puesto que la tenía, ella viviendo, se sustentaba de un delgado cabello, todavía, todavía ..." Y en este "todavía" se le pegó la lengua al paladar, de manera que no pudo hablar más palabra ni detener las lágrimas, que, como suele decirse, hilo a hilo le corrían por el rostro, en tanta abundancia, que llegaron a humedecer el suelo.[52]

There are several indications in this passage of the entropy of language, of its inadequacy in expressing strong affects. Ricardo's stammering (repeating the word *still*), along with the ellipsis that immediately follows in the text, represents inexpressible grief through the very failure or absence of language, symbolizing the affective limit experiences of the early modern Mediterranean. The irony is that Ricardo began his story precisely in order to reveal to Mahamut the cause of his sighs and tears, and it is these same tears that render him unable to finish it. As with most emotive scenes in Cervantes's texts, his affects are contagious, and Mahamut soon accompanies his friend in this "paroxysm." Although it delays his own desire to console him with words, eventually they both recover from their emotional stupor enough for the Muslim confidant to comfort his Christian friend.[53]

Mahamut defines this exchange with a medical analogy: "so that I may know what remedies or relief your affliction may have, you have to tell me about it, just as the patient's history is necessary to the physician, and I assure you that I shall confine it to the most hidden part of silence" (para saber qué remedios o alivios puede tener tu desdicha, es menester que me la cuentes, como ha menester el médico la relación del enfermo, asegurándote que la depositaré en lo más escondido del silencio).[54] In effect, Mahamut – as well as so many other characters with a comparable role in other works – performs the work of a physician throughout the story: having identified a symptomatology in the patient (his *muestras*), by means of his medical history, *relación*, or *historia(l)* he seeks to understand the affliction's etiology in order to venture a diagnosis and, finally, to prescribe a cure – all while maintaining the tenet of doctor-patient confidentiality.[55] One need only recall the malady of lovesickness to realize that the relationship between affectivity and early medical science is not fortuitous, in spite of a modern critical tendency to attribute an overly Manichaean slant to the body-soul distinction. More importantly, the palliative or therapeutic effect of sharing one's story aloud with another (even, to some extent it would seem, with the inanimate city walls) means that the promise of at least an initial cure is already offered by the story itself. In these characteristically Cervantine exchanges, the narrating of personal adversity falls, without exception, on sympathetic ears, prompting listeners to extend overtures of moral or material support and, oftentimes, to incorporate the aggrieved into the larger community of main characters. Fundamentally, however, the story itself entails partial relief of an emotional burden before and beyond the practical assistance tendered upon its conclusion. Although individuals may at first be reticent to speak, and despite what is sometimes the resistance of their affects to oral discourse, these hypodiegetic stories thus grant – like the similarly iterative *Arabian Nights* – a stay of one's less immediate fate, a temporary respite or deferral of subjective anguish through the shared act of communal storytelling. Such stories constitute a defining element of the literary Mediterranean.

The Affective Mediterranean

The saga of Captain Ruy Pérez de Viedma of the semi-autobiographical "Captive's Tale" in *Don Quijote* represents yet another example of a character whose release from an emotional burden hangs on the presence of an intra-diegetic audience. Upon his arrival at Juan Palomeque's inn with his beautiful Muslim saviour and future wife, Zoraida, the other guests exhort the captain to share the story of his capture and escape from the bagnios of Algiers. As I have argued elsewhere, his narration and acceptance by compassionate interlocutors partially relieve him of his shame, a feeling that is rooted in the perception of a social stigma and of the contaminating nature of Islam in early modern Spain. Thus, unlike Cervantes himself, who according to Garcés worked through the trauma of his captivity by means of the self-oriented process of writing, the captain relies wholly upon others for relief from this "specter of captivity."[56] His circumstances reveal not only how emotions in Cervantes's texts tend to be inherently social but also how they lay bare the trans-Mediterranean exclusionary practices of racial and religious othering, those that summon the Iberian programs of *limpieza de sangre* or blood purity and which, for Castro, are suppressed in Braudel's model.[57] What Ahmed calls these "cultural politics of emotion"[58] reflects my concern to show that affect in Cervantes's texts plays not just an aesthetic role in entertaining the idle reader but also a much more serious, ethical, and even subversive one, since emotions articulate and reinscribe the political conditions that rendered the Mediterranean an epicentre of imperial and ideological conflict. On the one hand, emotions can be regarded as the inverse or more human side of the logics of maritime profit, naval strategy, and military force, but, on the other, these forces traverse the subjective realm of affect and are quite often the very impetus to feeling. We need only think of Ricote's exile, Ruy Pérez de Viedma's captivity, or Zoraida's abandonment of her father to realize that a study of such feelings may help us understand both how people responded to these logics and the direction of these forces themselves.

Beyond the political capacity of emotions to shine back on the Mediterranean, there are remarkable similarities in the ways in which affectivity and the Sea have been theorized in recent years. Mobility and connectivity emerge as the most salient motifs in historiographical accounts of the early modern Mediterranean, and these same features have been distinguished as defining elements of emotion. At the most fundamental level, affectivity means to affect or be affected by, whether through the direct contact of physical touch or across what may be vast distances. These bidirectional and interpersonal vectors both move within and mirror the connectivity of a space like the Mediterranean. The historical mobility of the region finds its etymological analogue in emotion, a term whose origins in the idea of movement are clearly discernible: "*emotion* implies movement, a crossing between bodies, subjects, locations – or a failed attempt to make that crossing."[59] The early modern expression *movements of the soul* (*movimientos del alma*) manifests a kindred genealogy, as does our contemporary understanding of something that we find *moving* or that *moves* us. And, as work in the field of human and affectual geography has demonstrated, affects and emotions themselves are mobile, "interested in movements and circulations: in flows *between* people, and other things," sharing "a relational ontology that privileges the fluid over the fixed." "Affect," furthermore, "connects bodies, and makes them proximate, by flowing between them."[60] Such fluid or hy-draulic imagery is even more patent in the premodern period, when the dominance of humoralism ascribed emotional traits to liquid imbalances of blood, black bile, yellow bile, and phlegm that changed according to different environmental conditions.

The complementarity between sentiment and the Sea, however, amounts to far more than mutually felicitous figures for exploring what might otherwise seem isolated motifs, for there are several ways in which the Mediterranean comes to serve as a common yet singularly potent signifier of affect in Cervantes's texts. In *Persiles y Sigismunda*, the paronomastic relationship in Spanish of *mar* (sea) and *amar* (to love), a national literary topos, is never far from the surface.[61] It is therefore worth lingering momentarily on the pelagic qualities of *Persiles y Sigismunda* in particular. In contrast to the largely desiccated landscape of *Don Quijote*, Cervantes's last work might appropriately be called a "wet" novel. The first half of the text is soaked with an aquatic environment, beginning with the prologue, where Cervantes divulges that he suffers from dropsy or water retention, something that cannot be cured by "all the waters of the Ocean Sea made sweet" (toda el agua del Mar Océano, que dulcemente se bebiese).[62] After its *in medias res* opening, in a matter of a few short pages we encounter the first of many shipwrecks in the novel, with a vivid description of the waves that overcome the young Antonio, left for three days on the open sea but miraculously spared a worse fate. The maritime action of *Persiles y Sigismunda* circumscribes both the Mediterranean and the Northern Seas, which, as I will contend later, serve as a conveniently exoticized analogue of the Mediterranean itself, a means of introducing foreign and fantastic elements for defamiliarizing and thus reflecting on more proximate waters. The metaphorical ship of love, a Petrarchan conceit sung in sonnet form by the enamoured Portuguese soldier Manuel de Sosa Coitiño, stands as merely one example of the mutual relationship between sentiment and sea in *Persiles y Sigismunda*:

> Calm sea, fair wind, the bright and shining stars,
> a path untried but one most sweet and sure –
> all these will lead our rare and wondrous ship
> to find a pleasant, safe, and spacious port.
>
> Our ship fears neither Scylla nor Charybdis,
> nor does it stay its pure and virtuous course
> for fear of dangers that the sea may hide,
> but steers its way though open waters wide.

But if your hopes for anchor in this port
should start to waver, hesitate, or pale,
only a fool would think of shifting sail.

For love is [a] steadfast enemy to change
and only he who's constant as a gem
comes safely to a rich and worthy end.

Mar sesgo, viento largo, estrella clara,
camino, aunque no usado, alegre y cierto,
al hermoso, al seguro, al capaz puerto
llevan la nave vuestra, única y rara.

En Scilas ni en Caribdis no repara
ni en peligro que el mar tenga encubierto,
siguiendo su derrota al descubierto,
que limpia honestidad su curso para.

Con todo, si os faltara la esperanza
del llegar a este puerto, no por eso
giréis las velas, que será simpleza.

Que es enemigo amor de la mudanza
y nunca tuvo próspero suceso
el que no se quilata en la firmeza.[63]

Evoked in the midst of the perpetual nautical dangers weathered by the characters and considered an allegorical microcosm of the novel as a whole,[64] the poem calls upon lovers to summon the constancy and resolve of a ship's captain, lest their wanton "turning of the sails" causes the relationship to sink or run aground. Ironically, however, when Sosa shares the details of his life, it is revealed that this advice has utterly failed him. Having been promised marriage to Leonora, the most beautiful girl in Lisbon, he was conscripted for military service in Barbary for two years. Upon his return, as throngs of other noble suitors beheld at the wedding ceremony, Leonora proclaimed her betrothal to God instead, taking the devout orders of monastic life and leaving the forsaken Sosa at the altar. At the conclusion of his narration, Sosa falls over dead, his love and life ending as a shipwreck on the shoals of unrequited desire.[65]

In order to explain the dissonance between the values extolled by Sosa and the narrative resolution of his fate, Michael Armstrong-Roche observes that the episode "goes about annulling the promises announced by the sonnet, which is a way of saying that prose in *Persiles* rectifies the idealizing tendencies of its verse."[66] Isabel Lozano Renieblas, for her part, interprets this dissonance or what she calls Cervantes's "distanced attitude" in a didactic key, arguing that the poem refers not to the love between Sosa and Leonora but to that which the latter feels for Christ: "[T]he sonnet does not propose a lyric pathos. There is not a rhetoric of exaltation of the beloved. The lyric voice does not even refer to the passion or sentiment of the poet."[67] With this assessment it is almost as though Lozano has conflated Cervantes's sonnet with the broader tradition of shipwreck narratives, which in fact have been considered "the highest expression of realist writing, a model of exteriority in which sentiment finds no place."[68] I cannot agree, in any event, with the notion of limitations to pathos and feeling, in spite of the short circuit between lyric and prose. What exists here is precisely an excess of affect, which does of course lead to unexpected consequences (namely, Leonora's sudden change of heart). One must recall that a Mediterranean experience of separation – Sosa's military service in North Africa – precedes and begets these circumstances. This is significant because it suggests that, in the profound uncertainties of the Sea, perseverance and determination are sometimes futile qualities.[69] What we have, therefore, is not a "distancing" by Cervantes but just the opposite: a deep reflection on the affective repercussions of the Mediterranean on the part of an author whose own objectives had also been thwarted by an unexpected stay in Barbary.

The pairing of *peregrinatio vitae* and *peregrinatio amoris* bulwarks the very narrative foundation of *Persiles y Sigismunda*, but love is not the only affect to enjoy such a vital interrelationship with the sea in Cervantes's works. Jealousy, sadness, fear, and anxiety are all buoyed, as it were, by hydraulic or maritime imagery.[70] As Ernst Robert Curtius demonstrated long ago, the comparison between navigation and literary composition itself has been a commonplace since antiquity, breeding identifications between the work and the ship, the poet and the sailor, and the page and the surface of the water, among others.[71] Seafaring metaphors of this sort are not surprising, particularly among national traditions with extensive coastlines. Formulaic or clichéd though they may seem, however, these examples of what Hans Blumenberg calls the "nautical metaphorics of existence" reveal deeper philosophical and existential concerns.[72] It could be easily argued that humans, especially those who inhabit its shores or depend on it for their livelihood, have always possessed a powerful and innate affective relationship with the sea, and, in fact, neuroscientific research has begun to confirm this.[73] Whether it be characterized as one of fear, dread, reverence, joy, exhilaration, or awe, and even if Freud dismissed the "oceanic feeling" of eternity and self-empowerment as nothing more than symptoms of an under-developed ego,[74] one cannot deny that seas and oceans have exerted an immeasurable influence on the psyche, even as geographical, cultural, historical, and technological conditions have continually mediated and transformed the dynamics of the relationship.

In recent years this immemorial importance of marine bodies in the universal imaginary has increasingly captured the attention of multi-disciplinary scholars – giving rise to what have been dubbed "oceanic studies" and the "blue humanities."[75] Following in the wake of developments from various theoretical fields, these critics have sought to recuperate the liquid materiality of marine bodies and emphasize the linguistic and mimetic limits, as well as the radical possibilities, that one confronts when trying to convey the nature and dimensions of the seas. What miriam cooke calls "Mediterranean thinking" is a germane example of such possibilities. "A form of aquacentric inquiry," she explains, "Mediterranean thinking distinguishes between the materiality of earth and sea, juxtaposing the fixed and the fluid," and therefore obliges critics to think outside of the models of traditional area studies.[76] This epistemic, if admittedly abstract, potential of a water-based paradigm is evident in literary studies too. According to Philip Steinberg, "the combination of emotional intensity with material distance that characterizes our understanding of the sea has made for some excellent literature." And yet he continues by saying that "[t]he encounter from the shore, from the ship, from the surface, or even from the depths, while laden with affective feelings, captures only a fraction of the sea's complex, four-dimensional materiality."[77] What we have here, in essence, are two things that resist being adequately disclosed by language: on the one hand, the sea and, on the other, emotions. Due to their breadth, intensity, and complexity, both defy the expressive limits of words. For Cervantes, each one thus serves as a potent, complementary figure for relaying the meaning of the other.

Beyond any perceived natural or biological reaction, though, literature and other forms of cultural production have performed a pivotal role in constructing the mythos, allure, and affective associations of the marine environment. In antiquity the *nostos* theme of the epic hero's long and perilous maritime voyage home captivated audiences, and naval peripeteia was likewise a backbone of the Greek novel, such as Heliodorus's *Aethiopica*. Centuries later, with its boundless expanse, absolute horizon, unfathomable depth, and wellspring of natural force, the sea became a font of grand inspiration for the Romantics and a prime object of the aesthetic sublime. The genre of nautical fiction, popularized in the nineteenth century by the likes of Herman Melville, Robert Louis Stevenson, Joseph Conrad, and Édouard Corbière, is a further testament to the enduring pull of the open sea.[78] Their closest early modern analogue is not Cervantes but his fellow Iberian Luís de Camões, whose epic *Os Lusíadas* eulogized the Portuguese era of discovery and established him as a clear heir to Homer and Virgil.[79] Although the strictly maritime is far from the central concern of his works – his most famous characters, after all, hail from the arid Spanish hinterland – Cervantes does anticipate nautical fiction's focus on the adventures and psychological challenges of seafaring, particularly in *Persiles y Sigismunda*, as inspired by Heliodorus. These elements of *ars maritima* betray the eye of an author with extensive nautical experience himself, a curriculum vitae that Cervantes shared with his contemporaries Cristóbal de Virués, Luis Carrillo y Sotomayor, Luis Vélez de Guevara, and even Lope.[80] More importantly, Cervantes's writing evinces a profound interest in how individual and collective wills respond emotionally to the various trials that, whether in early modern history or fiction, almost necessarily arise at sea.

Such is the case when, near the end of *Don Quijote*, the protagonists arrive in Barcelona and witness the Mediterranean for the first time, a passage worth quoting in its entirety:

> Don Quixote and Sancho turned their eyes in all directions; they saw the ocean, which they had not seen before: it seemed broad and vast to them, much larger than the Lakes of Ruidera that they had seen in La Mancha; they saw the galleys near the shore, and when the canopies were raised, their pennants and streamers were revealed, fluttering in the wind and kissing and sweeping the water; from the galleys came the sound of bugles, trumpets, and flageolets, and the breeze carried the sweetly martial tones near and far. The ships began to move, performing a mock skirmish on the quiet waters, and, corresponding in almost the same fashion, an infinite number of knights on beautiful horses and in splendid livery rode out from the city. The soldiers on the galleys fired infinite pieces of artillery, to which those who were on the walls and in the forts of the city responded, and the heavy artillery shook the air with a fearsome clamor and was answered by the midship cannon on the galleys. The joyful sea, the jocund land, the transparent air, perhaps clouded only by the smoke from the artillery, seemed to create and engender a sudden delight in all the people.

> Tendieron don Quijote y Sancho la vista por todas partes: vieron el mar, hasta entonces dellos no visto; parecioles espaciosísimo y largo, harto más que las lagunas de Ruidera que en la Mancha habían visto; vieron las

galeras que estaban en la playa, las cuales, abatiendo las tiendas, se descubrieron llenas de flámulas y gallardetes que tremolaban al viento y besaban y barrían el agua; dentro sonaban clarines, trompetas y chirimías, que cerca y lejos llenaban el aire de suaves y belicosos acentos. Comenzaron a moverse y a hacer un modo de escaramuza por las sosegadas aguas, correspondiéndoles casi al mismo modo infinitos caballeros que de la ciudad sobre hermosos caballos y con vistosas libreas salían. Los soldados de las galeras disparaban infinita artillería, a quien respondían los que estaban en las murallas y fuertes de la ciudad, y la artillería gruesa con espantoso estruendo rompía los vientos, a quien respondían los cañones de crujía de las galeras. El mar alegre, la tierra jocunda, el aire claro, sólo tal vez turbio del humo de la artillería, parece que iba infundiendo y engendrando gusto súbito en todas las gentes.[81]

Salient in this rich description is the emphasis on the sensory experience of the sea, particularly of the senses of hearing and sight, with the incessant repetition of forms of the verb *ver* (*la vista, vieron, visto, habían visto*, and *vieron* again) underscoring the momentous nature of the maritime encounter.[82] The narrator goes on to report that, while marvelling at the spectacle, Don Quijote was "stupefied and astounded" (suspenso y atónito),[83] suggesting a sort of sensory overload, a transcendental state of awe reminiscent of the sublime, a notion supported as well by the superlative *espaciosísimo* and the repetition of the adjective *infinite*. Indeed, the onlookers' predominant feeling of pleasure before the "joyful sea" surges, so to speak, out of the blue ("sudden delight" [gusto súbito]).

Significantly, however, this experience is neither purely aesthetic nor limited to the realm of nature. Unlike Gustave Doré's decidedly romanticized, night-time tableau (fig. 2.1), Cervantes's representation involves the sights and sounds of war – soldiers, galleys, fortifications, cannons, and heavy artillery – as if to remind the reader of the uncompromising historical reality that in early modernity the Mediterranean Sea was a site not of unmediated ecological experience but of naval, military, and imperial exploits. The Barcelona harbour is, after all, the same stage on which the character of Ricote is tearfully reunited with his daughter, Ana Félix, after a byzantine series of events, Mediterranean crossings, and cultural encounters all set in motion by the Morisco expulsion. Among the cast of characters are Turkish pirates, a Spanish renegade, the king of Algiers, and Gaspar Gregorio, Ana Félix's Old Christian lover who is left in Barbary, impersonating a Moorish maiden. As the saga of the Ricote family poignantly illustrates, the Mediterranean is as much about hope as it is about tragedy, a realm of both separation and unity, frustration and fulfilment.

Figure 2.1. Gustave Doré, *Don Quichotte attendit le jour à cheval*, in *L'ingénieux hidalgo don Quichotte de la Manche* (Paris, 1863), p. 410. Wood engraving. Cervantes Project, Cushing Memorial Library, Texas A&M University.

True to character, Don Quijote compares himself with Gaiferos (a character from the Spanish ballad tradition said to have rescued Charlemagne's daughter, Melisendra, from the hands of Iberian Moors) and vows to place his knightly skills in the service of retrieving Gaspar Gregorio, an enterprise he reckons will prove too dangerous for others. His vow is met with disbelief by Sancho, who, in an unlikely lesson on Mediterranean geography, soberly reminds him that Gaiferos had escaped to France by land and that his master would have no means of returning to Spain from Algiers because "the sea's in the middle" (está la mar en medio). Adopting an equally matter-of-fact tone, Don Quijote retorts: "There is a remedy for everything [...] for if we have a ship along the coast, we can embark on that even if the whole world attempts to prevent it" (Para todo hay remedio [...] pues llegando el barco a la marina, nos podremos embarcar en él, aunque todo el mundo lo impida). Sancho's final remark on the matter aims to settle the dispute: "Your grace paints a very nice picture and makes it seem very easy [...] but there's a big ditch between discourse and deed" (Muy bien lo pinta y facilita vuestra merced [...] pero del dicho al hecho hay gran trecho).[84] Their exchange is deceptively simple, for, as is typical, beneath the overt humour of the proverbial refrains, droll banter, and peevish rapport lie deeper implications. Sancho's self-evident statement – "the sea's in the middle" – would seem to acknowledge the manifest risks of Mediterranean travel, the troubling uncertainties of passage on a body of water peopled with pirates and other threats too daunting for the chivalric pretensions of his master. Ever present in Cervantes's writing and an echo of the author's past, the Sea is the breach (trecho) between fable and fact, fiction and reality (del dicho al hecho). The Mediterranean is in the middle, literally and literarily.

Contesting a Sea of Discourses

If we look further afield, and in the spirit of the literary longue durée, Cervantes's writing challenges not only Romanticized conceptions of the Mediterranean but also commonplaces of a more insidious nature. One outcome of the environmental determinism of Mediterranean scholarship, and perhaps an orientalist remnant of the Romantic approach, has been the relentless characterization of Mediterranean civilizations as innately more impassioned and less given to reason than their northern counterparts.[85] Ostensibly more empirical studies performed in the very recent past have reinforced the popular notion that Mediterranean peoples are more expressive and "in touch" with their emotions,[86] while some Mediterranean countries have even embraced these associations, capitalizing on their marketing potential for the tourism industry, as Spain did in the 1990s with the promotional slogan "Passion for Life."[87] However, even when masquerading under seemingly innocuous cultural observations, such tropes have all too often served as alibis for reproducing a number of more troubling stereotypes. Erected from a predominately white, Christian North, these include the dismissal of people of the Global South as constitutionally less civilized; less reasonable; less in control of their sexual proclivities, emotions, and destinies; and disinclined to socio-economic development and progress.[88] The general equation of lower latitudes with lower aptitudes, in turn, casts them as the violent other and a threat to the well-ordered society of Protestant Europe, thus abetting imperial moves to conquer, coerce, and "civilize" the barbarians – tendencies that have existed on the continent since at least the seventeenth century.[89] In short, vaguely emotional typologies and psychological generalizations of the Mediterranean have historically attended more explicit race-, religion-, and nation-based forms of discrimination. Such commonplaces served as theatrical fodder for Cervantes's literary adversary Lope, whose Moorish character of Arbolán states in *Los esclavos libres* (The free slaves) that

> [...] love was born in Spain,
> And in Africa, jealousy.
> The Spaniard knows how to love
> and the Moor to be suspicious of;
> the Christian only to flare,
> the African to fear;
> one to serve, the other to stifle.

> [...] el amor nació en España,
> Y en el África, los celos.
> Sabe el español amar
> y sabe el moro guardar;
> el cristiano sólo arder,
> el africano temer;
> servir uno, otro celar.[90]

The simplistic emotional dichotomies that seesaw across these verses underscore the ease with which such stereotypes circulated, particularly in so far as they implicated those on the other, non-Christian side of the Mediterranean.

Indeed, the Muslim Arab community has borne the brunt of the purportedly irrational nature of Mediterranean civilization, even as it was recognized, albeit reluctantly, as the source of medieval knowledge.[91] For centuries this community was accused of lacking emotional and intellectual curiosity, as though it were bereft of epistemophilia, *amor studentium*, or wonder – that emotion which Descartes famously inducted as "the first of all the passions."[92] To deprive Arab Muslims of the desire for knowledge subtly performs the dual function of barbarizing them and of justifying the imperial conquests of European Christians conducted precisely under the banner of curiosity and exploration. As Nabil Matar has demonstrated in his penetrating study of seventeenth-century Arabic travel writing, however, Muslims exhibited both wanderlust and a similar zeal for knowledge of others, but the affect of fear tempered their enthusiasm for trans-Mediterranean voyages and *multaqa*, or encounters.[93] This fear – experienced by ordinary citizens and, as various accounts show, by sailors, merchants, and even ambassadors – was rooted in the historical memory of invasion, captivity, enslavement, piracy, and other forms of violence that Muslims had suffered at the hands of Christians. Later, these associations came to include the expulsion of the Moriscos, an event that gave rise not only to fear but also to prolonged feelings of loss, sadness, bitterness, and resentment – feelings to which Cervantes's Morisco character Ricote only partially, if poignantly, bears witness. An inordinate scholarly emphasis on the terror felt by Spaniards and other Europeans regarding North African and Ottoman threats has tended to imply that Mediterranean violence was unidirectional, that those on the "other side" lived free from corresponding fear and anxiety.[94] This is not to exempt North Africans and Ottomans from responsibility for what, in some cases, are historically comparable examples of violence but rather to contest the reflexive tendency, in the premodern era as today, to demonize or overstate the threat of Islam and impute fearfulness to its practitioners. These examples alert us to the often subtle yet powerful work performed by affect in a given socio-historical context and to the necessity of critically examining our scholarship for a better understanding of how affect has abetted certain ideological and political agendas.

The engagement with alterity in Cervantes's texts unsettles these popular fictions, illuminating the point at which they diverge from historical "reality." His writing casts emotions as complex, protean phenomena that are neither wholly pernicious nor praiseworthy, never entirely condemnatory nor redemptive – and yet anything but negligible. In this sense they reflect the curiously antithetical quality of the Mediterranean's most popular appellations, christened the "Great Sea" by ancient Syrian and Phoenician texts and the Hebrew Bible, and known among the Greeks and Romans as the "Corrupting Sea." While the most historically and politically suggestive episodes of Cervantes's oeuvre engage with and critique the concept of affect as a tool for othering, emotions just as frequently constitute an equalizing force that affects people of all national, religious, and ethnic identities – positively or negatively, but equally. It is for these reasons that an expressly literary, Cervantine approach to the region has the potential to destabilize the unquestioned stereotypes of Mediterranean individuals and to contest the grand narratives that, in their geographical and pseudoscientific fervour, have tended to neglect the individual altogether.

Such an approach does not mean a renunciation of worldly passions, a retreat to the solipsism symptomatic of the neo-Stoicism championed by Cervantes's contemporaries. We can situate Cervantes's representation of emotion, rather, within a philosophical genealogy that foregrounds affect as a form of knowledge whose relationship with rationality can be characterized as one not of diametric opposition but of mutual immanence. To quote Feliciano de Silva's satirical treatment in the second paragraph of *Don Quijote*, Cervantes manifests a marked interest in exploring "unreason's reason" (la razón de la sinrazón) – a most fitting précis for Cervantine affectivity.[95] Although Cervantes was acquainted with El Brocense's neo-Stoic writings[96] and was almost certainly aware of the broader neo-Stoic movement, his own writing activates emotion not just as a compelling aesthetic device but also as a potentially powerful ethical tool. In this way the author rejects excessive sentimentality for its own sake while echoing a long philosophical genealogy that, beginning with Aristotle, sought to vindicate the virtues of emotion and sentimentalism: from Augustinian humanism, the moral sense theory of David Hume and Adam Smith, and other cognitivist models that materialized in the later seventeenth and eighteenth centuries; to the pivotal affect theories of such figures as Spinoza, Nietzsche, and Deleuze and Guattari; to, more recently, the popular philosophical writings on emotion by Martha Nussbaum, Jesse Prinz, Robert Solomon, Victoria Camps, and Eugenio Trías; to a panoply of contemporary self-help literature imploring us to "get in touch with our feelings."[97]

Here it behooves us to recall Seneca's maxim, popular throughout the Renaissance, of "longum iter per præcepta, breve per exempla," or the idea that poetry can teach morality more efficiently than philosophy can. To grasp the lesson, however, the reader or listener must first be *moved*

Figure 2.2. Cesare Ripa, *Ragione*, in *Iconologia* (Rome, 1603), p. 425. Print. Image property of the Biblioteca Nacional de España, Madrid.

to admire (*admiratio*) the exemplary comportment of a fictional work's characters. But unlike Seneca and many of his own poetic forbears and literary peers, Cervantes did not conceive of the passions solely as a force to be dominated by reason.[98] By and large, his works eschew the deterministic strands of Stoic thought by establishing emotions as an ethical choice – not merely a judgment to be repressed – based on the free will and voluntary faculties of the subject.[99] Cervantes recuperates a sense of virtue before it is sundered from emotion. In contrast to the turning away and inward of Stoic doctrine, inoculated against the vagaries of happenstance and loss, Cervantes espouses an ethics that, like Aristotle's, is both more communal and vulnerable. His texts reveal an ideology that is subtly yet eminently more worldly, open to contingency, and more responsive to the travails and triumphs of the Mediterranean world that he and his characters inhabit. Unlike reason, whose popular iconography promotes a warring entity that yokes ignoble and unruly passions (fig. 2.2), the "unreason" of emotion becomes an ethical alternative for the *unreasonable* violence of the early modern Mediterranean.[100]

Deviations from Reason in a Sea of Diversity

For an example of an emotional ethics in times of violence, let us turn to Cervantes's theatre. Set in the far-off Mediterranean of the ancient Roman Empire, Cervantes's historical tragedy *Numancia* would have nonetheless struck some of its sixteenth-century spectators as uncannily familiar. The play represents the author's most sobering meditation on the aftermath of war and imperial conflict – those chronically recurrent themes of the Sea to which Cervantes himself also bore witness.[101] Throughout the four acts of the drama, the citizens of Numantia struggle in despair to resist the increasingly destructive Roman siege of the settlement, historically waged by the general Scipio Africanus the Younger as part of the Celtiberian Wars of the second century BCE. Suffused with tragic pathos, *Numancia* juxtaposes the indiscriminate violence of an occupying force with the everyday lives of individuals, bringing into stark relief not only the physical toll but also the varying emotional effects of the blockade. During a heated exchange in the midst of battle, the character of Leoncio accuses his friend and fellow citizen Marandro of being unduly swept away by amorous passion and therefore distracted from the task of defending the city:

> LEONCIO: How your amorous thought
> makes you lose your head! [...]
> Yes, if loving is not calculated,

> as reason has dictated,
> with when, how, and whom.
> MARANDRO: You want to put rules on Love?
> LEONCIO: Reason can supply them.
> MARANDRO: Reasonable they may be,
> but not of much subtlety.
> LEONCIO: To amorous endeavours,
> reason is foreign.
> MARANDRO: Love does not go against it,
> even though it deviates from it.

> LEONCIO: ¡Cómo te saca de seso
> tu amoroso pensamiento! [...]
> Sí, si a el querer no se mide,
> como la razón lo pide,
> con cuándo, cómo y a quién.
> MARANDRO: ¿Reglas quies poner a Amor?
> LEONCIO: La razón puede ponellas.
> MARANDRO: Razonables serán ellas,
> mas no de mucho primor.
> LEONCIO: En la amorosa porfía,
> a razón no hay conocella.
> MARANDRO: Amor no va contra ella,
> aunque de ella se desvía.[102]

Leoncio's admonition that Marandro discipline his love with reason encapsulates the widespread early modern paradigm of the opposition between rationality and emotion. Believing this to be a disservice to his feelings, however, Marandro rejects his friend's advice because he sees neither love and war nor emotion and reason as incompatible pairs. Towards the end of the play, after the city has been all but lost, Leoncio recognizes the truth in Marandro's philosophy and regrets his prior thinking: "it is made clear to us / that in love there is no cowardly breast" (se nos muestra claro / que no hay cobarde enamorado pecho).[103] In a general sense, Leoncio's words reflect the Platonic concept of an army of homosexual men in love, originally described in the *Symposium* as the Sacred Band of Thebes, whereby soldierly valour was mutually guaranteed by the potential for shame before one's fellow lover, should conduct on the battlefield be anything less than honourable and heroic.[104] Leoncio's conclusion goes further to suggest that love can serve as a form of resistance to imperial violence, even when that love ultimately implies wilful self-annihilation. In other words, the Numantians' eventual collective decision to either die of starvation or commit suicide – as Bariatro does by throwing himself from the tower in an act of fraternal solidarity at the end of the play – denies Scipio the trophy or symbolic victory that even a single prisoner of war would have afforded him. It is the bonds of *philia* that foreclose just such a possibility.

More importantly, Marandro's words betray a subtle yet critical insight into Cervantes's philosophical approach to emotion: "Love does not go against [reason], / even though it deviates from it." By asserting that such amorous deviations are worthwhile, the very use of the verb *desviar* seems to deviate from the binary oppositions of reason and emotion to which many of Cervantes's contemporaries subscribed. Deviation thus becomes a meaningful figure for the Cervantine representation of Mediterranean experience. It also signals yet another convergence of emotional and maritime language because it happens to be the same word used to describe the vicissitudes of fortune in the Mediterranean, for the mercurial and unexpected nature of life on the Sea. Its capricious winds and underwater currents are responsible, for instance, for the deviations of galley ships in "The Captive's Tale," leading directly to Captain Ruy Pérez de Viedma's initial capture and subsequent imprisonment in Algiers. Later in the story similar "deviations" threaten to return the protagonist to captivity when his escape ship begins to drift back towards the North African coast.[105] As we can glean from these examples, in the Mediterranean context such deviations can sometimes mean the difference between freedom and captivity or even life and death. But they are an integral and inevitable facet of the Mediterranean experience and, therefore, of emotional experience as well. Moreover, it is these same deviations that on the narrative plane pique and hold our interest as readers, when a character's emotional reaction deviates from reason, or the plot deviates from its expected course, thereby producing surprise, building suspense, or ushering in a new conflict or twist in its resolution. In part, this is how and why affect (and Cervantes's works themselves) can *affect* us so much as readers, and why it can be so subversive. Just as Don Quijote loosens the reins on Rocinante in order to deviate from a set or rational course – and, in doing so, subverts the Platonic metaphor of emotions as wild horses that must constantly be tamed by the whip, chomp, and bit of reason – Cervantine affectivity veers from the well-worn path prescribed by emotional repression. Going astray in such a way can serve, as in the case of Cervantes's Numantians, as a means of defying and resisting imperial logics. More broadly, these deviations suggest not only unpredictable mobility but also disruptions to rational stability and disturbances to homeostatic order. They signify an encounter with difference, with ideas and identities that lie outside the dominant, and considerably narrower, discourse. Deviations may imply marginality, misalignment, and even deviance – deviance from racial, ethnic, religious, sexual, gender, or other social norms. By splitting off from a single, normative path, deviations mean, most simply, diversity.

In fact, there could hardly be a more appropriate contextual analogy than the Mediterranean for the emotions that share its diversity, complexity, non-fixity, dynamism, and interconnectivity. Cervantes's Mediterranean was not an early modern version of what Arjun Appadurai has called a "community of sentiment," "a group that begins to imagine and feel things together."[106] Although Cervantes's writing portrays various scenes of cross-Mediterranean exchange and interconfessional reconciliation, it just as often depicts the differences that underpinned the disparate and conflictive reality of the region. In complementary fashion, the discussion in *Don Quijote* of individual interpretations of chivalric romance highlights the value of a literary work capable of producing myriad emotional responses in its readers and listeners, as evidenced by the aesthetic preferences of the innkeeper Juan Palomeque's daughter:

> [T]he truth is that even if I don't understand them, I like to hear them, but I don't like all the fighting that my father likes; I like the laments of the knights when they're absent from their ladies; the truth is that sometimes they make me cry, I feel so sorry for them.

> [E]n verdad que aunque no lo entiendo, que recibo gusto en oíllo; pero no gusto yo de los golpes de que mi padre gusta, sino de las lamentaciones que los caballeros hacen cuando están ausentes de sus señoras, que en verdad que algunas veces me hacen llorar, de compasión que les tengo.[107]

While reproducing the gendered discourse that limited women's literary taste to the trifles of sentimentalism, the young girl's precocious, if slightly naive, interpretation contrasts with Don Quijote's own defence of the books of chivalry before the canon: "read these books, and you will see how they drive away melancholy if you are so afflicted, and improve your spirits if they happen to be low" (lea estos libros, y verá cómo le destierran la melancolía que tuviere y le mejoran la condición, si acaso la tiene mala").[108] Despite its coarse, lowbrow qualities, these characters affirm that even chivalric romance can produce varying emotional responses, from sadness and compassion to hope and therapeutic enjoyment.

Lest this incongruity of reception appear but a parodic critique of the genre, may we recall the advice for Cervantes's own novel offered by the anonymous friend of the prologue: "Another thing to strive for: reading your history should move the melancholy to laughter, increase the joy of the cheerful, not irritate the simple, fill the clever with admiration for its invention, not give the serious reason to scorn it, and allow the prudent to praise it." (Procurad también que, leyendo vuestra historia, el melancólico se mueva a risa, el risueño la acreciente, el simple no se enfade, el discreto se admire de la invención, el grave no la desprecie, ni el prudente deje de alabarla.)[109] The friend's counsel mirrors the words of the priest towards the end of the 1605 novel, who makes a plea for the "good" comedia:

[F]or having heard an artful and well-constructed play, the audience would come out happy with the comic portions, instructed by the serious, marveling at the action, enlightened by the arguments, forewarned by the falsehoods, made wiser by the examples, angered at vice and enamored of virtue: *a good play should awaken all these affects in the soul of its audience.*

[P]orque de haber oído la comedia artificiosa y bien ordenada saldría el oyente alegre con las burlas, enseñado con las veras, admirado de los sucesos, discreto con las razones, advertido con los embustes, sagaz con los ejemplos, airado contra el vicio y enamorado de la virtud: *que todos estos afectos ha de despertar la buena comedia en el ánimo del que la escuchare.*[110]

These interventions open an essential window onto Cervantes's philosophy of emotional aesthetics – namely, that the excellence or sublimity of a fictional work can be measured precisely by its capacity to engender a multiplicity of affective responses in the reader or spectator.[111] I would suggest that the author thus refashions the Renaissance trope of *variatio*, which aspired to evoke the diversity already found in nature in order to relieve monotony and produce pleasure, for the modern demands of the novel.[112] Lauded in his time for their variety, Cervantes's narrative works lend themselves not only to the collective reception of public spectators but also to the greater emotional diversity of a growing body of private readers. The hodge-podge of modes, styles, verses, and genres in *Don Quijote* that has been regarded as a defining element of the modern novel itself,[113] or the stylistic innovations that Mercedes Alcalá Galán calls "unfettered writing" (escritura desatada),[114] finds its complement in the vast assortment of affective reactions that the text continues to elicit today.

Hutchinson has recently proposed the existence of what he terms "Mediterranean frontier literature," a distinguishing feature of which is an encounter with difference. In his view such frontier literature is not thematic but rather constitutes an entirely distinct genre, one of whose principal exponents is Cervantes. In their Mediterranean interfaces with doctrinal and ethnic diversity, characters of this genre are also confronted with "limit situations that oscillate between life and death, power and slavery, cruelty and compassion, love and hate."[115] Shakespeare serves as an illustrative example of this generic distinction: although some twenty of the Bard's works are set in the ancient or early modern Mediterranean, only two of these plays – the Venetian ones, *Othello* and *The Merchant of Venice* – exhibit the characteristics of Mediterranean frontier literature that Hutchinson describes, namely in the interreligious themes embodied by their respective characters of Othello and Shylock. As Hutchinson recognizes, this contrast between Shakespeare and Cervantes reminds us that a chronotope alone – in this case, the early modern Mediterranean – is insufficient for determining the more fundamental attributes of a genre or body of literature. In part, it is precisely this limitation that in the last few years has prompted critical attempts to move beyond the paradigm of national literatures. In doing so, however, we must take care not to reinscribe the same deficiencies in a Mediterranean model, to ensure we are not merely scaling up national frameworks. In this "project of reterritorialization" that Sharon Kinoshita identifies as that of Mediterranean literature, recalling the risks of Mediterraneanizing mentioned earlier is also crucial.[116] For these reasons I would extend Hutchinson's definition of "Mediterranean frontier literature" to suggest that, in order to be considered Mediterranean as such, a literature must necessarily involve a transaction across or a transgressing of borders. To join a Mediterranean republic of letters, it is not enough for a narrative to take place in the Sea. It must be pluralistic in a number of different ways – plurilingual, interconfessional, cross-cultural, trans-ethnic, multiracial, polysemic, heterogenous. It must by definition include an encounter with alterity.[117]

Although the scope of the present study prevents me from considering at length the debates around Cervantes's own engagement with linguistic, religious, and racial otherness, may it suffice to recall the studies by Castro, Carrasco Urgoiti, Márquez Villanueva, and others that have documented the author's uncommon and often heterodox approach to those who dwell on the "other side" of the Mediterranean.[118] In essence, these critics have established that a defining trait of Cervantes's writing is not only an acceptance of difference but also a defence of tolerance, particularly when it comes to the Muslim, Moorish, Turkish, and Berber communities that habitually comprised the Spanish imperial adversary. As Barbara Fuchs perceptively observes, moreover, Cervantes's "emphasis on the permeability of the [Mediterranean] contact zone and on the fluidity of the subjects who inhabit it effectively undoes the orthodox narratives of homogenous and fully realized national identity put forth by the Spanish Crown."[119] Forged in the crucible not only of *convivencia* but also of conflict, his works bear the marks of a hybrid existence and therefore signal Cervantes as a prime candidate for laying the groundwork of a literary Mediterranean, for mapping its possibilities as well as its limitations. Cervantes's writings at once expand and circumscribe the semantic field of the Sea, directing us, once again, towards a critical Mediterranean Studies.

Likewise, the lived experience of the former soldier, captive, prisoner, and poet – from Alcalá de Henares to Algiers, Madrid to Italy, Lepanto to Lisbon, Orán to Rome, and everywhere in between – was nothing if not diverse.[120] My purpose in highlighting this fact is not to recover an autobiographical motive for Cervantine affectivity but merely to establish that Cervantes already had at his disposal a plethora of real-life people, heart-rending material, personal adversity, and first-hand experience on which to draw when composing the affective profile of his works. Verisimilitude, which scholars have perennially certified as a distinguishing quality of Cervantes's writing,[121] finds its corollary in the emotional realism of his characters. If the aesthetic inspiration for *variatio* was culled from the natural world, then what better model could Cervantes have had than human nature for the development of his highly varied and preternatural affectivity? And what better form than the novel – with its heterogeneity, hybridity, and open horizons – for expressing it? Prose narrative accorded him the ideal medium through which to convey a multitude of variation, from that afforded by its formal properties, to the abundant emotions of his characters, and to the diversity of the Mediterranean where they circulate. According to Don Quijote himself, it is through "so varied a pattern that art, imitating nature ... seems to surpass it" (una variada labor, de manera que el arte, imitando a la naturaleza, parece que allí la vence).[122] We therefore have reason to agree with Hutchinson that, though "they are still within the modalities of the human, [...] some characters, rather than being less than real persons, may be more than real persons, and their emotions may be more than those of real persons."[123] A conglomeration of multiple frontiers, topographies, and ecologies, the Mediterranean is, as Franco Cassano has described it in an essay vindicating the region's cultural practices in the face of the market-driven logics of

Northern and Western Europe, "a place where the richest and the most complex personalities are gathered," where "one can experience diversity."[124] As if to pay homage to this diversity of which he was, as an early modern author, uniquely and undeniably conscious, Cervantes endows his characters with "the most complex personalities" as well, allowing their multifaceted affects to intervene in the political, ideological, and racialized economies that traversed the Mediterranean of his time. Revealing the interiority of these characters, he also reveals something about the larger world outside the work; their micro-stories of emotional affliction reflect back on the macro-structures of history. The nearly endless variety of their affects transcribes the affective geographies of a sea of diversity.

PART TWO

Quixotic Passages

Shadows of the Inquisition: Honour, Shame, and a Cervantine View of Mediterranean "Values"

The art of punishing, then, must rest on a whole technology of representation.

Michel Foucault

If ... the lowering of the eyelids, the lowering of the eyes, the hanging of the head is the attitude of shame, it may also be that of reading.

Eve Sedgwick and Adam Frank

The seventh of November 1604 was to have been a memorable day for the residents of Triana, a suburb of Seville on the banks of the Guadalquivir River that had hosted the headquarters of the Spanish Inquisition since 1481. Preparations for an auto-da-fé scheduled for that day were nearly complete, and, on the eve of the infamous act's celebration, throngs of ardent spectators filled the streets to witness the solemn procession of the Green Cross, all while the prisoners awaited their fate in the town's castle. And then, at eleven o'clock that night, an urgent royal decree was received. Fernando de Acevedo, a canon, inquisitor, and statesman for King Philip III, described the scene: "When Seville and all its suburbs are waiting for the celebration of the auto-da-fé, they hear the voice of a town crier saying that for legitimate reasons it was being suspended, and then a great sentiment began to form among everyone, an interior sadness as though each one were the offended [*agraviado*] [...] in this feeling and outcome were recognized the love and respect, along with fear, that is felt toward the Inquisition."[1] As the most visible face of the Inquisition's varied activities, the general auto-da-fé capitalized on its increasingly theatrical qualities as a Baroque spectacle to become a potent force in the imagination of the Spanish populace, a source of public fervour as well as a repository into which it was strategically channelled. Acevedo's account, however, also illustrates the range and intensity of the emotions that such a spectacle (or, in this case, its last-minute cancellation) could stir in its attendees, from a generalized feeling of affliction and internal sadness to seemingly contradictory sentiments of love, respect, and fear. The observation that the jilted bystanders felt as though they were affronted, by internalizing the feeling of offence typically reserved for the accused, suggests at least two more: honour and shame, concepts that underwrote the effectiveness of inquisitorial practice in the early modern Mediterranean and have been perennially cited as unifying features of the region as a whole.

Although the aggrandizing, propagandistic identification of "love" and "respect" for the Inquisition in Acevedo's description might contrast rather starkly with the affective associations of ordinary citizens with the institution, this disparity alerts us to the rhetorical, discursive, and performative praxis of inquisitorial attempts to appropriate and exploit certain collective emotions towards politico-religious ends. In Pierre Bourdieu's terms, honour and shame thus constituted an emotional "habitus" that structured social and political practices, actuated through a kind of recursive function or feedback loop whereby the affective content of lived experience was absorbed and instrumentalized by an institution like the Inquisition, only to percolate back down to shape the feelings of everyday life.[2] This phenomenon is perhaps most clear in the morphological distinction between *shame* as a noun (the feeling of being ashamed) and *shame* as a verb (the action of shaming), one that will form a prominent line of analysis in this chapter. Literature and other forms of cultural production intervene in this tension as well, and Cervantes's writing, in particular, reveals a distinct interest in exploring the affective valences that inevitably attend historical practices, even one at first blush as cold and calculated as the inquisitional auto-da-fé. While a more or less explicit representation of an auto-da-fé in *Don Quijote* has long been recognized by critics,[3] I identify a similarly inquisitorial discourse in the principal character's encagement throughout the final chapters of the 1605 novel. Until now, the critical attention paid to Don Quijote's encagement has chiefly focused on either its historical use as a treatment for madness or its precedents in the romances of chivalry.[4] Without discounting these intertextual parallels, my close reading of these chapters uncovers a potentially more subversive influence: that of early modern methods of dealing with criminality, and especially those informed by inquisitorial and popular practices of public shaming. As far as I am aware, this particular element has yet to be recognized as a historical undertone of Don Quijote's encagement. Beyond recovering an alternative historical context for these episodes, my purpose in this chapter will be to suggest how, by attending closely to the characterological manifestations of an emotion like shame, we stand to gain a more nuanced – if ultimately less unified – view of the ways in which it was expressed, manipulated, transformed, and exchanged in the affective economy of the early modern Mediterranean. My consideration of the heuristic possibilites opened by shame will allow me to conclude by gesturing towards an ethical re-evalution of its role in the constitution of supposed Mediterranean "values," a role that stands to challenge dominant structures of power through an affirmation of defeat and to prescribe an ethics dwelling at the intersection of personal virtue and political, non-violent dissent.

Rooted in Roman Catholic doctrine and practised in Spain, Portugal, France, Italy, and the Papal States, the Christian Inquisition – despite its more limited practice in other parts of Europe and its later expansion to some Asian and American colonies – was a decidedly Mediterranean phenomenon. Although the Spanish Inquisition's primary mandate was to enforce compliance with Catholic orthodoxy, inordinately affecting the conversos and Moriscos, the inquisitor's manuals, instructions (*instrucciones*), and amendments (*cartas acordadas*) that governed the Holy Office's procedures were circulated and reprinted across the Mediterranean and thus partook in its dynamic networks of exchange. In Cervantes's works, shame (as well as emotion more broadly, as noted previously) is often framed by historical structures that, like the Inquisition, govern significant swaths of the Mediterranean at large, as well as by those that, on a smaller scale, adhere locally to cultural, regional, national, and imperial lines. By focusing on these structures or shame's enabling conditions, one can draw a more complete map of these lines, in addition to the nodes and flows between them. This approach is consistent with the Braudelian model of the Mediterranean as a space both incapable of being grasped independently of what lies outside of it and undermined by an adherence to rigid boundaries. The very nature of shame is such that it may be provoked precisely by a transgression of these boundaries, at once calling our attention to their existence while highlighting the fluidity and interdependence of cultural contact zones. In short, the geographical unity of the Mediterranean should not be taken as a priori evidence of emotional uniformity. My analysis in this chapter, therefore, supposes two complementary yet divergent conceptual manoeuvres: one that forestalls the reification of a homogenous or monolithic "Mediterraneanism," and one that demystifies the honour-shame dyad by recovering the material and corporal conditions of shame. Doing so will allow me to plot further the shared profits and perils that emerge when interrogating affectivity within a Mediterranean framework and, finally, to rehabilitate local (hi)stories that are all marked by blood: the blood of shame's blush, that which was shed through violent conflicts, and that which governed the politics of *limpieza de sangre* or blood purity.

Anthropologies of Mediterranean Honour and Shame

I will situate my analysis against the backdrop of the ongoing and often polemical debates surrounding honour and shame in the Mediterranean. An overt assumption that honour and shame are counterparts of the same cultural phenomenon has coloured many anthropological and historical studies of these so-called Mediterranean values. In the introduction to *Honour and Shame: The Values of Mediterranean Society*, for example, J.G. Peristiany discusses honour and shame as merely "two poles of an evaluation,"[5] and David D. Gilmore refers to them as "moral twins."[6] More recently, Horden and Purcell concur that honour and shame "might suitably be interpreted as the values of Mediterranean microecologies."[7] Such conflations are at least partly responsible for the disproportionate level of critical attention allocated to honour over its complementary "pole." It is true that, as a fictional theme, honour is nearly ubiquitous in the comedia, especially the dramas of Calderón, Tirso, and Lope, who even prescribed it as the most reliable means of moving a theatrical audience.[8] Castro wrote extensively on the importance of honour in Cervantes's works, and it was no less omnipresent, so the story goes, as a social phenomenon: it was the linch-pin in relations between gentlemen, the sine qua non of female worth, the watchword of early modern Spanish society at large. Bartolomé Bennassar went so far as to claim: "If there was one passion capable of defining the conduct of the Spanish people, it was the passion of honor."[9] Shame, by comparison, remains inconspicuous in early modern historiography and textual criticism. The emotion is nevertheless not only distinct from honour and a meaningful object of study in its own right but also an essential narrative feature of *Don Quijote*, even if it is not as immediately discernible as honour.

There is a variety of reasons why shame sits uneasily alongside honour and why a reassessment of their conjugation is overdue. Modern psychologists and personality theorists such as Silvan Tomkins, whose work on emotion has inspired many publications in the field of cultural studies, have identified a number of other contrasting emotions for shame and placed them on "axes" that correspond to the affect's polyvalent attachments, such as shame-pride, shame-humiliation, shame-guilt, shame-fear, and shame-rage.[10] The extended idea in classical, medieval, and early modern thought that shame could signify virtue – in effect, a quality seen as honourable – further serves to deconstruct a facile honour-shame dichotomy.[11] By remarking on these complexities, what I wish to stress is not that shame was entirely independent of the "honour code" that has been taken for granted as a fundamental characteristic of Mediterranean societies, but rather that the emotion often functions in modes that are quite different from honour, modes overshadowed by such received generalizations.[12] The picaresque novel, a genre for which we might identify yet another axis for shame – shamelessness – patently attests to this reality: although honour was reserved for a relatively small sector of society, shame could be experienced universally, even if the very idea of the picaresque is borne by the figure of the *sinvergüenza*. Unlike honour's dependence on social, economic, religious, and racial privilege – namely the distinction of possessing Old Christian blood untainted by Moorish or Jewish ancestry – shame was an emotion available to all. This, along with its visual, material, and bodily qualities, means that shame operates in ways that subtly yet radically trouble its conventional association with honour.

These distinct complexities of shame also inhere in the semantic registers of the word itself, for which caution must be exercised in the practice of translation. As noted previously, although the translation of nearly any term or concept must necessarily confront the challenges of capturing its peculiar cultural milieu, this is particularly true of emotions, and even more so of shame. Yakov Malkiel has suggested "five distinct shadings" of the classical Latin *verecundia*, from which the Spanish *vergüenza* derives: "(1) 'reserve,' 'restraint'; (2) 'delicacy,' 'decency,' 'bashfulness,' 'chastity'; (3) 'sense of shame,' 'blush'; (4) 'respect,' 'esteem' (for somebody else); (5) 'timidity,' 'self-consciousness,' 'embarrassment.'" He further notes that *vergüenza* underwent "a significant extension of meaning" beyond these connotations of its Latin precedent and speculates that such diversification owes to the "inherently ambiguous" nature of shame as an affect.[13] The term *vergüenza* is even included in Barbara Cassin's recent *Dictionary of Untranslatables*, an ambitious collection of singular terms from various languages whose meanings hold valuable philosophical insights yet defy straightforward translation. Unlike the French *vergogne*, for example, which has become obsolete except in its negative form (*sans vergogne*), *vergüenza* is steeped in nuance, especially in the uniquely lexicalized *vergüenza ajena*. Betokening a truly untranslatable essence of "social solidarity" and "sense of community," the concept of *vergüenza ajena* highlights the deeply social nature of emotion in the Spanish Mediterranean.[14] In addition to *vergüenza*, a plethora of other sixteenth- and seventeenth-century words could connote shame, especially those whose etymologies bespeak its physiognomic qualities, such as *acato, afrentarse, atajarse, confusión, correrse, cortedad, deshonra, desprecio, empacho, encogimiento, infamia, pudor, pundonor, recato, rubor, sonrojo,* and *turbar.* The proliferation of such terms bears ample witness to the mutual influence between language and affect, while underscoring the abiding complexity of their mediation by early modern Spanish culture.[15]

Yet it bears recalling that honour and shame have often been entangled in the kinds of stereotypical or unquestioned essentialisms that sought to subordinate Mediterranean societies to a more irrational and uncivilized status than that of their Northern European counterparts, a phenomenon not unrelated to the imperial and ideological interests behind the Black Legend (which was partially fuelled by Spain's association with the Inquisition). In the nineteenth century these gestures bequeathed a binary strain of Spanish cultural and literary criticism: on the one hand, ethnocentric attempts to repudiate Southern Europeans as hopelessly impassioned, bellicose, and obsessed with honour; and, on the other, their no less vocal defenders, who toiled to elevate the supposedly exceptional valuation of personal honour as a Spanish national virtue – to claim honour itself as a badge of honour, as it were. Of the former camp, the words of Adolf Friedrich von Schack may ring stridently to modern ears: "This custom [of honour] was so generalized and absolute that no-one could dodge its empire [...] The impassioned nature of this southern people felt its thirst for revenge grow through the influence of public opinion."[16] Among honour's apologists, Menéndez Pidal responded in kind by excoriating his "hyper-Spanish" (españolísimo) compatriot and Golden Age literary champion Menéndez y Pelayo for his suggestion that honour was impelled by a "sickly egotism" (egoísmo enfermizo): "it is very improper to call *egotism* that which impels vengeance based on honour [...] Every dignified man must maintain intact the precious patrimony of social honour of which each one is a depository and guardian." "To not defend that patrimony," he alleged, "is bastard cowardice, it is to make oneself an accomplice of the abuse committed by the offender at the expense of collective honour."[17] Menéndez Pidal, along with Castro (who also suffered his fair share of accusations of having tainted the purity of an essential Spanishness), endeavoured to trace the concept of an eminently Iberian sense of honour back to a stockpile of possible historical and literary sources: from the epic[18] to the Italian drama,[19] as well as the casuists,[20] Arabs, Goths, romances of chivalry, and, quite simply, Spanish national character.[21] It would be difficult to cite examples as compelling as these of how the affective valences of premodern literature have continued, centuries later, to exert such a powerful influence over critical reception, stirring sentiments of disdain, pride, rancour, indignation, and, indeed, honour among philologists ostensibly detached by professional objectivity from the national canon. While denouncing Menéndez y Pelayo's "emotive evaluation," even Menéndez Pidal himself pondered the peculiarity of this emotional investment, ascribing it to the idea that "honour remains in a near past that prolongs its effects among us and that we still look at with a passion of the present."[22]

The reception of *Don Quijote* – the work that would eventually attain the honour of being the most famous and celebrated in Spanish literary history – kindled similarly passionate debate among critics who regarded the novel as calamitous for national pride, honour, and dignity. In his mid-eighteenth-century defence of Spanish theatre, Tomás de Erauso y Zavaleta averred that *Don Quijote*'s fame was "not good fortune nor an honourable title of the Nation as many believe," since the novel "is more smear than lustre, in which Foreigners find testimony of their concept that we are ridiculously vain, rigid, boastful, and [...] proud of such a high and serious chivalry that it makes us laughable."[23] To the classicist argument that Cervantes's untoward innovation had failed to uphold traditional standards of verisimilitude and other poetic precepts, Erauso y Zavaleta added the complaint that it had made a mockery of Spaniards themselves, and in this he was not alone. Critics both within Spain and beyond fretted that *Don Quijote* had not only scandalized the national literary reputation but also tarnished the moral one, as epitomized by a mid-eighteenth-century poem of dubious authorship: "Spain applauded the work / Without realizing, unaware / That of the honour of Spain / Its author was the knife and executioner."[24] In effect, the perception among the seventeenth- and eighteenth-century Spanish elite that "Don Quijote is ridiculing the nobility and the sense of honour of their time" reveals that "what they felt was the shame of the fact that foreign readers could identify a character and see him essentially as ridiculous as they themselves."[25]

In his introduction to the first edition of *Don Quijote* by the Real Academia Española (Royal Spanish Academy) of 1780, Vicente de los Ríos intervened in the polemic by vindicating the novel not as a caricature of Spanish society in general or of the nobility in particular but as merely a critique of the outmoded romances of chivalry, and specifically of the vices or "the false point of honour [*pundonor*] of knight errantry." Expounding that knight errantry was itself a broader European phenomenon, Ríos concurrently tried to stifle the debate over the novel that had roiled the aristocracy and foreign critics since its publication, to consecrate its station in the national canon, and to deflect from Spain the moral grievances it had engendered, concluding that Cervantes was "too honourable to be creative [*ingenioso*] at the expense of his nation."[26] By absolving Cervantes of the allegation that he was the "knife and executioner" of Spanish honour, Ríos not only resuscitated the victim but, ironically, also paved the way for the author to become lionized as a mainstay of Spanish literature and a point of pride for the country at large. In the same stroke Ríos disavowed the national shame that *Don Quijote* had earlier piqued, because his attempt to advance a new interpretation of the novel, according to Agapita Jurado Santos, responded to "none other than feeling ashamed of what depicts [Spaniards] as ridiculous."[27]

The portrayal of *Don Quijote* as the death blow to Spanish honour corroborates my argument, which I develop in what follows, about the potential of the novel and its principal character to undermine the honour discourse of the early modern Mediterranean through shame. What this critical history makes even plainer is that with honour we are dealing not so much with the affective reality or feelings of a discrete epoch as with a *discourse*, one with a lengthy and freighted trajectory in various spheres of Mediterranean culture, historiography, and the popular imaginary. By this I do not mean to imply that seventeenth-century everyday life was devoid of honour or that the Spaniard, noble or otherwise, did not *feel* honour. On the contrary, its extreme popularity in the comedia stands as singular proof of the fact, as Scott K. Taylor's albeit sceptical study of the Iberian honour code concedes, that "honor gripped the imaginations of early modern Castilians themselves."[28] It is clear, rather, that the proliferation of discourses of and about honour has exceeded the conditions that enabled its emergence; the signifier has eclipsed the signified, not to mention its oft-polarized counterpart of shame. Although one could be tempted to argue that shame is just as discursive a phenomenon – for it is true that the discourse of shame, to a great extent, empowers it as a tool of politico-religious persuasion, coercion, and punishment – the physiognomic qualities of shame, as I will detail in the following section, both render it more palpable and destabilize fundamentally its yoking with honour.

These examples, furthermore, alert us to the care that must be taken whenever ascribing emotional characteristics or moral values to a collective social group, and even more so when that group encompasses a geographical and cultural area as vast and diverse as the Mediterranean. In effect, Peristiany's *Honour and Shame* became the touchstone for a disciplinary and ideological debate among anthropologists in the decades following its publication.[29] This debate was led by Michael Herzfeld, who sounded a warning bell regarding the ethical stakes of an honour-shame–based Mediterranean and its inherent danger of giving "the impression that the objective of anthropological analysis is to generalize about the cultural characteristics of particular regions," adding that Mediterraneanism "thus becomes one of several means whereby anthropology risks aiding and abetting the perpetuation of cultural stereotypes."[30] Current interdisciplinary momentum in affect theory and the history of emotion stands as a compelling invitation to reopen the debate about these phenomena that were of such ostensibly central importance to the early modern Mediterranean – especially shame, whose social, cultural, and literary substance has been relegated to the dialectic shadow of honour far too long. And yet I hasten to add that as literary scholars we must exercise similar prudence not to fall prey to the pitfalls of Mediterraneanism. Although temporal and methodological distance may dampen the impact of such questions (i.e., the study of sixteenth- and seventeenth-century cultural production as opposed to ethnographies of living populations), it should not blunt the precision, critical scruples, and historical acumen with which we engage our texts. We must also remain mindful of these lessons from cultural anthropology in order to avoid perpetuating generalizations, reducing complexities, and reproducing essentialisms – for example, that of a putative early modern Spanish "honour society." Given the growing interest in the multidisciplinary field of Mediterranean Studies, if anything the onus is now even more urgent, particularly in the psychological realm, whose lack of a universal vocabulary for analysing emotions makes an oversimplification of Mediterranean affectivity almost unavoidable. In the midst of these cautionary cases and caveats, however, an affect like shame, when contextualized within discrete socio-historical practices, offers considerable purchase for understanding how various forms of cultural production have intervened in a distinctly Mediterranean affective economy, as well as for disentangling the more localized threads of everyday emotional experience that were gradually interwoven across this dynamic space to form the complex, knotted tapestry of values, valorizations, and re-evaluations that confront cultural historians and literary scholars of the Mediterranean basin today.

Visual Topographies of Shame

Turning now to the problem of shame itself, it will be profitable to take up for a moment its theoretical genealogy, particularly as it relates to the sense of sight. With a nod to the popular proverb that "shame is in the eyes" and with an emphasis on the public sphere, Aristotle ascribes the affect a markedly visual aura. In *Nicomachean Ethics* he defines shame as a "kind of fear of disrepute," and in the *Rhetoric* he elaborates on its utility as an oratorical device for manipulating public opinion: "Since shame is imagination [*phantasia*] about a loss of reputation [...] necessarily a person feels shame toward those whose opinion he takes account of [...] And they feel more shame at things done before these people's eyes and in the open."[31] For Aristotle, shame not only is irreducibly social but also asserts itself with varying intensity according to social status and another's capacity for providing favours or material gain. In these visual registers of shame resides what the Stagirite regarded as its virtuous function: the concern with one's appearance before the polis served to deputize shame as a social vehicle for developing and regulating ethical citizens, for mitigating the behavioural transgressions of those seen as lacking innate virtue (in Ancient Greece, women, slaves, and the young).[32]

Nowhere is the visuality of shame more evident, however, than in the blush, a spontaneous response described by Annibale Pocaterra, a sixteenth-century Italian physician who wrote the first book-length treatise dedicated exclusively to the emotion, *Due dialogi della vergogna*. Understood as part of shame's will to conceal, blushing, for Pocaterra, was nature's mechanism for curtailing exposure to judgment after wrongdoing, "by covering the face with a crimson veil of blood, intending to cover the sinning soul as well." Additional physiological manifestations of shame – including the covering of the face with the hands, the diversion of the gaze, and the lowering of the head and eyes – were believed to perform a similar function. "We have proof of this," Pocaterra explains, "when we observe those who, feeling shame and being unable to hide themselves otherwise, cover their face with their hands and lower their eyes as though they wanted their whole face to disappear under their brows."[33] Inducing the subject to physically evade the cause of emotional discomfort, Pocaterra's early modern deliberations underline the recognizable power of shame to assert itself in the body. These gestural indicators of shame likewise facilitated the emotion's representation in pictorial arts and literature: as an affect that could be visibly observed, it was exceptionally well suited to narrative descriptions of a character's emotional state.

More recently, practitioners of cultural studies have contended that shame is not merely an emotion to be repressed, overcome, or, indeed, ashamed of, but that it is attached in an affirmative way to what Tomkins called "interest."[34] Eve Sedgwick and Adam Frank, inspired by

Tomkins, tell us that "the pulsations of cathexis around shame [...] are what either enable or disenable so basic a function as the ability to be interested in the world."[35] Shame thus has the potential to "[highlight] unknown or unappreciated investments," to indicate where one's interests lie even when they are not self-evident.[36] These interests or investments roughly correspond to what I have already referred to as shame's enabling conditions, or the cultural, historical, and aesthetic factors that invariably attend its expression in Cervantes's texts. Therefore, just as fictional narrative can be an effectual medium for exploring shame as a lived experience, for uncovering what is "unknown," "unappreciated," or poorly understood about these factors, so too can shame reveal fresh yet historically responsive insights into Cervantes's writing. In *Don Quijote* the author fashioned a psychologically complex protagonist capable of self-reflection, inner doubt, and emotional dynamism, qualities shaped not only by poetic conventions of the novel but also by Cervantes's keen awareness of the historical and political landscape of the early modern Mediterranean. Propelling Don Quijote's behavioural evolution throughout the novel are the affective binds between, on the one hand, the heroic impulse of his chivalric ethos and, on the other, the increasing social demands of modernity, the courtly strictures of the "civilizing process," the rise of the state, the development of modern warfare and military professionalism, and popular and inquisitorial forms of punishment. As an affect that is culturally inflected – which is to say that shame was felt in the seventeenth century for reasons that are different from those of today – shame alerts us to these tensions as, like the blush on Don Quijote's face, a kind of red flag signalling the various anxieties behind its emergence.

The physiognomic and visual registers of the emotion play a central role in auguring shameful moments in the novel, beginning with Don Quijote's very first discursive exchange as a knight errant, when at the inn he mistakes two prostitutes for maidens: "when they heard themselves called maidens, something so alien to their profession, they could not control their laughter, which made Don Quijote feel ashamed" (Como se oyeron llamar doncellas, cosa tan fuera de su profesión, no pudieron tener la risa y fue de manera que don Quijote vino a correrse).[37] Later, when he discovers that the sounds of thunderous pounding in the night are not a sinister threat but an occurrence that is, so to speak, much more run-of-the-mill – fulling hammers – he produces a parallel reaction: "When Don Quixote saw this he fell silent and sat as if paralyzed from head to toe. Sancho looked at him and saw that his head hung down toward his chest, indicating that he was ashamed." (Cuando don Quijote vio lo que era, enmudeció y pasmose de arriba abajo. Mirole Sancho y vio que tenía la cabeza inclinada sobre el pecho, con muestras de estar corrido.)[38] (See fig. 3.1.) In general, Cervantes's characters are remarkably adept at reading the emotional states of one another by observing behaviours, demeanours, gestures, and facial expressions, and here Sancho immediately intuits that Don Quijote has become ashamed. But the typically involuntary nature and visible signs of shame, in particular, facilitate such immediate recognition; the blush of the face and the lowering of the head serve as semiotic features that lend shame a narrative role which functions quite differently from that of honour's. A similar emotional exchange occurs several chapters later with the priest and barber's fabricated story of their assault by a gang of galley slaves, which leaves Don Quijote blushing in grim silence: "He changed color at each word and did not dare say that he had been the liberator of those good people" (Se le mudaba la color a cada palabra, y no osaba decir que él había sido el libertador de aquella buena gente).[39] Soon thereafter he is again shamed in front of his friends when the young Andrés, prodded by the proud knight to corroborate his account of a heroic confrontation of Juan Haldudo, reveals that Don Quijote only served to aggravate his cruel master's abuse: "Don Quixote was deeply ashamed by Andrés's story, and it was necessary for the others to be very careful not to laugh so as not to shame him completely" (Quedó corridísimo don Quijote del cuento de Andrés, y fue menester que los demás tuviesen mucha cuenta con no reírse, por no acaballe de correr del todo).[40]

Predicaments of this nature will dog Don Quijote throughout the novel, his public façade cornered by the great many episodes that feature an intra-diegetic audience.[41] On the one hand, as readers we are invited to share in the humour and incipient Schadenfreude towards the protagonist that such infelicities and failings produce in the text, a tone that is, moreover, characteristic of a large part of the novel as a whole. On the other hand, these moments hold out the subjective possibility of empathy through an identification with Don Quijote's suffering of shame, suggesting that we temper our laughter, just as his friends did in their sympathetic attempt at mitigating his emotional discomfort ("so as not to shame him completely").[42] Yet beyond their unique capacity to induce both parody and pathos – and, therefore, to trouble the oft-exaggerated distinction between the "Romantic" and the "hard" critical approaches to the novel – these shameful moments point to an ethical reflection on the part of Don Quijote, who recognizes that his actions have not achieved the desired results but, in reality, have degenerated the life conditions of the very people he aspired to help. Shame delineates the contours of his madness by involuntarily escaping the

Figure 3.1. José Jiménez Aranda, detail in *"Quijote" del centenario: El ingenioso hidalgo don Quijote de la Mancha* (Madrid, 1905–8), ch. 2, p. 15. Reproduction of original sketch in Chinese ink and gouache white. Cervantes Project, Cushing Memorial Library, Texas A&M University.

customary justifications he supplies in times of impotence, defeat, or failure, namely the excuse of enchantment. In the mendacious story of the robbery by galley slaves as well as in the case of Andrés, Don Quijote finds himself suddenly incapable of furnishing an alibi for his actions, and, in its place, blood rushes forth to redden his cheeks. In my primary example, however, the character's shame becomes so acute that he is left no alleviation from its effects but to passively encloister himself in the psychological comforts of denial and disavowal that his otherwise accursed enchanter affords him. The priest and the barber's deceptive ploy to return Don Quijote home at the end of part 1 of the novel begins, in actuality, when they observe the potent effect on the knight errant of their feigned story of robbery by the galley slaves. In other words, they have perceived Don Quijote's susceptibility – or, in Bourdieu's terms, his "disposition" – to shame and consequently decide to exploit it as a means of manipulation towards a concrete end (which will in turn produce further shame for the titular character, thus recalling the emotional feedback loop invoked in this chapter's opening pages). It is in fact hard to imagine a more effective vehicle of manipulation, parody, and punishment than shame for a character whose chivalric ethos – in the words of Tomkins, his "interest" – is defined by such antithetical values of pride, renown, and fame.

Shame Punishments and Cervantes

The theatrical quality of the stratagem employed to convince Don Quijote to abandon his folly and return home has been registered,[43] but I would like to suggest that these episodes represent the staging of a historic practice, while equally dependent on theatricality, of a more sinister nature: that which was well known in the sixteenth and seventeenth centuries as "exposing to shame" (sacar a la vergüenza). Turning to Covarrubias, "[t]o expose one to shame is a penalty and punishment that is usually given for some crimes, and these [delinquents] are typically tied to the pillory for a certain amount of time so that they are ashamed and affronted [avergonzados y afrentados]."[44] The juridico-religious practice of public shaming or *escarnio público* is referenced earlier in the episode of the galley slaves when one of the prisoners is overcome with emotion and unable to describe his crime. Another condemned man offers himself as spokesperson to explain: "This honest man is going to the galleys for four years, having been paraded through the usual streets in robes of state and on horseback" (Este hombre honrado va por cuatro años a las galeras, habiendo paseado las acostumbradas, vestido, en pompa y a caballo). Sancho then immediately confirms his acquaintance with the practice by responding: "That, it seems to me [...] means he was shamed in public" (Eso es [...] lo que a mí me parece, haber salido a la vergüenza).[45] The mobilization of shame undergirds many well-documented forms of popular and inquisitorial punishment in medieval and early modern Europe, among them the charivari, stocks, yellow badge, pillory, sanbenito, and auto-da-fé. Francisco de Goya dedicated several of his darker and most socially disturbing paintings and engravings to the practices of the procession, the sanbenito, and the auto-da-fé (figs. 3.2 and 3.3). Without exception, the victims immortalized by the artist in these works adopt a stance nearly identical to Pocaterra's physiological descriptions of shame, as well as to Don Quijote as he is described in the text and portrayed in various illustrations (fig. 3.4): cowering posture, lowered head and gaze, a silent and motionless state.

Goya's medium performed a homologous yet inverse function to the *pittura infamante*, a form of defamatory painting in Renaissance Italy that bestowed on representational art the mandate of municipal justice in order to shame common criminals through frescoes depicting delinquents and their crimes.[46] Like Nathaniel Hawthorne's proverbial "scarlet letter," the practice of branding was another violent yet permanent means of inscribing shame on the body of slaves and criminals. The correspondence between particular iconographies of branding and national or linguistic conventions attests to their widespread use across the Mediterranean: the fleur-de-lis in France, the keys of Saint Peter in the Papal States, and the *L* for *ladrones* (thieves) in Spain all marked their victims with popularly recognized symbols for adjuring their crimes. Many of these practices, as was the case with inquisitorial procedure generally, were heirs to ancient Roman law, which prescribed, for example, that fugitive slaves be branded with the letters *FUG* to alert others to their status as *fugitivus*, serving to stigmatize the bearer and deter further transgressions. In Castile, similar customs survived in the *Fuero Juzgo* and Alfonso X's *Siete Partidas*, bodies of law that called upon popular ridicule as a method of punishment and compliance through such public acts as beatings, the carrying of chains, the amputation of limbs, or being disrobed and covered in honey and flies.[47] Although to some extent a commutation for penitents of the capital crimes of heresy and apostasy, a shame punishment nonetheless was regarded as exceedingly severe, since, according to Inquisition scholar Henry Charles Lea's famous study, "those exposed to it regarded death as a mercy, preferring to die rather than to endure a life of infamy."[48] Whether in popular or inquisitional form, the exploitation of shame and infamy through penality at once capitalized on their affective

Figure 3.2. Francisco de Goya, *Nohubo remedio*, in *Los caprichos* (1799), p. 24.
Etching and burnished aquatint. Real Academia de Bellas Artes de San
Fernando, Madrid.

Figure 3.3. Francisco de Goya, *Auto de fe de la Inquisición* (detail; ca. 1815–19). Oil on wood panel. Real Academia de Bellas Artes de San Fernando, Madrid.

Figure 3.4. Ramón Puiggarí, in *El ingenioso hidalgo don Quijote de la Mancha* (Barcelona, 1876), p. 310. Wood engraving. Cervantes Project, Cushing Memorial Library, Texas A&M University.

capacity as guarantors of social control, while extending their viability in subjective consciousness and the public sphere.

As a young man Cervantes himself was even condemned to a shame punishment ("vergüenza pública") after wounding one Antonio de Segura in a duel in 1569, even though, by fleeing to Italy, he avoided the sentence of having his right hand cut off, ten years of forced exile, and other penalties.[49] Along with his typical penchant for referencing historical events and with the fact that the peak of the Inquisition's activities between the years 1590 and 1620 corresponds almost exactly to that of Cervantes's literary activity,[50] it is thus not surprising that the author contemplated public shaming – and reflected upon its ethical ramifications – several times throughout his works.[51] For a better understanding of this practice and before we return to Don Quijote's encagement, some examples of its emergence in other writings by Cervantes merit brief consideration.

In *Persiles y Sigismunda* Cervantes stresses the potency of shame punishments as a spectacle in the story of Ortel Banedre, a Polish man who laments his fate of having been humiliated by his wife after she absconded with a former lover. Expressing his vehement desire to avenge the affront to his honour, he tells the pilgrims he is on his way to Madrid to exact the penalty that he believes his adulterous wife and her lover deserve. Serving as the novel's habitual voice of tempered reason, however, Periando quizzes the jilted man: "What do you think will happen to you when the authorities hand your enemies over to you bound and submissive on public display and in view of countless people, with you up on the scaffold brandishing your knife and threatening to cut off their heads as if their blood, as you put it, could cleanse your honor? What other result could you expect, I ask you, but that of making the offense against you more public?" (¿Qué pensáis que os sucederá cuando la justicia os entregue a vuestros enemigos, atados y rendidos, encima de un teatro público, a la vista de infinitas gentes, y a vos, blandiendo el cuchillo encima del cadahalso, amenazando el segarles las gargantas, como si pudiera su sangre limpiar, como vos decís, vuestra honra? ¿Qué os puede suceder, como digo, sino hacer más público vuestro agravio?)[52] The logic of Periandro's counsel here revolves not around the law, justice, or personal virtue but around the degree of infamy that Banedre's act of vengeance would undoubtedly visit upon him. Recalling Aristotle's description of shame as *phantasia* or imagination of a future "loss of reputation," Periandro goes on to evoke the perpetual guilt that would imbue public memory of Banedre's disgrace, exposed to the gaze of the masses in the "public theatre" of the scaffold. The gallows (*cadahalso*) was in fact placed in the express service of shame punishments in the early modern era, and, as Michel Foucault famously elucidated in *Discipline and Punish*, the supplice was wielded to repress the populace through the utmost visibility of punishment, a spectacle of state absolutism. In this aesthetics of penality I would propose that shame becomes, to use Foucault's terminology, a supremely potent "technology of representation." Its increasing cogency was coextensive with the growth of metropolitan centres and the rise of the early modern city, evidenced when Periandro, comparing the disgraced couple's small town of Talavera with Madrid, cautions that the sheer size of the latter lends it a capacity for causing greater dishonour, contrary to what our contemporary assumptions about urban anonymity might suggest.[53] If the rural character of medieval Spain was more conducive to the defence of personal honour through the righting of an affront, then the high visibility of a city like Madrid would seem to frustrate traditional codes of gentlemanly honour by aggravating the affront through the very attempt at its conventional remedy.[54] Moreover, Periandro's emphasis on the public dimension of shame implies at once the waning of personal virtue alongside a legal-penal apparatus that is ineffective at meting out justice. In its place the early modern subject is interpellated to practise a regime of self-discipline for which shame is the primary motor. The vigour of such a system is confirmed by Periandro's ultimate success in dissuading Banedre from pursuing retribution and his adding, as though a mere afterthought to his advice, that "finally, I want you to consider that you're going to commit a mortal sin by taking their lives" (finalmente, quiero que consideréis que vais a hacer un pecado mortal en quitarles las vidas).[55]

An exemplary novel, *Rinconete y Cortadillo*, proffers further insights for understanding the Cervantine take on public shaming. When the eponymous characters and other professional *pícaros* in Seville are convened to review the week's business, their illiterate leader Monipodio asks Rinconete to recite the contents of his personal memory book, which notably includes the following subheading: "Note on common offenses, to wit, blows given with flasks filled with foul-smelling liquids, ointments made with strong-smelling juniper tar, tacking on doors signs for Jews and horns for cuckolds, rackets, frights, disturbances and fake knife fights, publication of libels, etc." (Memorial de agravios comunes, conviene a saber: redomazos, untos de miera, clavazón de sambenitos y cuernos, matracas, espantos, alborotos y cuchilladas fingidas, publicación de nibelos, etc.)[56] This diverse litany of disturbances and delinquency reveals the appropriation of rituals of public shaming by a group of private citizens. In particular, the hanging of sanbenitos and the publication of libellous acts represent a form of renegade justice lifted from the inquisitorial practices of the state. That these *outlaws* make use of punitive devices that fall well within the law of seventeenth-century Spain suggests that such shame punishments were persuasive enough in the public sphere to be adopted by criminals who presumably would have had recourse to any number of additional instruments of intimidation, vengeance, and coercion. Shame serves as a more injurious weapon than other, more explicitly violent means at the disposal of Monipodio and his hitmen for hire. Cervantes's portrayal testifies to the common familiarity of these practices among the Spanish citizenry, a fact that accounted for their very efficacy. Even more significant, however, are Monipodio's words as Rinconete continues to read the list of planned affronts but is stopped short of pronouncing the names of their targeted victims: "And don't read [...] the house or where it is, it's enough for the offense to be done without saying it in public, for that's a great burden on one's conscience. At least, I'd rather tack up a hundred horns and the same number of punishment lists for the Inquis'tion and be paid for my work than say it just one time, even if it was to the mother who bore me." (Tampoco se lea [...] la casa ni adónde, que basta que se les haga el agravio, sin que se diga en público, que es gran cargo de conciencia. A lo menos, más querría yo clavar cien cuernos y otros tantos sambenitos, como se me pagase mi trabajo, que decillo sola una vez, aunque fuese a la madre que me parió.)[57] The startling irruption of moral conscience in a figure otherwise portrayed as the unscrupulous ringleader of Seville's criminal underground is meaningful in and of itself. It is also curious and seemingly hypocritical that Monipodio so strongly adheres to a personal imperative never to publicly speak the name of the shamed (among fellow delinquents, no less), while at the same time perpetrating acts that expose them to even greater public infamy. But the fact is that Cervantes's choice to offer such an ethical reflection through the words of a criminal underscores the gravity and seriousness with which the author approaches the topic of public shaming. This particular class of "honour among thieves" lends *Rinconete y Cortadillo* – widely received as a jocund, entertaining picaresque novella – its own subtle exemplary tone.

If in the *Novelas ejemplares* a gang of commissioned outlaws appropriates legal forms of shame punishments, then another group of outlaws pays for their crimes several fold in the final chapters of *Don Quijote*. I am referring to the moments just before the principal characters are captured by Roque Guinart and his gang of brigands, when Sancho becomes frightened upon brushing against legs and feet dangling from some trees. Don Quijote reassures him by explaining that they "undoubtedly belong to outlaws and bandits who have been hanged from these trees, for in this region the law usually hangs them when it catches them, in groups of twenty or thirty" (sin duda son de algunos forajidos y bandoleros que en estos árboles están ahorcados, que por aquí los suele ahorcar la justicia, cuando los coge, de veinte en veinte y de treinta en treinta).[58] Although banditry was commonly associated with the Mediterranean enclave of Catalonia, this kind of penal spectacle transpired across much of Castile as well.[59] And while some regarded public shaming as more severe than death, both punitive methods coincide in this practice, which was essentially a makeshift extension of the pillory: in the absence of a *picota* or *rollo* (stocks or pillory), criminals were often hung from prominent trees, which, like their architectural counterparts of stone, were situated near the entrance to a town or municipal district so as to advertise to residents and visitors alike the potent authority of local "justice."[60] In fact, the tall, imposing structure of the pillory acquired an iconographic association with infamy and shame, as attested by its lexicological inheritance in contemporary idioms such as *poner en la picota* and *enviar / hacer ir al rollo* (akin to the English expression *to pillory*). It is ironic that the environs surrounding the pillory, as original epicentres of legal jurisdiction, came to gather a reputation for delinquency and infamy themselves, leading to speculation that some families even uprooted their homes to avoid these peri-penal zones.[61] An analogous phenomenon attended executioners or *verdugos*, whose profession garnered such figures a loathsome reputation as both dispatchers and depositories of shame, influencing urban development through inhabitants' desire not to live anywhere near them.[62] These examples disclose the epidemic nature of shame in the early modern popular imaginary, its seeming ability to spread and infect through spatial and interpersonal proximity. Like the ill-fated brigands in the novel, the suspended, lifeless bodies acceded to the dual historical objective of shaming criminals and their families and of deterring other citizens from like transgressions of legal and religious authority.

Blood Purity and the Art of Infamy in Don Quijote's Encagement

Although Don Quijote's own fate is not immediate or terminal, the ox-cart used to deliver him home performs a function homologous to that of the trees; as another kind of makeshift pillory it is the material structure responsible for ensuring that he is exposed to a protracted visibility before public spectators. Like the branches of the trees or *arbori suspendere*, the wooden bars of his cage can be said to suspend the feeling of shame, to hold it in place for all to see. Suffused with pathos, Doré's engraving of the scene (fig. 3.5) foregrounds this effect by placing viewers in the cage with Don Quijote and thus subjecting us to the same piercing gaze of the grotesque figures who crowd in from all sides to witness the spectacle. Similar practices were employed by the Spanish Inquisition to publicly shame citizens accused of perpetrating such petty crimes as theft. One account describes the events of January 1605 along the Guadalquivir River in Seville, where several confraternities had assembled to perform a "sad but Christian task": "[p]ulling up the cadavers of those drowned in the river or shot by the Holy Brotherhood and taking off of the hooks and from the cages the remains, which were displayed in the streets, of criminals whom

Figure 3.5. Gustave Doré, *Lorsque don Quichotte se vit encagé de cette façon*, in *L'ingénieux hidalgo Don Quichotte de la Manche* (Paris, 1863), p. 388. Wood engraving. Cervantes Project, Cushing Memorial Library, Texas A&M University.

justice had required be quartered." Later, as part of granting the deceased delinquents a proper Christian burial, the members of the pious orders prepared their remains for the procession of the bones (*procesión de los huesos*), "one of the strangest processions of which there is note in the annals of our ecclesiastic ceremonies," whereby the bones were paraded through the city by a motley entourage. "In front, carrying their standards and insignias, went all the confraternities of the city," followed by "a multitude of clergy and friars of all the orders"; "behind them, with a standard and cross, some brothers of Charity, and the sanctuary priests with the high cross; and in back, guided by other brothers, in large carriages covered with blue cloths [...] the remains of the drowned, shot, and quartered."[63] As with the hanging of bandits, this particular punishment was exacted to lethal ends, along with a public spectacle of infamy. Like the priest and the barber in *Don Quijote*, the inquisitional authorities used cages for displaying the victims that they paraded through the streets. Most significant is that both parties – executioners and redeemers – employed the procession as a mobile ritual for exposing the remains of former criminals to the eyes of the masses, first as punishment and later as pardon. The procession was seemingly just as efficient at procuring the redemption of those upon whom it had previously bestowed infamy and shame, at least for the already deceased.

The similarly visual, extravagant, and spectacle-like qualities of Don Quijote's encagement invite us to consider it as a narrative form of the *pitture infamanti*, commissioned by the priest's religious authority and ekphrastically produced throughout the final chapters of the 1605 novel. The centrality of shame in these episodes is confirmed by the intentions and actions of other characters, the proliferation of metaphorical references to the emotion in the narration, and, most importantly, Don Quijote's own behaviour and affective reactions to his treatment. Like the silent shame he displays in other moments of the novel, the demeanour of Don Quijote while he is in the cage confirms that he has intuited and internalized the shame of his punishment: "Don Quixote sat in the cage, his hands tied, his legs extended, his back leaning against the bars, and with so much silence and patience that he seemed not a man of flesh and blood, but a statue made of stone." (Iba sentado en la jaula, las manos atadas, tendidos los pies y arrimado a las verjas, con tanto silencio y tanta paciencia como si no fuera hombre de carne, sino estatua de piedra.)[64] In spite of the differing landscapes, composition, and technique, his physical stance in Puiggarí's image of this scene (fig. 3.4) greatly resembles that in Jiménez Aranda's depiction of his shame before Sancho (fig. 3.1): motionless state, lowered head, downward gaze, and a passive, cowering posture. To recognize that many of these outward cues might be featured in a representation of melancholia, we need only recall the angelic figure of Dürer's famous 1514 engraving of the same name. The Knight of the Sorrowful Face, the text reports, indeed felt melancholy in the cage, and the physiognomy of shame partly shared with this emotion serves to underscore, as noted earlier, the often complex interrelationality of affective states in lived experience as well as in the novel. But one might also envisage, had Jiménez Aranda and Puiggarí not worked in a black-and-white medium, that they would have complemented such bodily symptoms by adding a light dash of red to Don Quijote's cheeks.

When Don Quijote is first placed in the cage, the barber, masking his true identity, proclaims prophetically: "O Knight of the Sorrowful Face! Grieve not at thy imprisonment, for it is needful in order to more quickly conclude the adventure to which thy great courage hath brought thee. And this will come to an end when the wrathful Manchegan lion shall be joined with the white Tobosan dove." (¡Oh Caballero de la Triste Figura!, no te dé afincamiento la prisión en que vas, porque así conviene para acabar más presto la aventura en que tu gran esfuerzo te puso. La cual se acabará cuando el furibundo león manchado con la blanca paloma tobosina yoguieren en uno.)[65] While embellishing the performance of Don Quijote's capture, this statement also reveals a recognition of its capacity to produce shame. Specifically, *afincamiento* anticipates the potential for humiliation, and *manchado* represents a play on words between *manchego* and *mancillado* (tarnished). The *mancha*, or stain, on the man of La Mancha's reputation is effected precisely by the shameful spectacle of his public imprisonment. Later, when knight and squire have the opportunity to consult privately about what Don Quijote believes are the consequences of enchantment and what Sancho clearly sees to be a grand artifice, the latter hilariously attempts to persuade his master with empirical evidence: "speaking with respect, since your grace has been locked in the cage, enchanted, in your opinion, have you had the desire and will to pass what they call major and minor waters?" (Pregunto, hablando con acatamiento, si acaso después que vuestra merced va enjaulado y a su parecer encantado en esta jaula le ha venido gana y voluntad de hacer aguas mayores o menores, como suele decirse). Sancho's prefacing of his query "with respect" (con acatamiento) confirms the commonplace that bodily functions were of themselves considered shameful, and Don Quijote's response that "not everything is clean" (no anda todo limpio) reinforces the scatological quality of the scene while insisting on the stain – in this case literal as well as figurative – that may sully his honour as a result of his encagement.[66]

Even more consequential is the fact that these examples, tacitly yet unmistakably, point towards the far more troubling Iberian program of *limpieza de sangre*. Begging the priest to allow Don Quijote to momentarily vacate his cage in order to evacuate his bowels, Sancho declares that "if they did not let him out, his prison would not be as clean as decency demanded for a knight like his master" (si no le dejaban salir, no iría tan limpia aquella prisión como requiría la decencia de un tal caballero como su amo).[67] The metonymical remove here between the bodily fluids of "major and minor waters" and blood is minuscule enough as to leave little doubt of the latter's patent symbolism. Along with the metaphors of cleanliness ("manchado"; "no anda todo limpio"), these insistent details encode the historical forms of racial and religious persecution that haunted the Spain of Cervantes's time. The societal and institutional racism that sanctioned the forced conversion, expulsion, or execution of countless Moors and Jews on the peninsula, in fact, often masqueraded under nearly identical metaphors of blood purity, as attested by the proliferation of a *limpio-sucio* or clean-dirty motif in historical documents of official as well as popular natures.[68] Sancho's deceptively innocent observation "that these phantoms wandering around here are not entirely Catholic" (que estas visiones que por aquí andan, que no son del todo católicas) lays bare the original inquisitional mandate of prosecuting the crimes of heresy and apostasy that threatened the hegemony of Catholic doctrine, while stretching to the limit any latent ambiguity regarding the episode's suggestive subtext. "I have read many extremely serious histories of knights errant," admits Don Quijote, "but never have I read, or seen, or heard of enchanted knights being carried in this fashion." (Muchas y muy graves historias he yo leído de caballeros andantes, pero jamás he leído, ni visto, ni oído que a los caballeros encantados los lleven desta manera.)[69] Such a strikingly frank assessment by the condemned knight is perhaps the most compelling evidence yet for the reader that the stakes of this episode are more urgent than a mere parodic reworking of the romances of chivalry. That the referent is lost on Don Quijote only serves to underscore the persistence of the real and reinforce the historical gravity of the apparent novelty of his punishment. The distinction between history and fiction that is prescribed so emphatically by the priest and the canon throughout these same chapters of the novel asserts itself more forcefully here: the "many extremely serious histories" of Don Quijote's fictional world seem to pale in comparison to the reality of his first-hand experience of public shaming in the cage.

Further implicit indications that the shaming of Don Quijote is modelled on early modern inquisitorial practice abound. The presence of the policemen, priest, and canon – representing royal and ecclesiastical authority – and their oversight and endorsement of Don Quijote's punishment lend it an official juridico-religious quality. Moreover, the pomp and pageantry of the retinue resembles the aforementioned historical processions sponsored by the Holy Office in which the condemned were publicly paraded through the streets, often on the way to an auto-da-fé. This theme is complemented by the appearance of the *disciplinantes*, or penitential procession, whose self-flagellation would have recalled for the early modern reader familiar sacerdotal imagery of a similar context. The public auto-da-fé, like the choreographed scheme to return Don Quijote to his home, "was a meticulously planned, stage-managed theatrical event."[70] It is evoked when Don Quijote, "skinny and yellow" (flaco y amarillo), arrives at his village, "which they entered in the middle of the day, which happened to be Sunday, when everyone was in the square, and the cart carrying Don Quixote drove right through the middle of it" (adonde entraron en la mitad del día, que acertó a ser domingo, y la gente estaba toda en la plaza, por mitad de la cual atravesó el carro de don Quijote).[71] The general auto-da-fé (*auto de fe general*) also typically occurred on Sundays in the main plaza of the town and, as in my opening example of the events in Triana, always drew sizeable crowds of onlookers who came to take in the spectacle.[72] The yellowness of Don Quijote's complexion, in addition to the colour's association with melancholy and an indication of sheer depravity after six days of travelling in a cage, calls up the image of penitents whose sanbenitos of yellow signified their contrition and desire for reconciliation (as opposed to the black sanbenitos worn by the unrepentant).[73]

Indeed it is the act of reconciliation that colours the canon's exhortation to Don Quijote that he return to reason:

Come, come, Señor Don Quixote, take pity on yourself! Return to the bosom of good sense, and learn to use the considerable intelligence that heaven was pleased to give you, and devote your intellectual talents to another kind of reading that redounds to the benefit of your conscience and the increase of your honor!

¡Ea, señor don Quijote, duélase de sí mismo y redúzgase al gremio de la discreción y sepa usar de la mucha que el cielo fue servido de darle, empleando el felicísimo talento de su ingenio en otra letura que redunde en aprovechamiento de su conciencia y en aumento de su honra![74]

The figurative use of the expression *reducirse al gremio* is the most overt example of Cervantes's appropriation of an inquisitorial discourse throughout the episode; it referred to the historical practice of appearing before the Holy Office to undertake formal reconciliation with the Catholic Church after having apostatized.[75] Besides his direct entreaty to Don Quijote, the canon's sweeping indictment of the romances of chivalry could be said to perform a function parallel to that of the Sermon of Faith (*Sermón de la Fe*), a homily that always accompanied the auto-da-fé and served a pedagogical and proselytizing objective upon spectators. These sermons complemented the instructive potency of the processions and the staging of shame in the public exposure of the condemned, reinforcing social and religious conformity and the hegemony of the Old Christian model.

Don Quijote's response to his shame punishment indicates that it has been equally effective. His uncharacteristic passivity, resignation, silence, and acceptance of his fate of imprisonment, while manifesting the defeated knight's shame, also suggest that he is self-conscious and even repentant of his errant, and aberrant, behaviour. This self-consciousness, a mentally reflexive state commonly associated with shame, offers a space for reflection upon the chivalric ethos and the real consequences of Don Quijote's madness. Exasperated by Sancho's persuasive insistence that he is not in fact enchanted, and attempting to quell the debate, Don Quijote conspicuously disavows his shameful guilt: "I know and believe that I am enchanted, and *that suffices to make my conscience easy*, for it would weigh heavily on me if I thought I was not enchanted, and in sloth and cowardice had allowed myself to be imprisoned in this cage, depriving the helpless and weak of the assistance I could provide." (Yo sé y tengo para mí que voy encantado, y *esto me basta para la seguridad de mi conciencia*, que la formaría muy grande si yo pensase que no estaba encantado y me dejase estar en esta jaula perezoso y cobarde, defraudando el socorro que podría dar a muchos menesterosos y necesitados.")[76] Although not going so far as to completely renounce the knightly profession, as he will do after his humbling defeat at the end of part 2 of the novel, this moment of consciousness exposes the defence mechanisms that escape his madness.[77] The hackneyed excuse of enchantment notwithstanding, Don Quijote's wilful return to the cage implies a bid of atonement for his errant transgressions and links him once again to processional penitents, his shabby (and soiled?) underclothes standing in for the yellow scapulars of the sanbenitos.

The ritual shaming of Don Quijote portends even broader implications when juxtaposed with the canon's and the priest's damning portrayal of chivalric romance, for the interweaving of the encagement episodes and the novel's most direct and extensive critique of the literary object of its parody is no arbitrary convergence. Just as shame in the penal practices of early modern Spain constituted what in Foucauldian terms I have deemed a technology of representation, so it is deployed as a primary *techne* in the theatrical designs to return Don Quijote to his village. Yet shame performs an analogous role on the metanarrative plane: the denunciation of the romances of chivalry can be read as a public shaming of these second-rate works of popular fame. Their deleterious effects are embodied by Don Quijote, whose placement in the cage represents in turn a symbolic indictment of the books responsible for his madness. His foolish deviation from the normative medical and social standards of sanity corresponds to the aesthetic deviance with which the chivalresque flouted the prescriptive norms of Aristotelian verisimilitude. Don Quijote is thus simultaneously punished for his own crazy and misguided conduct and made to answer for the fallacious aesthetic logic of the books that gave birth to his character. His heightened visibility while he is in the cage renders him a shameful object of humorous ridicule and a vessel through which to effect a shaming of chivalric romance. The scrutiny to which both Don Quijote and these books are subjected recalls the earlier, inquisitionally inflected scene in which the priest and the barber judge which books to condemn to the fire, and the priest remarks to the canon that the book burning was satisfying yet ultimately futile in restoring Don Quijote's sanity. Just as shame punishments in early modern Spain were popularly feared for their efficacy over burnings at the stake, the public shaming of Don Quijote has proven (and will continue to prove) more persuasive than the incineration of his library in immobilizing him. Perhaps, in like fashion, the satirical treatment of the romances of chivalry by and within *Don Quijote* is more effectual in securing their infamy than the stricter policies of royal censorship openly desired by the priest and the canon. In any event, these episodes constitute a microcosm of the novel as a whole, staging through Don Quijote's emotions the parodic shaming of the chivalresque that is performed by the text in its totality.

Conclusion

I would like to conclude this chapter by suggesting an alternative interpretation of Don Quijote's shaming in the cage, one that underwrites an investment of even greater political stakes and harbours the potential to destabilize the honour discourse from the inside out. For Castro, Cervantes conceived of honour not as a good inherited through blood and nobility but as a personal virtue, "a quality more internal than external,"[78] an Erasmian notion broadcast in *Don Quijote*: "A poor man may have honor, but not a villain" (La honra puédela tener el pobre, pero no el vicioso).[79] So too can we perceive in Cervantes's writing an implicit rejection of violence as a means of responding to an affront to one's honour, as Sancho affirms: "There's no need [...] to take revenge against anyone, since it's not right for good Christians to take revenge for affronts" (No hay para qué [...] tomar venganza de nadie, pues no es de buenos cristianos tomarla de los agravios).[80] In point of fact, the renunciation of personal revenge was consistent with nascent ambitions of royal, governmental, and legal bodies to bring the management of disputes – traditionally settled through individual, familial, and clan-based claims to honour and retaliation – under the purview of the early modern state.[81] This renders the appropriation of inquisitorial discourse and practice in the encagement episodes all the more poignant: that individual citizens wield the political tool of punitive shame for controlling Don Quijote parodies not only the character, his madness, and the romances of chivalry but also the structures of power that increasingly sought to remit the matter of personal honour to administrative bureaucracy. While reflecting upon what a forceful weapon shame can be in the hands of authority, however, Cervantes suggests that the emotion may serve as a form of resistance to those very same structures of power.

Although recent historical studies have speculated that extra-literary honour was not reserved exclusively for nobles, Old Christians, and other elite members of society,[82] what remains clear is that shame was readily available and abundant for all. By its very nature, it is agnostic to privilege, whether cultural, social, economic, racial, or religious. As a kind of universal, democratic affect of the commoner, shame therefore contains the potential to disrupt the dominant order and the discourse of prestige that attended early modern historical claims to honour. Indeed, honour can be seen as a sort of shibboleth or cipher for the Iberian programs of *limpieza de sangre*, through which claims to honour were necessarily mediated – and quite often foreclosed – by one's ethno-religious past. The conversos, Moriscos, and Marranos were all surely well acquainted with the feeling of shame, even if they were privately able to maintain a certain pride in their traditions. One might even draw a parallel between the ontological status of crypto-Jews and -Muslims and shame's own will to concealment. If "the body's expressions – including that classic one of shame, the hanging of the head – act as a metonym for the wider structures of social domination,"[83] then there could hardly be a more striking reminder of the politics of blood purity than the blush whose appearance depends in an equally vital way upon the same bodily fluid. Along these lines, Don Quijote's compliance with his shame punishment can be suggestively read as an invitation to adopt the subject position of these members of history's defeated, as a kind of "virtue of losers": it represents, on the one hand, a rejection of the vengeance and violence that characterized the hegemonic discourse of honour in early modern Spain and, on the other, a refusal to conform to that very discourse by embracing shame as an alternative ontology. Instead of turning to external mechanisms of revenge – as we might expect in Lope's or Calderón's honour plays – and thus promoting or perpetuating systemic brutality, Cervantes proposes that shame may serve as a means of peaceful resistance to state-based and popular forms of violence, as a way of arresting the feedback loop.[84]

Moreover, as a tool for reflecting on the racial, religious, and imperial conflicts that traversed Cervantes's Mediterranean, shame holds a unique power to call forth the stories and subjects that risk becoming lost in the expansive dimensions and unifying interests of certain Mediterraneanizing projects. As I noted in chapter 2, such a risk is apparent in Castro's scathing rebuke of Braudel for relegating the human – and dehumanizing – elements of Mediterranean history to a grand economic system, as well as in the tendency to conflate honour and shame as merely two sides of the same essentialist coin. Recovering shame as its own distinct emotional currency corresponds, then, to rescuing the forgotten local (hi)stories of Mediterranean subjectivity. To pull them from the cage of the homogenizing logics of historiography is to remember the struggles of those punished by the dominant forces of history, a move analogous to Sancho's empathetic and disconcerting call to consciousness in directly confronting the priest: "I've said all this, Señor Priest, just to urge your fathership to take into account the bad treatment my master is receiving, and to be careful that God doesn't demand an accounting from you in the next life for my master's imprisonment." (Todo esto que he dicho, señor cura, no es más de por encarecer a su paternidad haga conciencia del mal tratamiento que a mi señor se le hace, y mire bien no le pida Dios en la otra vida esta prisión de mi amo.)[85] This is what makes the novel so unsettling: the reader is afforded no easy outlet from the suffering of shame and, having identified with Don Quijote as an "endurer of affronts" (sufridor de afrentas),[86] is therefore obligated to inhabit or embody it in a similar way, to consider the ethical repercussions of and possibilities within shame, to meditate on the "virtue of losers" from the defeated's own position and on their own terms, to adopt an anamorphic or bottom-up perspective on the world – as in Doré's depiction – from within the cage; in short, to acknowledge the marginalized of the Mare Nostrum by prompting an inversion or alternative view of Mediterranean "values." The novel's ability to make shame linger in this way is a prime example of Cervantes's investment in articulating the deep emotional registers of Mediterranean lived experience and his dexterity with affect as both a political and an aesthetic instrument. But that he makes Don Quijote sally forth again in 1615, pride intact, is perhaps the most powerful gesture of all.

A Mediterranean (Tragi)comedy: Sancho, Ricote, and the Emotional Politics of Laughter

[T]he power to laugh should be put among the passions of the heart.

Laurent Joubert

The writer is the archaeologist or geologist who gets the mute witnesses of common history to speak.

Jacques Rancière

One of the most poignant and unambiguously Mediterranean episodes of the Cervantine canon – not to mention one of the most frequently commented and divisive among critics – concerns the Morisco Ricote and his family in *Don Quijote* of 1615. It begins immediately after Sancho Panza abandons his governorship of Barataria, the "ínsula" accorded him as part of an elaborate prank engineered by the aristocratic characters of the duke and duchess in order to relish the simple-minded failures and misfortunes of the deluded squire. While making his way back to the ducal palace, Sancho encounters what appears to be a group of pilgrims, who, singing in a foreign tongue, promptly solicit him for alms. After sharing some food from his saddlebags – having left the *ínsula* no richer than he was before – he is recognized by one of the strangely dressed entourage, who declares himself the Morisco Ricote. Upon hearing the name and scrutinizing his countenance, Sancho finally recognizes and embraces his former neighbour, asking him, "Who the devil could recognize you, Ricote, in the ridiculous disguise you're wearing? Tell me, who turned you into a foreigner, and why did you risk coming back to Spain? It'll be very dangerous for you if they catch you and recognize you." (¿Quién diablos te había de conocer, Ricote, en ese traje de moharracho que traes? Dime quién te ha hecho franchote y cómo tienes atrevimiento de volver a España, donde si te cogen y conocen tendrás harta mala ventura.) The dispossessed Morisco retorts: "If you don't give me away, Sancho [...] I'm sure that nobody will know me in these clothes" (Si tú no me descubres, Sancho [...] seguro estoy que en este traje no habrá nadie que me conozca).[1] For the early modern reader, their exchange could not resonate with greater urgency. And scarcely could there be a more solemn corrective to the romantic notion of a free-flowing Mediterranean network than the plight of the Moriscos, who like Ricote were forced by royal decree to flee Spain from 1609 to 1614, casting asunder a vast diaspora across the region.[2]

As I have remarked in previous chapters, two notable tendencies of large-scale Mediterranean historiography have been to neglect the literary as well as to subsume the evidently marginal details of human subjectivity and affectivity under the rubric of geography, climate, or economics. However, the episode of Ricote, and its historical context of the Morisco expulsion, may well manifest a collective exception to these trends. Consider, for instance, the 1612 eyewitness account of Pedro Aznar Cardona, who, despite being an apologist of the expulsion, stirringly describes the displaced Moriscos as "tired, pained, lost, fatigued, sad, confused, ashamed, enraged, ill, vexed, bored, thirsty and hungry [... they] suffered at the beginning of their banishment incomparable travails, terrible bitterness and sharp pains and sentiments in their body and soul, and many died from pure affliction."[3] Although scholars have often overlooked its Mediterranean dimension,[4] the Morisco expulsion was an event that touched not only the most hardened defenders of the policy but also nearly every corner of the Mediterranean basin, with the compulsory emigration of hundreds of thousands of Moorish individuals and families to such far-flung destinations as Algiers, Ceuta, Fez, Genoa, Istanbul, Livorno, Marseilles, Oran, Rabat-Salé, Sicily, Tangier, Tetouan, Toulouse, and Tunis. As by far the most complete and well-known fictional representation of the expulsion, the Ricote episode in *Don Quijote* occupies a curious place in historiography, for numerous historical studies cite, if only in passing, Cervantes's Morisco character, appealing to a common referent among readers of what is decidedly non-fiction.[5] And this is so in spite of the likelihood that Ricote himself was named thus as a deft allusion to the Murcian valley of the same name, which since the thirteenth century had harboured an old Mudejar community. The Muslim descendants of Ricote Valley, like the family of their Cervantine namesake, suffered the "ethnic, religious and political cleansing"[6] and "genocide"[7] that was the expulsion. But the popular awareness of the Ricote episode suggests that it has exceeded its own historical referent, obscuring the borders between the fictive and the real in a manner not unlike the phenomenon by which Don Quijote has eclipsed his creator. This is one of the more patent ways in which the literary Mediterranean, subtly yet powerfully, has conditioned more ostensibly objective understandings of the region.

Yet Cervantes's representation of the Moriscos is not limited to typically negative emotions like those in Aznar Cardona's rousing description. Before Sancho has the chance to contemplate his dilemma – whether to reveal his knowledge of Ricote's illicit return or potentially to face the severe penalties for concealing it – the Morisco and his band of sojourners convene a modest yet savoury meal, along with a half-dozen wine-skins. Sancho heartily accepts their invitation to partake of both. Revelry ensues, and the text emphasizes the "gusto" and insouciant pleasure enjoyed by all: "They began to eat with great pleasure, savoring each mouthful slowly" (Comenzaron a comer con grandísimo gusto y muy de espacio, saboreándose con cada bocado).[8] From time to time they clasp hands with Sancho and exclaim, "Español y tudesqui, tuto uno: bon compaño!," and the erstwhile governor spontaneously adopts their patois himself, responding, "Bon compaño, jura Di!" After such exchanges the narrator reports that a lengthy bout of laughter overcomes him: "And he burst into laughter that lasted for an hour" (Y disparaba con una risa que le duraba un hora).[9] From a good-humoured and generally cheerful character who cracks up on many occasions, and in a work with no shortage of comedic material itself, this is one of the most singularly emphatic outbursts of laughter in the entire novel.[10] The sudden, explosive connotation of the verb *disparar* recrudesces through the use of the imperfect tense, denoting the renewal of laughter each time that the pseudo-pilgrims proclaim their unity with the Spaniard and he replicates their language. That such laughter is said to last an hour further stresses its zeal, while suggesting the timeless nature of what is nevertheless a fleeting encounter.

But what is the reader to make of such laughter? Is it the innocent product of gleeful inebriation or, as some critics have claimed, nothing more than an expression of relief upon leaving behind the austere demands of government and returning to carefree plebeian life?[11] Does Sancho's laugh perchance reveal something more profound, beyond the novel's designation by some scholars as a "funny book"? And what does it mean that the most exaggerated outburst of laughter proceeds from the makeshift use of what amounts to a Mediterranean lingua franca in the presence of a Morisco character? In order to answer these questions it will be necessary to trace the squire's steps back to his governorship and the other pranks played on him and Don Quijote by the duke and duchess, for it is not fortuitous that Sancho's encounter with Ricote takes place within the context of these larger episodes.[12] By studying the diverse ways that laughter functions therein, I contend that deeper insights stand to be grasped regarding not only their bout of shared laughter but also the broader stakes of humour in the novel. My analysis therefore serves as a corrective to two general tendencies of the foregoing scholarship on Cervantine humour. The first has been to conflate the generic concept of comedy with the psycho-physiological concept of laughter. By referring to early modern writings on the latter, I call for recuperating the understanding of *laughter itself as an emotion*. I thus approach Sancho's laughter as a highly charged emotional event, one that urges the reader to contemplate not the cause of this laughter but its effects, not what it says about why he laughs but who laughs – and with whom. The second prevailing trend I will attempt to redress is that of ascribing inordinate weight to premodern dramatic theories of comedy in support of the premise that *Don Quijote* was read by early moderns as an exclusively funny book. Although such aesthetic trea-tises as El Pinciano's *Philosophia antigua poética* certainly illuminate various aspects of the novel (for example, Don Quijote's conversation with the canon near the end of part 1), they are wholly inadequate for adducing the range and depth of laughter and humour represented in or occasioned by the text. Alternatively, and in line with my privileging of laughter over comedy, I maintain that early modern behaviour man-uals like those by Baldesar Castiglione, Giovanni Della Casa, and Lucas Gracián Dantisco are more useful for elucidating the emotional stakes of Cervantine laughter, particularly that experienced by and directed at Sancho. The textual juxtaposition of the Ricote scene with the courtly scorn and derision of surrounding chapters becomes exceptionally meaningful when examined through the lens of this conduct literature, allowing a return to the Mediterranean problem of the Moriscos in a new light.

One may easily argue, nevertheless, that the modern novel was itself responsible for inaugurating new understandings of all things jocu-lar. Laughter therefore resembles other passions, whose philosophical categories, as I have suggested in previous chapters, are often incom-mensurate with the complexity and hermeneutic variability of their representation in literature. In fact, I will propound that Cervantine laughter actually inverts both the dominant philosophy of humour of the early modern period – the so-called superiority theory – and what might be called its classic corollary, found in thinkers from Aristotle to El Pinciano, that a lack of compassion was a binding precondition for laughter. *Don Quijote* contains instances of what we could spatially define as laughing down (derisive laughter or, in the terminology I propose below, Schadenfreude), laughing up (critiquing elite structures of power through satire), and laughing across (an intersubjective, empathetic laughter such as that shared by Sancho and Ricote). We might also signal a circular laughter of the self-deprecating variety, whereby the Cervantes of the prologues proves fond of disparaging and poking fun at himself. Our own laughter too can participate in these multifaceted forms of mirth, even though I will be more interested to explore laughter in the text – and how it reveals intimate links with the social, cultural, and political context of the early modern Mediterranean – than to consider the reader's response, which in the case of *Don Quijote* has been mired in debates about whether critics have Romanticized its interpretation at the expense of its historical reception as a funny book. No other single issue has been as divisive as this one among Cervantes scholars, yet the approach to laughter as an emotion that I advocate in what follows may serve not only as a reconciliation of such divides but also as a corrective to Mediterranean scholarship's own Romantic tradition.

Gelotological Genealogies

According to a perennial anecdote, one day King Philip III – author of the Morisco expulsion – peered from the balcony of the Royal Alcázar of Madrid to find a student seated alongside the Manzanares River. A book in one hand, the young man was slapping himself in the forehead with the other, all while laughing uncontrollably and exhibiting "extraordinary movements of pleasure and happiness."[13] Bemused, the sovereign reckoned that the young man must have been either mad or reading *Don Quijote*. A courtier later confirmed for the king that the latter was indeed the case. Although the story may be apocryphal, it has been recounted as evidence that, shortly after the novel was published and while Cervantes was still living, its comicity had met with royal approval.[14] A similar moment occurs, we recall, in *Don Quijote* of 1605, when in chapter 9 the "second author" encounters in a Toledan market some old papers written in Arabic and asks a *morisco aljamiado* to translate them. Almost immediately after he begins reading, the young polyglot bursts out laughing. Naturally, the author-narrator asks him why, and he explains through further laughter that an annotation, scrawled in the margin of the manuscript, proclaims that Dulcinea del Toboso "had the best hand for salting pork of any woman in all of La Mancha" (*tuvo la mejor mano para salar puercos que otra mujer de toda la*

Mancha).[15] The quote reveals that not only do the papers, to the narrator's astonishment, augur the continuation of the story of Don Quijote (which had been abruptly interrupted in the previous chapter), but also that its humour would appear to transcend translation and multiple narrative levels.

Even if the boorish gloss fails to convulse our twenty-first-century diaphragms as much as the Arabic translator's, his laughter is comprehensible – in short, we get the joke. Explaining precisely what about a joke – not to mention a novel – makes it funny, however, is another story entirely. El Pinciano's *Philosophia antigua poética* of the year 1596, esteemed as the most complete treatise on literary aesthetics of sixteenth-century Spain, betrays no small difficulty when faced with the challenge of explicating the concept of humour. Although he ponderously identifies its primary trigger as "something, I know not what, about the awkward and ugly" (un no sé qué de torpe y feo), El Pinciano claims that the reader's everyday familiarity with laughter makes it unnecessary to define, concluding resignedly that "laughter is laughter" (la risa es risa).[16] If El Pinciano is to be considered one of the most acute influences on the writing of *Don Quijote*, then his struggle to articulate humour may help to explain the view of the critic Daniel Eisenberg, who has asserted, suggestively if hyperbolically, that humour "is the most understudied topic" of the novel. While some scholars have long regarded the text as a "funny book" – based on the notion that its primary historical purpose was to provide light-hearted entertainment – Eisenberg maintains: "The lack of discussion of humor in the work – that we are encouraged to laugh, but not to reflect on our laughter – is surely one reason why scholarship has avoided the topic of *Don Quixote*'s humor."[17]

Such pronouncements bespeak a contentious debate that has roiled Cervantism for decades, if not centuries. The seemingly innocuous question of whether *Don Quijote* is primarily comedic summons an entire history of critical scholarship on the novel, which, in turn, reveals the broader ideological tensions between philological and interpretative or theoretical approaches to Spanish literature. At the crux of the matter is whether Cervantes intended his masterpiece to be humorous – as it was purportedly received by King Philip III and his early modern compatriots – or that it harbours "deeper" insights into metaphysical, aesthetic, political, or other critical modes of thought characteristic of so-called high literature. In essence, a close historical examination of *Quijote* criticism reveals a number of competing yet interconnected attempts to make sense of how a funny book can simultaneously be that and much more. Neoclassicism first presupposed that *Don Quijote* was more satirical than burlesque by elevating its author as a heroic slayer of irredeemably deficient romances of chivalry. By emphasizing meta-literary parody over slapstick and grotesque comedy, such readings brought the novel into the hallowed fold of serious literature and established its place in the world canon. As Rachel Schmidt has effectively shown, the mid-eighteenth-century illustrated British editions at the forefront of this interpretative movement – such as Lord Carteret's, for which Gregorio Mayans penned the first biography of Cervantes – preempted Romanticism's own investment in seeing, beyond the farcical in the novel, something more formidable and far reaching. It was, however, the nineteenth-century German Romantics who were primarily responsible for crystallizing a serious approach to *Don Quijote*, ascribing it a "sentimental" ethos that epitomized their aesthetic and philosophical ideals.[18] This is not surprising when we recall the broader trends of Romanticism: it favoured emotion over Enlightenment reason, subjectivity over objectivity, and a celebration of the past over future-oriented teleologies. Spain, with its stereotypically intense emotions and medieval flair, arose as the premier Romantic locale, and the German Romantics became particularly enamoured of its popular folklore, Arab influence, the Spanish Baroque, and, of course, Cervantes's bestseller. Scarcely could one imagine a more superb idol for the movement than a moonstruck, spirited Spanish gentleman intent on resurrecting the exalted ideals of a medieval past.

Since then, much ink has been spilled by scholars who have espoused, or been accused of espousing, the Romantic or "soft" approach versus those who have defended the putatively more rigorous, historical, or "hard" reading of the novel as a funny book. With the North American academy's forays into theory, and Peninsular scholars doubling down on philology as the most legitimate method of textual interpretation, in the twentieth century these divisions intensified. The most adamant advocates of the hard approach were the British critics P.E. Russell and Anthony Close, with the former launching the opening salvo in the "*Don Quixote* as a funny book" war with his 1969 article of the same name, which claimed there existed "no grounds for suggesting that Cervantes himself thought of his book [...] as anything other than a funny book."[19] In 1977, Close commanded a more sustained barrage with *The Romantic Approach to "Don Quixote,"* asserting that "the Romantic tradition – serious, sentimental, patriotic, philosophical, and subjective – has pulled criticism directly away from the questions that the novel most obviously and naturally prompts." For Close, such "questions" concerned, quite simply, the writing of a book of light-hearted entertainment and burlesque humour that parodied chivalric romance. Levelling his sights on the likes of "Schlegel, Schelling, Coleridge, Menéndez Pelayo, Menéndez Pidal, and Américo Castro," Close added provocatively that "if a critical tradition so perversely ignores the obvious it must be suspected of having gone badly astray."[20] Not even Spain's own pre-eminent thinkers Ortega y Gasset, Unamuno, and Azorín were spared the withering volley of Close's critique.

In heavier, more uncompromising strokes the studies by Russell and Close drew the battle-lines of an engagement that had been brewing for some time, and, predictably, they were met with swift opposition from the other side. A number of book reviews exposed the limitations and often specious logic of the funny-book approach, while objecting to Close's "partisan rhetoric."[21] Many also noted the rhetorical and interpretative gymnastics that, somewhat ironically, were required to address the numerous instances in which Cervantes seems to undermine his own avowed objective of what Stephen Gilman aptly coined "comic prophylaxis":[22] writing a book that provided "amusement for the sad and melancholic breast on any occasion, at all times" (pasatiempo / al pecho melancólico y mohíno, / en cualquier sazón, en todo tiempo).[23] True to these words, *Don Quijote* does deliver on the promise of great comic diversity, which a handful of critics have recognized and I will survey in greater detail throughout this chapter.[24] Others like Eisenberg, Close, and Russell, however, have fallen into the trap of taking too literally the influence of El Pinciano as "the only contemporary theorist of the comic whose work Cervantes would likely have known."[25] According to Russell:

> It seems plain to me [...] that earlier readers of the book cannot have thought of identifying themselves *con amore* with Don Quijote or with Sancho; their clear-cut notions about insanity and folly, about the nature of laughter and the causes of the ridiculous, ruled out any such thing. The point is made very clearly by Alonso López Pinciano [...] In tragedy, he explains, the audience participates emotionally in the events depicted on the stage, feeling commiseration and pity towards the characters. A distinguishing feature of comedy is that no such process of identification occurs; the audience laughs but is emotionally indifferent."[26]

Russell's point is that only since the dawn of European Romanticism has anyone felt inclined to sympathize with knight and squire (or, one would suppose, a character like Ricote) and that early modern readers, as if by nature, would not identify with these characters but remain emotionally uninvolved. In a sense, this is already a highly subjective thesis.[27] As I remarked in my discussion in chapter 2 of the challenges confronting practitioners of the history of emotion, attempting to re-construct the feelings of premodern individuals is a fraught, though certainly not unworthy, enterprise. To claim, as Russell and Close do, that seventeenth-century readers did not *feel* any affective attachment to Cervantes's characters amounts to merely an inversion of the same critical practice. The most ardent champions of the funny-book thesis thus become ensnared in dual critical pitfalls: they succumb to a trans-posed version of precisely what they censure in Romantic critics (a sub-jective evaluation of the text) and, by leaning so heavily on El Pinciano, to the more general peril of taking the philological practice of tracing authorial influence too far. One need only recall his overt tautology – "laughter is laughter" – to realize that El Pinciano's coarse treatment of the concept pales in comparison to that contained in and stimulated by the novel.

In effect, a rigid adherence to precepts inherited from antiquity – circumscribed in their ability to account for the rise of the modern novel – has further plagued the staunchest advocates of the funny-book approach. Renaissance theorists were notoriously obdurate in their fi-delity to the neo-Aristotelian norms governing tragedy and comedy, airing fervid remonstrances of serio-comic hybrids or the concept, it-self developed in the Renaissance, of *serio ludere*. The Spanish humanist Francisco Cascales is only one of many sixteenth- and seventeenth-century writers who railed against tragicomedy as "monstrous" and "against nature."[28] Legion are such precepts in El Pinciano's discussion of the dramatic arts, right down to the emotions that each respective genre was meant to arouse or purge. Defining comedy as "an active imitation made to cleanse the soul of passions by way of pleasure and laughter," he importantly adds that when a funny situation or prank "brings about notable harm, compassion overcomes the ridiculous, and laughter is completely lost."[29] Although the full repercussions of these concepts will become clear in the following pages, here they are ger-mane for registering how they have hamstrung modern proponents of the funny-book approach who, in relying excessively on El Pinciano and dramatic theories, likewise see the reader's laughter as incompati-ble with compassion.[30] In other words, according to these critics' read-ing of the generic strictures of comedy, we cannot find Don Quijote and Sancho at once risible and pitiable. Since the latter quality would negate the former, so their logic goes, the novel can only ever be come-dic – thus suggesting, à la El Pinciano, another tautology: the novel is intended to be funny, so readers ought not sympathize with the pro-tagonists, because if they did, it would no longer be funny. Beyond this *reductio ad absurdum*, the problem is that such boiler-plate dramatic prescriptions fall short in accounting for the dynamic emotional range of such a path-breaking, genre-defying work as *Don Quijote*.[31]

Although the funny-book thesis could be further refuted, it is not my intention to reopen a debate that, for most Cervantists, has already been settled, for even if staunchly partisan supporters with an ideological axe to grind still linger on both sides of the hard and soft paradigm, such divisions have waned considerably in recent years.[32] Rather, this necessarily brief audit of their most salient trends reveals that these critical genealogies have bequeathed a curious legacy to specialists on *Don Quijote*: a scholarly landscape largely devoid of in-depth studies on either laughter or sentiment in the novel. Ironically, it is almost as though the historical versus Romantic polemic has engendered a heightened self-consciousness of these very divisions, which in turn has led to a sort of reflexive avoidance of the aspects with which they have been most closely associated. On the one hand, adherents of the historical approach have dismissed Romantic interpretations of *Don Quijote* as "sentimental." In response to such criticism, proponents of Romantic readings, on the other hand, have tended to undervalue or ignore the comical aspects of the novel. Put simply, both hard and soft approaches have failed to shed suitable light on Mediterranean emotions in the text, those which are so starkly apparent in the episode of Ricote. Moreover, the hard-soft dialectic is itself the dividend of a fundamental misunderstanding about laughter, one that has only been further obscured, albeit unwittingly, by inveterate, ossified stances on the subject. My argument, however, is that what Close identifies as the "sentimental" and "subjective" aspects of Romantic criticism are, in reality, perfectly compatible with humour. To conceive of laughter as an emotion is to be historically rigorous and yet attuned to how the text may reveal insights about that history, or those that otherwise lie beyond the hard approach of only ever seeing a funny book.

The Emotional Effects of Laughter, and Laughter as Affect

El Pinciano's unabashed tautology ("laughter is laughter") is significant for another reason. As a concept that defies analytical language, laughter is thereby situated among such things as love, desire, jealousy, and rage – emotions whose description has long posed a challenge for scientific and philosophical analysis, not to mention personal expression. That laughter should be just as ineffable is, in fact, consistent with most early modern theories of the passions. Hobbes, for instance, recalls El Pinciano's difficulties when he classifies laughter as "that passion which hath no name."[33] Descartes and Spinoza included laughter in the discussion of their distinct emotional taxonomies, and Malebranche and La Chambre too followed suit by counting it among the passions of the soul. Laurent Joubert, a French physician whose *Traité du ris* (*Treatise on Laughter*) of 1579 analysed the phenomenon exhaustively, similarly fixes laughter as an emotion, as quoted in the epigraph to this chapter. "Now, we say commonly," Joubert reminds the reader, "he laughs heartily, and not brainily, thus denoting the place from which the risible emotion proceeds."[34] The affiliation between emotion and humour is foreseeable given the latter's lexical heritage, deriving as it does from the humoral theories set in motion by Hippocrates, Galen, and, in early modern Spain, Huarte de San Juan. The belief that the four humours, along with certain environmental factors, influenced one's personality and emotional disposition led Huarte to posit a relationship between humoral imbalance and madness. However, since it was impossible to attain a perfect equilibrium, to one degree or another all individuals experienced an idiosyncratic temperament and exhibited the outward cues of folly. Although in the premodern period madness itself was regarded as amusing – one need only think of the countless characters entertained by Don Quijote's derangement – the etymology of *humour* suggests that everyday human behavioural and emotional follies could just as easily serve to make one laugh. After lamenting that the many philosophical attempts at pinpointing the cause of laughter have been incomprehensible, Huarte locates a humoral etiology for laughter in the sanguine or an excess of blood.[35] Even so, the physician and proto-psychologist, like many of his fellow early modern writers, refers to laughter as a "passion" (pasión).[36]

In spite of contemporary psychological, cognitive, and gelotological studies that have lent further scientific credence to the intimate relationship between laughter and affect,[37] modernity has, by and large, disposed of the idea of laughter as an emotion. In her recent book *Laughter: Notes on a Passion*, the comparative literary critic Anca Parvulescu remarks on laughter's conspicuous absence among those things ordinarily considered emotions today: "Importantly, when the list of passions is sifted into a list of emotions, although most names of passions are retained, laughter is left behind." Arguing that the "question [...] of the interior 'feeling' that causes the external 'expression of laughter' [...] is misconceived," Parvulescu advocates for a return to the conception of laughter not merely as the "accessory of an internal event" but as a passion in its own right.[38] Two general reasons, each not without its own problems, help to explain the omission. The first is that modern writers on humour have further pried apart and exploded the rift between compassion and laughter that was already present among some premodern thinkers. Henri Bergson's influential turn-of-the-century study is likely the most flagrant culprit in this regard. He rids laughter of its emotional undercarriage at the outset, remarking on what he purports to be "the *absence of feeling* which usually accompanies laughter," and claiming that "the comic demands something like a momentary anesthesia of the heart. Its appeal is to intelligence, pure and simple." "Indifference," he adds, "is its natural environment, for laughter has no greater foe than emotion."[39] Almost diametrically opposed to his early modern countryman Joubert, Bergson erects a stark dialectic and adduces it in support of his broader theory that at the root of humour lies a mechanistic representation of the human, "something mechanical encrusted on the living," or "the momentary transformation of a person into a thing." Curiously, the paradigmatic example that Bergson marshals is precisely Cervantes's hapless squire: "*We laugh every time a person gives us the impression of being a thing*. We laugh at Sancho Panza tumbled into a bed-quilt and tossed into the air like a football."[40] Responsive to the social effects of nineteenth-century industrialization though Bergson's model was, its foremost problem is that it reproduces the rigid dualism of emotion as contrary to reason, cognition, and intellect – a fallacy that, as demonstrated previously, was rebutted as early as Aristotle.

The second, albeit more dubious, explanation of why laughter began in modernity to shed its association with the passions is the proliferation of behaviour manuals and a preoccupation with etiquette as part of what Elias called "the civilizing process." Accordingly, then, laughter followed a course parallel to that of other emotions, whose public expression became increasingly governed by the astringent demands of proper conduct, moulded by a dialectic of prohibition and transgression. As with certain other outward emotional cues, to laugh passionately was either to commit a social faux pas or to thumb one's nose at propriety. The cardinal difference is that laughter never recovered its earlier conception as a passion itself, a fact that has led other scholars to focus instead on the rise of the smile as its diluted and more socially acceptable heir.[41] We should nonetheless be wary of accounts that lean too heavily on Elias, whose intellectually seductive hypotheses, as scholars specializing in the history of emotion have cautioned, appear to create as many problems as they solve.[42] The present monograph, indeed, is founded on the premise that emotions were not nearly as repressed as readers of the twentieth-century sociologist might be led to believe.

Whatever the ultimate reasons for laughter's evaporation from the affective domain, plentiful are the critical pay-offs of recuperating its early modern conception as a passion. Unlike Bergson's and other attempts at elucidating a theory of humour based on the trigger for laughter – a joke, a play on words, an absurdity, the grotesque – conceiving of laughter as an affect unshackles it from the limitations of a stimulus-response dichotomy, thus opening onto a more robust understanding of the textual, bodily, material, and political work it performs. Those critics of *Don Quijote* who have placed the sentimental and the comical at odds with one another have neglected, wittingly or not, these fertile and historically founded affiliations between affect and laughter, further alienating the intimate dependence of humour on an entire range of emotions. Recovering the emotional content and contours of laughter offers considerable purchase for comprehending its use (and abuse) in the novel, for escaping the reductionism of the funny-book designation. It would also enrich our understanding, for example, of the emotional and aesthetic work that laughter performs in the novel, and how that work relates to other emotions; how laughter's expression morphs according to different characters and their moods, social milieus, and narrative tones; and what sorts of historical prohibitions and transgressions are mapped onto its distinct irruptions in the text.

To be sure, instances of subdued laughing or attempts to control an outburst of laughter abound in *Don Quijote*, particularly in the space of the ducal palace, where the eminently courtly practice of dissimulation is mustered to conceal the comic delight of the duke, duchess, and their servants from the objects of their pranks. Upon the arrival of the protagonists, for instance, the narrator reports that "if the maidens who were serving [Don Quijote] had not been charged with hiding their laughter, for this was one of the precise orders their mistress and master had given them, they would have split their sides laughing" (a no tener cuenta las doncellas que le servían [a don Quijote] con disimular la risa (que fue una de las precisas órdenes que sus señores les habían dado), reventaran riendo).[43] Shortly thereafter, as Don Quijote's attendants perform the quintessentially burlesque ceremony of the soaping of his beard, "it was truly astonishing and a sign of great astuteness that they could hide their laughter" (fue gran maravilla y mucha discreción poder disimular la risa).[44] To achieve the desired comedic effect, these examples, as so many others contrived by the duke and duchess, hinge on a feigned gravitas that recalls two well-established theories of humour, the incongruity and the superiority theories. According to the incongruity theory, first devised in the eighteenth century, such situations are funny because they violate expected mental patterns; in this case, a solemn court ritual is hilariously mismatched with the image of a mad knight errant covered in soap bubbles. The attempts by members of the courtly entourage to suppress their laughter respond to three concerns: they avoid raising the suspicion of Don Quijote and Sancho that they are the butt of the jokes and thus ensure their continuation; they reproduce the decorous behaviour prescribed by conduct manuals and treatises on the royal court; and they lend the pranks the air of earnestness that is vital for catalyzing the incongruity needed for making such pranks funny in the first place.[45] The other theory subtending these episodes is the one that dominated early modern understandings of humour, the so-called superiority theory of laughter. From Plato and Aristotle to Cicero and Quintilian, its proponents held that turpitude – something ugly or deformed (*turpitudo et deformitas*) – was the primary trigger for humour. But it was essential that this "defect" not be so great as to rouse compassion, the idea being that, if one sympathized with the object of comedy, it would no longer be funny. In the Renaissance, Joubert still subscribed to the notion that sympathy was antithetical to humour: to experience the passion of laughter, one must not feel compassion for something potentially laughable.[46] If this seems paradoxical, then it may be so, once again, because modernity has dispensed with the concept that laughter itself was an emotion, independent of any given risible stimulus. Therefore, in the following section I would like to explore this class of humour through the feeling of Schadenfreude in order to understand better how Sancho contributes to the comedic qualities of the novel.

Sancho and Schadenfreude, or Courtly Comedics

My reasons for adopting the lens of Schadenfreude are several-fold. First, since this book as a whole is interested in how language goes about the work of expressing affect and how this work changes diachronically, the German loan-word offers a prime example of an emotional concept that is lexicalized and yet, to some extent, is also defamiliarized. In this way, Schadenfreude can afford critics a more precise analytical tool than simply humour, for example. Although it does not always imply laughter per se, the modern definition of *Schadenfreude* – "malicious enjoyment of the misfortunes of others" – does depend upon clearly emotional categories such as joy, pleasure, and happiness (and, conversely, often upon the shame of its object as well).[47] Hence not only are its affective registers more readily available, but also its meaning aligns with the predominant understanding of laughter in the early modern period, the superiority theory.[48] As Hobbes explains, "the passion of laughter is nothing else but a sudden glory arising from sudden conception of some eminency in ourselves, by comparison with the infirmities of others."[49] The term *Schadenfreude* helpfully evokes the malice, contempt, and scorn of this pre-Enlightenment laughter. One might even speculate that the adoption of this foreign concept – which entered into common usage in English in the late nineteenth century – became necessary only after newly differentiated understandings of laughter had begun to circulate. More recently, Schadenfreude has become the object of several studies, pop-culture references, and satire in the English-speaking world, especially in the last ten to twenty years.[50] In his *Schadenfreude: The Little Book of Black Delights*, Tim Lihoreau coins several facetious terms, based on classical Latin roots, for cynically describing the expanding lexicon of twenty-first-century opportunities for Schadenfreude, including *verolatophilia* ("delight in being visibly on a train which someone misses"), *cogecolloquophilia* ("delight in witnessing someone forced into conversation on a train"), *extrunophilia* ("delight in sailing past a queue because you're on the guest list"), *findophilia* ("delight in 'copying in' superiors on relevant emails"), and, finally, *ruinophilia res publica* ("delight in the downfall of a politician"), which he reasons affects over 99 per cent of the population.[51]

Yet we should not dismiss these phenomena too hastily as symptomatic of a pitiless, self-centred contemporary society, for early modern individuals seized ample opportunities for Schadenfreude as well. In effect, they underpin Vladimir Nabokov's notorious objection with *Don Quijote*, which he assailed as a "torture house" and "one of the most bitter and barbarous books ever penned." For Nabokov, the novel's "hideous cruelty – with or without the author's intent or sanction" actually "befouls its humor."[52] No character is more prone than Sancho to generating this class of derisive laughter, which is nowhere more prevalent than in the episodes at the ducal palace.[53] These chapters comprise an integral stage of what Henry W. Sullivan has deemed the "grotesque purgatory" of comical torments through which the protagonists must pass in part 2 of the novel.[54] The duke and duchess amount to early modern archetypes of what psychologists have lately termed "katagelasticists," or those individuals who enjoy laughing at others to an extreme.[55] Having already read the metafictional account of Don Quijote and Sancho's adventures, the duke and duchess reap immediate pleasure upon encountering them for the first time in the flesh, as is underscored by the text's repetitive use of such words as *pleasure* (*gusto*), *pleasant* (*agradable*), *amusing* (*gracioso*), and *content* (*contento*), especially in portraying the aristocratic characters' reaction to Sancho.[56] Soon thereafter, the narrator remarks on the squire's one-of-a-kind propensity to provoke laughter: "The duchess was dying of laughter when she heard Sancho speak, and in her opinion he was more amusing and even crazier than his master, an opinion held by many at the time."

(Perecía de risa la duquesa en oyendo hablar a Sancho, y en su opinión le tenía por más gracioso y por más loco que a su amo, y muchos hubo en aquel tiempo que fueron deste mismo parecer.)[57] According to Eduardo Urbina, it is in part 2 of the novel that Sancho's evolution as a character results in the "Sanchification" of the text, akin to what Bakhtin dubbed the "Pantagruelism" of Rabelais's eponymous work.[58] It is true, as many other critics have recognized, that Sancho is an eminently carnivalesque figure,[59] and while readers will surely agree that the character is funny (whether more or less so than Don Quijote), it befits the incisive grasp on laughter sought here to diagnose what precisely it is that makes him so comical.

In addition to the handful of examples in which Sancho intentionally uses his wit or tells a joke, I identify six basic elements of his characteristics and personality that induce other characters to laugh, many of which doubtless coincide with the reader's own mirth:[60]

1 Language (metaplasm, tendency to misspeak or mispronounce, excessive use of refrains, and general loquacity)[61]
2 Physical characteristics (corpulence, squatness, and relative clumsiness; related to the text's carnivalesque emphasis on bodily humour with the character)[62]
3 Mental characteristics (forgetfulness and simple-mindedness; as the duchess remarks, unlike his master he is not actually insane, but due to his naïveté he believes in Don Quijote's enterprise nonetheless)[63]
4 Temperament (a *dormilón* or sleepy-head, *comilón* or glutton, who is somewhat cowardly and generally keen to preserve physical comfort)[64]
5 Economic self-interest (eagerness to pursue material gain and subsequent delight at profit)[65]
6 Rustic nature (and, by extension, vulgarity and ignorance of chivalric, courtly, and other social protocols)[66]

Many of these risible qualities are interrelated and, when combined, work to enhance the comedic effect of given scenes. In fact, the duke and duchess actively exploit each of these traits throughout the course of the various pranks they devise for their amusement at Sancho's expense. The squire's governorship of Barataria, for instance, which represents the utopian consummation of all his desires, revolves around (1) his gullibility in believing in the promise of an *ínsula*; (2) the interest in material gain it would grant him; (3) a public stage for exposing the improprieties of his rustic nature; (4) the opportunity for verbal gaffes and linguistic crudeness through the feigned court cases; (5) the exploitation of his gluttony and penchant for sleep by denying him food and rest; and (6) taking advantage of his rotund figure during the "siege" of Barataria by strapping shields on either side of him and turning him into a giant "tortoise." By preying, in Hobbes's words, on the relative "infirmities" of Sancho – physical, mental, economic – it is not fortuitous that each of these comical situations, when brandished by the duke and duchess, exemplifies the early modern superiority theory of laughter. Since by design it is intended to produce pleasure for the ducal entourage through the failures and misfortunes of Sancho therein, Barataria can likewise be seen as an elaborate mechanism for manufacturing Schadenfreude.

From Sadism to Satire

Of greatest import, however, are the ways in which this Schadenfreude ultimately fails to be fully realized – or, stated in a different manner, the reason the duke and duchess yield a diminished return of pleasure on their significant investment in the performative economy of Barataria. For while he certainly supplies ample comedic material, on the whole Sancho turns out to be judicious, prudent, and surprisingly successful in his management of the *ínsula*.[67] The multiple disputes and litigation he resolves astound onlookers, as is evident in the sudden emphasis on the term *admiración* in the first chapter of his government. To cite merely a few examples: the narrator observes that Sancho's jurisprudence "moved the onlookers to amazement" (movió a admiración a los circunstantes), who later "were again amazed at the judgments and verdicts of their new governor" (quedaron admirados de nuevo de los juicios y sentencias de su nuevo gobernador). Finally, with a biblical metaphor of the sagacious judge par excellence, it is reported that "everyone was stunned, and they considered their governor to be a second Solomon" ([q]uedaron todos admirados, y tuvieron a su gobernador por un nuevo Salomón).[68] Here it is necessary to recall the "variegated meaning" of *admiración*,[69] which could connote light-hearted surprise and entertainment as well as excellence. In short, an islandish illusion plotted in part for Sancho's penitence ends up being his redemption.

Early modern behaviour manuals and treatises on the royal court, which circulated widely across Europe and prescribed, among many other things, moral limitations for laughter and practical jokes, aid in clarifying how and why Sancho, to everyone's astonishment, carries the day as governor. The most prominent example is Castiglione's *Il cortegiano* (*The Book of the Courtier*), which dedicates several pages to the sundry social benefits and hazards of humour. Although Castiglione derives much of this discussion from earlier thinkers such as Cicero and Quintilian, his book met with an avid readership in Spain, with the translation by Juan Boscán passing through numerous reprintings in the sixteenth century.[70] Unlike later thinkers, such as Bergson or Shaftesbury, who defended the laughter of mockery as expedient for the social order, early moderns like Castiglione tended to condemn this sort of humour, and, as such, we can learn a great deal from what the acclaimed medieval historian Jacques Le Goff would call their "casuistry of laughter."[71] According to Castiglione, "we must carefully consider the scope and the limits of provoking laughter by derision, and who it is that we deride." "Yet it is proper," he asserts, "to ridicule and laugh at the vices of those who are neither so wretched as to excite compassion, nor so wicked as to seem to deserve capital punishment, nor of so great a station that their wrath could do us much harm."[72] What translators have rendered "laughter by derision" is, for Castiglione, *ridere mordendo* or literally "biting laughter." On the more specific issue of pranks, he cautions that "the Courtier's practical jokes ought to be somewhat more removed from scurrility" and not tread into fraudulence or be "too rough."[73] As the name Barataria itself echoes the notion of a phony, cheap joke, it is not coincidental that the majority of disputes brought before Sancho involve fraud or deception. Likewise, it is clear that Castiglione would object, at the very least, to Sancho's treatment in the feigned battle to defend the *ínsula*, when he is bound between two shields and mercilessly trampled. It is here that the squire's objectification is more salient than at any other point of the novel, including his *manteamiento* or tossing in the air that inspired Bergson. Although "not even when they saw that he had fallen did those mockers have any compassion for him" (no por verle caído aquella gente burladora le tuvieron compasión alguna), after Sancho faints from the fear of his torment, "[t]hose who had deceived him regretted having carried the joke so far" ([y]a les pesaba a los de la burla de habérsela hecho tan pesada).[74]

In his widely read *Galateo español* of 1582, Gracián Dantisco – a friend of Cervantes who would approve the printing of *La Galatea* – details the genus of laughter of greatest concern here, the act of *escarnecer* or *escarnio*, alternately translated as "derision," "ridicule," "mocking," or "scorn." "Mocking," Gracián Dantisco explains, "is taking pleasure in the shame we cause another without any benefit to ourselves. Therefore in common behaviour and conversation diligent people should abstain from laughing mockingly at anyone." (Es, pues, el escarnecer un tomar deleite de la vergüenza que hacemos tener a otro sin ningún provecho de nosotros mismos. Por lo cual en el común trato y conversación se deben abstener los curiosos de mofar de na-die.)[75] Della Casa's *Galateo*, on which Gracián Dantisco modelled his own conduct manual, helpfully glosses what in Italian was known as *schernire* or *scherno*. Someone who engages in *scherno* is wont to "burst out in laughter and rejoice over an idiotic thing someone said; or to take pleasure in making others blush [...] Very similar to these are those buffoons who enjoy playing tricks and teasing, not because they want to scorn or deride, but simply for the fun of it."[76] Della Casa fur-ther details the minute difference between joking (*beffare*) and mocking (*schernire*), one that is based on the moral or emotional intentions of the individual behind the joke:

> Know that there is no difference between joking and mocking except in purpose and intention; for joking is done for amusement, and mocking is done to harm, while in common parlance these two words are often inter-changed: but whoever mocks is happy with the shame of another, while he who jokes is not satisfied but rather amused by another's error, and if the other man were ashamed, the joker would feel pained and sad [...] And so the same thing done to the same person, depending only on intention, will be either laughing with someone or laughing at someone. Since our intention is not easily clear to others, it is not fitting to indulge in practices so dubious and suspect, and one should avoid them.[77]

These proscriptions alert us once again to the emotional work per-formed by laughter and the affective interplay supposed by *scherno*, whereby the quantity of pleasure derived from such laughter corre-sponds with the degree of shame felt by its object. In the case of Sancho, however, the cumulative force of this mutually influential relationship between shame and Schadenfreude is curtailed. The reason is that his character rarely exhibits a capacity for shame, unlike Don Quijote, for whom the duke and duchess actually stifle their laughter to spare him such a feeling.[78] This contrast owes to each character's respective social class: the status of Alonso Quijano as an hidalgo of the lower nobil-ity, coupled with Don Quijote's aspirations of knightly fame, suggest a self-consciousness and acute awareness of courtly decorum that is ab-sent in Sancho, a poor farmer. As Castiglione and Della Casa recognize, the lower someone's estate and social capital, the farther the threshold of accepted comical decorum could be extended. Don Quijote himself alludes to this distinction when, after ticking off the various pieces of advice for Sancho's governorship, he admonishes him, "if you govern badly, the fault will be yours and mine the shame" (si mal gobernares, tuya será la culpa, y mía la vergüenza).[79]

Yet Don Quijote's most decisive counsel for underwriting Sancho's success in Barataria is that he embrace his ignoble, rustic background: "Take pride in the humbleness of your lineage, and do not disdain to say that you come from peasants, for seeing that you are not ashamed of it, no one will attempt to shame you." (Haz gala, Sancho, de la humildad de tu linaje, y no te desprecies de decir que vienes de labradores, porque viendo que no te corres, ninguno se pondrá a correrte.)[80] This insight acknowledges the a priori necessity of shame in a potential object of ridicule in order that the act of shaming – and therefore the humorous pleasure or Schadenfreude that results – be effective. Sancho's disinclination towards shame thus simultaneously ensures the success of his government, spares Don Quijote the embarrassment of its potential failure, and denies the duke and duchess the ultimate gratification of luxuriating in Sancho's humiliation. In this way, his unrefined, homespun nature functions as a kind of *pharmakon*: on the one hand, it is a primary source of comedy for fellow characters, and, on the other, it insulates him from much of the malicious laughter and derision that would otherwise befall him. His facility with folk wisdom, embrace of unpolished, provincial customs, and refusal to be ashamed of his humble lineage, while all contributing to his status as a comical figure, foreclose on the potential for those same qualities to produce even greater pleasure, gloating, morose delectation, and Schadenfreude for characters of a higher class. Sancho's rusticity is at once what produces laughter for other characters and safeguards him from its effects.[81]

The "fool's wisdom" that Sancho displays by prevailing as governor defies readerly expectations and thwarts the designs of the duke and duchess, spoiling their Roman holiday. One of their accomplices, the steward (*mayordomo*) of the *ínsula*, marvels at how Sancho's discreet success has caused their plan to back-fire: "Every day we see new things in the world: deceptions become the truth, and deceivers find themselves deceived." (Cada día se veen cosas nuevas en el mundo: las burlas se vuelven en veras y los burladores se hallan burlados.)[82] Later, after Don Quijote and Sancho are subjected to yet another round of pranks in the ducal palace, the narrator again emphasizes this point: "Cide Hamete goes on to say that in his opinion the deceivers are as mad as the deceived, and that the duke and duchess came very close to seeming like fools since they went to such lengths to deceive two fools." (Y dice más Cide Hamete: que tiene para sí ser tan locos los burladores como los burlados y que no estaban los duques dos dedos de parecer tontos, pues tanto ahínco ponían en burlarse de dos tontos.)[83] Ironically, it is the duke and duchess's own obsession with pleasure at any cost that is satirized by a peasant governor who puts the public good above his own selfish desires. Outwardly punctilious yet privately repugnant, the patrician class is left with no clothes. While performing a political function in parodying the excesses of the royal court (in the extended tradition of *de curialium miseriis*), and a moral function in taking to task the perpetrators of malicious pranks, these statements illustrate one of the foremost risks of Schadenfreude: biting humour can bite back. The ridiculer attracts ridicule, suggesting both a carnivalesque and a self-recursive effect that renders Schadenfreude a kind of *pharmakon* as well. The reader is invited to indulge in the satisfaction of seeing Sancho's tormenters turned into *tontos* themselves. Thus what began as little more than a humorous, if elaborately sadistic, plot for the purpose of blithe entertainment ends up producing a mordant satire.[84] In fact, one of the most widely accepted contemporary definitions of literary satire reproduces much of the same language as the early modern descriptions by Castiglione, Della Casa, and Gracián Dantisco of derisive laughter.[85]

The resistance of Sancho's character to becoming the full-blown buffoon or court jester offers further insights into the underlying enjoyment of laughter and the aesthetics of humour in the novel. For this suggests that the mirth Sancho induces is not without a ceiling – thereby prompting the question, why not? What literary pay-off is accrued by curbing the risible potential of this nevertheless comical character? On the one hand, the question itself would seem to challenge the notion of *Don Quijote* as merely a funny book, for within these limits of laughter lie, as already stated, some rather pointed social, political, and ethical implications. Attending to the emotional valences of laughter, as I have done in the spirit of its early modern conception as a passion, troubles the ostensibly historicist approach to the novel as a work of light-hearted diversion. Even after accounting for the possibility that seventeenth-century individuals did not find derisive laughter as reprehensible as modern readers do,[86] analysing the affective investments behind this laughter reveals that it is anything but innocent, at least in so far as it responds not to a given risible stimulus but to an entire range of emotional values. On the other hand, it could be argued that Sancho's divergence from the buffoon archetype bestows on the character a depth and a complexity that make him all the more pleasurable and, in some respect, funnier. Counter-intuitive though this may seem, it is consistent with the idea that the best joke is one that thwarts our own expectations. This "incongruity theory" of humour was not fully elaborated until the eighteenth century, and yet it is a concept that was surely not lost on Cervantes.[87] In fact, he dresses down Avellaneda for his failure to endow the apocryphal Sancho with the comicality engendered by such seeming contradictions; while Cervantes's Sancho is three-dimensional, Avellaneda's falls flat. So concludes Álvaro Tarfe, the character from Avellaneda's unauthorized sequel who appears towards the end of *Don Quijote* of 1615: "though he was famous for being very amusing, I never heard him say any witticism that was" (aunque tenía fama de muy gracioso, nunca le oí decir gracia que la tuviese). After the "real" Sancho concurs – "I'm the real Sancho Panza, and [...] without my knowing what I've said most of the time, I make everybody who hears me laugh" (el verdadero Sancho Panza soy yo [...] que sin saber yo las más veces lo que me digo hago reír a cuantos me escuchan) – Tarfe reckons that Avellaneda's Sancho "was more gluttonous than well-spoken, and more foolish than amusing" ([m]ás tenía de comilón que de bien hablado, y más de tonto que de gracioso).[88] As if to afford us a flash of his authorial thought process, earlier in the novel Cervantes, through the discerning words of Don Quijote, summarizes the comic genius of the character:

> Sancho Panza is one of the most amusing squires who ever served a knight errant; at times his simpleness is so clever that deciding if he is simple or clever is a cause of no small pleasure; his slyness condemns him for a rogue, and his thoughtlessness confirms him as a simpleton; he doubts everything, and he believes everything.

> Sancho Panza es uno de los más graciosos escuderos que jamás sirvió a caballero andante: tiene a veces unas simplicidades tan agudas, que el pensar si es simple o agudo causa no pequeño contento; tiene malicias que le condenan por bellaco, y descuidos que le confirman por bobo; duda de todo y créelo todo.[89]

It is these very incongruities and ambiguities that furnish readers "no small pleasure" as well, granting the opportunity for laughter not only to revel in but also to ruminate on.

Laughing with Sancho and Ricote

Having studied the dominant historical approaches to humour and a character who produces it for others, we can now return to the question of Sancho's own laughter and his encounter with Ricote that opened the present chapter. Although its scope does not allow for a complete consideration of the approaches to this copiously commented episode of the novel, may it suffice to note two principal camps bisecting criticism of the Ricote encounter: on the one hand, those who find Cervantes supportive of or, at the very least, ambivalent towards the edict of expulsion; and, on the other, those who identify a subtle yet powerful critique of the royally imposed plight of the Moriscos.[90] At the crux of the contention is the moment when, with the repast concluded and the wine depleted, Ricote and Sancho step aside to talk in private, and the Moorish exile voices approval of the edict of expulsion that has scattered his family and fellow Spanish converts across the Mediterranean and Europe. Deeming "so noble a resolution" (tan gallarda resolución) nothing less than "just and reasonable" (con justa razón) and "divine inspiration" (inspiración divina), Ricote rationalizes the course of action "not because all of us were guilty, for some were firm and true Christians, though these were so few they could not oppose those who were not, but because it is not a good idea to nurture a snake in your bosom or shelter enemies in your house" (no porque todos fuésemos culpados, que algunos había cristianos firmes y verdaderos, pero eran tan pocos que no se podían oponer a los que no lo eran, y no era bien criar la sierpe en el seno, teniendo los enemigos dentro de casa).[91] I share the view that it is fundamentally erroneous to take these words at face value or to ascribe them to Cervantes's own attitude about the expulsion.[92] With the ink of the royal edict scarcely dry, the sheer fact that a Morisco character of a major literary work is made to speak already constitutes what Jacques Rancière would call a "redistribution of the sensible," a highly political act inasmuch as it transforms the mode of visibility of the Moriscos and their circumstances in the world.[93] In spite of the serious demand to appease royal censors and to evade inquisitional persecution himself, the reality is that Cervantes was the only one of his literary contemporaries to dare confront the expulsion in such a direct fashion.[94]

Ricote's continuing narration of his circumstances since he was forced to leave Spain further bolsters the evidence of an unmistakable critique of royal policy and a sympathetic portrayal of Morisco identity:

> [N]owhere do we find the haven our misfortune longs for, and in Barbary and all the places in Africa where we hoped to be received, welcomed, and taken in, that is where they most offend and mistreat us. We did not know our good fortune until we lost it, and the greatest desire in almost all of us is to return to Spain; most of those, and there are many of them, who know the language as well as I do, abandon their wives and children and return, so great is the love they have for Spain; and now I know and feel the truth of the saying that it is sweet to love one's country.

> [E]n ninguna parte hallamos el acogimiento que nuestra desventura desea, y en Berbería y en todas las partes de África donde esperábamos ser recibidos, acogidos y regalados, allí es donde más nos ofenden y maltratan.

No hemos conocido el bien hasta que le hemos perdido; y es el deseo tan grande que casi todos tenemos de volver a España, que los más de aquellos, y son muchos, que saben la lengua, como yo, se vuelven a ella y dejan allá sus mujeres y sus hijos desamparados: tanto es el amor que la tienen; y agora conozco y experimento lo que suele decirse, que es dulce el amor de la patria.[95]

Although the reader importantly learns on the following page that, unlike his family, Ricote has not fully assimilated Catholic identity but ignored the strict injunction to renounce his Muslim faith, here the threat of ethnic and confessional difference is diminished by subsuming it under the rubric of national identity. He is Spanish in the "most radical sense, as the emigrant always is" because, as Fernando Plata poignantly observes, "only the 'uprooted' can, literally, know and feel and see the root of that Spanishness."[96] Both the material loss and the deep emotional pain of religious exile have prompted a renewed sense of patriotic devotion in Ricote, his lament for his former Spanish homeland itself a moving exegesis of the experience of trans-Mediterranean migration.

The great German writer Thomas Mann, himself compelled by the rise of the Nazis to flee from Germany, a country to which Ricote travels for its "freedom of conscience" (libertad de conciencia),[97] offers the most perceptive evaluation of the episode and its seemingly contradictory outlook on the expulsion. While he was crossing not the Mediterranean but the Atlantic in 1934, the only book he carried with him was Ludwig Tieck's four-volume edition of *Don Quijote*.[98] Even though he had not yet been forced to abandon Europe definitively, his feelings about his first transatlantic voyage strikingly attest to the affective experience of maritime migration that was surely felt by many an early modern traveller: "I have, quite simply, stage fright. And what wonder? My maiden voyage across the Atlantic, my first encounter with the mighty ocean, my first knowledge of it."[99] On each day of the journey Mann chronicled the happenings on board and his concomitant impressions of those taking place in the novel. As the ship neared the North American continent, and he neared the end of the book, he had this to say about Cervantes's representation of Ricote: "The artist's dilemma [...] speaks a more convincing language than his careful, obsequious tongue. He sympathizes with the persecuted and banned. They are as good Spaniards as himself or anybody; Spain is their true mother-land; she will not be purer, only poorer, after they have gone, while, once torn from her soil, they are everywhere foreign [...] He condemns the cruelty of the decree that he has just approved – not directly, but by stressing the love of the exiles for their homeland."[100] Thus Mann captures Cervantes's own *Weltanschauung*, the weaving together of an affective world that is irreducible to the seemingly rational, face-value convictions mouthed by the marginal figures who populate it.

In addition to the penetrating and suggestive importance of love in Ricote's account, sadness is yet another emotion that Cervantes does not shy away from incorporating, powerfully, into his narrative of the Morisco expulsion. After refusing to help Ricote unearth the family patrimony that he has risked returning to Spain to retrieve, Sancho assures him that he will not reveal the Morisco's clandestine presence: "be satisfied that I won't betray you" (conténtate que por mí no serás descubierto). Then he goes on to describe the circumstances of the departure of Ricote's daughter, Ana Félix, from their hometown:

> [Y]our daughter looked so beautiful when she left that everybody in the village came out to see her, and they all said she was the fairest creature in the world. She was crying and embracing all her friends and companions, and all those who came out to see her, and asking them all to commend her to God and Our Lady, His Mother, and she did this with so much feeling it made me cry, though I'm not usually much of a weeper.

> [S]alió tu hija tan hermosa, que salieron a verla cuantos había en el pueblo, y todos decían que era la más bella criatura del mundo. Iba llorando y abrazaba a todas sus amigas y conocidas y a cuantos llegaban a verla, y a todos pedía la encomendasen a Dios y a Nuestra Señora su madre; y esto, con tanto sentimiento, que a mí me hizo llorar, que no suelo ser muy llorón.[101]

Common prejudice and popular concern for blood-purity statutes seem to evanesce before the sight of the Moorish girl, yielding to the compassion engendered by her peerless beauty and appeals to God. The calamity of her retreat from the village becomes a communal emotional event for all, with both Ana Félix and her onlookers engaging in the shared act of leaving ("salió"; "salieron") and weeping ("iba llorando"; "me hizo llorar"). Even though Sancho humorously misrepresents his own predilection for crying, the tears shed for the expatriation of the young Spanish convert would appear to flow with particular abandon, bitterly foreshadowing the salty waters of the Mediterranean that await her passage to North Africa.[102]

Above all, Ricote's elegiac yearning for Spain and Sancho's testament of the Morisco family's departure defy, ipso facto, the evaluation of *Don Quijote* as a funny book. Perhaps this is why the episode is conspicuously absent in Close's study. Yet, as remarked in my opening excursus, the encounter is not devoid of revelry and laughter, those primal elements that for Close define the raison d'être of *Don Quijote*. My consideration of early modern and courtly approaches to laughter sheds contrasting light on the laughter that erupts from Sancho after his impromptu attempt at reproducing a jargon akin to a localized example of the Mediterranean lingua franca ("Bon compaño, jura Di!"), which is nothing if not consequential. As a performative speech act that introduces heteroglossic difference and cultivates communal bonds (with divine authority, no less), his utterance may well be one of the most meaningful discursive markers of the Mediterranean in the entire Cervantine corpus. It could be argued that Sancho laughs thereafter because of the incongruity of his sudden linguistic improvisation, the unexpected whimsy of his new-found proficiency in a foreign tongue. There is certainly a playful, ingenuous, and almost childlike sincerity to his intervention. The philosophy of laughter that comes closest to explaining Sancho's guffaw, however, may be that of Lodovico Castelvetro, a sixteenth-century Italian commentator of Aristotle who details an entirely different class of laughter: "We are pleased when we see, for the first time or after an absence, persons who are dear to us [...] our fathers, mothers, children, lovers, friends, and the like." Such people, Castelvetro explains, "embrace one another with laughter."[103] To my knowledge, Castelvetro is the only premodern thinker to describe such a laughter of affection. Perhaps it is not fortuitous that, like the Ricote family, Castelvetro was also exiled for heresy and separated from "those who were dear" to him.

One can also compare this affectionate laughter to that which Sancho and Don Quijote themselves share on numerous occasions, or what Alan Trueblood has called a "characteristically Cervantine [...] laughter of sympathy."[104] As readers – modern or otherwise, I would suggest – we may enjoy a similar kind of good-natured laughter, one that fully corresponds with neither the derision nor the intellectual detachment of more dominant theories of humour. What is perhaps most clear is that no single theory of comedy or laughter is adequate for explicating the range and depth of their deployment in Cervantes's novel.[105] Ultimately, then, the question of why Sancho laughs with Ricote, based on the affective approach to laughter for which I have advocated here, is misconceived. Most crucial is that, like his extemporaneous use of a lingua franca, Sancho's laughter partakes of and contributes to the ritual bonding and bonhomie that crystallize between communities of difference through emotive exchange. Any claim that Sancho displays a "cool demeanour" or "reservations about showing any emotions about

Ricote's situation"[106] thus becomes untenable. His laughter is, rather, a reminder of the reality that the intercultural encounters which have come to define the early modern Mediterranean are built upon not only linguistic communication but non-discursive yet more universal signifiers such as laughter as well.[107] Laughter, as I have already suggested with emotion more broadly, can itself become a lingua franca.

When one conceives of laughter as an emotion, then, the question becomes no longer to laugh *at what* but to laugh *with whom*.[108] The preposition *at* posits and reifies an object of laughter. It presupposes a stimulus for a laughing response, constricting laughter to a binary and unidirectional logic, while neglecting the emotional work that the act of laughter itself performs in the text. The examples studied earlier disclose power relations of laughing down (derision) and laughing up (satire), but to laugh *with*, in contrast, implies a horizontal, multidirectional affective exchange, apart from and with little concern for any given catalyst that might set it in motion. Instead of attaching to an object, laughter as an emotion speaks to the laughing subject. In the case of Sancho and Ricote, the squire's burst of laughter comes to signify fellowship, an intersubjective bond, and the capability of empathy (an emotional concept whose etymological roots, like passion itself, clearly derive from *pathos*). To laugh with the Morisco Ricote is to sympathize with his plight, thereby introducing an unassuming yet potent political gesture into an episode brimming with historical urgency. Sancho's impulsive, unrestrained laughter with Ricote is therefore significant for two reasons: rebuffing the predominant superiority theory of humour, it escapes from the cycle of objectification upon which the laughter of preceding episodes was erected; and – with the text's emphasis on its force, duration, and repetition – it renounces the hypocritical courtly prohibitions of the aristocratic class, with their dissimulated laughter thinly veiling the equally fine line between mirth and malice. Laughing outwardly and emphatically, moreover, Sancho shuns both the behavioural mandates and the political projects concocted at court. While his success as a governor inverted the object of the ducal pranks and established the decadent ruling class as an object of laughter itself, with Ricote the reader finds that laughter can also embody a peaceful form of resistance and solidarity with the subjects most affected by their half-baked policies. Cervantes thus reappropriates the weapon of satire and refashions it for a nobler yet no less scathing purpose. Masquerading under a universally benign ritual of entertainment – laughing over food and drink – laughter becomes an inconspicuous yet trenchant vehicle of dissent, the real stakes of cross-Mediterranean migration and exile entering public consciousness in a work purporting to be correspondingly light-hearted as well. Recognizing the emotional content of laughter is key to deciphering the seeming discrepancy of a Moorish character who extols the wisdom of his own expulsion. Our understanding of other episodes and aspects of the novel, of the constitutive contradictions that so often accompany Cervantes's writing, could likewise benefit from a critical engagement with laughter as a passion.

Conclusion

Equal parts satire and sympathy, parody and pathos, Sancho's laughter is an omnidirectional emotional event, reverberating across multiple vectors of the text, while threatening to disrupt the structures of power that lie beyond it. It is a laughter that refuses to objectify, revealing instead the bonds of shared subjectivity. Mann was keenly aware of this commingling of the burlesque and the serious, or what he deemed the novel's "comic pathos," "sympathetic humour," and "melancholic humour."[109] A Mediterranean encounter or a book that makes us laugh can also make us cry, as exemplified by Gogol's formula of "laughter through tears," or even Freud's concept of "broken humour," that which "smiles through tears."[110] Already in the Renaissance, Joubert had recognized that "weeping is not so contrary to laughter that it does not sometimes receive it with itself," deeming as "bastard laughter" that which is experienced while one is sad or afflicted.[111] In other words, a work that sounds the deepest chasms of bathos can also carry the reader to the furthest reaches of pathos. It can at once evoke both Democritus and Heraclitus. It need constitute neither a singular monument to the *agelastoi*, those laughless individuals allergic to humour and derided by Plato, nor a pathologized instantiation of gelotophilia. Stated simply, wit and sentiment are not mutually exclusive concepts.

Symbolically, Sancho's laughter resounds as a spontaneous, irrational clarion call that defies impulses both empirical and imperial, particularly the pseudo-scientific approaches to the Mediterranean that posit an object in the positivist dualism of stimulus and response. It also contests the supposedly historical yet ultimately reductionist interpretations of the novel as a funny book, which in similar fashion have reduced it to an object of the reader's laughter. Recovering the conception of laughter as a passion, and its intersectionality with other emotions, invites us instead to view Cervantes's text as a vessel for reflecting on our own positionality as laughing subjects. On the one hand, the critical spirit of my analysis – with its close reading of a discrete encounter and singular emotional event – can be seen to represent a contrapuntal take on Braudel, of his avowed inclination to see the individual "imprisoned within a destiny in which he himself has little hand, fixed in a landscape in which the infinite perspectives of the long term stretch into the distance both behind him and before."[112] It is true that certain details of the Ricote family saga are possible only in fiction – one need only recall its closure towards the end of the novel when Ana Félix, having travelled from Barbary in the guise of a Turkish pirate, is reunited with her father on the shores of Barcelona, leading to the local authorities' vow to ensure the safe and legal reintegration of the Morisco family back into Spain. Although some Moriscos did manage to return to their homeland,[113] such a happy ending is definitively the purview of fiction, so as not to say fantasy. On the other hand, however, as literary characters in a work with a four-hundred-year critical history, Sancho, Ricote, and family have made an indelible mark on the manners in which readers and the popular imaginary have understood Moorish culture and the Morisco diaspora throughout the centuries. It is no longer merely a case of "fiction posing as history," as one critic describes Cervantes's use of irony in the episode.[114] Here, rather, literature comes to function as a preservation of history, enshrining in story the struggle of a minority group that was largely effaced from the Spanish macro-landscape. Approached in this way, the protracted lives of literary individuals, as suggested previously, can affect the longue durée to an even greater extent than historical figures can, perhaps even rivalling in certain ambits the influence of the geological events singled out by Braudel.

Paraphrasing El Pinciano, who professed that "laughter is laughter," we can affirm that laughter in Cervantes's texts is, in fact, more than simply laughter, or at least that it is more than what modern critics have conventionally granted it. Among the austere panorama of Mediterranean historiography, laughter represents fertile ground not only for further study but also as a vigorous challenge to some of its dearest and longest-held assumptions. *Homo risibilis* may disrupt the dominance of *Homo economicus*. Like the shame examined in the foregoing chapter, the self-reflexive irreverence of humour might serve to further erode a rigid honour-based paradigm. In the case of the Ricote episode, laughter encodes transculturation and modulates the seemingly less ambiguous feelings of maurophobia and maurophilia. While emotional, empathetic laughter of this sort can be a rousing agent for intercultural and interreligious exchange in the Mediterranean, it also productively troubles Romantic approaches to both *Don Quijote* and the region at large. It reminds us that Cervantine comedy is a rich and varied terrain, an integral feature of the vaster affective geographies of the text. We ought neither reduce humour to a homogenous standard-bearer of the novel nor banish it unwittingly from its shores.

PART THREE

Other Ports of Call

Suspended Admiration: Wonder, Surprise, and Emotional Exemplarity in *La española inglesa*

[E]xpression is the clarification of turbid emotions.

John Dewey

Beyond his vast biographical seafaring experience, it is in the paraleptic prologue of *Don Quijote* of 1605 that Cervantes finds himself figuratively at sea. Hunched over a blank page, with a pen in his ear, an elbow on the desk, and a hand propping up the head that is hopelessly lost in thought, the author is suffering the early modern symptoms of what we would not hesitate to diagnose as writer's block (fig. 5.1). Perhaps even those of us disinclined to share in this kind of parodic self-effacement should be heartened to know that the condition afflicted Cervantes's literary self as well. As if to underscore the implacable despair of this authorial impasse and implicate us in its resolution, with the urgency of the present progressive tense Cervantes directly interpellates the reader of "the preface you are now reading" (esta prefación que vas leyendo). His languishing state of being "perplexed," "confused," and "baffled" (imaginativo, confuso, suspenso) is ameliorated only by the unexpected arrival of a friend, to whom he proceeds to confess his prefatory quandary.[1] Soliciting his interlocutor's goodwill to help overcome his "perplexity and abstraction" (suspensión y elevamiento), Cervantes implores, "How do you intend to fill the void of my fear and bring clarity to the chaos of my confusion?" (¿[D]e qué modo pensáis llenar el vacío de mi temor y reducir a claridad el caos de mi confusión?) As a rhetorical foil and voice of practical reason, the anonymous friend promises in short order to assuage "all the problems that you say bewilder you and make you fearful" (las faltas que decís que os suspenden y acobardan), while

Figure 5.1. Philippe Joseph Auguste Vallot, title page in *L'ingénieux chevalier Don Quixote de la Manche* (Paris, 1821). Engraving. Cervantes Project, Cushing Memorial Library, Texas A&M University.

incredulously pondering, "How is it possible that things so trivial and so easy to remedy can have the power to perplex and absorb an intelligence as mature as yours, and one so ready to demolish and pass over much greater difficulties?" (¿Cómo que es posible que cosas de tan poco momento y tan fáciles de remediar puedan tener fuerzas de suspender y absortar un ingenio tan maduro como el vuestro, y tan hecho a romper y atropellar por otras dificultades mayores?)[2] As we recall, Cervantes's literary self – by composing the hilariously deformed dedicational sonnets that follow – ends up taking the unabashedly picaresque advice of his friend to pay lip-service to the formalities of a prologue. But, far from putting the matter to rest, the questions exchanged between the prologue's two characters raise even more: What are the further aesthetic stakes of the "suspension" that Cervantes purports to have suffered? Beyond the intervention of a clever friend, how are such stalemates to be resolved? Given the author's posture, critics have associated it with Dürer's iconographic angel of melancholy, and Cervantes references his own fear as well. But what other affects are mobilized through the repetition of words commonly, if imprecisely, translated as "bafflement," "bewilderment," "perplexity," and "confusion"?

There is a clue in one of Cervantes's other prologues. In the *Novelas ejemplares* he inaugurates a unique variant of the Horatian dictum "delectando pariterque monendo," by articulating the simultaneously entertaining and exemplary aspects of the novellas:[3]

> I mean that the amorous remarks you will find in some of them are so chaste and so moderated by reason and Christian discourse that they will not move either the careless or the attentive reader to any ignoble thought. I have called them exemplary, and if you consider this carefully, there is none from which one cannot derive some edifying example.

> Quiero decir que los requiebros amorosos que en algunas hallarás, son tan honestos y tan medidos con la razón y discurso cristiano, que no podrán mover a mal pensamiento al descuidado o cuidadoso que las leyere. Heles dado nombre de ejemplares, y si bien lo miras, no hay ninguna de quien no se pueda sacar algún ejemplo provechoso.[4]

The reader, in other words, may at the very least reap enjoyment from the text without risking moral corruption (since it is tempered with "reason and Christian discourse") and, with a discreet and careful eye, may even discover the exemplarity that lends the novellas their collective title yet often lies beneath the surface of their more light-hearted features. Like the medieval precedents of religious *exempla* and troubadouresque *novas*, the *Novelas ejemplares* erect their moral authority not only on Aristotelian grounds that poetry is more universal and therefore truer than history but also that it is more useful.

Tellingly, however, Cervantes's rationale reads more like an apologia than an exposition. Beyond blazing the trail for the short-story genre in Spanish,[5] it thus suggests something more audacious: the implication that "amorous remarks" and "edifying example[s]" do not just occupy different pages of the same tale, but that the elevated concept of exemplarity may be found precisely among such base elements as love, desire, and other human passions. On the one hand, this deviates from the early modern emphasis on rationality, the neo-Stoicism of many of Cervantes's contemporaries, and other philosophical traditions that promoted an oppositional or sublating relationship between reason and emotion, as I demonstrated in chapter 1. On the other hand, the unlikely companionship of affect and exemplarity approximates the novellas to the poetic theories of Antonio Minturno, who in the sixteenth century appended a third element to Horace's classic formula to propose that fiction should not only teach (*docere*) and delight (*delectare*) but also move the spectator or reader emotionally (*movere*). I will examine this more closely, but for now I merely want to stress that, for Minturno as well as a handful of other Renaissance critics, the didactic potential of a literary work was predetermined by its affectivity, and the responsibility to move the audience or reader, in turn, principally fell on *admiratio*, a complex concept usually rendered as awe, marvel, or wonder. The eminent Cervantes scholar E.C. Riley observed long ago that, though "[i]t is not easy to fix the variegated meaning of the word," admiratio "is evidently a powerful sensation for Cervantes." The critic also astutely recognized its moralizing abilities: "Seventeenth-century writers aimed to startle and impress their readers not only because this was pleasant, but in order to engage their attention and put them in a receptive frame of mind in which a moral lesson could be driven home, a universal truth conveyed."[6] Little work has been done to clarify just how such a receptive frame of mind is achieved, and yet more equivocal is the tacit assumption in recent studies on admiratio that such processes are inherently more intellectual than emotional, relegating it to the authorial, mechanical act of emplotment. Almost inexplicably, even scholars shaped by the history of emotion have been complicit in "cognitivizing" wonder.[7]

The cardinal aim of this chapter, then, will be to rescue the emotionality of admiratio and that of related concepts to which I will collectively refer as suspension, including such difficult-to-translate terms as *turbación*, *confusión*, *sobresalto*, and *suspensión*. A cursory inventory of the

Novelas ejemplares indicates that these words comprised for Cervantes a favoured means of expressing emotional upheavals, since they populate each and every novella to a striking degree.[8] In *La española inglesa* (*The English Spanishwoman*) alone, from which I will draw several examples, these five vocables and their corresponding variations appear thirty-five times. Their irruption in the text alerts the reader to situations of heightened tension, unexpected events, surprising revelations, outcomes of chance and contingency, or reversals of fortune – in short, they perform the basic aesthetic function of building suspense throughout the novellas. A more global exploration of their lexical heritage and usage in other ambits like music, theatre, pictorial art, and mysticism, however, reveals that in early modernity suspension was not simply a narrative trope or abstraction, but it encircled a dynamic range of emotions expressed through the body, mind, and soul. Attending closely to these material, gestural, visual, and physiognomic manifestations of admiratio and like terms will be key to unlocking their affective as well as ethical valences, for in prompting a sudden withdrawal from the temporal flow of the narrative, I argue that suspension is what enables, in Riley's words, the "receptive frame of mind" through which to contemplate the specifically edifying content of the novellas. Suspension can be thought of as a narrative brand of *coups de théâtre*, or what Lessing and Diderot would later characterize as the "pregnant moments" of a visual or theatrical text, those that constitute in Barthes's words a "condensation of meaning that transports the spectator's emotions and beliefs."[9] Recalling Bakhtin's theory that "[i]n literature and art itself, temporal and spatial determinations are inseparable from one another, and always colored by emotions and values,"[10] a secondary though no less vital ambition of this chapter, therefore, will be to recover the temporality of the Mediterranean chronotope that has been so often neglected in studies of the region.[11] Ultimately, the novellas' deep engagement with maritime contingency, whether Mediterranean or Atlantic, means that their emotional exemplarity is at once more worldly and responsive to the surprises, unexpectedness, and unforeseeable events that arise in everyday life as well.

In effect, the Mediterranean makes its presence felt in all manner of ways in the *Novelas ejemplares* and *La española inglesa*. For the moment I should like to highlight merely a couple, one structural and the other geographical. Unexpected events at sea, first of all, actively trade in the novellas' narrative economy of suspense, for the perils and adventures of maritime travel captivated the early modern imagination. Legion are the examples, literary and historical, of sudden turns of fate on the Mediterranean, even if it bears reiterating my view that such elements are for Cervantes secondary to the affective, interpersonal, and human relationships in his stories. Most significant is how in *La española inglesa* events at sea mirror more exclusively emotional forms of suspension on land or in the heart, and how the text subtly interlaces the seagoing with the sentimental through the use of shared imagery, metaphors, and narrative pacing and structure. Curiously, the second major aspect of the Mediterranean in *La española inglesa* is as conspicuous as it is neglected. Although historians have established the North Atlantic as a major node of the region's broader network – for reasons the novella itself makes abundantly clear – its relatively faraway setting of England distinguishes it as one of only two major works by Cervantes that feature extended scenes outside the Mediterranean zone (the other being *Persiles y Sigismunda*, the subject of the following chapter).[12] Not unjustifiably, this anomaly has inspired several scholarly studies on the text's representation of England and the country's diplomatic relations with Iberia, and especially on Cervantes's benign characterization of Queen Elizabeth vis-à-vis the historical enmity between her and Habsburg Spain.[13] Yet overlooked has been the plain fact that the Mediterranean still plays an essential role in the novella. It bookends the narrative, beginning in Cádiz and ending when the protagonist has come full circle and returned to her origins in Seville. In between, Gibraltar, Jebel Musa and Larache in Morocco, Portugal, Rome, Genoa, the Papal State of Acquapendente, the southern coast of France, Valencia, and Algiers all make at least a marginal appearance, such that nearly the entire last third of the text transpires in Mediterranean locales. Thematically, too, the Mediterranean is more pervasive than we might initially expect – from piracy, commerce, captivity, and ransom to interreligious conflict. There is even an appearance by Arnaut Mami, the historical Ottoman Albanian renegade who not only became one of the most feared Islamic corsairs of the Mediterranean but also had captured Cervantes himself in 1575. Try as he might to escape it, the author always returns – even in the short scope of a single novella – to the Sea he knew so well. Like the dual nationality of the work's titular character, whose familial, Spanish roots are imprinted on her soul even after she has spent most of her life in England, Cervantes's Mediterranean experience indelibly conditions his writing.

Aesthetics of the Unexpected

Before I delve into how these concepts are borne out in the novella itself, it will be helpful to briefly rehearse the ways in which thinkers both classical and contemporary have pursued the problem of surprise and its literary accessory of proairetic suspense. "As in everyday life, narrative in fiction is inherently disposed towards the relation of the unexpected," as Mark Currie observes in his recent study of surprise and narrative time.[14] One could also contend that the unforeseeable nature of literary narrative constitutes a defining quality not only of emplotment but also of the genre itself, as well as a principal source of our sustained investment as readers. Nothing seems to grab and hold our attention quite like a well-timed surprise and the suspense that crescendoes towards it, from the latest book we cannot put down to, arguably perhaps, the favourite story we have read on countless occasions. It is, quite simply, one of the primary reasons we read. These observations were not lost on Aristotle, even if he was more concerned with sustaining the attention of a live theatrical audience than that of private bookworms. Oftentimes the terms of suspension that intrigue me coincide with moments of peripeteia or anagnorisis in the novellas, or what Aristotle believed were "the most powerful elements of emotional interest in Tragedy."[15] Yet even when it does not directly correlate with the Stagirite's two most favoured poetic topoi, suspension in the *Novelas ejemplares* plays a decisive role in the plot by staking out moments of surprise and piquing "emotional interest" for characters and the reader alike. José Antonio Maravall intimates as much when he identifies suspension as a keystone of Baroque aesthetics and notes in passing its ability to similarly "reinforce the consequence of emotional effects."[16]

Cervantes, of course, was well acquainted with such techniques. While prescribing the need for fictional works to create suspense in the reader, in his meta-literary disquisition in *Don Quijote* the canon employs the very terms of interest here: "Fictional tales must engage the minds of those who read them, and by restraining exaggeration and moderating impossibility, they enthrall [*suspendiendo*] the spirit and thereby astonish [*admiren*], captivate [*suspendan*], delight, and entertain, allowing wonder [*admiración*] and joy to move together at the same pace." (Hanse de casar las fábulas mentirosas con el entendimiento de los que las leyeren, escribiéndose de suerte que, facilitando los imposibles, allanando las grandezas, suspendiendo los ánimos admiren, suspendan, alborocen y entretengan, de modo que anden a un mismo paso la admiración y la alegría juntas.)[17] If the *techne* of suspension proved a reliable vehicle for entertaining and enthralling the reader, then its promise is even more fully realized in the unique genre of the *Novelas ejemplares*. Although Aristotle had already ordained literature a temporal art, following Bakhtin's study of time and chronotopes we might well conclude that the genre of the novella – with its "suddenlys" and "at just that moments" – is even better suited to captivating its consumer.[18] I would add that with suspension "[t]ime, as it were, thickens, takes on flesh, becomes artistically visible."[19] Its tendency to arrest, delay, dilate, rupture, or, indeed, suspend narrative time, coupled with the relatively short length of each novella, suggests that the *Novelas ejemplares* already serves up a concentrated dosage of what could be called sentimental suspense.[20]

Other thinkers offer suitable waypoints for analysing the unforeseeable in lived experience and literature. For Aristotle, peripeteia is a main ingredient of emplotment, such that *reversals* of fortune are necessary, somewhat paradoxically, for advancing the plot *forward*. Paul Ricoeur elaborated on this notion to suggest that a plot is essentially "a discordant concordance, and a synthesis of the heterogeneous" – a germane figure for Cervantine suspension because its disparate emotions interrupt the unfolding of the narrative while contributing to its unity.[21] If for Aristotle and Ricoeur unexpected events fall under the purview of the plot, for Derrida the unforeseeable undergirds the very nature of his theory of "the event" itself: "an event worthy of the name cannot be foretold. We are not supposed to see it coming." Appealing to a spatial metaphor, he concludes that the event must always arrive "from above," catching us unaware in a manner that something we see on the horizon cannot; to be eventful, it must surprise us.[22] What Bakhtin called the "eventness" of an occurrence was, for him, similarly related to its "surprisingness," but the Russian critic also considered it, significantly, a hallmark of decision making, of the freedom to choose. This kinship between event, choice, and surprise will inform my discussion of how Cervantine suspension opens an emotional space for reflecting upon the ethics of our decisions. What is apparent from all of these thinkers is that the interrelated concepts of the unforeseeable, discordance, unexpectability, and surprise underwrite an event that somehow arrests or interrupts the flow of (narrative) time. Likewise, something eventful implies an emotional impact; an unexpected event (even if for Derrida this is pleonastic) must perforce produce an emotional response or judgment to be designated as such. As Currie explains, "in the affective operations of stories more generally, surprise is the one that takes us, theoretically, straight to the heart of narrative dynamics."[23] Let us proceed, then, to a close reading of *La española inglesa* to grasp the affective content of the unexpected, of its expression in the text, and of the reader's experience of suspension.

The novella begins in the Mediterranean, where during the sack of Cádiz – likely an allusion to the same historical event of either 1587 or 1596 – the character of Clotaldo abducts a young Spanish girl, Isabela, as illicit spoils and takes her back to England for him and his wife to raise as their own daughter. Spellbound by her superlative beauty, their son Ricaredo falls in love with his younger stepsister, and his parents, convinced it is the only cure for the lovesickness that has slowly consumed him, give in to his desire to marry Isabela. But it is not, as the modern reader might expect, incest that is the problem, but rather the failure to secure nuptial consent from the queen and, graver still, that all the family members are devout Catholics secretly practising their faith in Reformation England. With this detail it is as though Cervantes has transposed to the North Atlantic the multi-confessional landscape that I have suggested be a mandatory and distinguishing feature of Mediterranean literature as such. Appropiately, then, anxieties about the family's religious identity occasion the first moment of suspension in the text, when Queen Elizabeth I summons the crypto-Catholics to her court just days before the wedding ceremony, news that "disturbed all their good cheer" (turbó todo su regocijo) and left "everyone's bosom filled with perturbation [*turbación*], alarm [*sobresalto*], and fear" (llenos los pechos de todos de turbación, de sobresalto y miedo).[24] Upon their arrival, however, it is the queen herself who is left in a speechless state of "suspensión," stupefied by the unparalleled beauty of the young Spanish bride.[25] Isabela thus makes an ideal payment – the text constantly casts her as a commodity[26] – which the queen exacts as compensation for Clotaldo's insolence in not following the royal protocol of securing the queen's blessing of all marriages. Ricaredo too must pay for his father's dereliction, a realization that leaves him correspondingly "trembling and alarmed" (temblando y con sobresalto) when he prostrates himself before the monarch to request an appropriate reparation through which to demonstrate his worthiness of Isabela. The "emotions on the part of the two lovers" (afectos de los dos amantes) seem infectious, as Isabela, "astonished [*suspensa*] and amazed to see Ricaredo's humility and pain," begins to cry "so quietly and with no movement at all, it was as if an alabaster statue were weeping" (Isabela, que estaba suspensa y atónita de ver la humildad y dolor de Ricaredo [...] tan sesga y tan sin movimiento alguno, que no parecía sino que lloraba una estatua de alabastro).[27] As I will detail, this posture is one of the most emblematic physiological representations of suspension.

With Isabela under her royal aegis, the queen requires Ricaredo to serve her privateering interests as captain of a ship of corsairs so that he might prove his worth and recuperate his beloved. The narrator represents the emotive scene of the enamoured captain's departure in the following way:

> Ricaredo kissed the queen's hands, valuing greatly the kindness she had done him, and he went to kneel before Isabela, and wishing to speak he could not because a lump in his throat tied his tongue, and tears filled his eyes, and he attempted to hide them as much as possible.

> Besó las manos Ricaredo a la reina, estimando en mucho la merced que le hacía, y luego se fue a hincar de rodillas ante Isabela, y queriéndola hablar no pudo porque se le puso un nudo en la garganta que le ató la lengua, y las lágrimas acudieron a los ojos, y él acudió a disimularlas lo más que le fue posible.[28]

The emotional intensity of this tableau is characteristic of myriad examples in Cervantes's writing of lovers or family members who are tragically separated, only to be rapturously reunited later in the narrative, as will eventually be the case with Ricaredo and Isabela. This exchange also reveals the entanglement of several different emotions, including sadness, shame (for crying, as the queen immediately recognizes), and likely fear (of losing Isabela, who is being courted by another nobleman), as well as the futility of inhibiting the outward expression of powerful affects. More importantly, though the specific terms of concern to us (*suspensión*, etc.) are themselves withheld in favour of a description of Ricaredo's physiological condition, the effect is similar. Like Cervantes's self-description in the prologue of *Don Quijote*, the character appears incapable of tempering his thoughts with reason or of translating them into action. Minute differences in bodily expression notwithstanding (Cervantes's stoop over his desk versus Ricaredo's stoop in front of the queen, along with his uncontrollable tears), both characters experience a sort of discursive impasse or paralysis (fig. 5.2). In Ricaredo's case, the act of falling to his knees – like the knot in his throat – is a telling symptom of suspension; it is not only a gesture of reverence towards the queen but also an involuntary effect of his emotional turmoil, akin to feeling weak in the knees, a sensation that often precedes fainting. The ability to stand, to speak, and to control his emotions is suspended.

Compelled by duty to his queen and devotion to his bride, Ricaredo nonetheless gathers the fortitude to overcome this suspension and carry out the former's bidding. Six days after setting sail from London, he is diverted by the prevailing winds, as if by fate, directly to the Mediterranean gateway of the Strait of Gibraltar, where suddenly the fleet admiral dies of apoplexy, a "shock" (sobresalto) that leaves Ricaredo in command of the two-ship flotilla.[29] The swift promotion works in his favour in so far as his authority to call the shots, as it were, spares

Figure 5.2. D. Valdivieso, in *Novelas ejemplares* (Madrid, 1854), p. 113. Lithograph. Cervantes Project, Cushing Memorial Library, Texas A&M University.

him the burden of conscience that firing on fellow Catholics would entail, something that he nonetheless has resolved to abstain from at any cost, even if it means exposing himself to accusations of both heresy and cowardice and losing Isabela as a result. His convictions are put to the test when two Turkish galleys mount a brazen yet failed bid to besiege Ricaredo's militarily superior squadron, whose ruse of flying the Spanish flag instead of the English – as though a nod to the characteristically fluid, unstable, and often duplicitous nature of Mediterranean identity[30] – had duped the Turks into inferring it to be easy commercial prey from the Indies. The young captain gives the order to spare the Christian captives who have escaped the bowels of the sinking galleys to take refuge on a large merchant vessel, even after it is revealed that they are legitimate Spaniards and the ships, the property of none other than Arnaut Mami. If Ricaredo's naval prowess secures the booty of a galleon laden with New World spices, jewels, and other riches – an argosy that will prove supererogatory in reclaiming the sentimental and, for him, far more valuable treasure of his Spanish bride – then his clemency introduces misgivings among his men, which, on course back towards England, are quelled only by fortune:[31]

> The wind, which had shown signs of being favorable and steady, began to die down a little, and this calm raised a storm of fear in the English, who blamed Ricaredo and his generosity, saying the freed men could tell them in Spain about what had happened, and if by chance there were battle galleons in port they might come looking for them and cause them trouble, and they would be lost. Ricaredo knew very well they were right, but vanquishing them with his words, he calmed them [*los sosegó*]; the wind calmed them even more, because it began to freshen so that with all sails unfurled, with no need to shorten or temper them [*templallas*], in nine days' time they found themselves within sight of London.

> El viento, que daba señales de ser próspero y largo, comenzó a calmar un tanto, cuya calma levantó gran tormenta de temor en los ingleses, que culpaban a Ricaredo y a su liberalidad, diciéndole que los libres podían dar aviso en España de aquel suceso, y que si acaso había galeones de armada en el puerto podían salir en su busca y ponerlos en aprieto, y en término de perderse. Bien conocía Ricaredo que tenían razón, pero, venciéndolos a todos con buenas razones, los sosegó; pero más los quietó el viento, que volvió a refrescar, de modo que, dándole todas las velas, sin tener necesidad de amainallas ni aun de templallas, dentro de nueve días se hallaron a la vista de Londres.[32]

Here Ricaredo relies on his superior command not of naval but rhetorical strategy to stifle the obscure threat of mutiny, even though, as the narrator is quick to stress, his adeptness at oratory pales in comparison to the natural power of marine weather to mollify the agitated crew. Of still greater substance is the degree to which the text muddies the metaphorical waters between maritime and psychological occurrences. The nautical winds appear as fickle and erratic as the sailors' whims. *Calm* at once describes the mariners' temperament and the personified air currents, which in turn "[raise] a storm of fear" in them. Even the ships' sails, with their lack of need for "tempering," connote behavioural and emotional traits. Such mutually allusive properties of winds, sails, and souls (the natural, technological, and psychological) disclose the deeper affinities between sentiment and the sea in Cervantes's writing that are the subject of this book as a whole.

Early Modern Cultures of Suspension

Before seeing how the novella's events at sea play out on land, however, I want to suspend my close reading of the text in favour of an equally close examination of the terms of suspension that appear throughout. As ubiquitous in the *Novelas ejemplares* as they are crucial for comprehending the collection's emotionality, to uncover the early modern nuances of these terms demands a thorough exploration of their etymological, lexical, and cultural connotations. The one term of suspension to have been studied at some length, as noted earlier, is that of *admiración*, with critics observing its seemingly contradictory potential to evoke, on the one hand, comic merriment and mirth before things of a trivial nature and, on the other, a class of wonder and curiosity before those of an elevated status or profound substance.[33] Related to *mirabilia*, in classical philosophies this latter form served as an epistemological precursor to knowledge itself, and this is why Descartes famously considered wonder to be "the first of all the passions."[34] Early modern understandings of *admiratio* exceed facile translation and signify something only remotely similar, at best, to the modern English term *admiration*. But beyond its utility as an aesthetic device and philosophical concept, which I will discuss momentarily, even admiratio could stir affects and produce corporeal reactions. It was not only conceptually but also emotionally capacious.

El museo pictórico y escala óptica (The pictorial museum and optical scale), by the Spanish Baroque painter Antonio Palomino, published between 1715 and 1724, sheds much needed light on this neglected aspect of *admiración*. Although the third volume's biographies of early Spanish painters brought him international notoriety, the other two, dedicated to the theory and practice of painting, were largely ignored. It is here that, in a kind of technical ekphrasis, Palomino describes the bodily expression and physiognomy of *admiración*: "*Admiración* is an affect, which has great variety in its expressions, since at times it arches the eyebrows, opening the eyes a lot, and the mouth somewhat. Other times it closes the mouth, burying the lips, and wrinkling the forehead, and maybe taking hold of the beard, if it has grown. At others, it lowers the eyebrows to the eyes, and with them half-open, looking towards the act that causes surprise, it helps itself to the hands, extending them, and stretching out the fingers."[35] Shortly thereafter, he sketches the closely related term *espanto*: "*Espanto* has many parts of *admiración*, but nonetheless is distinguished by the loss of colour and shrinking, showing timidity, which it always carries with it; and dread and astonishment [*pavor y estupor*] are the same, since all are synonyms."[36] These ekphrastic depictions bring into focus the ways that suspension functioned not only as a dramatic, narrative, and literary device but also as an emotional experience, producing often intense affects that were felt, actuated, expressed, and observed through the body as well.

So too do the early understandings of the additional terms of suspension evoke phenomena at once mental, social, psychological, and physiological. According to Covarrubias, the word *confuso* signifies "he who is perturbed [*turbado*] and does not know how to make himself understood, mixing one reason with another without distinction,"[37] and the *Autoridades* dictionary adds that *confusión* is akin to an "obstacle and difficulty to disturb the soul and the senses," or a "restlessness, disturbance [*turbación*], and uneasiness [*desasosiego*] of the soul, proceeding from some strong consideration or another affect and motive that alters and perturbs it." Importantly, *confusión* may be "occasioned by some news or unexpected motive."[38] The verb *sobresaltar* signifies "to startle, distress, and alter some event," while *sobresalto* means "fear or sudden shock" and, in its adverbial form, "unexpectedly."[39] As for *suspensión*, *suspender* means to "grab hold of the soul, and detain it in wonder [*admiración*] of something strange."[40] Likewise, someone who is *suspenso* is "he who is stopped and perplexed,"[41] and *suspensión* is "arresting of some movement of the soul."[42] *Turbación*, by the same token, "also means confusion, disorder, disconcertion,"[43] while *turbarse* means "to have a certain kind of fright [*espanto*] or shock, which in a certain manner takes away sense, disturbs reason, and alters memory."[44] Finally, *turbar*: "Metaphorically it means to surprise or to stun someone, making him blush in some act, in such a way that he cannot manage to speak or continue what he was going to do."[45]

Beyond the observable fact that these terms are interrelated and largely synonymous – each denoting an abrupt disturbance of tranquillity, syncopating peaceful repose with strong, unexpected affects – there are several worthwhile points to recognize in their definitions.[46] First is the diversity of emotions provoked by or related to these states of suspension, including fear, wonder, surprise, and shame. One should give particular heed to the repercussions of such states in the faculty of reason, "perturbing," "perplexing," "altering," or confounding rational thought. With *confuso*, this means that the person becomes unable to distinguish one "reason" from another or is faced with obstacles to understanding, and all of these terms similarly blur the distinctions between emotional, rational, sensory, and cognitive faculties, even to the point of affecting memory and destabilizing the *sensus communis* itself. The contrasting metaphors of movement employed to convey such effects should draw our attention as well: on the one hand, *suspender* denotes a detention, halting, or arresting of an action, while, on the other, *turbarse* seems to imply the very movement, stirring, and turbulence of an otherwise calm, still, and nearly static state. These conceits are in keeping with the Aristotelian notion that the human soul maintains a state of constant motion and is thus responsible for our passions and desires.[47] At stake, however, is not just spatiality – the arresting of movement – but the temporal associations of these terms, the arresting of time, which is underscored by the musical acceptation of *suspensión* as "the detention of the voice on some point longer than what corresponds to it by its interval."[48]

In a sense, the subtle delay in which a singer indulges before moving on to the next note evokes the sensation that readers experience when stumbling upon certain phrases – such as *became astonished* (*quedó suspenso*) – in a piece of literature. In both cases – musical composition and literary text – the artfulness hinges on the skill or licence of the composer, performer, author, or rhapsodist to extend or hang upon a point, note, or word longer than strict notation would allow. It is these subjective, interpretative indulgences that constitute art as such and, I would add, endow it with emotion. The same could be said of any number of additional arts, from the painter's brush-stroke or the visual artist's use of colour to the dancer's distinctive style or what Barthes codified as the elusive *punctum* of a photograph, for such sublime yet slippery things are art's pièce de résistance, if not its very raison d'être.[49] Without conflating the subtleties of these art forms or straying into the realm of comparative aesthetics, I would like to momentarily dwell on the example of music in order to highlight, rather, its utility for thinking about the narrativity and temporal qualities of emotion.

I am not alone in the view that, at least until quite recently, musical critics have pursued the problem of emotion more thoroughly and cogently than their literary counterparts have, beginning with the *Affektenlehre*, a catalogue of musical passions devised to legitimize Baroque instrumental composition.[50] Their success, however, may also owe to a sort of self-fulfilling prophecy foretold by the notion that music is a more impassioned art, that it possesses a peculiar, a priori potential to elicit and sustain emotions in its listeners more readily than literature. Renaissance humanism's deep interest in the topic likely had a hand in perpetuating the commonplace that music is the "language of the soul." One might gather as much from the written conventions for directing the performer as to the proper emotional connotations of individual passages – from *affettuoso, passionato, con anima,* or *con amore* to *con dolore, flebile,* or *lacrimoso,* and everything in between: *molto, pochettino,* and *ma non troppo.* Were the interpretation of emotions in literature so easy! The other side of this coin, and equally disputable, is that music likewise lacks the power of narrative, that it is more form than content. Such claims would clearly vary were their scope reduced to more discrete genres, since there are substantial differences in the narrative and emotional potential of, say, a Baroque fugue and a modern rock song, or epic poetry and a contemporary romance novel. So too would the dubious merit of such comparisons depend upon a gamut of additional factors, such as whether the music was performed live or pre-recorded, whether it was enjoyed publicly or privately, the quality of the performance venue or recording, and the individual taste of the listener. Evidently, a Bach prelude could trigger the same feeling of melancholy in one listener as could the Beatles' "Hey Jude" in another, and that same listener might experience anger or disgust from either song depending on their prior mood, disposition, and changing fancies. The same can be said of literature. But reflecting on emotions through music can productively compensate for the comparably impoverished critical vocabulary for talking about them in narrative fiction, or at least for talking about them in different ways.

In the *Novelas ejemplares,* like the singer who holds a well-timed note "longer than what corresponds to it by its interval," the text lingers on emotive moments in order to have a greater impact on the reader. Notes of suspension in the novellas could be said to announce their arrival, as it were, by a *staccato,* pointedly accentuating the affective tension of a scene by introducing an unexpected conflict. The inharmonious or atonal notes that follow might be marked, depending on the desired effect of the particular scene's phrasing, by a *fermata* or *caesura,* thus deferring its resolution. A *lunga pausa* could be added to further prolong the effect. And a veritable ensemble of additional musical techniques – like syncope, counterpoint, and, indeed, suspension – may serve as evocative analogues for vivifying the tone and temporality of Cervantes's text. It is not coincidental that terms like *suspension* exist in a number of different arts, vocations, and fields. Beyond their common etymological antecedents (like the Latin *suspendere*), these fields not only wilfully borrowed and appropriated such terms but also mutually influenced one another, as rendered manifest by the intimate relationship between music and rhythmic poetry, for example.[51] The affinities between music and theatre, in particular, would seem to align with Cervantes's own nostalgia for Spanish drama of the likes of Juan del Encina and Lope de Rueda, perhaps because he recognized the raw emotional power of live musical performance without the distraction of, so to speak, the modern bells and whistles of Lope de Vega's *comedia nueva*.[52]

Indeed, if the art of music has aided in making vivid the temporality of suspension, then the art of early modern theatre will help to animate its physicality. In his study of Calderón's *La vida es sueño* (*Life Is a Dream*) and acting techniques, Agustín de la Granja highlights the complex network of emotions that encircle suspension itself: "*Suspensión* as well as *turbación* enclose, in the depths of the soul, a complex chain of feelings or 'affects' (from sensual love to the rage of jealousy) that forcefully imprison those who suffer them."[53] As for how these feelings materialized in theatrical praxis, it behoves us to recall that "Renaissance theoreticians of gesture," as Kevin Dunn explains, "always understood the difference, the gap, between gesture as code and gesture in its fuller sense of expression, an expression that both registers and provokes desire – gesture, in short, as affect."[54] An examination of the declamation and histrionics that an early modern theatrical audience could expect to see in a representation of suspension, then, may address the similar gap that exists in literature between suspension as a narrative trope and its expression as a deeply emotive experience. In the *corrales* of seventeenth-century Spain, Granja speculates that there were numerous bodily means by which actors might communicate to the audience the suspension or perturbation of their characters, from using the eyes or gaze to "improvising a bodily agitation sufficiently visible to the audience"; from "a supposedly uncontrollable stammering or trembling to suddenly falling silent; from the abrupt dropping of an object to irregular breathing," or even fainting.[55] The most widespread and convincing theatrical method for relaying suspension, he surmises, was for the actor abruptly to become motionless and silent like a statue. In addition to many less explicit examples, this is the stance that Ricardo, in a passage seething with ire in *El amante liberal*, adopts when he sees Leonisa alone with his rival Cornelio: "I was like a statue, unable to speak or move" (me quedé como estatua, sin voz ni movimiento alguno).[56] Although the image in figure 5.3 does effect a depiction of the scene, due to the intrinsically static nature of the pictorial arts such a posture is far less appreciable than in the live action of the theatre, where to freeze in this way would be palpable for playgoers. Granja explains: "There is no doubt that the 'action' an actor of the seventeenth century develops according to stage directions like 'become suspended [*suspenso*]' or 'act pensive' is precisely that of remaining 'like a stone,' without moving feet, nor hands, nor tongue, nor eyelashes [...] arresting the body and repressing speech, they *communicate* to the audience the emotional turmoil of the soul."[57] While underscoring how performers overcame the abiding demands of emotional expression on the stage generally, this example evinces a paradox at the heart of suspension in particular. Just as an unforeseeable event can stupefy the subject, disturbing rational and sensory faculties, here too the modus operandi of actorly technique is interrupted; arresting both movement and time, the theatrical performance itself becomes suspended by suspension.

Beyond these physical and kinetic methods one of the uniquely theatrical possibilities for acting out intense perturbation was the aside, through which the performer could momentarily suspend the action to explain to the audience, directly or indirectly, the affective circumstances of a given scene.[58] Another advantage for actors (or even readers of plays) was the existence of stage directions, which, akin to musical notations, could advise them on the most favourable modes of representing suspension.[59] The *didascalia* in one of Calderón's dramas, for example, coach the actor to appear *"as in ecstasy, in the manner of a statue."*[60] In *Jorge Toledano*, a Lopean captivity play, however, the instruction to freeze and become silent is implicit within the dialogue itself, peppered with ellipses to simulate a tongue-tied confession of love: "I've taken a liking to you ... / And am liking you so / and of ... liking so ... flustered / Oh, Allah, flustered I am!" (Aficionada te estoy ... / Y estoy tan aficionada / y de ... afición tan ... turbada / ¡Ay, Alá, turbada estoy!)[61] The *comediante* portraying this scene would presumably pause in between words, speak in fits and starts, and appear to stutter or stammer. But if one of Lope's characters expresses suspension by losing control of her speech, then another loses control of an even more primitive physical function. The following verses describe a pivotal juncture in *La Gatomaquia*:

Figure 5.3. D. Valdivieso, in *Novelas ejemplares* (Madrid, 1854), p. 241. Lithograph. Cervantes Project, Cushing Memorial Library, Texas A&M University.

Astonished and stunned was the audience
At seeing, armed with sword and fury,
A cat in a wedding,
Where pomp is proper, and not steel,
Everything was disrupted;
And Zapaquilda, seeing him so fierce,
Wet the estrade [...]
In this shock, everyone perturbed, [...]
It left them fearful and awestruck.

Suspenso y como atónito el senado
De ver de acero y de furor armado
Un gato en una boda,
Donde es propia la gala, y no el acero,
Alborotóse todo;
Y Zapaquilda, viéndole tan fiero,
Humedeció el estrado [...]
En esta suspensión, todos turbados, [...]
Los dejó temerosos y admirados.[62]

In addition to the sobering feelings of fear, pity, and despair, this scene airs with burlesque pageantry the fact that an experience of suspension could take on a humorous tone as well. What all of these cases show is that dramaturges, directors, and actors alike had a diversified repertoire of technical, dramatic, discursive, gestural, and bodily resources at their disposal for expressing suspension before their audiences. Likewise, the spectators of a theatrical performance – which in Cervantes's Spain almost always implied the intimate setting of the palace or the *corral* – enjoyed the ability to descry the affective state of suspension by observing a vast array of visual beacons, including asides, stuttering, speechlessness, rhetorical silence, trembling, fainting, wide eyes, dumbfounded expressions, the dropping of an object, or paralyzing stillness.[63] While "it is difficult to determine what [actors] think, unless their faces and their 'gestures' betray their interior affects," the reader of prose lacks the benefit of all such cues and stage directions, rendering the "interior affects" of characters even more inscrutable.[64] Maybe this is another reason why literary critics traditionally have shied away from emotions.

One final cultural context, however, will serve to make greater sense of the narrative figuration of suspension as an emotionally mediated concept, especially its epistemic foundations. The practice of mysticism, whose lasting influence on early modern Spanish culture through such figures as San Juan de la Cruz and Teresa de Ávila was perhaps second only to Cervantes's own, also shared a common lexicon with many of the terms of suspension analysed thus far.[65] The words *admiración* and *suspensión* were frequently invoked to characterize the prodigious mental, spiritual, and phenomenological states of mystical visions, which, qua disjunction, recall these terms' irruption in the novellas. Spanish mystics signalled the concept of *suspensio animi*, closely related to the expression of admiratio, as a vector of suspending cognitive judgment, transcending consciousness, and losing the self in an ambiguous mode of ecstasy that was receptive to truths deemed inaccessible through the more conventional faculty of human reason. The parallels between mysticism and literature here are not fortuitous. The ancient doctrine of *furor poeticus*, revived in the Renaissance by Marsilio Ficino, ascribed the ecstatic mania of poetic inspiration to divine provenance. Early erotic poetry exploited verbal confusion for symbolizing the ecstasy of orgasm, and the idea that the reader may be removed, transported, or obliged to contemplate a literary work from a critical distance is innately Baroque. Góngora's prosody, for instance, often draws readers into a state of suspension while they are searching for the main verb of a sonnet or deciphering a stubbornly hermetic metaphor.[66] Becoming entranced and enraptured by these poetic puzzles – as well as the gratifying epiphany of resolving them – therefore mirrors the mystic experience of accessing esoteric knowledge or spiritual arcana through *suspensio animi*. Elena del Río Parra has even mused that the act of reading literature – regardless of form and content – is itself a form of suspension, a way of "leaving" ourselves.[67]

Further similarities between suspension of the mystic variety and the specifically Cervantine kind warrant closer examination. In his preface to the *Obras espirituales* (Spiritual works) of San Juan de la Cruz, the seventeenth-century theologian Diego de Jesús Salablanca details how during a mystic vision the rational and sensory faculties "are as though dazed [*admiradas*] in suspension [*suspensión*] and without acting." Such a state, he explains, "is not so much a manner of movement and action as a form of stillness and suspension [*suspensión*]," "and so what is there on the part of understanding is a simple, arrested, and suspended bewilderment [*suspensa admiración*]."[68] The receiver of mystical experience is conveyed to a higher plane of consciousness, one simultaneously conditioned by an increased intimacy with the divine and a diminished command of rational faculties (or *potencias*). To be thus severed from human reason, according to Teresa de Ávila and Diego de Jesús, unseals alternative epistemes, namely the soul's "habitual disposition of amorous inclination towards God."[69] "We act," says the mystic annotator, "but like someone who is stopped and does not move. We speak, but in the manner of silence. We look, not as someone who gazes [*mira*], but as someone in a daze [*se admira*]; and we understand more by recognition [*reconocimiento*] than by cognition [*conocimiento*]." Such a description, fraught with paradoxes as it is, could just as easily chronicle the experience of characters in the *Novelas ejemplares* who, withdrawn by the shock of surprise or anagnorisis (another type of recognition), find themselves suddenly deprived of sensory, motor, and rational control. Diego de Jesús, in fact, remarks that "these spiritual actions are instantaneous,"[70] and it was this spontaneity that led Teresa de Ávila to feel anxiety and embarrassment about succumbing to mystic visions in public, as she confesses in her autobiography.[71] This abrupt nature of mystical suspension, unexpectedly interrupting the flow of normal consciousness, represents yet another parallel with the literary form, suggesting that Ricoeur's, Derrida's, and Bakhtin's theories of the unforeseeable might apply to mystic encounters as well. Indeed, mystic ecstasy is an event of the most Derridean kind – it comes "from above."

Yet mystical suspension differs in one essential way. If in this tradition orthodox forms of reason are suspended in favour of an altered state of consciousness, then it also implies a "lack of affection," or a detachment from human emotion.[72] As Michel de Certeau observed in his penetrating study *The Mystic Fable*, "the works of Teresa are 'esteemed by everyone'" precisely "because they 'circumcise the desires and affections.'"[73] Poles apart, suspension in the *Novelas ejemplares*, in addition to the majority of its lexical definitions and cultural connotations, is nothing if not affective. It is, rather, a happening at once profound, multifarious, often vehement, and always thoroughly emotional. Although "it is paradoxical that both concepts are conjoined in one definition,"[74] in this paradox – as invariably is the case with those favoured by the mystics – lies a subtle insight: both kinds of suspension (the unexpected, affective variety and the detached, mystical sort) share a circumvention of standard cognitive reasoning. Suspension in the *Novelas ejemplares*, like its mystical counterpart, opens onto forms of knowing that are enabled by a lapse, however fleeting, of reason. It affords access to other modes of thinking about – and, indeed, feeling – unexpected events and the hardships, quandaries, and quagmires that may follow in their wake, whether at sea or in the heart. If the revelations reaped through mystical experience necessarily shepherd adherents towards the divine, then this knowledge in the novellas steers readers towards ethical solutions for what, in the mundane realm of human emotion, perturbs us in the first place.[75]

Tempering Fears, Tempering Sails

To make further sense of how suspension functions in the text as an invitation to ethical reflection, especially in so far as the semantic field of the sea comes to inform interpersonal events on land, let us now return to the narrative thread of the novella. The winds of fortune that had guided Ricaredo and his crew to safe harbour now intervene proverbially to carry Isabela's biological parents back to their long-lost daughter, for among the Spanish captives whom he spared are the aging and bereaved *gaditanos*, who request passage to her kidnapper's commonwealth of England. The spectacle of the returning ships sailing up the River Thames – which leaves a crowd of onlookers "baffled" (suspenso)[76] – corresponds not only with the gallantry of Ricaredo's subsequent entrée to the queen's palace in full military regalia but also with the sight of "so much grandeur and luxury" before the eyes of Isabela's parents there a day later, leaving them "awestruck and astonished" (admirados y suspensos de ver tanta grandeza y bizarría junta).[77] Even more bewildering for them is the sight of Isabela herself, a scene whose emotional weight is described by the narrator in meticulous detail:

> As Isabela looked up, her mother looked at her, and stopped to look at her more carefully, and in Isabela's memory *confused* recollections began to awaken which led her to understand that she had seen the woman before her long ago. Her father was in the same state of *confusion*, not daring to credit the truth his eyes were showing him. Ricaredo very attentively watched the emotions and feelings of the three doubtful, perplexed souls so *perturbed* [*confusas*] by the question of whether or not they recognized one another. The queen perceived their *suspension* and even Isabela's *uneasiness* [*desasosiego*], because she saw her cold perspiration and how she kept raising her hands to arrange her hair.

> Ansí como Isabela alzó los ojos, los puso en su madre, y detuvo el paso para mirarla más atentamente, y en la memoria de Isabela se comenzaron a despertar unas *confusas* noticias que le querían dar a entender que en otro tiempo ella había visto aquella mujer que delante tenía. Su padre estaba en la misma *confusión*, sin osar determinarse a dar crédito a la verdad que sus ojos le mostraban. Ricaredo estaba atentísimo a ver los afectos y movimientos que hacían las tres dudosas y perplejas almas, que tan *confusas* estaban entre el sí y el no de conocerse. Conoció la reina la *suspensión* de entrambos, y aun el *desasosiego* de Isabela, porque la vio trasudar y levantar las manos muchas veces a componerse el cabello.[78]

Shortly thereafter the narrator adds that the queen has been left "astonished" (admirada) by the events of the family's reunion – a fitting reaction to one of the most acutely emotive and heart-rending scenes of the entire collection of novellas.[79] Such moments of anagnorisis, frequent in Cervantes's texts, are already some of the most impactful, given that, as Hutchinson observes, "few literary techniques can involve as much emotive participation by readers as a well-executed anagnorisis."[80] Here Cervantes has orchestrated a masterful crescendo of sentimental suspense, with both intra- and extra-diegetic audiences anxiously awaiting the resolution of the international and inter-familial conflict. The heightened tension seems to sharpen everyone's senses, with each character scrutinizing the other ever more intently to discern the significance of movements and affects.[81] This explains the queen's canny ability to identify Isabela's emotional state of "suspension" and "uneasiness" through such minute bodily and non-verbal cues as her breaking into a cold sweat and obsessively fixing her hair. As readers, we become keenly attuned to the details of the tableau through a reciprocal kind of suspension and unrest as we await its resolution – to evoke the etymology of the term, we are left "hanging" on these moments of suspension.

Any hopes of swift closure for the displaced family and sundered couple, however, are just as quickly stymied when Arnesto, son of the queen's principal lady-in-waiting and desperately infatuated with Isabela, challenges Ricaredo's legitimacy as her future husband. After royal guards thwart the suitors' attempt to duel, the queen condemns the insolent Arnesto to prison, and his mother, fearing his life is at stake so long as Isabela is in the picture, cravenly poisons her, leaving her terribly disfigured.[82] Note the metaphorical language used to contrast Ricaredo's emotional state of being "very happy about the proximate hope of possessing Isabela with no fear [*sobresalto*] of losing her" (contentísimo con la esperanza propincua que llevaba de tener en su poder a Isabela sin sobresalto de perderla) with the abrupt effect of these events on his psyche in the "brief time" since he had dropped anchor in England: "[W]hen he thought the ship of his good fortune was sailing before a favorable wind toward the desired port, bad luck raised on his sea a storm so great he feared a thousand times that it would sink him" (Mas en aquel breve tiempo, donde él pensaba que la nave de su buena fortuna corría con próspero viento hacia el deseado puerto, la contraria suerte levantó en su mar tal tormenta, que mil veces temió anegarle).[83] So too is a maritime conceit deployed in reference to Isabela and her parents' equally inconstant fate: "All these things tormented the hearts of Isabela and her parents, who saw the sea of their tranquility so quickly agitated [*turbado*]" (Todas estas cosas atormentaban el corazón de Isabela y de sus padres, que tan presto veían turbado el mar de su sosiego).[84] A hydraulic, meteorological, or nautical metaphor figures, in each of these examples, a sudden reversal of fortune and its resultant emotional effects. Here as elsewhere, unforeseeable events at sea correspond with those of an emotional nature, such as the disruption of desire, the deferral of familial stability, and the fear of losing not only life and limb but also love. The untimely ups and downs of his fortune while Ricaredo is serving as captain of the English fleet inevitably govern the temporal and affective parameters of the satisfaction of his longing to return to his beloved, consummate their marriage, and recuperate a sense of calm. Figurative language reinforces these parallels, mutually evoking the turbulence of the sea and that of emotions themselves. The emotional tide can turn as suddenly as the literal one.

As if to drive this very point home, Ricaredo's parents raise the emotional stakes even higher when, in the midst of these imbroglios, they send for Clisterna, a Scottish lady whom they had initially arranged to wed their son. Their covert intention is to betroth them before the convalescing Isabela can recuperate her original physical beauty. Upon Clisterna's arrival, "Ricaredo was startled [*sobresaltose*] at the unexpected sight of the young lady, and he feared that the shock [*sobresalto*] of her arrival might end Isabela's life" (Sobresaltose Ricaredo con la improvisa vista de la doncella, y temió que el sobresalto de su venida había de acabar la vida a Isabela). In Ricaredo's situation, his *sobresalto* is doubly disturbing because he experiences the shock of Clisterna's precipitate arrival and concomitantly fears that such a trauma might be enough to kill Isabela in her already weakened state. Nevertheless, by way of yet another vocable shared by seafaring and psychology, he almost immediately converts these passions into action, issuing to Isabela's bedside "to temper this fear" (para templar este temor).[85] With the verb *templar* signifying the action of transforming (or returning to their original state) materials or qualities that are discordant, disproportionate, and dissonant into those that are concordant, proportionate, and harmonious, we effectively have the antonymous counterpart to *sobresalto* and similar words of suspension.[86] It should come as no surprise, then, that this is the same term used to describe the management of the sails when Ricaredo was at sea. "[T]o moderate and proportion the sails to the wind, rolling them up if it is very strong, and extending them if it is smooth or soft" (moderar, y proporcionar las velas al viento, recogiendolas, si es mui fuerte, y extendiendolas, si es suave, ò blando") – as the *Diccionario de autoridades* glosses this acceptation of *templar* – thus becomes a felicitous means of describing the management of one's emotions.[87] The erstwhile mariner, in effect, appears as capable of navigating the high seas as he is his feelings.

When Ricaredo reaches Isabela, his tack involves a measured discourse for appraising the situation and professing his love, explaining to his deformed lover that "although your corporeal beauty captivated my senses, your infinite virtues captured my soul" (puesto que tu corporal hermosura me cautivó los sentidos, tus infinitas virtudes me aprisionaron el alma). He then goes on to ask for her hand in marriage, leaving his onlookers in a correspondingly dazed state and bringing the emotive suspension of the scene full circle: "Isabela was suspended by Ricaredo's words, and her parents amazed and astonished" (Quedó suspensa Isabela con las razones de Ricaredo, y sus padres atónitos y pasmados).[88] Instead of allowing the mortal shock of Clisterna's arrival to suspend him indefinitely or drive him to any number of detrimental or destructive emotions (such as rage, despair, melancholy, or even love for Clisterna), Ricaredo seizes the affective turmoil of his situation as an opportunity to make a different choice. It is the sudden irruption of this very shock that prompts him to propose to Isabela, an outcome rendered more meaningful by the subterfuge of his parents in summoning Clisterna, a threat that Ricaredo intuitively perceives. Since he was already emotionally vulnerable (as Isabela was physically vulnerable), they had hoped to take advantage of the element of surprise and its tendency to encourage one to act impulsively. We might expect that their plan for him to exchange ugliness for beauty would have worked were it not for Cervantes's insistence that moments of suspension give rise not to further impassioned impulses but to reasoned reflection and virtuous action. To be sure, these events perform the narrative functions of accentuating the impact of a turn in the dramatic trajectory and of reinforcing the ethos of the protagonist, as the reaction of Ricaredo's intra-diegetic audience amply demonstrates.

Beyond their purely aesthetic purpose in creating suspense, however, I suggest that these moments open a self-conscious space for the characters and the reader alike in which intense emotion leads to a meditation on the moral and ethical insights contained in each novella. The accumulation of confusion in the scene of family reunion at the English royal court (wherein the term *confuso* is repeated three times) underscores the dissonance between sensory input (i.e., the startling sight of seeing someone unexpected) and innate intuition (i.e., the unshakeable feeling of knowing someone). Here the Platonic notion that the soul – emotion's home turf – is imprinted with past memories intervenes in favour of the displaced family members, leading

Isabela and her parents to confirm the veracity of what they see. In spite of the initial confusion, the implication is clear: following one's feelings, though seemingly irrational, may lead to the truth. The very presence of suspension and confusion in the passage facilitates this kind of pre-modern emotional intelligence. That such heartfelt, emotive exchanges take place in the royal court, moreover, stands in stark contrast to the idea prescribed, popularized, and often parodied in courtly literature that successful courtiers had to repress and dissimulate their true feelings. Although characters in the novella recognize and at times express shame or regret for transgressing this directive of decorum in front of the queen (including Ricaredo and Isabela's parents), the fact that they are explicitly condoned, accepted, and even praised for their emotional outbursts in this milieu is surely significant. By representing the court as a space where emotions such as love, desire, shame, sadness, and wonder circulate among characters of distinct genders, nationalities, and socioeconomic profiles, Cervantes forges affect as a medium of interpersonal exchange and potential resistance to dominant political structures and social expectations. This is not to imply that rationality and inborn virtue are not qualities that he reveres in their own right, as they are obviously another weight-bearing pillar of the didacticism of the *Novelas ejemplares*. But the reality is that here, as in numerous instances throughout the text, such qualities proceed directly from *an unexpected emotional event*. It is the commingling of reason and emotion therein that furnishes an uncommon prescription for ethical behaviour and, at the same time, a narrative resolution for the compelling ups and downs of Cervantine suspension.

Ethical Solutions through *Admiratio*

A return to the more abstract, philosophical acceptation of *admiración* unveils the mechanisms responsible for this latent ethical potential in suspension, beginning with Covarrubias, who notes that "the capacity to wonder [*ser admirativo*]" is a human trait that produces "inquiring, scrutinizing, and reflecting on what is offered [...] until reaching calm with the knowledge of the truth," adding tersely that whoever "does not wonder [*no se admira*] about anything either has knowledge of all effects," or they "are simpletons, stupid and moronic."[89] His definition renders more translucent the concept of suspension as an invitation to further reflection: the agitated state of uncertainty is mollified only by "knowledge of the truth," itself arrived at through scrutiny, thought, and questioning (recalling the extreme attentiveness of Isabela, her parents, and the queen during the scene in the English court). The feeling of being awestruck thus precedes rational knowledge; the truth becomes predicated on an emotional event that produces epistemophilia or the *desire* to know. To fully appreciate the concept of admiratio, however, we must first locate its place among the pan-European debates on tragedy that were a hallmark of Renaissance literary theory. As we know, Aristotle's ancient blueprint held that tragic catharsis ought to purge the feelings of pity and fear in spectators, a dramatic precept that easily found its way into aesthetic treatises of the Renaissance. It was as though, for centuries, these feelings had enjoyed a duopoly on the audience's temperament. By the late sixteenth century, however, even some of the staunchest neo-Aristotelians, many of whose adherence to the *Poetics* was legendarily rigid, began to concede that tragedy might stir other emotions – namely, admiratio. Wonder, then, gradually displaced the supremacy of pity and fear in the psychological domain of the spectator. Although several critics would eventually jump on this dramatic bandwagon – from Pierre Corneille in France to Philip Sidney and later John Dryden in England – it was the Italian Antonio Minturno who first brought admiration into fashion and, more importantly, awoke its dormant emotional potential for literature.[90] His *De poeta*, a popular treatise on poetic theory published in Venice in 1559, proposes, as noted previously, that the work of fiction should not only teach (*docere*) and delight (*delectare*) but also move the spectator or reader emotionally (*movere*). For Minturno, this addendum to Horace's classic recipe was indispensable for ensuring that the audience be receptive to the work's didactic aims, an impact accomplished precisely by admiratio. Despite the novelty of Minturno's logic among pre-modern poetic theories, it is almost self-explanatory: the poet should endow the marvels, conflicts, and reversals of the plot with emotive elements, for otherwise the reader – and here we glimpse the modern usage of the term – will not *admire* the heroic comportment of the protagonists, and the moral lesson will go unlearned.[91] When it comes to fiction, the dispassionate reader is antithetical to ethical instruction.

What this entails is that instances of *admiración* in the novellas subtend not only the surprise and ethical revelation of the characters but also those of the reader, as Riley observed: "Cervantes refers to [*admiratio*] repeatedly as an audience-reaction to events."[92] The sixteenth-century Toledan humanist Alejo Venegas bolsters this claim, having asserted that "the principal aim of ancient poetry was to direct men to the precepts of moral philosophy 'by way of *admiratio*,'"[93] as does the great Renaissance comparativist Joel Elias Spingarn, who considered admiratio "the logical consequence of the Renaissance position that philosophy teaches by precept, but poetry by example, and that in this consists its superior ethical efficacy."[94] We thus have a more lucid picture of the paradoxical dual signification that inheres in *admiración*, of its capacity to produce both unexpected moments of light-hearted entertainment and opportunities for moral edification – or, more suitably, *exemplarity*. Given the intimate, often synonymous relationship that existed in the early modern mind among the terms of suspension examined herein, it is reasonable to surmise that, in addition to *admiración* in particular, each of those terms could perform a correspondingly didactic function. Put simply, it is not just the characters who experience suspension, but also we as readers.

Much more recent scholarship concurs that fictional events of this sort affect the reader to an equal or greater extent than they do the characters. In his study of narrative temporality Currie stresses the need to reconnect writer and reader through the feeling of surprise.[95] Hutchinson, for his part, relates these ideas specifically to anagnorisis, which to bear affective fruit must "involve us emotionally" and make us "capable of imagining how the characters feel."[96] Much the same evidence has emerged from the fields of empirical aesthetics and neuroaesthetics, which have studied the emotional effects of reading and the psychological impacts of literature on the brain.[97] It is precisely in moments of suspension – during which an interruption of narrative temporality opens what Riley calls a "receptive frame of mind" in the reader – that the transmission of or reflection upon a "moral lesson" or "universal truth" is most opportune. In effect, this ratifies the provocation inherent in the *Novelas ejemplares* and announced in its prologue to commingle "amorous remarks" (requiebros amorosos) and "edifying example[s]" (ejemplo[s] provechoso[s]). Focusing on the unambiguously affective mechanisms of suspense, as I have done here, reveals that these unlikely companions not only coincide but also interrelate and that intense emotions do not simply harbour the capacity to provide exemplarity, but that there is essentially no better place to go searching for it. Although critics have seldom agreed on the form and extent of this exemplarity, I would suggest that this is precisely where the ethical kernel of the novellas germinates: in the triple potential of unexpected emotional events to attain a level of aesthetic admiration, of moral imitation, and – following Minturno, crucially – of moving inspiration. Exemplarity arises at the same time as the surprisingness that generates narrative suspense and thus induces us to continue reading – in short, it is suspended in suspension.

Conclusion

The interdependency between the maritime and the affective, crystallized in moments of suspension, further urges us to contemplate an emotional exemplarity for Mediterranean life. Although I am unable to ponder its particularities in detail here, other scholars have cogently sketched some of the parameters that Cervantes established for an expressly Mediterranean ethics. Luis F. Avilés, for example, has shown that the expansive quality of liberality in *El amante liberal* allows for a corresponding expansion of the self, thereby prescribing a virtuous alternative to the Mediterranean's libidinal economies and those based on forceful possession.[98] We might consider this a prime avatar of what Hutchinson, in his broader study of the same name, calls Cervantes's "ethical economy," in which similarly liberal exchanges are transacted pursuant to mutually recognized, humanist principles of equality.[99] One of these principles is love, whose potency for Hutchinson depends upon scenes of public recognition, those that arise time and again in Cervantes's narrative. Regardless of the finer contours it adopts, a cornerstone and common denominator of such an ethics is free will, which Marsha Collins and David Boruchoff, respectively, have distinguished as a theme of *La española inglesa* and of the *Novelas ejemplares* as a whole.[100] So, too, is choice essential for navigating the field of potential outcomes in a given (narrative) situation, a process to which, if only by implication, readers are necessarily privy – from Ricaredo's sudden decision to propose to Isabela to Ricardo's unexpected and unprecedented display of liberality near the end of *El amante liberal* when he yields to Leonisa's choosing of the course of her own romantic future (merely two of countless examples).[101] But, as I remarked earlier, choice also inheres in the unexpected events responsible for producing suspension in the first place, with Currie concluding that the unforeseeable "is decisively linked to freedom, or to the possibility of momentous choice in the present of a kind that is consistent with surprisingness."[102]

Maritime contingency in Cervantes's fiction thus shapes an ethics that is eminently more responsive to the travails of the (Mediterranean) world than is the staid detachment of neo-Stoicism or the constraints of pure philosophical conjecture. This is true even when the text appears to champion a more stolid form of resilience, as it portrays Isabela with yet another nautical metaphor: "Isabela was like a rock in the middle of the sea, touched but not moved by the waves and the winds" (estaba Isabela como roca en mitad del mar, que la tocan, pero no la mueven las olas ni los vientos).[103] The titular character successfully negotiates not only the national and religious binaries that traverse her and her surroundings (English and Spanish, Protestant and Catholic) but also the adversities of Mediterranean life (enduring the seduction of her many suitors in Seville while awaiting Ricaredo and the fulfilment of their nuptial vows), herself embodying an exemplar that the reader can both marvel at and admire.

Although I concur with the spirit of recent sceptical readings of the novellas' exemplarity and of critical attempts at exposing its "cracks,"[104] this is an ethics that, if generically indebted to the classical and medieval exemplum, strays far from the "moral certainty" that more earnest interpretations of Cervantes's didacticism are sometimes presumed to espouse.[105] While certain novellas – namely those with picaresque leanings like *Rinconete y Cortadillo*, *El coloquio de los perros*, and *El casamiento engañoso* (*The Deceitful Marriage*) – may well ironize the collection's self-avowed moralization, they can neither undermine the ethical force of others nor enfeeble poetic fiction's generally edifying potential, even when it is realized precisely through or alongside the singularly literary function of irony.[106] If anything, the final words of *La española inglesa* – by far the most explicitly didactic of any of the *Novelas ejemplares* – underscore this reality by broadcasting under the guise of authorial clarity a moral lesson whose applicability to either text or reader is sufficiently ambiguous as to inspire multiple interpretations: "This tale could teach us how much virtue can accomplish and how much beauty can do, for they are fairly close and each by itself can inspire love even in enemies, and how heaven knows how to extract from our greatest adversities our greatest benefits." (Esta novela nos podría enseñar cuánto puede la virtud y cuánto la hermosura, pues son bastantes juntas y cada una de por sí a enamorar aun hasta los mismos enemigos, y de cómo sabe el cielo sacar, de las mayores adversidades nuestras, nuestros mayores provechos.)[107] With Ricaredo and Isabela finally accorded the closure of marriage and a peaceful, happy life, what is perhaps most clear at the novella's end is that emotions undergird a uniquely Cervantine species of virtue.[108]

Lest such emotional exemplarity appear a facile or even quixotic solution to Mediterranean life's tumult, however, these words also remind us that feelings may just as easily lead us astray, even to the point of occasioning the "adversities" from which we might otherwise "benefit." We would be remiss to ignore the text's insistence that such ideals as prudence, moderation, and discretion, in addition to the faculty of reason, are exigent guarantors of an impassioned yet virtuous existence, for Cervantes leverages the *Novelas ejemplares* to alert us to a sort of anti-exemplarity of emotion as well. *El celoso extremeño* (*The Jealous Extremaduran*) may be the single most effective demonstration of the potentially destructive force of strong passions and the imperative to temper them with rationality and other virtues. The very last words of this novella reify an inverse, inimical example of suspension not as an opportunity to convert passion into action but as an impasse responsible for the bitter injustice of the protagonists' fate – the covetous old man's erroneous belief that his young wife had committed adultery leading to his death and her disgrace. "What I do not know," the narrator laments, "is the reason Leonora did not beg forgiveness with more zeal and let her jealous husband know how pure and without offence she had emerged from these events, but perturbation [*la turbación*] tied her tongue, and the speed with which her husband died left no room for her excuses." (Sólo no sé qué fue la causa que Leonora no puso más ahínco en desculparse y dar a entender a su celoso marido cuán limpia y sin ofensa había quedado en aquel suceso, pero la turbación le ató la lengua, y la priesa que se dio a morir su marido no dio lugar a su disculpa.)[109] This is not some unsubtle deus ex machina by negligence or narrative sin of omission. By way of a contrasting example in which *turbación* fails to effect justice, Cervantes's choice to end *El celoso extremeño* in such a fashion actually reinforces the directive, abundant throughout the collection of novellas, to seize suspension as an invitation to ethical reflection as well as action.

A similar move of negative reinforcement in the text casts the Mediterranean as a convenient pretence for avoiding something emotionally arduous or confounding, most often through the trope of the character who travels to Italy or another foreign locale to escape an uncomfortable predicament. A religious pilgrimage to Rome not only serves as the foundational alibi for *Persiles y Sigismunda*, but also becomes a pretext for Ricaredo himself in *La española inglesa* so that he might circumvent the hurdles to his and Isabela's marriage by reuniting with her later in Seville. Not incidentally, this plan almost back-fires, as he narrowly avoids being killed by his rival Arnesto in Italy, only to be captured and held for ransom in Algiers. He reaches his beloved at the eleventh hour just before she, believing him dead, cloisters herself in a convent – thus enabling the novella's fittingly miraculous, wonder-inducing ending: "All of this added surprise to surprise and astonishment to astonishment" (Todo esto fue añadir admiración a admiración y espanto a espanto).[110] A variation on this theme surfaces in several other novellas, including *La ilustre fregona* (*The Illustrious Scullery Maid*), *La gitanilla*, and *La fuerza de la sangre*. Here the Mediterranean offers not an opportunity for expanding the ethical dimension of the self but a geographical mobility and anonymity whereby deceit and duplicity work to defer the resolution of narrative conflict. As a plot device, such detours function to lay an anagnorisis or reversal, to incubate suspense for the reader, and to hatch in their aftermath an about-face for what is always a male character, whose road to redemption leads him home (principal female characters typically appear as modest and virtuous from the start). Although on occasion the Mediterranean is a transient accomplice for indulging in picaresque wanderings or subterfuge, in Cervantes's writing, without exception, it returns characters who, eventually, have grown from their ordeal and display greater ethical and emotional maturity as a result.

While awaiting in suspense the outcome of these Mediterranean experiences, which often go unresolved until the last page or two of each novella, the reader must exercise a suspension of judgment as to the overall exemplarity of these characters. At an aesthetic level, their ensuing adoption or recovery of a moral stance augments our admiratio all the more, while at the same time sounding a harmonious note as a culminating counterpoint – in the classical and Renaissance tradition of *discordia concors* – to the necessary convulsion that preceded it. An analogous idea emerges in the homiletic final words of *La española inglesa*, where, as noted earlier, readers are told that "from our greatest adversities" may arise "our greatest benefits." The intense affects of suspension mark the calamities, conundrums, and adversities we are invited to work through and benefit from, underwriting a characteristically Cervantine kind of exemplarity. The *Novelas ejemplares* advances the bold yet noble idea that affect and reason can – and perhaps should – go hand in hand. The proliferation of the techniques of suspension analysed in this chapter likewise suggests the benefits – aesthetic, emotional, and ethical – of a momentary lapse of reason. In sum, just as Cervantes's literary self overcame his suspension in *Don Quijote*, and just as positive upshots can proceed from the trials of the Mediterranean, so too can we profit from our turbulent emotions, which may aid us in navigating the death-dealing conditions of the open sea as much as the doldrums of everyday life. To recall the dual usage of the verb *templar* in the text – "to moderate and proportion the sails to the wind, rolling them up if it is very strong, and extending them if it is smooth or soft" – Cervantes proposes that, rather than stoically folding the sails completely, we actively manage our emotions according to the conditions of a particular environment. If at intervals unbridled feelings may lead us to drift off course or even to capsize, at others it is the very embracing, accentuating, or indulging of them that promises to propel us safely forward. The conceit might apply to literary narrative as well – the ups and downs of the wind corresponding with the alternately tranquil and suspended states of emotive tension – with Cervantes as the skilful mariner who always seems to know how and when to adjust the sails.

Chapter Six

Aporias of Love: Articulating the Ineffable in *Los trabajos de Persiles y Sigismunda*

To try to write love is to confront the muck of language: that region of hysteria where language is both too much and too little, excessive [...] and impoverished.

Roland Barthes

The sauce of stories is the property of language, in whatever thing is said.

(*La salsa de los cuentos es la propiedad del lenguaje, en cualquiera cosa que se diga.*)

Cervantes

When Cervantes suggested with a mixture of self-deprecating irony and hubris that his last work would be "either the worst or best ever composed in our language" (o el más malo, o el mejor que en nuestra lengua se haya compuesto), it is as though he had preordained how *Los trabajos de Persiles y Sigismunda* would divide critics for the next four centuries.[1] The author himself considered it his crowning achievement, and it quickly passed through several international editions within the first few years of its posthumous publication in 1617. Yet until the latter half of the twentieth century it mostly languished in the imposing shadow of *Don Quijote*, stymying critics who were unable to fathom why Cervantes would abandon the modern, path-breaking spirit of its hallowed predecessor to consummate his literary career with a work they regarded as deeply flawed.[2] For them, *Persiles y Sigismunda* had failed, quite simply, to meet Cervantes's own expectation, audaciously announced in the prologue, to compete with Heliodorus, author of what is widely esteemed as the greatest extant Greek romance, the *Aethiopica*. Even among the scholars who revived interest in *Persiles y Sigismunda*, the formal elements that were deemed as worthy of either praise or opprobrium diverge as much as do the labyrinthine meanderings of the plot for which the novel had previously been so roundly condemned.[3] In the words of Bradley J. Nelson, "the distinct critical postures brought to bear on the text [...] are so radically contradictory" that *Persiles y Sigismunda* "has arguably produced more totalizing interpretations than all of [Cervantes's] other works combined."[4] This owes in part to what José Manuel Martín Morán has described as a sweeping temptation to reduce the novel to a singular semantic unity and to read *Persiles y Sigismunda* as an allegory.[5] In her *Allegories of Love*, a penetrating and pioneering inquiry into the representation of women, marriage, and sexual difference in the text, Diana de Armas Wilson nevertheless sounds a corresponding note of caution when asserting that Cervantes's last work is "resistant to any totalitarian critical approach."[6]

It is not my intention here to rehash the disparate critical history of a text that by now has become universally accepted into the fold of Cervantism and, thanks to a recent blossoming of nuanced and pluralistic studies, has transcended prior polarizations. I want to take the dissent and bewilderment of this earlier history, rather, as an invitation to explore that which already inheres in the text itself, for the emotional language of *Persiles y Sigismunda*, upon close examination, exhibits analogous tendencies. Like the simultaneous economy and excess, humility and pretension, deprecation and elevation of Cervantes's self-assessment ("el más malo, o el mejor"), the characters of his last work negotiate a world rife with discord, polarity, paradox, and uncertainty. Paying subtle tribute to Wilson's study, this chapter mines the text not for allegories but for *aporias* of love, for the myriad ways in which the emotion resists the very act of interpretation. I thus respond to the presumption, hitherto unchallenged, that *Persiles y Sigismunda* is a love story whittled from the wooden stock of sentimental fiction, which has permitted some critics to tout the work's "detailed analysis of the psychology of love," while remaining poised to defend its governance by the laws of sentimentalism.[7] In this chapter I aim to highlight how the novel breaks these supposed laws of love, how it frustrates and destabilizes its very categorization as a love story. It does so, I will argue, by activating a variegated aesthetic strategy for the representation of affect, one that surpasses the bounds of sentimental fiction in favour of a paradigm not of "life [as] subject to the rules of art"[8] but ultimately of an art that throws out the rules in order to more closely resemble life.

While it is indisputable that Hellenistic romance and sentimentalism influenced the writing of *Persiles y Sigismunda*, these designations are an inadequate lens for comprehending the complexity of emotions in the novel.[9] Here Cervantes is concerned with not only the excesses of love but also its shortcomings, pitfalls, and impossibilities when it is mediated by human discourse – unlike the conventions of sentimental fiction, the pastoral apotheosis of amorous devotion in his own *Galatea*, or even the strenuous love of *La española inglesa* with which *Persiles y Sigismunda* has often been compared.[10] The aphoristic words of the principal character of Periandro, cited in the epigraph to this chapter, encapsulate the fact that in his last work the author was deeply invested in language. By employing what I identify as tropes of aporia, ineffability, and materiality, Cervantes confronts and defies the limitations of mimetic representation, holding in abeyance the capacity of poetic language to pigeonhole intense emotions such as love and desire into transparent, universal categories. The inherently indeterminate and irresolute nature of these emotions evokes both the early modern conception of the human soul as marked by a perpetual state of movement and the protracted series of interruptions, interdictions, digressions, and deferrals that constitute the narrative structure of the text itself. Inscribed at the very core of linguistic representations of intense love is paradoxy – whereby the emphasis on inexpressibility actually becomes an effective means of expression.[11] For readers of *Persiles y Sigismunda*, emotion thus comprises a vessel through which to scrutinize not only the ambiguities of *peregrinatio amoris* but also the uncertainties of knowledge in Counter-reformation Spain.[12]

May it nonetheless be acknowledged at the outset that some of the tropes I will analyse here have undergone a peregrination as long and roving as that of the novel's protagonists. From the Neoplatonists to Petrarchan poets, from medieval monastic thinkers to the troubadours, the ineffable, for example, has historically proven to be a vexing yet fertile concept for a host of philosophical and cultural spheres. We would be equally remiss to neglect that, to some extent, the discordant qualities evident in *Persiles y Sigismunda* had already been woven into the fabric of the epic and the Byzantine romance, generic patterns that Cervantes in turn stitched into the tartan patchwork of his own final literary experiment. As Sonia Velázquez reminds us, for theorists like Lukács, Benjamin, and Bakhtin, "the babelization of epic resulted positively in the birth of characters that are individuals with contradictory desires rather than types," and the latter critic in particular "located the modernity of the novel in the echo chamber of different voices and discourses present throughout the text"[13] – features that are consistent with my analysis of *Persiles y Sigismunda*. Rather than tracing the salient philological precedents for the tropes I survey, or rehearsing at length the iterative deliberations as to the genre of the text,[14] however, my reading tends to privilege the role of authorial invention. In this vein, it behoves us to recall, for instance, how the "multiplicity of micronarratives radically distinguishes the *Persiles* from its model," the *Aethiopica*, and that it "bears little resemblence to its predecessor in formal structure, mood, and occasion."[15] A close reading of the emotional language of the text discloses a comparably radical investment in innovation that, on the whole, differs from anything that his predecessors or Cervantes himself had written before.[16] Particularly when we catch sight of its relationship with the Mediterranean, this emotional language constitutes what can appropriately be called a sea change.

To wit, the text's emotional vernacular paradoxically destabilizes knowledge while advancing an endemic concept of truth, one which, based on difference, suggests a verisimilar relation to everyday life and thus a potentially subversive political ideology. These qualities reflect the historical uncertainties of lived experience in the early modern Mediterranean, where one's fortune – like that of the characters in the novel – could easily be interrupted, deferred, or reversed. I read the novel's setting in the septentrional seas, like the *mundo al revés* trope that recurs throughout, in part as an exoticized analogue for the meridional geographies of more immediate concern to the story's seventeenth-century audience. I am hardly the first critic to decode the northern setting of *Persiles y Sigismunda* as a pretence for Cervantes to reflect on and critique locales more relevant to his readers, such as the New World or even Spain,[17] or to detect the novel's proclivity for collapsing, conflating, and upending the distinction between Barbarian North and Catholic South.[18] In my view, for Cervantes the remote unfamiliarity of northern climes was not, as has often been assumed following Torquato Tasso's prescription, a distancing device for evading the threat to neo-Aristotelian precepts of verisimilitude that would otherwise be posed by talking wolves and other outlandish features of *Persiles y Sigismunda*. Nor was the setting elected merely because of the "internal necessities of the book."[19] A close reading of its emotional language indicates, rather, that the Septentrion serves as a geopoetic medium for countervailing the ineffability of the toilsome and vexing events born of the Mediterranean that Cervantes knew so intimately, as well as an imagined yet definitively remote guise for magnifying the repercussions and geographical reach of these events. The various maritime metaphors that populate the text to refer to emotions, as I suggested in chapter 2, signal the fact that both sentiment and the sea are exceedingly unstable and prone to engendering all manner of turmoil, for intense emotions inevitably attended the uncertainties of life in the Mare Nostrum. This raises the following questions: How can such emotional intensities and uncertainties be conveyed to readers, especially those historical individuals who had never abandoned the relative safety of Spanish shores? How can language, poetic or otherwise, be called upon to express sentiments as mutable and turbulent as the great Sea itself? How, indeed, can the powerful force of the feeling of love – tenuous though it may be in this space – be expected to transfer to the comparatively inert, receptive act of reading?

Beyond Sentimentalism

Cervantes is far from the first writer to confront these questions or to show an awareness of what has been called "affective false consciousness," the idea that upon attempting to verbalize emotion, one reverts to a superficial, glib sentimentalism.[20] Many pre-modern poets laboured to depict love with greater realism and regularly chided their predecessors for lacking authenticity, with the courtly love tradition being a seasonal butt of critique. So it was that Petrarchism, the *trovadorismo* of Portugal and Galicia, and the innovations of Ausiàs March would all lay claim to a sincerity and naturalness that they found to be absent among the early troubadours.[21] It was a formidable balancing act to reconcile poetic form with verisimilitude while writing about things as arduous as lust, infatuation, anguish, and amative devotion. In his comparative literary study of what he calls the "vehement passions," Philip Fisher employs the terms *disposition* and *passion* in order to underscore the opposition between, respectively, those emotions that readily lend themselves to linguistic forms of expression and those like love that, through their "vehemence," confound representation by defying the very nature of language.[22] The simultaneous excesses and inadequacies of expressing love have more lately been explored by Richard Terdiman, who succinctly considers the ontological challenges that such an opposition poses to literary scholars, vitally dependent as we are upon language to decipher texts so suffused with the topic of love that "'love studies' [are] as uncompassable as literature itself": "Love challenges language. But language is the foundation of our discipline."[23] What Fisher and Terdiman have sought to address in the last few years, then, is fundamentally a dual problem, likely as old as literature itself – how to express intense affects like love and how to transmute this fervour into a form legible to readers.

The proliferation and enduring popularity of genres dedicated, wholly if implicitly, to love certifies that this problem is not so daunting as to preclude the historical development of poetic formulae for addressing it. The Greek romance, medieval literature of courtly love, the *novela sentimental* (germ of many a best-seller in fifteenth- and sixteenth-century Iberia), *les Amours* of seventeenth-century French literature, eighteenth-century English-language sentimental fiction, and the *novela rosa* or *roman à l'eau de rose* of the European Romantic movement, as well as contemporary pulp romance novels (which in North America continue to outsell by far all other literary genres), leave little doubt of this reality.[24] Even outside of these popular examples in which its presence is obvious, stories of love span an archive of almost Borgesian proportions. Cervantes's writing is certainly no exception to the subtle notion that the term *literature of love* is often redundant. From the *Galatea*'s foray into pastoral feelings to the comparatively brief lessons on love that comprise a major plot point of nearly all the *Novelas ejemplares*, amorous passion is frequently the engine that gives Cervantine narrative its thrust. To write a book on emotions in Cervantes's texts without studying love would betray, perhaps, more than just a conspicuous oversight.

Yet it is this very ubiquity, I would submit, that has prevented a more thoroughgoing examination of the rhetorical means by which Cervantes confronts the "hysterical region" of language to which Barthes alludes, that oppositional divide between the "too much and too little, excessive [...] and impoverished."[25] In *Persiles y Sigismunda* this critical lacuna is especially pronounced at the latter pole, the one ruled by poetic language's inadequacies in expressing love. Barthes's words perform a suggestive epigraphic function here because in reactivating the Greek romance – a genre known almost exclusively for its sentimental excesses – *Persiles y Sigismunda* has been received as yet another instantiation of sentimental fiction and subjected to a prevailing critical paradigm that tends to censure just this sort of excess. But in trudging headlong through what Barthes called the "muck" of language, Cervantes fashions an idiom of love that is marked by its impoverishment as much as its excess, by meiosis (understatement) as much as auxesis (exaggeration), by poetry's impotence as much as its power.[26] Such language recalls what Frank Kermode has called Shakespeare's "turbulent thinking," the stylistically verisimilar innovations that Cervantes's English counterpart also developed to express the muddled speech patterns of a conflictive age.[27]

The almost reflexive tendency to lump *Persiles y Sigismunda* in with sentimental fiction runs the risk of incurring additional distortions that have dogged such fiction, namely that the genre is bereft of meaningful political content and that it merely indulges a consumerist desire for immediate pleasure, whether judged to be licentious or benign.[28] In effect, the increasing popularity of the fifteenth-century sentimental novel has been assumed to correspond with a growing thirst for escapist diversion among the aristocracy.[29] Although it rose to prominence more than two centuries after its Southern European counterpart, similar appraisals attended traditional criticism of anglophone sentimental fiction, such as Sterne's *Tristram Shandy* and *A Sentimental Journey*, as well as that of authors of the Romantic period like Austen, Brontë, and Eliot. In addition to peddling the simultaneously bourgeois yet lowbrow commodities of "fine feeling" and "cheap sentiment," the excessive sentimentalism of late eighteenth-century English fiction was accused of fomenting such psychopathological and sociopathic conditions as nervousness and oversensitivity among the reading public.[30] The Marxist philosopher and literary critic Georg Lukács took foreseeable umbrage with sentimental fiction on different, though related, grounds. Basing his analysis on Hegel's distinction between world and mind, Lukács bemoaned the literary turn towards sentimentality, melancholic sensibility, and self-reflective inwardness, inaugurated by such works as Flaubert's *Sentimental Education*, as a turning away from the world. By focusing on the mind, sentimental fiction for Lukács amounted to little more than an aestheticized form of navel-gazing at the expense of objectivist or materialist representations of reality. In proclaiming *Don Quijote* the first modern novel, he even pitted the protagonist's picaresque heroism and Cervantes's "abstract idealism" against what he termed the "disillusioned romanticism" of writers like Flaubert.[31]

In spite of such critiques, recent scholarship has probed the cultural and political registers of sentimentalism to establish that even its refined sensibilities are not entirely devoid of subversive elements. In his study of Spanish sentimental fiction, Cortijo Ocaña describes the genre as a hybrid, intertextual body capable of revealing distinct social realities, polyphony, crisis, and ruptures of uniformity and homogeneity, in addition to a highly developed feminine voice.[32] Recalling major plot points of the Greek novel, he goes so far as to assert that "[l]ove is an equalizing force, and lovers, after multiple vicissitudes and contretemps, pulled to catastrophe by a blind and stubborn fate, end up demonstrating that love defeats or spreads calamity"; he adds rhetorically: "Could an ideal of greater subversive power be found?" For Cortijo Ocaña, the democratic, egalitarian nature of love in the newly emerging forms of sentimental fiction harboured the potential to disrupt the dominant order of the fourteenth- and fifteenth-century Iberian Peninsula. Nevertheless, he concludes that sentimentalism is "deliberative," a rhetorical exercise far removed from affective reality: "There are not masculine or feminine personages of flesh and blood, but rhetorical possibilities of argumentation made into characters."[33] This is, above all, the distinction I wish to make with respect to *Persiles y Sigismunda*: though relying on various rhetorical techniques to do so, Cervantes distils his characters from the often messy, unstable, and discordant emotions of everyday life, preserving a verisimilar relation to the "flesh and blood" of lived experience. Not only does this emotional realism stand to threaten the cultural politics of representation, aesthetic decorum, and social hierarchy to a greater degree than the "deliberative" nature of sentimentalism, but also, in Hegelian terms, it could be said that the novel thus manages to synthesize world and mind.

The omnipresence of the specifically Mediterranean world in *Persiles y Sigismunda* is a keystone of the text's imbrication with the quotidian, and therefore of its distinction from prior exemplars of romance. We should recall that fully half of the narrative – books 3 and 4 – is set in the Mediterranean, including the disembarkation of the characters in Lisbon and their trek across Spain, southern France, and northern Italy, culminating with their arrival in Rome. But even among the remote northern latitudes of the first two books, the Mediterranean makes frequent, if subtle, incursions. Many of the characters who appear in the Septentrion – including the Spanish Antonio, the Portuguese Sosa, the Italian Rutilio, and the French Renato – recount stories from the Mediterranean of their origins.[34] When the entourage's ship runs ashore in the lands of King Policarpo, an old man explains to a crowd of stunned onlookers that the voices coming from inside are not a miracle but merely the foreign nature of a galley that has overturned and trapped its passengers inside. The survivors are rescued only because the man, having witnessed a similar event on the Genoese coast years prior, draws on his Mediterranean experience, and begins his intervention thus: "I remember, my Lord, having seen in the Mediterranean Sea ..." (Yo me acuerdo, señor, haber visto en el mar Mediterráneo ...).[35] A few pages later, the Granadan Morisca Cenotia appears, having fled inquisitorial persecution in her native Spain. Among the northern climes of books 1 and 2, even the poetic language of the text betrays its Mediterranean pedigree. After a storm forces some of the characters to take refuge in a dinghy, which then drifts onto a snowy island, the narrator remarks that "the fortunes of the sea are miserable and frightening" ([m]iserables son y temerosas las fortunas del mar).[36] According to Romero Muñoz, *fortunas* is "an essentially Mediterranean term" to describe tempestuous weather.[37] Indeed, the narrative action of the first half of the novel traffics not only in squalls and shipwrecks but also captivity, slavery, piracy, intercultural commerce and violence, multiple languages, and religious and racial difference – in essence, all those elements identified earlier as the defining traits of Mediterranean literature.

In chapter 2, I remarked at length on the "wetness" of *Persiles y Sigismunda* and how it serves as a foil for the largely desiccated landscape of *Don Quijote*, since most of the Byzantine novel's first half transpires at sea or on islands and coasts.[38] This is yet another way in which the Mediterranean can be seen to infiltrate the distant and peregrine nature of the Septentrional backdrop of the text. It is widely accepted that Olaus Magnus's *Historia de gentibus septentrionalibus* of 1555 inspired Cervantes to elect the locale as a setting for his last work; however, Magnus's tome devotes strikingly few pages to the open sea and islands, focusing instead on the continent and the folkloric traditions of the northern peoples.[39] Although Tasso had singled out the Septentrion as an ideal poetic space for marvels,[40] behind this exoticism there lurks in *Persiles y Sigismunda* a more fundamental engagement with the Mediterranean. This specificity distinguishes the novel from the Greek romance that, as Cervantes tells us in his ambition to compete with Heliodorus, inspired its genesis. Even though critics like Northrop Frye have pegged the classical genre for its Mediterranean setting and Levantine characters,[41] and despite the fact that Heliodorus's *Aethiopica* (and, for that matter, Lope's *El peregrino en su patria*) is more overtly Mediterranean, Bakhtin perceptively describes the "size and diversity" of the Greek romance's land- and seascapes as "utterly abstract." "For a shipwreck one must have a sea," he explains, "but which particular sea (in the geographical and historical sense) makes no difference at all [...] The adventuristic events of the Greek romance have no essential ties with any particular details of individual countries that might figure in the novel[; ...] the place figures in solely as a naked, abstract expanse of space." Due to the reasons just enumerated and the examples that follow, the Septentrional world is not an abstraction but a reflection, albeit defamiliarized, of the Mediterranean world to which Cervantes bore witness. "A depiction of one's own world – no matter where or what it is," Bakhtin concludes, "could never achieve that degree of abstractness necessary for Greek adventure-time."[42] Setting aside the bigger, thornier question of the novel's verisimilitude, or lack thereof,[43] for Cervantes the Northern Seas afforded a stage not so much for beguiling the reader with wonders that strained its precepts but for pondering more proximate waters, for vicariously feeling the Mediterranean experiences and emotions that themselves challenged the bounds of poetic language. In what follows, a close reading of various moments of the text will serve to chart how not even the extremes of language, in attempting to represent the intense affects of this experience, fully escape the semantic field of the sea.

Aporias

The narrative action of *Persiles y Sigismunda* is founded upon a secret –
that of the amorous relationship between the two protagonists, Periandro
and Auristela, who masquerade as siblings until the very end of the
work. Owing to the fantastic nature of their wanderings and the need
to conceal vital biographical details, they and other characters circulate
in an affective economy of undecidability. Populating the novel are numerous instances in which an intra-diegetic audience finds itself at odds
over how to respond emotionally to an event or to another character's
narration. Likewise, an uncertainty or inability to effectively interpret
another's emotional state – contrary to the majority of cases in Cervantes's
other works – pervades many of the novel's interpersonal exchanges,
often originating or sustaining narrative conflict. This impenetrability
recalls not only Ludwig Wittgenstein's concept of "private language,"
or that which communicates individual sensations and is therefore un-
intelligible to others,[44] but also the Renaissance proverb, rescued from
antiquity by Alberti and others, that lamented the lack of a window
on the chest that would allow one to know another's true feelings.[45]
At other times, the text emphasizes the wide disparity of emotional responses that a given event or story may provoke in its spectators, an
effect accordant with Alcalá Galán's portrayal of *Persiles y Sigismunda* as
a "seedbed of stories," as a text whose ultimate outcome, after the con-
templation of an endless range of possibilities, seems to arise as much
by happenstance as by a fixed authorial ideal or intention.[46]

Boundless and equivocal qualities leaven the emotional states of
characters, too. Among the "amorous schemes and machinations" (tra-
zas y máquinas amorosas) of Policarpo's palace, for example, the narrator stresses "the hearts of the confused lovers: Auristela was jealous;
Sinforosa, infatuated; Periandro, disturbed; and Arnaldo, obstinate"
(los pechos de los confusos amantes: Auristela, celosa; Sinforosa, en-
amorada; Periandro, turbado y, Arnaldo, pertinaz).[47] Though of a piece
with my prior discussion of the constitutive diversity of Cervantine
affectivity, this quotation reveals how the difficulty already inherent
in articulating inner emotional states is exacerbated when everybody
is feeling something completely different. Earlier, in the aftermath of
the holocaust that destroyed the barbarous island, the mixed emotional
reaction among the party of survivors is underscored when they dis-
embark, "shedding tears of grief but also showing signs of happiness"
(entre lágrimas de tristeza y entre muestras de alegría),[48] and this deceptively simple trope of "between sad and happy" (entre triste y alegre)
reappears incessantly throughout the novel.[49] In many such examples

this emotional variability materializes not only among the distinctive members of a group but also within single characters, oscillating at the level of the interpersonal as well as the individual. These antitheses, not uncommon in the *cancionero* and in Petrarchan prosody, divest meaning from polar extremes (*alegre* and *triste*) and deposit it in an intermediary space, a space of in-betweenness, consigning true semantic responsibility to the preposition *entre*. It is as though the conventional, ossified signifiers of emotion have lost their capacity to carry meaning, relegated at best to the status of catachresis and denoting something no linguistic term can adequately convey.

As an oxymoron, the juxtaposition of two contradictory ideas reveals a conceptual paradox, one that need not be confined to poetic language or be foreign to everyday encounters – to cite two of the most hackneyed examples from the emotive realm, bittersweet feelings or the shedding of tears of joy. It therefore bears reiterating that Cervantes's insistence on creative, contradictory, and often disorderly linguistic constructions is evocative of the lived reality of affective experience, of the emotional paradoxes and conflictive internal sentiments that are part and parcel of human existence. Beyond a mere *contradictio in terminis*, however, oxymorons such as "sad happiness" strike with a double blow: the left hook of a negative emotion followed instantly by the right jab of a positive one, leaving language reeling from the jarring impact of a one-two punch. Such a move itself is paradoxical because it underscores the impossibilities of language (i.e., the lack of a word to fully express a complex emotional state) while highlighting its extreme possibilities (i.e., the inventive cobbling together of antagonistic terms to express a complex emotional state). It is precisely these impossible possibilities that undergird the inventiveness of Cervantes's emotional language. As a kind of metasememe and like the language of mysticism that shares identical tropes, such oxymorons *leave* language by deviating or escaping from conventional linguistic signs.[50] This rhetorical deviation – analogous to the geographical deviation of *Persiles y Sigismunda*'s protagonists – continually destabilizes language in the text.

By foreclosing on language's tendency of coming to rest in a monolithic signifier, these affective aporias mimic the Augustinian understanding of the soul as marked by perpetual motion. The narrator invokes this concept while explaining the amorous desire that overcomes Arnaldo for Auristela:

Since our souls are in continual movement and can't stop or rest [*sosegar*] except at their center – which is God, for whom they were nurtured – it's no wonder our thoughts are changeable; we take this one up, drop that one, follow one, forget another. But the thought bringing us closest to inner peace [*sosiego*] will be the best, provided it's free from mistaken ideas.

Como están nuestras almas siempre en continuo movimiento, y no pueden parar ni sosegar sino en su centro, que es Dios, para quien fueron criadas, no es maravilla que nuestros pensamientos se muden, que éste se tome, aquél se deje, uno se prosiga y otro se olvide, y el que más cerca anduviere de su sosiego, ése será el mejor, cuando no se mezcle con error de entendimiento.[51]

The continuous yet capricious nature of desire can be arrested only with the death of the soul and its return to God, its "center," which – like affect – tends to confound language.[52] Yet this conception of desire as lack would seem at variance with the "most important" axiom of the novel,[53] the last one of the "Flower of Unusual Aphorisms" (Flor de aforismos peregrinos), a metacollection of "maxims taken from truth itself" (sentencias sacadas de la misma verdad): "Don't desire anything and you'll be the richest man in the world" (No desees, y serás el más rico hombre del mundo).[54] Although the character of Antonio, marvelling at the sagacity of the aphorism, later summarizes it by dint of reference to the notion of lack,[55] here we have yet another aporia, one that constitutes a veritable axis of the novel: how is one to achieve the lofty goal of ceasing to desire when the interminable movement of the soul impedes it? How is one to fulfil a lack (to go from *desasosiego* to *sosiego*) that originates in the soul's estrangement from its divine centre?[56]

The association of desire with lack, articulated as early as Plato, was taken up by Jacques Lacan in his theory that desire is never expressed in relation to an object but to lack (*manque*) itself, a lack that comes to represent that of the signifier in the "Other" and, along an unending metonymic chain of desire, of the individual self. In his study of travel and motion in Cervantes's works Hutchinson takes issue with the Lacanian model in so far as it exerts an arresting effect on movement and neglects "how desire deploys its energies, how it's felt and how strongly, how it interacts with the desired other and redefines human relationships, how it improvises, fluctuates, emerges, and submerges."[57] Although I agree with Hutchinson that *Persiles y Sigismunda* mobilizes a more dynamic representation of desire than can be understood solely through the static nature of lack, my reading suggests that these two approaches are not incompatible but, rather, form a productive tension throughout the text. Amorous desire therein is propelled forth by the unrelenting drive to satiate itself, yet its momentum is impeded at every turn by the competing wants of other characters and by all manner of narrative hurdles, interruptions, and digressions. The vigour of the soul comes up against the impossibility of satisfying its continual movements and attachments, a phenomenon that finds its correlative in a plot whose forward progress is constantly stymied by the lack of narrative closure. The consummation of Periandro and Auristela's desire is likewise deferred until the "center" of the Catholic Church, Rome, and very end of the text. This protracted frustration of desires, contrary to erstwhile critiques of the novel, is precisely the point of Cervantes's aesthetic craft, as showcased by Hutchinson's keen assessment of emotions as movement: "As motion, emotions thrive on discursive disorder and discontinuity; their pathways are no simple lines here, but instead irregular routes whose traveling involves leaps and unexpected moves of the mind choreographed so as to let emotions exert themselves."[58] What I have classified as affective aporias generate narrative and interpersonal friction while allowing emotions to "exert themselves," attesting finally to *Persiles y Sigismunda*'s intensification of affect that is produced, paradoxically, through the very forbearance and withdrawal of emotion.

Ineffability

A further catalyst for the aporetic withholding of emotional signifiers unfolds in the form of ineffability.[59] Operating at both intra- and extra-diegetic levels, the topos varies from the explicitly stated unrepresentability of certain feelings to more subtle accounts in which silence becomes the salient figure. In the latter case, the text is perforated by productive silences, which not only bear witness to the abiding difficulty of communicating internal emotional states but also stand as sites of signification in their own right. When the pilgrims encounter the love-stricken Portuguese soldier Manuel de Sosa Coitiño, for example, he describes bidding farewell to his beloved Leonora just before his departure on a military campaign to Barbary thus: "I didn't know what to do, nor could I do anything but keep still and let silence express my confusion" (ni supe ni pude hacer otra cosa que callar y dar con mi silencio indicio de mi turbación). Leonora's father replies, "it may be that this silence speaks more in your favor than any other eloquence" (puede ser que este silencio hable en su favor de vuesa merced más que alguna otra retórica).[60] Although language may fail them in expressing intense affects, the text endows these characters with the consciousness that such a failure may ultimately do more justice to their feelings than words ever could. The validation of Sosa's silence corroborates the long-standing belief that rhetorical arts were not as reliable as nonverbal cues for judging the veracity of another's emotions; the dubious sincerity of love preoccupied real-life individuals as well, especially as forms of amorous expression became increasingly codified.[61] Although Luhmann concludes that this question was resolved by the *honnestes gens,* or those sectors of the early modern populace who due to their nobility were presumed to be more truthful, in *Persiles y Sigismunda* love remains unstable and resists certainty, even among such aristocratic characters as Periandro and Auristela, whose relationship finds itself in jeopardy until the last pages of the novel.[62] Even if they manage to overcome their doubts in time for a happy dénouement, Sosa's fate, as remarked earlier, is less forgiving: after he has been jilted at the altar, his silence eventually gives way to death from a broken heart.

In his study of the philosophical implications of ineffability, William Franke underscores the irony of meaningful silence, remarking that "what ultimately defeats all articulation remains nevertheless the object-elect, the darling, of copious discourses."[63] One of the most striking examples of this phenomenon corresponds with what is perhaps the most sudden and intense irruption of affect in the entire novel, when Periandro all but perishes after falling from a tower near the end of book 3. Auristela, believing him dead, desperately rushes to her lover's broken body in an attempt to capture a part of his soul through his expiring breath, a traditional act of piety that, not incidentally, the narrator reports would have been impossible: she "placed her mouth on his, trying to gather into herself some small part that might be left of his soul; but even had there been something left, she couldn't have taken it in, for his clenched teeth wouldn't let her" (puesta la boca con la suya, esperaba a recoger en sí alguna reliquia, si del alma le hubiese quedado; pero, aunque le hubiera quedado, no pudiera recibilla, porque los traspillados dientes le negaban la entrada). Constanza, in contrast, "overcome by emotion" (dando lugar a la pasión), finds herself completely immobilized by the shock of the occurrence and unable to help her troubled companions. Bartolomé, their mule-driver and guide, is the only one who outwardly emotes, "crying bitterly" and "show[ing] in his eyes the great pain he felt in his soul" (mostró con los ojos el grave dolor que en el alma sentía, llorando amargamente). Yet as the narrator observes, all of the characters' reactions share one trait in common – that of silence: "everyone was suffering the bitter affliction I've described, without yet expressing their feelings in words" ([e]stando todos en la amarga aflicción que he dicho, sin que hasta entonces ninguna lengua hubiese publicado su sentimiento).[64]

Silence thus becomes synonymous with inexpressible grief and affliction, representing the paralysing effect that a traumatic event exerts on the body and on the capacity for language. The delayed reaction that accompanies extreme shock is then delayed even further by the subsequent interruption of the scene by the seemingly casual arrival of Deleasir,

Belarminia, and Félix Flora, three French maidens with whom the group had become acquainted earlier; this is followed immediately by the appearance of a cadre of armed men intent on kidnapping Félix Flora. The abrupt arrival of these characters serves to lade the affective weight of the episode by incorporating additional witnesses to the accident and by once again postponing its resolution. The piling of one unexpected conflict on top of another also disorients the reader, who is forced to bracket the original event and await its resolution only after the secondary conflict has been introduced (but not yet resolved either). The narrative voice, always astutely conscious of its complicity in these types of trickery, returns to the moribund Periandro only after reiterating the silence of the scene: "their tongues have wrapped their laments in bitter silence" (las lenguas, en amargo silencio tienen depositadas sus quejas).[65] Here we can interpret *tongue* or *lengua* in the dual meaning of the word – it denotes the organ responsible for producing language as well as, synecdochically, language itself. The fundamental message is clear: tongues falter and fall silent when faced with the challenge of expressing intense emotional affliction.[66]

In addition to these instances of productive silence, language calls attention to its inefficacy in vocalizing affect in more explicit ways. When Auristela is released from captivity on the barbarous island, the use of adynaton allows the narrative voice to openly ponder its own limitations in portraying Periandro's feelings: "What tongue could say, or what pen could write, what Periandro felt when he knew Auristela was the condemned person now set free?" (¿Qué lengua podrá decir, o qué pluma escribir, lo que sintió Periandro cuando conoció ser Auristela la condenada y la libre?)[67] With consistency to the unremitting interruptions of the narrative action, at other times Cervantes figures the affect of startled surprise with a sudden break or reversal in the text itself, such as when Auristela, already overcome by her jealousy of Periandro's many suitors, laments her fortune on board a ship in book 1.

[T]he ship's captain listened very carefully to her words without knowing what conclusion to draw from them; he only said that ... But he didn't say anything because in an instant and split second a wind came up so suddenly and so strongly that it snatched the words out of his mouth and made him get up without responding to Auristela.

[E]scuchaba atentísimamente el capitán del navío y no sabía qué conclusión sacar de [sus palabras]; sólo paró en decir ... Pero no dijo nada, porque, en un instante y en un momentáneo punto le arrebató la palabra de la boca un viento que se levantó, tan súbito y tan recio que le hizo poner en pie sin responder a Auristela.[68]

Owing to Cervantes's use of yet another rhetorical figure, aposiopesis (a sentence rendered incomplete because of an inability to continue), Auristela is denied the cathartic possibility of a complete dialogic exchange with her interlocutor, his own words arrested by the pregnant pause that advertises yet another precipitous turn in the narrative. The affective tension of the episode is prolonged and suspended, as it were, by the *puntos suspensivos* of the text.

In fact, I would argue that the novel is exceedingly adept at propagating and sustaining what I have already termed a kind of sentimental suspense, *pace* the popular view that "Cervantes did not write a suspenseful book, largely because he chose to delay and even arrest its plot by some dozen subplots."[69] Although such "retarding elements" have often been bound up with epic poetry – leading prominent critics to debate whether they augment or diminish suspense, or exert no effect on it[70] – from my perspective it is precisely these delays that in *Persiles y Sigismunda* prohibit the timely resolution of the characters' emotional affliction and thus permit readers to maintain their own affective investment in the plot, hanging by the dearth of emotional dénouements.[71] Just as the etymological ancestors of the word *suspense* evoke the same uncertainty and deferment of the affective aporias addressed earlier, so these narrative obstacles mirror the course of an amorous relationship in real life; according to Luhmann, the culmination and the demise of love nearly coincide, "and one therefore almost had to fear such a point, defer it or attempt to avoid it [...] Precisely for this reason one had to hold resistance, detours or obstacles to one's love in high regard, because only through them does love endure."[72] Paradoxically, the chronic setbacks that Periandro and Auristela encounter to the consummation of their relationship allow not only their love but also the reader's emotional investment in the text to endure.

Such sentimental suspense is unambiguously palpable during the several chapters set in King Policarpo's palace, with the plurality of love triangles, jealousies, and unrequited desires that fill their pages. When it seems that the restless tension of these conditions has become unbearable to the characters themselves, Policarpo implores his daughter Sinforosa to begin to release it by breaking her silence and articulating her affliction: "No more suspense, daughter, no more silence, my friend – no more" (No más suspensión, hija; no más silencio, amiga; no más). Shortly thereafter, the motif of suspension resurfaces in the tense exchange between Clodio and Rutilio: "Rutilio's words struck Clodio dumb, and with his surprised silence the author of this great story brought the chapter to a close" (Suspendióse Clodio con las razones de Rutilio, con cuya suspensión dio fin a este capítulo el autor desta grande historia).[73] The author of this great story, indeed, plays upon the suspended emotions of his characters to ferry those of his readers across the rupture of the chapter break. Although its abruptness threatens to breach the flow of the plot, such a calculated risk betrays the purpose of its design: the readers' desire for narrative resolution echoes the characters' desire for emotional resolution, and both are dashed by a text bereft of the will to swiftly fulfil them. On the one hand, this quintessentially Cervantine move could be seen to parody the romance genre through its heavy-handed recourse to the authorial bag of tricks, but, on the other, it is an acute technique in its own right for circumventing readerly eagerness for closure and prolonging the sentimental suspense.

At the beginning of the following chapter we find this suspense intact: "They all had someone to share their thoughts with; Policarpo had his daughter and Clodio had Rutilio; only the perplexed Periandro was reflecting alone, for Auristela's words stirred up so many thoughts he didn't know which one to turn to in order to alleviate his grief." (Todos tenían con quien comunicar sus pensamientos: Policarpo con su hija y, Clodio, con Rutilio; sólo el suspenso Periandro los comunicaba consigo mismo, que le engendraron tanto las razones de Auristela, que no sabía a cuál acudir que le aliviase su pesadumbre.) The "suspended" Periandro, addled by doubts about Auristela's motives, goes on to indulge in a disquietingly modern soliloquy of self-lamentation. So overcome by his emotions is the forlorn lover that he unwittingly pronounces, for the first time in the novel, his and his "sister's" true names (Persiles and Sigismunda), startling and obliging himself to verify that nobody has overheard him. Anxious for relief from this emotional strain, he proceeds to brood over Auristela's jealousy and his own feelings for her, eventually concluding that "my love has no terms that can encircle it nor words that can declare it" (mi amor no tiene términos que le encierre ni palabras que le declare).[74] This is one of the most expressly inexpressible instances of the novel. Accentuating an already psychologically fragile moment of the text with his inability to articulate its closure, Periandro's resignation gestures towards a love that defies all verbalization. This frenzy of *je ne sais quoi* ultimately produces his decision to abandon the spoken word in favour of putting his feelings to paper in the form of a letter, thereby managing to defer even longer his therapeutic release of emotional tension and, likewise, that of the reader, who is forced to wait until a few pages later to read the letter (which itself is neither delivered nor recited to its intended recipient, Auristela).

Forthright confessions of the inability to express emotion aside, the topos of ineffability crops up more subtly in the mere refusal to articulate a feeling in words. While recounting his life story and the circumstances that have carried him to the barbarous island, the young Antonio, in one of the novel's best-known episodes, describes the moment he found himself on another island overrun by wild wolves. Claiming to have been warned "with a clear and distinct voice and in my own language" (en voz clara y distinta y en mi propia lengua) by a lone, merciful wolf to flee before he ended up being "torn apart by our claws and teeth" (hecho pedazos por nuestras uñas y dientes), he consigns the designation of his emotional state in this situation to his interlocutors: "I'll let you decide whether I was frightened or not" (Si quedé espantado o no, a vuestra consideración lo dejo).[75] Although this statement could easily be dismissed as a rhetorical convention or means of mitigating the threat that a protracted description of his fear might pose to his masculinity, its status as an utterance of ineffability is consonant with the tenor of the examples we have already seen. Yet the implications of this locution are even more substantial due to its immediate juxtaposition with a perfectly fluent, Spanish-speaking wolf. According to the widely known Aristotelian doctrine, the two characteristics that distinguish humans from animals are our capacity for reason and our use of language. Here, however, as in numerous other instances of the novel, we are presented with a character who is incapable not only of tempering his feelings with reason but also of fully articulating them in spoken language.[76] In effect, the text depicts language as something that undermines the silent tranquility of the soul by stirring up the passions, as the words of Auristela bear out: "While I kept quiet, my soul was at peace; then I spoke up and was at rest no more" (Mientras callé, estuvo en sosiego mi alma; hablé, y perdíle).[77]

Rarefaction of this sort, the almost nihilistic tendencies of linguistic forms of emotional expression, looms even as the pilgrims draw near their final destination. Upon entering Milan, they are informed that the most outstanding sight to behold in the city is the "Academy of the Elite" (Academia de los Entronados), an institution of world-renowned scholars. On this particular day, the visitors are told, the academy would be disputing whether love can exist without jealousy, and, when the topic is broached, the characters weigh in with their own thoughts on love. Auristela, verbally reproducing the most prevalent archetype of ineffability, claims, "I know not what love is, although I know what liking is" (no sé qué es amor, aunque sé lo que es querer bien), to which Belarminia retorts, "I don't understand this way of talking, or the difference between loving and liking" (No entiendo ese modo de hablar, ni la diferencia que hay entre amor y querer bien). Venturing a clarification, Auristela adds: "[T]hat thing people say is called love, which is a vehement passion of the soul, as they say, even when it doesn't cause jealousy, it can cause fears strong enough to take a person's life, and it seems to me that love can never ever be free from such fears." ([A]quello que dicen que se llama amor, que es una vehemente pasión del ánimo, como dicen, ya que no dé celos, puede dar temores que lleguen a quitar la vida, del cual temor a mí me parece que no puede estar libre el amor en ninguna manera.)[78] Her cumbersome gloss of love anticipates Fisher's classification of the emotion as precisely a "vehement" passion, challenging the efficacy of language in a way suggested by Belarminia ("No entiendo ese modo de hablar").

More importantly, Auristela's attempt at an elucidation hinges on a number of aporetic and negative utterances ("aquello que dicen que se llama," "no," "en ninguna manera"), thus distancing and estranging the very concept of love. The only assuredly affirmative content of her explanation is itself predicated on a negative: love is defined by a fear of loss that may, in turn, lead to the loss of life. Apophatic discourse also permeates Periandro's assenting reply immediately thereafter: "There's no one in love who, possessing what he loves, isn't afraid of losing it. There's no good fortune so solid it can't sway from side to side. There's no nail so strong it can stop the spin of the wheel of fortune." ([N]o hay ningún amante que esté en posesión de la cosa amada que no tema el perderla; no hay ventura tan firme que tal vez no dé vaivenes; no hay clavo tan fuerte que pueda detener la rueda de la fortuna.)[79] This anaphoric litany of negative impossibilities, along with the corresponding subjunctive mood, further emphasizes the abiding difficulties of limning the desires of the heart. Although Periandro expresses confidence that he could testify to the relationship between love and jealousy in a disputation with the Academy of the Elite, his apparent certainty is offset by his refusal to actually follow through with proving the assertion. Significantly, the debate never takes place in the text, and the group never hears the world-famous experts opine on a topic of utmost relevance to so many of the characters. The meaning of such an omission is unequivocal, for not even the erudite Socratic talents of renowned scholars are sufficient for bridging the gulf between theory and praxis, rhetoric and feeling, semantics and experience, that is insistently borne out in *Persiles y Sigismunda*. To try to describe love is to become entangled in syntactic binds, negative expressions, vacuous rhetoric, circumlocutions, and impossibilities of the sort uttered by what is nonetheless a plenitude of enamoured characters in the novel. The text thus points up the persistent correspondence between the *trabajos* or "trials" of love and those of language itself.

Materiality

The Cervantine impulse to mobilize affect through modes that challenge and expand the bounds of conventional language may be instructively analysed by means of one final categorization, that of materiality. Although I discussed at length in chapter 2 the specifically marine materiality of *Persiles y Sigismunda*, because this is a concept charged with a rather long history of critical divergence, I feel it necessary to clarify my understanding of the term in two principal, interrelated ways. First, I locate materiality in the slippages between content and form, a perception of *material* that proceeds from its vernacular usage as that which pertains to matter. In a more discrete sense of this definition, I also take *materiality* to mean that which designates the body as opposed to the soul or the spirit. Second, my approach responds to what cultural theorists of late have broadly denominated "non-representational theory," which undertakes the ways in which various forms of cultural production can be seen to collapse the Platonic distinction between appearance and the real.[80] Non-representational theory, of which affect has been a crucial focal point, seeks to demystify the privileged status of the Idea, while staking a claim for the inherent, sui generis meaning of material things themselves. The modern Peninsular literary critic Jo Labanyi has called for such "ways of thinking beyond, or outside of, representation" to be "a stimulus to new forms of research which [...] have not been tried in Spanish studies," citing affect and materiality as two avenues in need of further scholarship.[81] Along with the aporias and ineffability contemplated previously, here I will suggest that Cervantes, *avant la lettre*, provides an early modern response to this call for an exploration of non-representational forms through materiality, even though I maintain that his writing remains within – if at the outer limits of – the orbit of literary representation.

One of the most rudimentary devices for prodding and prying at these limits is the appeal to visual and ekphrastic realms, a recurrent motif in *Persiles y Sigismunda* upon which critics have seized in studies of the varying uses of painting, sculpture, and other pictorial arts in the novel.[82] Like the eleventh-century Al-Andalus thinker Ibn Hazm, who declared love to be as mutable as the iridescent colours of the dove's neck, Cervantes turned to visual modes to supplement conceptual language and render more intelligible the aporias of love.[83] As I have detailed in foregoing chapters, however, the representation of affect also relies on the semiotics of gesture, the gaze, and corporal manifestations such as sighs, cries, moans, and tears. The sense of sight was particularly prone to rouse emotions, a commonplace of Cervantes's era that the narrator evokes while describing the vengeful anger of the recently widowed Ruperta: "Anger, it is said, is a violent disturbance of the blood flowing near the heart, stirring in the chest at the sight of the offending object or sometimes merely at its memory" (La ira, según se dice, es una revolución de la sangre que está cerca del corazón, la cual se altera en el pecho con la vista del objeto que agravia y tal vez con la memoria). After naming the sundry objects that awaken her fury – a silver box with the likeness of her deceased husband, the sword that killed him, and the tunic she imagines still dripping with his blood – the narrator accents the material qualities of her rage:

> Enough tears rained down from her eyes to wet the relics of her suffering, and such sighs broke loose from her chest that the air near and far was thick with them [...] and sometimes it seemed that not tears, but fire, was pouring out of her eyes, and from her mouth, not sighs, but smoke, so tightly was she gripped by her emotions and her desire for revenge.

> Llovían lágrimas de sus ojos, bastantes a bañar las reliquias de su pasión; arrancaba suspiros del pecho, que condensaban el aire cerca y lejos [...] parecía que arrojaba por los ojos, no lágrimas, sino fuego y, por la boca, no suspiros, sino humo: tan sujeta la tenía su pasión y el deseo de vengarse.[84]

Hence the text enlists the visual register to substantiate the potency of her smoldering wrath, assigning to the already material manifestations of emotion (tears, sighs) more visibly forceful elements (fire, smoke).

It is true that these examples, their vivid imagery notwithstanding, are ultimately just as dependent on language as any other form of verbal representation is – they are, after all, still words on a page, and poetry has by definition always enjoyed extensive recourse to visual imagery. But when they are considered as a whole and alongside the techniques enumerated here, it becomes clear that a more robust investment in hypostasizing, in giving shape to, affect is at stake. Notice how the narrator further dramatizes the image of the bereaved Ruperta: "Can't you see her weeping? Can't you see her sighing? Can't you see her beside herself with rage? Can't you see her brandishing the murderous sword? Can't you see her kissing the bloody shirt, her sobs interrupting the words?" (¿Veisla llorar? ¿Veisla suspirar? ¿Veisla no estar en sí? ¿Veisla blandir la espada matadora? ¿Veisla besar la camisa ensangrentada y que rompe las palabras con sollozos?)[85] This sudden anaphoric apostrophe to readers demands that we reflect upon the mental *phantasia* that Ruperta's emotions materialize, implicating us in the task of verifying the efficacy of their visual representation. That the widow's sobbing "breaks" (rompe) her words underscores moreover the superior might accorded to materiality over discursive language.

Similarly antagonistic juxtapositions between words and non-linguistic signifiers of affect emerge elsewhere in the novel, the latter always being given the upper hand. After Auristela, consumed by jealousy of Sinforosa's pursuit of Periandro, attempts to rationalize her feelings to him, the narrator imparts the following: "At this point Auristela finished her speech and began to weep tears that undid and erased everything she'd just said" (Aquí dio fin Auristela a su razonamiento y principio a unas lágrimas que desdecían y borraban todo cuanto había dicho).[86] It is as though her tears spill over the extra-diegetic boundary of the text, soaking the page and causing the ink to run and blur into a state of unintelligibility, her words negated by the material manifestation of her true feelings. These tears do not serve to reference a prior, more authentic signified, but rather embody and circulate meaning in and of themselves. Although it cannot ultimately qualify as non-representational, this is the most patent example of how the novel's emotional language grates against the limits of conventional poetics, defying Platonic distinctions between diegesis and mimesis or appearance and the real. Tears perform other remarkably active roles in the novel as well, to the point of constituting a veritable leitmotiv or what Romero Muñoz has coined a "hyperbole of tears."[87] Here are just two of many examples of the text's fondness for lachrymose characters: "[I] increased the waters of the sea with some that poured from my eyes" (aumenté las aguas del mar con las que derramaba de mis ojos);[88] "Periandro's eyes filled with tears like two fountains, while those of the others present overflowed like rivers" (hiziéronse fuentes los [ojos] de Periandro y ríos los de todos los circunstantes).[89] The hyperbolic and hydraulic force of these tears threatens to drown the purely linguistic, desiccated signifier in a deluge of materiality, neutralizing the discursive logic of the text, just as Auristela's weaping washed away her words of reason.

Lest we conceive of this materiality as a solution to the aporetic and ineffable, however, we should observe that affect continues to pose problems of undecidability and impossibility. Despite their edge over language in relaying internal emotional states in the text, the visual, gestural, and material remain equally vexing and susceptible to the vagaries of subjective interpretation, which is liable and indeed likely to engender the same discord and uncertainty among characters. Such is the case with two examples involving Auristela: "Auristela gave no answer to all this, but tears came to her eyes and began to bathe her rosy cheeks. Arnaldo was very confused by her reaction and couldn't figure out if it came from distress or happiness." (A todo esto no respondió palabra Auristela, antes le vinieron las lágrimas a los ojos, que comenzaron a bañar sus rosadas mejillas. Confuso Arnaldo de tal acidente, no supo determinarse si de pesar o alegría podía proceder semejante acontecimiento.)[90] As ubiquitous as they are, tears buoy an unstable semiotics, as singularly insufficient as words for determining with any degree of certitude Auristela's true feelings.[91] Later on, "she was watching Sinforosa in almost the same way and with the same affects, even though each had different intentions: Sinforosa was watching with simple benevolence, but Auristela with jealousy." (Auristela casi por el mismo modo y con los mismos afectos miraba a Sinforosa, aunque en las dos eran diferentes las intenciones: Auristela miraba con celos y, Sinforosa, con sencilla benevolencia.)[92] Here again, outward emotional cues can prove deceptive, since nearly identical bodily affects and manners of gazing belie inward emotional states of an entirely discrepant nature. Facial legibility is precarious, in spite of Auristela's own avowed talent for physiognomy.[93] The early modern popular faith in this practice meets with utter failure in communicating love in the novel, this time in Renato's account of his relationship with Eusebia: "[O]nly my eyes let her know I adored her, but she, either because she failed to notice or failed to care, did nothing with either her eyes or her tongue to let me know she understood me" (sólo con los ojos la di a entender que la adoraba, y ella, o ya descuidada o no advertida, ni con sus ojos ni con su lengua me daba a entender que me entendía).[94] Although characters in Cervantes's other works are remarkably adept at intuiting the emotional states of one another, especially when accompanied by a visual cue, those in *Persiles y Sigismunda* often founder at understanding, deciphering, and sharing emotions, even when they produce a visible, material, or corporeal response unmediated by subterfuge or pretence. Here affect confounds discursive as well as sensory modes of interpretation, each one as tenuous a hermeneutics of emotion as the other.

Conclusion

Cervantes's recognition that love "is a vehement passion of the soul" and that its "manifestations are as diverse as they are inscrutable and its laws as numerous as they are variable" (las condiciones de amor son tan diferentes como injustas y sus leyes tan muchas como variables)[95] prefigures Fisher's distinction of love as a "passion" that resists verbal representation.[96] As though goaded by this challenge, however, Cervantes coaxes this resistance into an emotional language that, as

I have illustrated, encompasses various rhetorical figures (including hyperbole, meiosis, auxesis, anaphora, apostrophe, adynaton, and aposiopesis); the appropriation of classical topoi (such as the paradox and antithesis); the taking up of eminently mystical concepts (oxymora, ineffability); the leveraging of alternative idioms (ekphrastic and visual language); and the probing of aesthetic horizons beyond the bounds of monolithic signifiers and diegetic convention (materiality). On the one hand, these *techne* manage to countervail the vehemence of love, to ballast the contentious and indeterminate nature of emotions across multiple narrative levels. But, on the other hand, from the text's refusal to fully resolve the instability of affect we can infer a number of subtler yet more significant conclusions. First, it reflects both the larger narrative structure of *Persiles y Sigismunda* itself, with its interruptions, interdictions, digressions, and deferrals prolonged until the very last pages, and Cervantes's concern to avoid the blithe sentimentalism of the Greek romance while pressing the classical genre into the service of his own literary innovation. Second, and more fundamentally, the aporetic qualities of the novel signal a wariness towards logocentric forms of language, universalizing logics, and apodictic discourse. The denial of a singularly effective hermeneutic for interpreting affect suggests portentous implications for knowledge in Counter-reformation Spain, as well as an almost postmodern scepticism of consensus and grand narratives, advocating instead for a collective plurality in which dissent is not repressed but productively valued.[97] In short, in fashioning a different practice of language, Cervantes offers us a *language of difference.* In book 3 the narrator makes a kindred statement about the diversity of stories in the text: "Long pilgrimages always bring with them diverse occurrences, and since diversity is composed of different things the situations encountered will all necessarily be different as well" (Las peregrinaciones largas siempre traen consigo diversos acontecimientos y, como la diversidad se compone de cosas diferentes, es forzoso que los casos lo sean).[98] And yet, while insisting on the relative nature of subjective experience, *Persiles y Sigismunda* does not reject out of hand the concept of absolute truth, as would be expected, say, in a Derridean model of aporia. Rather, it subsumes the normative standards of truth under its own affirmative valuation of difference.

The periodic discussions of history and fiction in the novel corroborate this, from the aforementioned passage that equates history with poetry;[99] to the directive to endow the latter with "accurate details" and "an appearance of fact" to compensate for the foundational lie of fiction ("guisar sus acciones con tanta puntualidad [...] y con tanta verisimilitud"); to the ambivalence between history and story that dwells in the work's own subtitle of *Historia septentrional*.[100] More concretely, this prompts us to recall once again the perseverance with which the Mediterranean makes historically trodden inroads into the otherwise outlandish setting of the Septentrion. This is, after all, where a character like the Moorish Cenotia can lament thus:

> [P]ersecution in Spain by those known as Inquisitors tore me from my homeland, for when one is forced to leave it, one doesn't simply leave but feels torn away. I came to this island by strange roundabout ways, through countless dangers, and since I almost always felt as if they were nearby I kept turning my head around, thinking those dogs – which I fear to this day – were nipping at my skirts.

> La persecución de los que llaman inquisidores en España me arrancó de mi patria, que cuando se sale por fuerza de ella, antes puede decirse arrancada que salida. Vine a esta isla por extraños rodeos, por infinitos peligros, casi siempre como si estuvieran cerca, volviendo la cabeza atrás, pensando que me mordían las faldas los perros, que aun hasta aquí temo.[101]

Here the geographical remoteness of the Northern Seas not only serves in an arbitrary or abstract fashion to exoticize the familiar or even to sidestep censorial scrutiny from the very institution named in the passage.[102] The fictitious setting actually functions in a more straightforward and historically conscious way to inflate the distance travelled by the Morisco diaspora and therefore to sharpen the critique of a policy whose effects did in truth redound well beyond the Mediterranean itself. The expulsion that stripped Cenotia of her homeland leaves her with the enduring dread, latent paranoia, and psychological trauma of the tortuous and hazardous flight from Spain. Her fear becomes yet another testament to the ineluctable link between affect and the Mediterranean, its tribulations having undoubtedly bred and exacerbated emotional predicaments not only for those historical individuals who found themselves subject to its misfortunes but also for their friends, spouses, and lovers who awaited news on terra firma with similar anxiety. If scholars are correct in asserting that the Greek novel's early modern rediscovery and surge in popularity was due to sixteenth-century conversos, who "could 'identify' with the heroes of Byzantine romance, whose literary lives of wandering and travail adumbrated their own very real *trabajos* during the Second Diaspora,"[103] then the material, contemporary Mediterranean of *Persiles y Sigismunda* must necessarily have felt even more relatable. So it is that the Mediterranean's frequent incursions in the text, whether implied or overt, make waves that ripple far beyond it. The Septentrion serves less as a loophole for evading the poetic strictures of verisimilitude than as a loupe through which to magnify the Mediterranean presence therein, which nips at the narrative's heels at nearly every Northern turn, haunting the text in a way not unlike that of Cenotia's inquisitors.

Moreover, by depicting emotions in all their deferrals, discordance, and difficulties, the language of the text can be seen to amplify the very limits of verisimilitude, enlarging the *impossible possibilities* that undergird language. Unlike in the novel's forbear of the romance genre, which according to Frye tends to avoid "the ambiguities of ordinary life, where everything is a mixture of good and bad,"[104] in *Persiles y Sigismunda* the consciously ambivalent and indeterminate qualities of emotion echo the uncertainties of love and desire in lived experience. "The language of this work," Wilson contends, "is at times so innovative, so gnostic in its stance toward authority, that it disrupts the signifying order, expanding the bounds of the possible."[105] According to Aristotelian poetics, upon which the narrator's metafictional reflection noted earlier is based, history represents what *did* happen while fiction imagines what *could have* happened. However, a fictional representation should always adhere to a standard of verisimilitude, such that a verisimilar impossibility is always preferable to an "inverisimilar" possibility.[106] What may well be a pre-eminent truth of *Persiles y Sigismunda* lies conspicuously in this distinction: its affective impossibilities are verisimilar. In real life, emotion – and love, specifically – is often aporetic and ineffable. It can be hindered by obstacles, misunderstandings, and differences. Love can be a *trabajo* or trial that is difficult to resolve, and the more cynical of us might even claim that "true" love is in fact impossible.[107] Perhaps it is this engagement with the Byzantine feelings of everyday life, this poetics of the prosaic, that makes his last story one of Cervantes's most human, as well as a fitting culmination to the literary career of an author whose own life and work converged on the affective experience of the Mediterranean. As though a spectral voice were beckoning to Braudel from the torrid expanse of the literary longue durée, in his expiring breath Cervantes enjoins readers to remember, and revel in, the individual stories that movingly immortalize this experience in a language loosened from its moorings.

Afterword

Let us close by visiting one final micro-narrative, among those which, as I have suggested in preceding examples, comprise the very fabric of Cervantine affectivity and the literary Mediterranean. These themes are epitomized in the oft-commented episode of the false captives in *Persiles y Sigismunda*. In brief, it begins when the band of pilgrims encounters in a nameless Spanish village two young men attired in the garb of recently rescued captives. Displaying an elaborately painted canvas that depicts the Mediterranean Sea itself – replete with ships and galleys, skirmishes between Christian and Turkish forces, and the port city of Algiers – the men dramatically narrate, with the additional visual and aural aid of whips and chains, the circumstances that led to their apparent capture and imprisonment. Among the crowd of spectators, however, are two elderly mayors of the town, one of whom, like Cervantes himself, had served in the royal galleys before enduring five years of captivity in Barbary. When he perceives holes in the young men's tale, the mayor challenges them to corroborate various details about their supposed ordeal, a test they promptly fail. Resolved to swiftly punish such a vile deception, he dispatches a man to fetch donkeys on which to parade the counterfeit captives through the streets in public shame. Before any asses can be located – a touch of comic relief in a place where, the mayor grumbles, there is a surplus of the animal – the impostors remorsefully confess to having fleeced the crowd with a cock-and-bull story, and Periandro intervenes to join them in pleading for leniency. Urged by the natural forbearance of his colleague, the mayor eventually acquiesces, determining not only to refrain from castigating the false captives but also to redress voluntarily the factual oversights of their tale so that "from now on no one will catch them making mistakes in their Latin, I mean, in their made-up story" (de aquí adelante ninguno les coja en mal latín en cuanto a su fingida historia).[1] Later on, the main group of characters encounters them, as promised, "well coached by the mayor" (industriados del alcalde)[2] and on the way to spin their yarn in Valencia, historically a principal point of re-entry for former Spanish captives and where Cervantes himself had spent several weeks shortly after his redemption. For readers, this is a rather startling twist to an episode whose deeply biographical subtext might lead us to expect Cervantes, in spite of his already-demonstrated aversion to shame punishments, to ratify the first mayor's initial insistence that the hoax be rectified, or at least the need to right a fictional wrong and an affront not only to the compassionate, paying spectators who are conned but also to the real captives whose suffering is debased in the process.

The fact is, however, that the author and former captive forgoes the facile opportunity to pontificate, albeit obliquely, on the moral scourge and threat to truth that a good many of his contemporaries saw in fiction. Instead, the episode's conclusion suggests a number of insights into the literary Mediterranean. First, if it is moving to readers and spectators and if it appears plausible to boot, then the story possesses intrinsic value beyond the question of whether or not it is actually true. Even when they are of specious provenance or a *fingida historia*, Mediterranean stories merit being shared, as though the contents and setting themselves required wide dissemination over and above public demand. To add a spurious tale to those already in circulation represents, moreover, an affirmation of the diversity and plurality of these stories. Because sixteenth- and seventeenth-century Spain contended with similarly mendacious mendicants in real life, the canard of the false captives and their painted canvas attest, if nothing else, to the ways in which fiction historically has conditioned the popular reception of the Mediterranean. They remind us that the field of Mediterranean Studies is incomplete without a consideration of how the literary has sculpted the cultural imaginary, generated knowledge and associations about the space, and influenced the ways in which people across the centuries have imagined, and felt about, the Sea.

For Cervantes, emotions are not frivolous adornments or by-products of formal aesthetic convention, nor do they materialize exclusively on the side of the reader's "subjective" response. They comprise, rather, a bona fide staple of his oeuvre's content and context and, therefore, have something vital to say about the author, his works, and the broader social, cultural, and political milieu from which they emanated. *Persiles y Sigismunda* registers how affect tends to disrupt the critical impulse to extract a singular, unified meaning – authorial or otherwise – from a text, and is thus a testament to the heterogeneity and diversity of emotion in Cervantes's writing. The author, however, does not merely lift the affective complexity of lived experience and deposit it in his texts. Acutely conscious of the linguistic and literary challenges that inhere in emotional expression, and by exploiting, adapting, improvising, and experimenting with poetic language and its limitations, he moulds this complexity into a signifying figure in and of itself. From recycling classical tropes with just enough ironic distance to achieve a novel effect, to appropriating cultural forms from theatre and mysticism, to punctuating narrative temporality with events of suspension, to laying bare the harsh materiality of intense affects, and to mobilizing innovative rhetorical constructions of his own invention, Cervantes manages to countervail the limitations of expressive language even while dwelling upon its own lack. So deftly does the author vary these strategies that, just when we as readers think we know the script, another well-timed narrative twist exploits a kind of affective hysteresis, in which our emotions are piqued even before we are cognizant of it.

The examples highlighted throughout this study indicate that Cervantes's literary and rhetorical dexterity with all things emotional ramifies beyond the pages of his texts as well. True to the Mediterranean that so often shapes it, his representation of affect is equally nimble at *mediating* text and context – serving as a *medium* through which to articulate manifold moral, racial, religious, and social anxieties and as a central staging ground between the otherwise largely sovereign cultural spheres of politics, history, aesthetics, and ethics. Or, to invoke Braudel and Castro once more, between the Mediterranean basin and far more localized communities, between the macro and the micro, the economic and the human, the material and the sentimental, the structural and the subjective, the collective and the individual, the public and the private, and the exterior and the interior. Along correspondingly diaphanous lines, Cervantine affectivity tends to elide the reason-emotion dialectic itself. That these multiple border crossings take place in the vastness and variety of the Mediterranean world is not fortuitous, for even beyond a biographical approach that ascribes the affective and geographical magnitude of Cervantes's texts to that of the author's own life, these crossings are reciprocally enabled by the equation "Mediterranean experience = emotional experience." This textual, topographical, and emotional mobility is useful not simply because it breeds mutually felicitous metaphors. It is crucial for thinking through, between, and around problems that otherwise abut against the firmness of more typically hermetic conceptual boundaries, for it encourages us to push off from the relatively static and rational comforts of terra firma to explore the dynamic emotional horizons of the open sea, whose aleatory currents in turn open ever more foreign epistemological itineraries or "deviations" from reasoned thought. We are thus called upon to consider not only "unreason's reason" (la razón de la sinrazón) but also what we might conversely call *reason's unreason*. No wonder Plato distrusted sailors as much as unbridled passions.

Indeed, according to this model, the Platonic and Horatian metaphor of the ship of state as a majority-ruled democracy begins to take on water. If we follow the diversity of Cervantine affectivity to its logical (or illogical) ends, we might well imagine that the implied stakes of emotional *variatio* are greater than the concern to accommodate readers' differing aesthetic tastes. When the priority granted in *Don Quijote* to fomenting an entire range of emotional responses is weighed alongside the entropic failure of discrete emotional terminologies to capture fully the complexity of affect in *Persiles y Sigismunda*, we already have what amounts to an intriguing psychological world-view. Recalling the latter work's valuation of difference through affective aporias, it is not a stretch to infer an even more suggestive paradigm, one that admits a suitably differentiated spectrum of political ideologies and devotional creeds. If Cervantes's emotional philosophy of diversity is to be any guide, then this multitude would not be subject to the potential tyranny of the majority or, in contemporary terms, to the veiled yet exclusionary effects of multicultural liberalism and coalition politics – and, for this, one need look no further than the Mediterranean of today, the site of a tragic, ongoing humanitarian crisis of migration. A more genuinely egalitarian model such as this would be situated in opposition to the hegemonic, colonizing discourse of reason and the logic of *reductio ad unum* that have so often abetted imperial conquest and domestic projects of forcible assimilation. In fact, it would be difficult to envisage a more appropriate – and appropriately complex – politico-ethical proposition for early modern Spain, where a compliant Old Christian majority witnessed the expulsion of a sizeable minority population of conversos, Marranos, and Moriscos. Plato's metaphorical ship of state takes on a whole new meaning when we envision it steered not by representatives of the rational majority but, like the character of Ricote, by members of a stricken minority and a Mediterranean diaspora in search of "freedom of conscience" (libertad de conciencia).

As the discordant affects of *Persiles y Sigismunda* attest, this model is imperfect yet, partly for that very reason, is also eminently more human. Along with its complexity and heterogeneity, this humanizing element forms another salient landmark of the often asperous Cervantine emotional topology, whence the potential recognition of the racial and religious other is perhaps even more apparent. To focus on the individual is neither to retreat to the neo-Stoic solipsism espoused by many of Cervantes's contemporaries, nor to neglect the historical materialist conditions that determine the hierarchical structures of society at large, but rather to remain open to both contingency and the transformative power of story. Ricote is only one example of the ubiquitous Cervantine phenomenon whereby a character's emotional affliction becomes the impetus to sharing one's life experience through narration. These individual stories of encounter with difference and adversity, the lifeblood of Cervantine fiction and a hallmark of Mediterranean literature, lead to the building and sustaining of intersubjective bonds, and stand as yet another instantiation of the mediating role performed by affect in the middle sea. Once again, these bonds should not be construed as betokening complete unity, in contrast to the Romantic impulse of many interactionist approaches to the Mediterranean. Seldom does Cervantes allow the reader to forget the imperial, ethnic, and interconfessional conflict that was a perpetual reality of the early modern Mediterranean. In complementary fashion, the narrative's reliance on discord introduces sentimental suspense, polyphony, and, in the case of the *Novelas ejemplares*, a rupture in narrative temporality, which in turn opens an exemplary space for meditating on an emotional ethics.

Alternative epistemes such as these, part and parcel of what I have deemed Cervantes's literary longue durée, invite us to conclude by reflecting on their stakes for our scholarship as well. I have remarked on the homogenizing tendency of certain Mediterraneanizing logics, especially that which has established honour as a value of Mediterranean society, or, along national lines, the equally spurious distinction of Spain as an honour society, all while tacitly excluding those inhabitants proscribed from attaining this very same value (i.e., conversos, Marranos, and Moriscos). But affect may also be seen to mediate certain disciplinary ideologies of Cervantism itself, such as the oft-exaggerated distinction between hard and soft approaches to *Don Quijote*. A critical attention to the affective dynamism of the text, including the recuperation of laughter as a passion, not only obviates the reductive notion that it is nothing more than a "funny book" but also foils rigid, bipolar interpretations of a comparable nature. Shame, in its potential to incite at once parody and pathos, sympathy and Schadenfreude, singularly exemplifies these slippages, and it also reveals how the humoralism of a binary choleric-melancholic paradigm is wholly inadequate for elucidating the range and depth of Don Quijote's emotions in the novel. This does not mean that the alternative resulting from these slippages, however, must yield a nebulous scholarship or a critical landscape inhospitable to broader schools of thought and interpretation. On the contrary, the decisive implications of Cervantine affectivity do not endorse a monolithic, binary, or formless model but confirm a multitude of methodologies. Hutchinson grants that "there is no guarantee we are going to coincide on the emotional qualities we attribute" to a text like *Don Quijote*.[3] The analysis I have advanced in the preceding pages substantiates that this is precisely the point: as readers we are entreated to enjoy an untold diversity of affective responses equal to or greater than the emotional variety that animates the text and its characters. Yes, these responses are subjective – if by that term we mean an innate and inalienable condition of the human subject, and one that as such remains receptive to individual differences – as opposed to top-down, structuralist, or militantly historicist. But these complex, diverse, humanizing, and subjective elements are what not only make Cervantes's writing such an opportune object of aesthetic pleasure and critical inquiry but also convene a propitious place for the individual and the literary, whose integration in Mediterranean Studies is long overdue. The subjective essence of affect should no longer be put to use as a bridle for reining in ostensibly less rational and therefore less valid readings but, through a renewal of literary scholarship on emotion and the Mediterranean, as a spur to setting forth across new geographical, disciplinary, and critical frontiers.

Notes

1. Introduction

1 Cervantes, *Comedias y tragedias*, 11–12. Cervantes achieved this through his use of allegorical characters (E.C. Riley, "The 'Pensamientos Escondidos'"). The translation is my own, as will be the case, unless otherwise noted, for all others throughout the book, with the exception of the three major works of Cervantes analysed here and for which an adequate translation already exists: for *Don Quijote* and the *Novelas ejemplares*, I follow Edith Grossman's translations (*Don Quixote* and *Exemplary Novels*, respectively), and for *Persiles y Sigismunda*, that of Celia Richmond Weller and Clark Colahan (*The Trials of Persiles and Sigismunda*). Text references are to book, chapter, and page. As Hutchinson notes, the imagination (*imaginación*) was always associated with "a great emotional intensity, an immediacy and liveliness" ("Afinidades afectivas," 185), while Covarrubias's dictionary also makes clear that the interiority suggested by *imaginación* implies an emotional as well as a cognitive content (*Tesoro*, 1091).

2 Braudel innovatively divided historical time into three categories: the *longue*, *moyenne*, and *courte durées* (respectively, geographical, social, and individual time). For him, the least important was the latter, which includes the *histoire événementielle* or history of events that had previously dominated historiography. While in the interest of specificity I will employ these lexicalized terms in the original French, when citing Braudel's *The Mediterrananean World* I will use the English translation by Siân Reynolds, unless otherwise noted.

3 In addition to a hodge-podge of edited volumes on the region, scholars have recently traced the importance of urban culture (Cowan), religion (Husain and Fleming), the prehistoric origins of the Sea (Broodbank), and the popular focus on ecology (Grove and Rackham), among other studies (Catlos and Kinoshita; Guarracino; Harris; Watkins and Reyerson;

and Horden and Kinoshita). Among historians, after Horden and Purcell the most prominent voice has been that of David Abulafia, whose *The Great Sea* represents a conservative return to the *histoire événementielle* that Braudel had shunned. With few exceptions, references to literature in these studies are scant, at best, though Hutchinson's *Frontier Narratives*, in press at the time of this writing, promises to remedy this lacuna by concentrating on the representation of the early modern Mediterranean's "liminal lives." The Mediterranean in Hispanism has remained under-explored (Fuchs, "Another Turn," 417). Exceptions include Hamilton and Silleras-Fernández, *In and Of the Mediterranean*; Hutchinson and Cortijo Ocaña, "Cervantes y el Mediterráneo"; and Hutchinson, "Escribir el Mediterráneo" and "Literatura fronteriza mediterránea." For the Spanish–North African frontier specifically, see Hess, *The Forgotten Frontier*, and García-Arenal and Bunes, *Los españoles*.

4 Interdisciplinary scholars have explored at length the interstices between politics and affect, especially in so far as the latter suggests an alternative representational paradigm; for example, Ahmed, *Cultural Politics*; Massumi, *Parables for the Virtual*; Protevi, *Political Affect*; and Thrift, *Non-representational Theory*. For a critique of the "affective turn" and its supposedly ambiguous relationship to political engagement, see Leys, "The Turn to Affect."

5 Anderson and Smith, "Emotional Geographies," 9; Pile, "Emotions and Affect," 6.

6 Quoted in Horden and Purcell, *Corrupting Sea*, 36.

7 Bloom, "Introduction," xxii.

8 Egginton, *The Man Who Invented Fiction*, xxiii, xxii.

9 Attridge, *Singularity of Literature*, 22.

10 Aristotle, *Poetics*, in *Complete Works*, vol. 2, 1451a35–1451b30; 2340–1.

11 Jurado Santos, "El rídiculo 'Quijote.'"

12 Wimsatt and Beardsley, "Affective Fallacy." For an overview of the resistance to the study of emotions in narrative, see Keen, "Narrative and the Emotions."

13 Philology's "name does not signify knowledge of the *logos* [...] but affection for, friendship with, inclination to it. The portion of *philía* in this appellation was forgotten early on [...] Philology loves and in the beloved forgets love" (Hamacher, "95 Theses on Philology," 26). Further attempts to revindicate the field by so-called critical, liberation, or post-philologists are described in a recent special issue of the journal *postmedieval* (Warren, "Philology"); the contribution by Willis ("Art of Befriending the Text") therein is particularly apposite.

14 The few studies on emotion in early modern Spanish literature remain limited to individual feelings such as jealousy (Wagschal, *Literature of*

Jealousy), love (Muñoz Sánchez, *De amor y literatura*), or melancholy (Bartra, *Cultura y melancolía*). Melancholy is the most thoroughly explored, which is partly due to the broad semantic field of premodern understandings of the term; besides Bartra, see Layna Ranz, *La eficacia del fracaso*, 217–92; Soufas, *Melancholy and the Secular Mind*; Peset, *Las melancolías de Sancho*; Flor, *Era melancólica*; Orobitg, "El sistema de las emociones"; and Redondo, *Otra manera*, 121–46. Continuing momentum of the "affective turn" is evidenced by the founding of three major research centres on emotion (in Berlin, London, and Australia), and the establishment in 2014 of three new book series on the history of emotion, in addition to a slew of monographs and edited volumes on emotions. As for the early modern period, see Broomhall, *Early Modern Emotions*; Cummings and Sierhuis, *Passions and Subjectivity*; Paster, Rowe, and Floyd-Wilson, *Reading the Early Modern Passions*; Marculescu and Morand Métivier, *Affective and Emotional Economies*; Perfetti, *Representation of Women's Emotions*; and Tausiet and Amelang, *Accidentes del alma*. For an approachable neuroscientific study of emotions, see Damasio, *Looking for Spinoza*.

15 "The rationalistic temper may be observed in critical literature almost at the very beginning of the sixteenth century. This spirit of rationalism is observable throughout the Renaissance; and its general causes may be looked for in the liberation of the human reason by the Renaissance, in the growth of the sciences and arts, and in the reaction against mediæval sacerdotalism and dogma" (Spingarn, *History of Literary Criticism*, 148).

16 The narrative of Spanish imperial declension has been increasingly challenged in recent years; see Storrs, *Resilience*, especially 7–12.

17 See Gitlitz, "Inquisition Confessions"; Amelang, *Flight of Icarus*; and Amelang, "Tracing Lives" for how the "involuntary autobiography" of inquisitional persecution inspired other forms of first-person writing.

18 In *canción* 4, for instance, the poetic self recounts a battle in which reason is defeated at the hands of desire ("mi razón vencida"), an outcome that causes him profound shame (Garcilaso de la Vega, *Obra poética*, 153). Consider as well the subject of Garcilaso's *égloga* 2, and "the indisputably pathological nature of his new feelings" (Morros, "Noticia," 45). For a provocative analysis of the Stoicism of Garcilaso's elegies, see Graf, "From Scipio to Nero."

19 They do so in an epistolary exchange; Mendoza, *Poemas*, 413; see also 358–66. Blüher provides the most thorough discussion of Stoic influence on Spanish lyric poetry (*Séneca en España*, 298–318).

20 "No ai mayor señorío que el de sí mismo, de sus afectos" (Gracián, *Oráculo manual*, 26).

21 Maillo-Pozo, "Motivos neoestoicos," 355.

22 Quevedo, "Epicteto traducido." Sánchez de las Brozas (hereafter El Brocense) and Correas had already published their own translations of Epictetus's work (in 1612 and 1630, respectively), but Quevedo's of 1635 was distinguished for being written in verse; see Castanien, "Quevedo's Version." Quevedo espoused similar tendencies in his *Defensa de Epicuro*, published the same year. For studies of Quevedo's neo-Stoic ideology, see Blüher, *Séneca en España*, 427–86; Ettinghausen, *Francisco de Quevedo*; and Schwartz, "Justo Lipsio en Quevedo."

23 From "his scornful attitude toward love" to "that stoic and disillusioned attitude of someone who is reeling from so many things desired and not achieved," Serrano Poncela locates "Quevedo's peculiar *black humour*, at once so original and personal" in a distant "infancy deprived of affects and responsible for a certain insensitivity toward tender and sentimental things, with his corresponding taste for shamelessness [*impudor*] and obscenity" ("Estratos afectivos en Quevedo," 38, 43, 46). Except for an apparently healthy dosage of spleen, aggression, and ressentiment – a biting example of which Quevedo's own *Bilis negra* provides – if these accounts are to be believed, then he was a living example of the self-evacuation of emotion. Even if Serrano Poncela's creative imagining of the Quevedian psyche amounts to little more than speculative biographical fiction, Quevedo's sustained enthusiasm for neo-Stoicism serves as an instructive contrast for Cervantes.

24 Respectively, Greenblatt, *Renaissance Self-Fashioning*; and Orozco Díaz, *El teatro*, 87–118. For worthwhile critiques, see Martin, "Inventing Sincerity, Refashioning Prudence," and Martin, *Myths of Renaissance Individualism*, where he details the existence of various "selves," including the "prudential," "performative," and "sincere" self (32–8).

25 For example, Della Porta, *De humana physiognomonia*; and Cortés, *Phisonomia*.

26 Alexander and Selesnick, *History of Psychiatry*, 16–17. Enrique Fernández has recently explored how "the great process of internalization" and "growth of the inner realm" were also bound up with the science of dissection (*Anxieties of Interiority*, 4).

27 "There can be no doubt that the seventeenth century, the latter half of Hapsburg domination in Spain, was a period the equal of which in dismal depression and sordid melancholy it would be difficult to find in modern history" (Klein, *The Mesta*, 244). Books like Andrés Velázquez's *Libro de la melancholia* and Santa Cruz's *Sobre la melancolía* evinced this fascination in print, while King Philip II himself was fabled to be a melancholic.

28 For instance, Santos, *Las tarascas de Madrid*. St Ignatius of Loyola's facility with weeping was the stuff of legend; see his *Personal Writings*.

On the *lloronas*, see Amelang, "La viuda alegre"; on religious weeping more generally, Christian, "Provoked Religious Weeping"; and Tausiet, "Agua en los ojos"; and on tears in Cervantes, Dopico Black, "Las lágrimas de Sancho."

29 Paul Michael Johnson, "Feeling Certainty, Performing Sincerity."

30 "Whether the patient was on horseback or in a carriage or on a boat, the rhythms of the journey were as much part of the cure as the air was. So also were the emotions induced. Among the 'non-natural' determinants of health in late antiquity were the 'passions of the soul,' in effect positive emotions" (Horden, "Travel Sickness," 188).

31 Eliot, *Harvard Classics*, vol. 50, 3, 9.

32 See, for instance, Jáuregui, *Diálogo entre la Naturaleza*.

33 Rodríguez Cuadros, *Técnica*, 402.

34 Berenson, *Lorenzo Lotto*, 255. He adds that Lotto "seems always to have been able to define his feelings, emotions, and ideals, instead of being a mere highway for them" (255). See also Dal Pozzolo and Falomir, *Lorenzo Lotto: Portraits*. Cf. da Vinci's *moti mentali*.

35 Although Le Brun's *Méthode pour apprendre à dessiner les passions* (1698) is generally considered to be the authority on pictorial representations of emotion, the seventeenth century produced an abundance of treatises on painting, many of which also describe the gestures of specific emotions, including Carducho's *Diálogos de la pintura* (1663); Palomino's *El museo pictórico y escala óptica* (1715–24); da Vinci's *Trattato della pittura* (1651); and Pacheco's *Arte de la pintura* (1649).

36 Lope de Vega, *Arte nuevo de hacer comedias*, 148, vv. 305–12.

37 Minturno, *De poeta*. Lope too advised dramaturges to "describe lovers with affects / that move to an extreme whoever is listening" (*Arte nuevo*, 146, vv. 272–3; describa los amantes con afectos / que muevan con extremo a quien escucha).

38 "From almost all the documented examples, then, it is deduced that the new rhetoric of the actor requires emphasizing emotive values" (Rodríguez Cuadros, *Técnica*, 409).

39 "But now *decorum* is affirmed above all in the affects and their expression [...] The rational key gives way to emotivity, [...] aspiring to surpass nature, something reachable only insofar as emotion can transfigure the image, moving from considering it merely a mirrored reflection of reality to carrying it beyond its natural possibilities" (Rodríguez Cuadros, *Técnica*, 401). Alonso López Pinciano (hereafter El Pinciano), for his part, stresses "how important it is that actors do their job with much skill and very truly [*muy de veras*]; since they take our money truly and make us wait here two hours, it is only fair that they should do their acting with lots of truth [*con muchas veras*]" (*Philosophia antigua poética*, 3:284). And Leone

de' Sommi, the Jewish-Italian author of the most complete treatise on theatre in the Renaissance, echoes El Pinciano's insight when stressing that players must perform their part in a "lively" and "very vivacious way" (*vivezza; vivacissima maniera*) (*Quattro dialoghi*, 46).

40 For examples, see Cotarelo, *Bibliografía*, 122b, 560a.

41 Quoted in Noreña, *Juan Luis Vives and the Emotions*, 141. In contrast to the Stoics and the neo-Stoics, Vives's indebtedness to the Aristotelian concept of *metriopátheia*, or the golden mean of moderate passion, is clear in his conviction that only an excess of affect is prejudicial to the well-being of the soul.

42 Like the Stoics, in the *Tusculan Disputations* Cicero established the existence of four primary passions (distress, fear, lust, and delight), under which he enumerated several sub-passions. Aquinas, "Treatise on the Passions," however, brought what he considered to be eleven distinct passions into a bipartite division between the irascible (hope, desperation, fear, and daring) and concupiscible passions (love, hate, desire, aversion, joy, and pain), in addition to the special case of anger.

43 Some contemporary psychologists have been just as given to producing easily digestible menus of feelings; for example, Du, Tao, and Martinez, "Compound Facial Expressions," in which the authors identify through computational models twenty-one different emotions, which they note is a significant increase from previous studies, such as Ekman, *Emotion in the Human Face*.

44 Bouwsma, *Waning of the Renaissance*, 26, 25.

45 An egregious example is Garrote Pérez, who fails to even acknowledge the competing currents of thought surrounding emotion in early modernity, which enables him to conclude that Cervantes "conforms to accepting the scientific and moral explanations that, with regard to the passions, are accepted by all men of the era" (*La naturaleza*, 80).

46 Note the several articles that Hutchinson has authored on the topic ("Affective Dimensions," "Afinidades afectivas," "Anagnórisis," "Poética de la emoción," and "'Los primeros movimientos'"), as well as a more general attention to emotion in his books *Cervantine Journeys* and *Economía ética en Cervantes*. Carrera has also demonstrated an interest in these problems ("The Emotions," "*Pasión* and *afección*," and "The Social Dimension"), while Redondo, "En busca del 'Quijote,'" and Camacho Morfín, "El lenguaje de las emociones," have recognized the importance of emotion in *Don Quijote*, albeit with limited analysis.

47 Hutchinson, "Affective Dimensions," 74.

48 Cascardi, *Discourse of Politics*, and Byrne, *Law and History*, both published in 2012.

49 "The origin of transmitted affects is social in that these affects do not only arise within a particular person but also come from without" (Brennan, *Transmission of Affect*, 3).

50 Mancing's description of Don Quijote's defeat in Barcelona is a serviceable example: "His thoughts, we infer, are filled with confusion and emotional anguish; they are, very literally, affective – he *feels* them, physically as much as mentally. The reader knows this, but the narrator does not intervene to drive the point home. The reader has the obligation of creatively and sympathetically imagining what Don Quixote's thoughts and feelings are. And most of all, the empathetic reader perceives the anguish, the uncertainy, the confusion, the self-doubt, and the pain Don Quixote is feeling" ("Don Quixote's Affective Thoughts," 641).

51 On these points, see Close, "Cervantine Irony"; Avilés, *Avatares de lo invisible*, 17–58; and Espejo Madrigal, who in "Fin del amor cortés" details the Cervantine critique of courtly love. According to Schmitz, Cervantes also parodies Neoplatonic tropes, such as that of having the beloved engraved in the soul or heart ("Cervantes's Language," 175–7).

52 As for the broader question of satire and the novel, critical work must still be done. Since I cannot recommend more recent monographs on Cervantine satire (such as Reichenberger, *Los enigmas peligrosos* and *Hermeneutics of Satire*), Parr's *Anatomy of Subversive Discourse* remains the primary referent on the whole, along with Darnis's work on Menippean satire (*Don Quichotte*). Even if, according to John J. Allen, "it is not a satire," "*Don Quixote* abounds in subtle, perceptive, devastating satire, compounding ironies and deflating presumption and pretention" ("Transformation of Satire," 6–7), in spite of Cervantes's own ironic claim that "[n]ever did my humble pen fly through the satirical region" (*Poesías*, 321; [n]unca voló la pluma humilde mía / por la región satírica). Useful, but more general, waypoints for understanding satire include Etreros, *La sátira política*; Scholberg, *Sátira e invectiva*; Schwartz Lerner, *Metáfora y sátira*; and Arellano, "Las mascaras de Demócrito."

53 Paul Michael Johnson, "Don Quijote avergonzado."

54 "To meet the historian's demands [...] the Mediterranean must be accepted as a wide zone, extending well beyond the shores of the sea in all directions. We might compare it to an electric or magnetic field, or more simply to a radiant centre whose light grows less as one moves away from it, without one's being able to define the exact boundary between light and shade" (Braudel, *Mediterranean World*, 1:168).

55 Pratt, "Arts of the Contact Zone."

56 For the purported "waning" of the Mediterranean, which coincided with European access to the Atlantic and Indian Oceans and a shift of the "world economy" towards Northern Europe, see Tabak, who in *Waning of*

the Mediterranean critiques the inordinate historiographical emphasis on Mediterranean decline by establishing that the picture is more complex and that the Mediterranean continued to command an important stake in world affairs.

57 Braudel, *Mediterranean World*, 2:1088.

58 Penco Valenzuela, *El origen judeoconverso*, is only the latest to advance this possibility, which Castro first suggested long ago ("Taller de existencialidad"; *Casticismos*, 34). Luciano G. Egido goes so far as to ascribe Cervantes's "sentimentality" to his supposed converso roots, "isolated in a society of Old Christians, tinged by a cold and hard racism of hate and irrational fears" (*La razón de la sinrazón*, 233–4). I agree with Rey Hazas that some elements of Cervantes's life "allow one to maintain some suspicion as to his 'tainted' blood without there being a way to confirm it" (*Poética de la libertad*, 10–11).

59 Cervantes, *Comedias y tragedias*, 361, vv. 3069–72.

60 In addition to Garcés's study, on his captivity see Cervantes's two most autobiographical texts: the "Epístola a Mateo Vázquez" (in *Historia de una polémica literaria*, by José Luis Gonzalo Sánchez-Molero) and the *Información de Argel*, just published in a new edition by Adrián Sáez.

61 *La española inglesa* and *Persiles y Sigismunda* explore the North Atlantic yet also include significant portions in the Mediterranean; *El rufián dichoso*'s second act takes place in Mexico but begins in Seville; and even *La conquista de Jerusalén*, questions of authorship aside, transpires in the broader Mediterranean region, meaning that no major work by Cervantes fully escapes the Sea.

62 Spain is "a fascinating test case for some of the fundamental insights of Mediterranean scholarship" (Akbari, "Persistence of Philology," 10–11).

63 Hutchinson and Cortijo Ocaña, "Prólogo," i.

64 Horden and Purcell, *Corrupting Sea*, 126–7.

65 Maíllo Salgado, *El perfume de la amistad*, 74.

66 The fourteenth-century Moroccan Ibn Battuta or the seventeenth-century Turk Evliya Çelebi, both of whom journeyed widely in the Mediterranean and beyond, are two notable examples.

67 Matar, "Arab Travelers," xxxii. For instance, those by Ahmad bin al-Mahdi al-Ghazzal and Mohammad bin abd al-Wahab al-Ghassani are rich with insightful observations about the Spanish climate, terrain, history, and religious, administrative, political, and social life, yet, with the notable exception of al-Ghassani's angry denouncement of the expulsion of his co-religionists from al-Andalus, their accounts largely lack personal details.

68 As its title advertises, Antonio de Sosa's *Topographia e historia general de Argel* (1612), for example, meticulously records the layout of Algiers as well as the customs of the city's diverse inhabitants and captives.

69 Benítez Sánchez-Blanco, "El Mediterráneo de Cervantes"; or Franco Sánchez, "Cervantes y el mar," for instance.

70 Historically, "certain kinds of people (slaves, women, homosexuals, ethnic or raced others) have been understood as determined by their bodily appetites and intense emotions and thus as inferior to citizens – white heterosexual, able-bodied men, presumed to transcend the corporeal through reason" (Jensen and Wallace, "Facing Emotions," 1254).

71 It should nonetheless be noted that, for Aristotle, emotions were an unequivocal cornerstone of accomplished tragedy, as his discussion of pathos in the *Poetics* makes readily apparent. For an insightful look at how the concept of catharsis and its various translations have evolved over the years and thus inform the history of emotion, see Gobert, "Behaviorism."

72 Yet Freud was mostly allergic to emotions because, by associating them with repression and sublimation, he considered them a barrier to the psychoanalytic process. See O'Neill, *Freud and the Passions*; and especially Carveth, "Psychoanalytic Conceptions," for alternative interpretations. Naturally, Cervantes has been placed on the metonymical couch of several psychoanalytical studies of his works, which has led to more than a few "breakthroughs." Carroll B. Johnson, *Madness and Lust*; El Saffar and Wilson, *Quixotic Desire*; and Combet, *Cervantès* are three of the most prominent examples.

73 Dewey, *Art as Experience*, 43. It is for these reasons that "poet and novelist have an immense advantage over even an expert psychologist in dealing with an emotion. For the former build up a concrete situation and permit *it* to evoke emotional response. Instead of a description of an emotion in intellectual and symbolic terms, the artist 'does the deed that breeds' the emotion" (Dewey, 70).

74 Rogerson, "The Art of Painting the Passions," 68.

75 For instance, Canavaggio, "Alonso López Pinciano."

76 López Pinciano, *Philosophia antigua poética*, 1:64–96.

77 Paul Michael Johnson, "Don Quijote avergonzado," 477. Soufas's *Melancholy and the Secular Mind* argues that the influence of Huarte on Cervantes is not as acute as has been defended by critics like Salillas, *Un gran inspirador*; and Green, "El Ingenioso Hidalgo." This is not to suggest that humoral paradigms or Huarte's text is impoverished, even if they remain largely outside the scope of the present study. Arikha's *Passions and Tempers* represents the most recent and ambitious attempt to recover the richness of humoralism and its relationship to the emotions, even though Huarte is mystifyingly absent in her study.

78 This is what Doody identifies as "[t]he homeland of the Western Novel" (*True Story of the Novel*, 18).

79 "The absence of Muslims and Moriscos, and the attempted erasure of a Semitic past, created an aperture that Spaniards could not address within their pre-existing literary forms. This aperture created a radical break from previous genres of narrative and could only be articulated via a new, capacious, fictional narrative" (Quinn, *The Moor and the Novel*, 27).

80 Along these lines, I fully concur that "Cervantes was an acute observer of human behavior and the body's physiological experience of emotion" (Schmitz, "Cervantes's Language," 180).

81 Perhaps it is Lope who, referring to the printing of his comedias, most succinctly highlights the visual traces of theatricality that remain in the journey from stage to page, comparing the text to a body whose soul is the actors: "I'm certain that in reading them you will remember the actions of those who for this body served as the soul" (quoted in Rodríguez Cuadros, *Técnica*, 70). At other times, nevertheless, Lope disparages actors as well as the *vulgo* for spoiling the ostensible perfection of a comedia in its textual form; see Couderc, "El autor."

82 Noting the "overt reliance upon novelistic elements" of the interludes, Reed proposes that "Cervantes' mastery of literary prose and its conventions may, in fact, be partially responsible for the alleged theatrical inadequacy of his dramatic work" ("Novelization of Drama," 66, 65).

83 Remarking on *Don Quijote*, the expert on early modern drama Melveena McKendrick notes that "it would be difficult to conceive of a more extensively theatrical novel" ("Writings for the Stage," 133). See also Syverson-Stork, *Theatrical Aspects*; and Torres, *Cuerpo y gesto*.

84 De Armas, *Writing for the Eyes*. Bass (*Drama of the Portrait*), Bergmann (*Art Inscribed*), and de Armas (*Ekphrasis*) also study the popular themes of painting and ekphrasis in early modern Spanish literature. For the importance of the visual in Cervantes's works, see Laguna, *Pictorial Imagination*, and, for a germane example, Infante, "Painting."

85 The iconography of illustrations from Cervantes's works can be accessed in Urbina, "Iconografía textual del *Quijote*," and Lucía Megías, "Banco de imágenes." For theoretical approaches to these images, see Urbina and Maestro, *"Don Quixote" Illustrated*; Lucía Megías, *Leer el "Quijote" en imágenes*; and Schmidt, *Critical Images*. Lord Carteret's 1738 edition of *Don Quijote* is remarkable as the first to explicitly highlight the novel's emotional contours, both in the reflexive commentary that graces its preface and in the illustrations themselves; see Paul Michael Johnson, "Of Fine Arts."

86 Ahmed, *Cultural Politics*, 89–92.

87 Ahmed, *Cultural Politics*.

88 Williams, *Marxism and Literature*, 128–35.

89 Heidegger, *Being and Time*; Bartra, *Cultura y melancolía*. While maintaining shades of difference, Williams's "structure of feeling" and Heidegger's "mood" can be compared with Adorno's concept of "atmosphere" (*Aesthetic Theory*, 274) and Benjamin's concept of "aura" (*Illuminations*, 222), which Ngai does while explaining her decision to adopt her own term, *tone* (*Ugly Feelings*, 87).

90 Horden and Purcell, *Corrupting Sea*, 464–5.

91 In a constructivist model the symbolic order of language informs the type, range, and intensity of emotional experience. It was the view of William James that language itself was responsible for our emotions; in other words, we are sad because we weep, and not the other way around (*Principles of Psychology*, 1065–70).

92 Examples include Ngai's coining of the terms *stuplimity* and *animatedness* and the decision by the English editors and the translators of Oliva Sabuco's *Nueva filosofía de la naturaleza del hombre y otros escritos* to use the portmanteau *angry grief* for a feeling unserved by the idea of "depression" (*New Philosophy of Human Nature*, 6–7). Conversely, there are those emotions that seem no longer to be felt in the same way, such as ancient and medieval acedia, the nineteenth-century condition of neurasthenia or "Americanitis," or the phrenological concept of "amativeness." For more on these slippages in Spanish and English, see Díaz-Vera, "Reconstructing the Old English Cultural Model for Fear," and Díaz-Vera and Caballero, "Exploring the Feeling-Emotions Continuum."

93 *Emoción* is absent in Palencia's *Universal vocabulario en latín y en romance* (1490; Universal vocabulary in Latin and Romance), Covarrubias's *Tesoro de la lengua castellana o española* (1611; *Treasure of the Castilian or Spanish Language*), as well as the *Diccionario de autoridades* (1726–39; Dictionary of authorities), and would not be granted official recognition until the mid-nineteenth century. Nevertheless, Cervantes would likely have recognized the term *emoción*, since it does appear in a sixteenth-century poem by Fray Luis de León and in Cabrera de Córdoba's *Historia de Felipe II* (1619; History of Philip II). See the Real Academia Española's *Corpus diacrónico del español* (Diachronic corpus of Spanish) and Crespo, "Emotions in Spain," 210.

94 Hutchinson discusses in detail the close relation (etymological, analogical, and philosophical) of motion and emotion ("Los primeros movimientos"; *Cervantine Journeys*, 15–37). Gil-Sotres likewise notes that "for medieval physicians and philosophers, *pasión* indistinguishably designated all the affective movements of the sensible soul. In this way, its meaning is closer to the word *emoción* of our conventional language" ("Modelo teórico," 184).

95 On this point, see Dixon, *From Passions to Emotions*.
96 Covarrubias, *Tesoro*, 49.
97 See for example Ngai, who briefly contextualizes the affect-emotion polemic while justifying her decision to use the terms interchangeably (*Ugly Feelings*, 25–8).

2. Connected (Hi)stories

1 The first large-scale work of Mediterranean historiography to be published since Braudel's *Mediterranean World* is Horden and Purcell's *Corrupting Sea* (2000), itself partly responsible for inaugurating the recent
explosion of interest in Mediterranean Studies. Castro's influence on
cervantismo can be found in Close's "La aproximación romántica" and
Dopico Black and Layna Ranz's *USA Cervantes*. Subirats's *Américo Castro*
explores how Castro's standing has been both embraced and elided in
Spanish historiography.
2 Castro, *Edad conflictiva*, xxvi, xx–xxi.
3 Although Braudel does discuss the Morisco (esp. in 2:780–97) and Jewish
(2:802–25) communities in his book, Castro's largely forgotten rebuttal is
not the only one to have been lodged at Braudel, whose crowning work
has been chided for its failure to embrace religion in general (Amelang,
"Braudel"), its "surprisingly reductive and simple account" of Islam
in particular (Husain, "Introduction," 10), and its saturation by French
colonialism (Strachan, "Colonial Cosmology"; Chambers, *Mediterranean
Crossings*, 148). Its "relegation of culture to the status of epiphenomenon"
(Amelang, "Braudel," 229) is also noted by McNeill ("Fernand Braudel,
Historian"). As for the issue of emotion, despite this chapter's epigraph,
in his book Braudel maintains "a different posture, as if 'I' as a subject
with feelings and emotions had been dismissed"; he "dispossessed the
people he studied from their dreams, their fears, their expectations,
and their beliefs, silenced their voices, and played as a soloist" (Valensi,
"Problem of Unbelief," 17, 31). Paradoxically, despite the fact that "a
strong case can be made that it is *the* single most important historical
work to appear" in the twentieth century, Braudel consigned literature
and culture to a marginal place in a work that itself was "too 'literary,'
too poetic," to be imitated (Piterberg, Ruiz, and Symcox, introduction to
Braudel Revisited, 3, 8).
4 For the related dynamics that undergird debates about *convivencia*, and
Castro's role in popularizing the concept, see Szpiech, "Convivencia
Wars."
5 Subrahmanyam, "Connected Histories," 750; for an example of this
model see Subrahmanyam, "Holding the World in Balance."

6 Horden and Purcell, *Corrupting Sea*, 28.

7 Horden and Purcell, 30.

8 "Mediterranean discourse has suffered from Mediterranean discursiveness: sun and sea, scent and color, sandy beaches and islands of fortune, girls maturing young and widows shrouded in black, ports and ships and *invitations au voyage*, journeys and wrecks and tales thereof, oranges and olives and myrtle, palms and pines and cypresses, pomp and poverty, reality and illusion, life and dreams – such are the commonplaces plaguing the literature, all description and repetition" (Matvejević, *Cultural Landscape*, 12).

9 Horden and Purcell, "New Thalassology."

10 "The Great Sea is the one that flows from the Ocean out of the West, turns to the south, and finally stretches to the north. It is called 'great' because the other seas are smaller in comparison with it. This is also called the Mediterranean because it flows through the 'middle of the land' (*media terrae*) all the way to the East, separating Europe, Africa, and Asia" (Isidore of Seville, *Etymologies*, 277). See also Broodbank, *Making of the Middle Sea*.

11 Anderson, *Imagined Communities*; and Said, *Orientalism*, 49–73.

12 Balibar, *Politics and the Other Scene*, 75–86.

13 Loomba, "Mediterranean Borderlands," 14. Particularly promising in this regard are Fuchs's proposal of "imperium studies," which avoids the sometimes complacent tendency of the Mediterranean interactionist paradigm to lose sight of imperial conflict ("Imperium Studies") as well as the pitfalls of transnationalism, a term that "suggests that the early modern nation is an achieved entity rather than the messy category in process that it was" (Fuchs, "Another Turn," 415). Dangler, in *Edging toward Iberia*, proposes the network theory of Manuel Castells and world-systems analysis of Immanuel Wallerstein as tools for rethinking medieval Spain and avoiding the Eurocentrism that I will discuss. Also see Doyle, "Inter-Imperiality"; Lynn and Rowe, *Early Modern Hispanic World*; and, in relation to Cervantes, Childers, *Transnational Cervantes*.

14 The same dynamic emerges in the political sphere, for example the so-called Union for the Mediterranean of the 1990s (cooke, Göknar, and Parker, *Mediterranean Passages*, 322). Picard's *La mer des califes*, first published in 2015 and translated to English as *Sea of the Caliphs* in 2018, is a welcome and long-overdue corrective to these tendencies.

15 Many of these debates have already taken place within the field of anthropology and thus can be helpful for understanding similar pitfalls faced by other disciplines, as I discuss in chapter 3 with regards to the honour-shame question. For more detailed critiques of Mediterraneanism, see Herzfeld, "Practical Mediterraneanism"; Pina-Cabral, "The

Mediterranean as a Category"; Hamilton and Silleras-Fernández, introduction, xvi; and what Horden and Purcell recognize as "restricted comparativism" (*Corrupting Sea*, 486–7).

16 Pinet, "Between the Seas," 76. Morris even ascribes the proliferation of Mediterranean frameworks to globalization: "Globalization has created winners and new losers; Mediterraneanization did the same" ("Mediterraneanization," 51).

17 Ahmed, *Cultural Politics*, 89–92.

18 Curiously, even Braudel, known for his stylized writing, pondered: "Is history, perhaps, though aspiring to be a science, a matter of writing, of literary style?" ("Personal Testimony," 464).

19 Kinoshita, "Mediterranean Literature," 322.

20 Juan de Mariana, quoted in Kamen, *Spanish Inquisition*, 131.

21 Kagan, *Clio and the Crown*.

22 Friedman, *Cervantes in the Middle*, 16–17. On the interactions between fiction and history in Cervantes, see Byrne, *Law and History*, 108–41; Quinn, *Moor and the Novel*, 101–33; and Wardropper, "Story or History."

23 Cervantes, *Comedias y tragedias*, 131, vv. 3133–4.

24 Cervantes, *Persiles y Sigismunda*, 3.14.570–1; *Persiles and Sigismunda*, 3.14.272.

25 McNamer, "Literariness," 1435. Nevertheless, at least until lately, cultural historians have been more willing than literary scholars to explore emotion and thus can provide valuable theoretical and analytical tools for the task. Early forays into the cultural history of emotion by such figures as Huizinga (*Autumn of the Middle Ages*) and Febvre (*Combats pour l'histoire*) were revitalized in the 1980s by Stearns and Stearns in "Emotionology." More recent yet equally foundational are Reddy's *Navigation of Feeling* and Rosenwein's *Emotional Communities*. Matt and Stearns's *Doing Emotions History* and Plamper's *History of Emotions* provide a theoretical overview and bibliography. For an application of the history of emotion to early modern drama, see Paul Michael Johnson, "Estudio introductorio."

26 McNamer, "Literariness," 1436.

27 Verdon, *Travel in the Middle Ages*, 55.

28 Braudel, *Mediterranean World*, 2:46–7.

29 Abulafia, *Great Sea*, 380.

30 Goitein, *Mediterranean Society*, 1:273. Purcell manages to avoid taking sides in the debate with his commonsensical observation that "there is unfortunately no incompatibility between fear and misery and frequent and necessary use, and it is clear that, for all the perils and the images of disaster, the Mediterranean has not usually been a frontier itself in the way that oceanic spaces are" ("Boundless Sea," 18).

31 Cervantes, *Persiles y Sigismunda*, 1.18–19.250–1; *Persiles and Sigismunda*, 1.18–19.87.

32 Cervantes, *El amante liberal* and *El licenciado Vidriera* (*The Glass Lawyer*), in *Novelas ejemplares*, 194, 352; in *Exemplary Novels*, 78, 175–6.

33 A telling demonstration arises just before the scene of the sinking ship when Mauricio asks: "[I]s it surprising that while sailing in a wooden ship I'd fear lightning bolts from the sky, clouds in the air, and water from the sea? But what most confuses and perplexes me is that if some harm threatens us it won't come from any natural element [...] but from treachery forged [...] in some lustful hearts" (Cervantes, *Persiles and Sigismunda*, 1.18.86). ¿Qué mucho que, yendo navegando en un navío de madera, tema rayos del cielo, nubes del aire y aguas de la mar? Pero lo que más me confunde y suspende es que, si algún daño nos amenaza, no ha de ser de ningún elemento [...], sino de una traición, forjada [...] en algunos lascivos pechos (*Persiles y Sigismunda*, 1.18.249).

34 See, for example, Green, Chatham, and Sestir, "Emotion and Transportation"; Gerrig, *Experiencing Narrative Worlds*; and Oatley, *Passionate Muse*.

35 Hochschild, "Emotion Work."

36 Kinoshita, "Mediterranean Literature." Hershenzon studies the case of Muley Zidan's Arabic manuscripts in his appositely titled article "Traveling Libraries." As for *Don Quijote*, the most compelling evidence of its own rapid transmission is the fact that in 1607 – only two years after its initial publication in Madrid – its protagonists were represented in a local festival in Peru, as attested by a manuscript of Francisco Duarte, president of the Casa de Contratación de las Indias at the time.

37 Mallette, "Boustrophedon," 254.

38 Mallette, 265, 264.

39 "The Arabs! I hate the whole lot [...] You know them as doctors; I know them as poets. Nothing more insipid, nothing softer, nothing more limp, nothing more obscene [...] I will not be persuaded that any good can come from Arabia" (Petrarch, quoted in Mallette, "Boustrophedon," 258).

40 For the broad cultural efforts to expunge Arabic thought from medieval and early modern Europe see Akbari and Mallette's edited volume *A Sea of Languages*, and for the politics of speaking Arabic see Tolan's contribution therein ("Forging New Paradigms"). On the wider links between language and identity in the early modern Mediterranean, see Dursteler, "Language and Identity."

41 Cervantes, *Don Quijote*, 2.54.1169; *Don Quixote*, 2.54.812.

42 Cervantes, *Don Quijote*, 1.9.118; *Don Quixote*, 1.9.67–8.

43 For Abulafia, the lingua franca is the greatest single proof of Mediterranean unity: "it was its fluidity and changeability that expressed most clearly the shifting identities of the people of the early modern Mediterranean" (*Great Sea*, 487). For the Mediterranean lingua franca, Dakhlia's *Histoire d'une langue métisse* is *de rigueur*, and Epalza's "La naturaleza" analyses its appearance in Cervantes.

44 Cervantes, *La Galatea*, 1.168.

45 Cervantes, *Don Quijote*, 2.10.764; *Don Quixote*, 2.10.514, translation modified. Don Quijote conversely claims to be able to extrapolate the physical
features of chivalric heroes from their moral character: "by means of the
deeds they performed and the circumstances in which they lived, and
by using sound philosophy [*fisonomía*], one can deduce their features,
their natures, and their stature" (Cervantes, *Don Quixote*, 2.1.466); por la
aprehensión que tengo de que fueron como sus historias cuentan, y por
las hazañas que hicieron y condiciones que tuvieron, se pueden sacar
por buena fisonomía sus faciones, sus colores y estaturas (*Don Quijote*,
2.1.693). For more examples and analysis, see Gernert, *Lecturas del cuerpo*,
esp. 393–413.

46 As he does in the episode of Mambrino's helmet, for example (Cervantes,
Don Quijote, 1.21.246; *Don Quixote*, 1.21.155).

47 Johnson, "Don Quijote avergonzado," 480, 482.

48 Wilson, *Allegories of Love*, 36. Note this critic's analysis of *Persiles y Sigismunda*: "This rupture of narrative by a multiplicity of micronarratives
radically distinguishes the *Persiles* from its model: unlike the personal
stories in Heliodorus, Cervantes's stories are not integral to the plot"
(Wilson, 36). For the importance of such stories in *Don Quijote*, see El Saffar, *Distance and Control*.

49 Cervantes, *Comedias y tragedias*, 11–12.

50 Cervantes, *El amante liberal*, in *Novelas ejemplares*, 179; in *Exemplary Novels*,
69.

51 Cervantes, *El amante liberal*, in *Novelas ejemplares*, 180–1; in *Exemplary
Novels*, 70.

52 Cervantes, *El amante liberal*, in *Novelas ejemplares*, 197, ellipsis in original;
in *Exemplary Novels*, 80.

53 Mahamut summarizes the situation thus: "Now I know [...] that what
people say is true, that what can be felt can be said, though sometimes
sentiment silences the tongue; whatever the case, Ricardo, whether your
sorrow reaches your words or they keep ahead of it, you will always find
in me a true friend" (Cervantes, *The Generous Lover*, in *Exemplary Novels*,
80). Ahora he hallado ser verdadero [...] lo que suele decirse, que lo que
se sabe sentir se sabe decir, puesto que algunas veces el sentimiento en-
mudece la lengua; pero, comoquiera que ello sea, Ricardo, ora llegue tu
dolor a tus palabras, ora ellas se le aventajen, siempre has de hallar en mí
un verdadero amigo (Cervantes, *El amante liberal*, in *Novelas ejemplares*,
198). Reifying the notion that "what can be felt can be said," Cervantes
here defies the commensurate limitations of representation while affirm-
ing the very efficacy of mimesis itself.

54 Cervantes, *El amante liberal*, in *Novelas ejemplares*, 179–81; in *Exemplary
Novels*, 70.

55 Cervantes is not the first to have used a medical analogy to define friendship and its bonds of intimacy. See for example Plutarch, "How to Distinguish a Flatterer from a Friend," in *Essays*, 61–112.

56 Paul Michael Johnson, "Soldier's Shame."

57 Castro, *Edad conflictiva*, xxvi, xx–xxi.

58 Ahmed, *Cultural Politics*.

59 Jensen and Wallace, "Facing Emotions," 1252.

60 Pile, "Emotions and Affect," 10, 8. For an overview of work on
affect in the field of human geography, see Bondi, "Making
Connections."

61 The most notable example may be Martorell and Galba's *Tirant lo Blanc*, a
work admired by Cervantes and that evokes "all those who will navigate
the sea of love" (201; tots aquells i aquelles que en la mar d'amor nave-
garan). Worthy of mention, too, is that in Catalan the two lexemes are
homophonous and nearly homographic (*la mar / l'amar*).

62 Cervantes, *Persiles y Sigismunda*, prologue, 122; *Persiles and Sigismunda*,
prologue, 19.

63 Cervantes, *Persiles y Sigismunda*, 1.9.196; *Persiles and Sigismunda*, 1.9.56.

64 Casalduero, *Sentido y forma*, 46.

65 I concur with Armstrong-Roche that the literary Sosa and Leonor could
have been inspired not by the Manuel de Sousa Coutinho that Cervantes
met in captivity in Algiers but by Manuel de Sousa Sepúlveda and his
wife, Leonor de Sá, whose shipwreck on the *São João* in 1552 became
the stuff of legend across sixteenth-century Europe (Armstrong-Roche,
Cervantes' Epic Novel, 220–2). "They are," according to Blackmore, "shipwreck experience personified" (*Manifest Perdition*, xix).

66 Armstrong-Roche, *Cervantes' Epic Novel*, 39.

67 Lozano Renieblas, "'Mar sesgo,'" 304–5.

68 Blackmore, *Manifest Perdition*, xxiv. The critic is referring precisely to the
wreck of the *São João*, even if the notion of the absence of sentiment is,
even here, "overstated."

69 In a notably direct explanation of similar symbolism, the narrator remarks that "the sea is a symbol of the inconstancy of our lives, neither
one promising safety or stability for any length of time" (Cervantes, *Persiles and Sigismunda*, 2.17.178); la inconstancia de nuestras vidas y la del
mar simbolizan en no prometer seguridad ni firmeza alguna largo tiempo
(*Persiles y Sigismunda*, 2.17.396).

70 For an example of how seafaring metaphors also intersect with economics, see Brewer, "Jealousy and Usury," 16–18.

71 Curtius, *European Literature*, 128–30.

72 Blumenberg, *Shipwreck with Spectator*, 7.

73 Such is one of the conclusions of Nichols, *Blue Mind*.

74 Freud was responding to Romain Rolland, who had suggested that such oceanic feelings of grandeur constituted an alternative "source of religious sentiments." "I cannot discover this 'oceanic' feeling in myself," admitted Freud, adding tellingly that "[i]t is not easy to deal scientifically with feelings" (*Civilization and Its Discontents*, 10–11).

75 Respectively, Blum, "Oceanic Studies," and Mentz, "Shakespeare's Ocean." In her plea that the field not fall back on familiar tropes, the former unequivocally states that "[t]he sea is not a metaphor" (Blum, "Oceanic Studies," 670).

76 cooke, "Mediterranean Thinking," 294.

77 Steinberg, "Of Other Seas," 157, 156.

78 On the robust relationship between the sea and the novel, see Cohen, *Novel and the Sea*, and Raban, *Oxford Book of the Sea*.

79 Burningham, nevertheless, finds satirical echoes of Camões in Cervantes, particularly in the episode of the enchanted boat in *Don Quijote* ("Os Manchíadas"); Percas de Ponseti sees in the same episode parallels with Cervantes's own Mediterranean experience (*Cervantes y su concepto del arte*, 618–20).

80 See Socorro, *El mar*. Of course, an author need not have travelled the seas to write about them, as a plethora of sentimental romances and books of chivalry demonstrate. Catalan and Galician authors were, for obvious reasons, particularly attracted to the sea, but medieval Castilian writers also became increasingly enamoured of its hold, despite some early critics' dismissal of the importance of the sea to those from inland regions. Navarro González rectifies the notion in his extensive *El mar en la literatura medieval castellana*. For newer approaches see Delpech, *L'imaginaire*, and Pinet, "Between the Seas." Finally, it bears recalling Eugenio de Salazar's curious *Navegación del alma* of 1600, an allegorical maritime journey across the stages of life, recently updated in an edition by Carriazo Ruiz and Sánchez Jiménez.

81 Cervantes, *Don Quijote*, 2.61.1234–5; *Don Quixote*, 2.61.862, translation modified. A remarkably similar scene takes place in *Persiles y Sigismunda*, 1.2.144–5; *Persiles and Sigismunda*, 1.2.28–9.

82 Don Quijote has no doubt imagined such an encounter through the lens of his books of chivalry, as *Amadís*, *Esplandián*, and *Tirant lo Blanc* all feature maritime adventures. Along similar lines, it is not fortuitous that the prime form of payment to Sancho is an *ínsula*, as islands were favoured sites of intrigue in such books. For more on these precedents see Navarro González, *El mar*, 241–317. I owe to María Antonia Garcés this particular insight of the repetition of the sense of sight.

83 Cervantes, *Don Quijote*, 2.61.1235; *Don Quixote*, 2.61.862.

84 Cervantes, *Don Quijote*, 2.64.1254; *Don Quixote*, 2.64.884, translation modified.

85 "There is now a long tradition of giving our deepest psychological impulses a Mediterranean embodiment," a tendency that inscribes a "symbolic geography" "that roughly follows human anatomy: the south is assigned the emotive, viceral [*sic*], genital, spontaneous qualities and the north the cognitive, cerebral, control, and management qualities" (James W. Fernandez, "Consciousness and Class," 170).

86 See, for instance, Pennebaker, Rimé, and Blankenship's social-psychological study "Stereotypes of Emotional Expressiveness of Northerners and Southerners: A Cross-Cultural Test of Montesquieu's Hypotheses," which "confirms" the stereotypes referenced in the article's title, largely unaware of the problematic nature of Montesquieu's original conjectures (for which I direct readers to Dainotto, "Does Europe Have a South?").

87 On the phenomenon of self-stereotyping, see Herzfeld, "Practical Mediterraneanism," 52, 57; Bowersock, "East-West Orientation," 168; and Dainotto, "Does Europe Have a South?," 39.

88 To cite merely one example, Gilmore emphasizes "the flamboyant virility complexes of Mediterranean males" ("Introduction," 16). Herzfeld would assert the need to recognize that such Mediterranean claims are "performative in Austin's sense; they do not so much enunciate facts as create them" ("Practical Mediterraneanism," 50). On the myth of the Mediterranean as an erotic, libertine space, particularly for gay men, see Aldrich, *Seduction*.

89 Montesquieu claimed the need to legislate controls over southern sensibilities and the liabilities they engender: "As you move toward the countries of the south, you will believe you have moved away from morality itself: the liveliest passions will increase crime; each will seek to take from others all the advantages that can favor these same passions" (*Spirit of the Laws*, 234).

90 Lope de Vega, *Los esclavos libres*, 92.

91 "[S]ome of the authors who praised the Arabs for their erudition and for their unflinching devotion to reason portrayed Islam as an irrational cult based on violence and lechery" (Tolan, "Forging New Paradigms," 65). On the refusal of other European thinkers to recognize the contributions of medieval Muslims to the growth of science, knowledge, and culture in the Renaissance, also see Mallette, "Boustrophedon."

92 Descartes, *Passions of the Soul*, 350. Unfortunately, modern scholars such as Bernard Lewis, Sylvain Gouguenheim, Serafín Fanjul, and Samuel P. Huntington have levelled analogous accusations. The widely discredited Pirenne thesis – that Muslim conquest caused the collapse of the Roman Empire and contributed to European decline by thwarting access to the Mediterranean – represents a similarly spurious idea that was influential for Braudel (Strachan, "Colonial Cosmology," 81–2). For a more

balanced approach to emotions in the Muslim Mediterranean see Ostle, *Sensibilities*.

93 Matar, "Arab Travelers," xxv.

94 Taylor, "The Enemy Within and Without" is one example. See also Delumeau, *La peur en Occident*, 262–72, and Matar, "Arab Travelers," xxvii.

95 Cervantes, *Don Quijote*, 1.1.40; *Don Quixote*, 1.1.20, translation modified.

96 Blüher, *Séneca en España*, 386n.

97 Aristotle is fundamental for understanding and anticipating modern attempts at distinguishing the rationality inherent in affect (*De Anima, Nicomachean Ethics,* and *Rhetoric;* see also de Sousa, *Rationality of Emotion*). The most complete attempt at recovering the oft-neglected influence of Greek and Roman philosophy on Cervantes is that of Barnés Vázquez, who identifies in *Don Quijote* alone more than 1,200 references to the classical world and 62 different classical authors (*La tradición clásica,* 3). See also Hume, *Treatise of Human Nature;* Smith, *Theory of Moral Sentiments;* Spinoza, *Ethics;* Nietzsche, *Gay Science;* Deleuze and Guattari, *What Is Philosophy?;* Nussbaum, *Political Emotions;* Nussbaum, *Upheavals of Thought;* Prinz, *Emotional Construction;* Prinz, *Gut Reactions;* Solomon, *In Defense of Sentimentality;* Camps, *El gobierno de las emociones;* and Trías, *Tratado de la pasión.*

98 We must nonetheless acknowledge that for Cervantes, unlike for many of his contemporaries, we lack any extant document in which he might lay out his own thoughts and ideology, a paradox described by Sliwa, *Documentos cervantinos,* 1–2.

99 Castro, in his broader project to link Cervantes to Erasmus – who had flirted extensively with Stoicism – observed several examples of a generally Stoic morality in Cervantes's literary works. It is certainly true that Cervantes extols the virtues of reason and the wisdom of accepting one's fortune; however, Castro himself was the first to recognize that the morality espoused across the Cervantine corpus is "quite complex" and that, even if it "appears strongly tinged by Stoic elements," it does not preclude other world-views, among other qualifications and caveats (Castro, *El pensamiento de Cervantes,* 346; see also 329–53). Unfortunately, I cannot subscribe to the belaboured and often bewildering argument recently advanced by Lorca in his *Neo-Stoicism and Skepticism.*

100 In an early English translation Ripa explains the allegory thus: "Reason alone can bring valiant Men upon the *Stage,* and into *Credit.* The Sword intimates the *extirpating Vice,* that wars against the Soul. The Bridle, the *Command* over *wild Passions*" (*Moral Emblems,* 64). For Cervantes's more general tendency to resist dualism, see Wilson, "'Unreason's Reason.'"

101 On these themes, see Rupp, *Heroic Forms.*

102 Cervantes, *Comedias y tragedias*, 1035–6, vv. 685–708.

103 Cervantes, 1068, vv. 1575–6.

104 Plato, *Symposium*, 178d–179a. For an alternative interpretation see Gil-Osle, *Amistades imperfectas*, 76–81.

105 Cervantes, *Don Quijote*, 1.39.497–8, and 1.41.527–8; *Don Quixote*, 1.39.337, and 1.41.359–60.

106 Appadurai, *Modernity at Large*, 8; he describes the concept more fully in "Topographies of the Self."

107 Cervantes, *Don Quijote*, 1.32.405; *Don Quixote*, 1.32.268.

108 Cervantes, *Don Quijote*, 1.50.625; *Don Quixote*, 1.50.430. In his "Aprobación" of *Don Quijote* of 1615, Josef de Valdivielso commends the 1605 volume for having done just that: "uplifting withered souls and melancholic spirits" (alentando ánimos marchitos y espíritus melancólicos; Cervantes, *Don Quijote*, 2.666).

109 Cervantes, *Don Quijote*, bk. 1, prologue, 19; *Don Quixote*, bk. 1, prologue, 8.

110 Cervantes, *Don Quijote*, 1.48.607; *Don Quixote*, 1.48.417, translation modified (emphasis mine).

111 This recalls Alberti's prescription for variety in painting, which advises "be careful not to repeat the same gesture or pose. The *istoria* will move the soul of the beholder when each man painted there clearly shows the movement of his own soul" (*On Painting*, 77).

112 Related to the Aristotelian concept of unity and expressed by El Pinciano as "unity and variety" (*Philosophia antigua poética*, 2:39), the principle of *variatio* was a *locus classicus* that Cervantes evoked several times in his works, with Fernando Bermúdez y Carvajal even eulogizing Cervantes's facility with *variatio* in the dedicational verses preceding the *Novelas ejemplares* (86), *Exemplary Novels* (8). Studies on the trope, however, have focused almost exclusively on the digressions of the interpolated stories (Martínez Mata, *Cervantes on "Don Quixote"*; and Campana, "Apuntes sobre la *variatio*"). It bears noting, moreover, that Horden and Purcell, in *Corrupting Sea*, regard as the supreme characteristic of the Mediterranean "diversity in unity," which is effectively a classical and Renaissance concept related to *variatio* and *discordia concors* or enantiosis, which have been identified as hallmarks of Cervantes's writing (Leland H. Chambers, "Coincidence of Opposites").

113 Bakhtin, *Dialogic Imagination*, 262.

114 Alcalá Galán, *Escritura desatada*.

115 Hutchinson, "Literatura fronteriza mediterránea," 1436.

116 Kinoshita, "Mediterranean Literature," 314. Here she also suggests that the discrete motifs of "piracy, slavery, and commerce" are "illustrative" of Mediterranean literature, themes that recur across Cervantes's works. For Childers, such topics "bespeak a concern with suturing the widening

gulf between the northern and southern shores of the Mediterranean" (*Transnational Cervantes*, 42).

117 Stated another way, even if the Mediterranean constitutes what Foucault would call a "heterotopia" (after all, he did deem the ship in a sea "the heterotopia par excellence"; "Of Other Spaces," 27), its literature ought to reflect difference beyond the virtues of its setting.

118 Castro, *Obra reunida*; Carrasco Urgoiti, *Vidas fronterizas*, 113–31; Márquez Villanueva, *Moros, moriscos y turcos*; and Márquez Villanueva, *El problema morisco*. See also Garcés, *Cervantes in Algiers*; Martínez de Castilla Muñoz and Gil Benumeya Grimau, *De Cervantes y el islam*; Schmauser and Monika, *El encuentro*; and, for a useful summary, Santos de la Morena, "El tema musulmán."

119 Fuchs, *Passing for Spain*, 10.

120 Consider, for example, Hutchinson's description of the city of Algiers, where Cervantes spent five years of his life as a captive from 1575 to 1580: "the Algiers of that time – with its ethnic, linguistic, and religious diversity, its high index of renegade immigrants and *morisco* emigrants, its dependency on corsairs and enormous population of slaves from all parts, its peculiar institutions and exercise of power, its luxuries and famines, its festivals and sexual practices – resembled no other city on Earth at the same time that, in its unique configuration, it reunited people from so many places near and far" ("Escribir el Mediterráneo," 648).

121 Riley, *Cervantes's Theory of the Novel*, 179–99.

122 Cervantes, *Don Quijote*, 1.50.624; *Don Quixote*, 1.50.429.

123 Hutchinson, "Affective Dimensions," 79.

124 Cassano, *Southern Thought*, 63.

3. Shadows of the Inquisition

1 Acevedo, "Caso," 108. After the Grand Inquisitor appealed to Philip III himself, the auto-da-fé was eventually rescheduled and carried out, much to the satisfaction, according to Acevedo, of the population of Triana, whose "happiness and consolation was twice as great as the distress they had received from the past slight" (111). For the reasons behind its original suspension see Domínguez Ortiz, *La clase social*, 86.

2 Bourdieu, *Logic of Practice*, 52–66.

3 In Sancho's parodic trial in the ducal palace (Cervantes, *Don Quijote*, 2.69.1294–1301; *Don Quixote*, 2.69.907–12).

4 Respectively, Shuger, *Don Quixote in the Archives*, 128–30, and Riquer, *Aproximación al "Quijote,"* 129, for instance.

5 Peristiany, *Honour and Shame*, 9.

6 Gilmore, "Honor, Honesty, Shame," 90.

7 Horden and Purcell, *Corrupting Sea*, 518.
8 Lope states that "the cases of honor are best, / because they move every-one with more force" (*Arte nuevo*, 149, vv. 327–8; los casos de honra son mejores, / porque mueven con más fuerza a toda gente). On honour in the comedia see Arellano, "Casos de honor"; Caro Baroja, "Religion"; Castro, *Semblanzas y estudios españoles*, 317–402; García Valdecasas, *El hidalgo*; Larson, *The Honor Plays*; McKendrick, "Honour/Vengeance"; Pitt-Rivers, "Honour and Social Status"; and Scott K. Taylor, *Honor and Violence*. For an even more extensive bibliography see Artiles, "Biblio-grafía." Although the precise meaning of honour can vary according to genre and time in the seventeenth century (Arellano, *Historia del teatro*, 114), it is clear that the body of scholarship on honour dwarfs that of shame.
9 Bennassar, *Spanish Character*, 213.
10 Tomkins, "Varieties of Shame"; Tomkins, *Affect Imagery Consciousness*, 511–12. In his study of Renaissance concepts of shame, Gundersheimer notes a few, but not all, of these axes as well ("Renaissance Concepts," 34–6).
11 Something similar happens when the theoretically antonymous terms *shameful* and *shameless* coincide to describe a brazen and deplorable action, one that ought to have produced shame – and yet seems to lack it entirely. *Shame* is thus a kind of contronym or Janus word, a striking example of what Freud called words of "antithetical meaning," or those that contain in a single term both a defining quality and its opposite ("Primal Words," 99); also noted in Allen, "Waxing Red," 204.
12 The most comprehensive critique of the overstated importance of honour in seventeenth-century Spain is to be found in *Honor and Violence* by Scott K. Taylor, who advocates instead for a "rhetoric of honor" by undermin-ing the rigidity of the honor code through an examination of criminal jus-tice proceedings. The fallacy and limitations of the honour-shame binary are also underscored by Wikan, "A Contestable Pair," 635–6; Brandes, "Reflections," 122–3; and Kressel and Arioti, "Vergogna e genere." Wil-liam Ian Miller, for his part, underlines the need to "rid ourselves once and for all of the idea that honour-based culture produces shallow inner lives" ("Deep Inner Lives," 200).
13 Malkiel, "Development of *Verecundia*," 514.
14 Cassin, *Dictionary of Untranslatables*, 1196.
15 The multiple refrains involving shame further corroborate its cultural importance in early modern Spain; see *Diccionario de autoridades*, 3:464; Covarrubias, *Tesoro*, 1523; and Sbarbi, *Diccionario de refranes*, 2:442–3.
16 Quoted in Castro, *Semblanzas y estudios españoles*, 321–2.
17 Menéndez Pidal, "Del honor," 357; 361–2.

18 Menéndez Pidal, 365.
19 Castro, *Semblanzas y estudios españoles*, 329.
20 Castro, 350–4.
21 Castro, 324.
22 Menéndez Pidal, "Del honor," 361.
23 Quoted in Jurado Santos, "El rídiculo 'Quijote,'" 272.
24 Quoted in Jurado Santos, 273–4.
25 Jurado Santos, 273–4.
26 Ríos, "Juicio crítico," 275.
27 Jurado Santos, "El rídiculo 'Quijote,'" 275.
28 Scott K. Taylor, *Honor and Violence*, 5.
29 In the mid-1980s, Herzfeld ("Honour and Shame," "The Horns," "Of
    Horns and History") and Galt ("Straw Horns") carried out an exchange
    of mutual criticism in the journal *American Ethnologist* that centred largely
    on the honour-shame question in Mediterranean cultures. Boissevain's
    "Social Anthropology," Davis's *People of the Mediterranean*, Gilmore's
    Honor and Shame, and Horden and Purcell's *Corrupting Sea*, 485–523, 637–
    41, are also useful for contextualizing the polemic of Mediterraneanism
    since the publication of Peristiany's volume.
30 Herzfeld, "The Horns," 439.
31 Aristotle, *Nicomachean Ethics*, in *Complete Works*, vol. 2, 1128b11; 3826; and
    Rhetoric, in *Complete Works*, vol. 2, 1384a22–36; 4726–7.
32 Palencia, in a similar vein, defines *verecundia* as "honest shame with tem-
    perance fearing reprimand of a vice" (*Universal vocabulario*, cccccxx *verso*).
33 Pocaterra, *Two Dialogues on Shame*, 43.
34 Tomkins, *Affect Imagery Consciousness*, 13.
35 Sedgwick and Frank, "Shame in the Cybernetic Fold," 97.
36 Probyn, *Blush*, 14.
37 Cervantes, *Don Quijote*, 1.2.53; *Don Quixote*, 1.2.26. I have modified this
    translation to correspond more faithfully to Covarrubias's definitions,
    which underscore the physiognomic traits of shame inherent in the act of
    blushing: "*Correrse* means to be affronted, because the blood rushes [*corre*]
    to the face [...] *Corrimiento*, confusion or shame." Similarly, *affront* [*afrenta*]
    is defined as "the act that is committed against someone in his dishonour,
    even if it is done with reason and justice, like whipping someone or ex-
    posing him to shame; and to this person we say that they have affronted
    him [...] *Affront* is said, as though in the forehead [*frente*], because from the
    shame felt by the affronted, colours appear on his face and particularly on
    the forehead, due to the blood that rises to the brain" (*Tesoro*, 618, 51).
38 Cervantes, *Don Quijote*, 1.20.239; *Don Quixote*, 1.20.150, translation
    modified.
39 Cervantes, *Don Quijote*, 1.29.377; *Don Quixote*, 1.29.249.

40 Cervantes, *Don Quijote*, 1.31.402; *Don Quixote*, 1.31.266, translation modified.

41 On the importance of the figure of the spectator in *Don Quijote*, see Avilés, "En el límite de la mirada."

42 Elsewhere I have studied in greater detail the importance of shame in these and other episodes from the novel, including its relation to humoral theory and the protagonist's emotional evolution ("Don Quijote avergonzado"); as a "technology of the self" for Don Quijote ("Las tecnologías cervantinas"); its poetic embodiment ("End(lessnes)s of Infamy"); and its association with Mediterranean captivity in "The Captive's Tale" ("Soldier's Shame").

43 Díaz-Plaja, *En torno a Cervantes*, 115; Syverson-Stork, *Theatrical Aspects*, 32–6.

44 Covarrubias, *Tesoro*, 1523.

45 Cervantes, *Don Quijote*, 1.22.261; *Don Quixote*, 1.22.166. In order to fulfil the pressing needs of Philip II's armadas, the galleys became an alternative to the shame punishment of the sanbenito by way of a 1567 judicial decree that "suggested – suggestion being equivalent to an order – that sentences to the galleys could be substituted for those to prison and sanbenito" (Lea, *History of the Inquisition*, 142).

46 On what Edgerton calls these "effigies of shame," see his *Pictures and Punishment*. Mills discusses their probable use in other parts of medieval Europe (and analogues such as the German *Schandbilder*), though, conspicuously, not in Spain (*Suspended Animation*, 42–9). For shame's relationship to penality and criminality as a broader European phenomenon see Hamblet, *Punishment and Shame*; Sère and Wettlaufer, *Shame between Punishment and Penance*; and Nash and Kilday, *Cultures of Shame*; and for the ethics of shaming in the modern legal system see Nussbaum, *Hiding from Humanity*, 172–305.

47 See especially Partida VII, título 14, ley 18 (617); and Partida VII, título 31, ley 4 (709–10).

48 Lea, *History of the Inquisition*, 138. Lea's statement reflects what was inscribed in law by the *Siete Partidas*: "The one with infamy, even if there is no guilt, is dead with regards to good and honour in this world" (quoted in Menéndez Pidal, "Del honor," 358); and in letters by Lope: "Because there is no greater punishment, Than giving life to someone affronted" (quoted in Castro, *Semblanzas y estudios españoles*, 338; Porque no hay mayor castigo, Que dar vida a un afrentado).

49 Even though the sentence itself has been lost, the royal arrest order ("Para que un alguacil vaya a prender a Miguel de Cervantes") is preserved in the Archivo General de Simancas. Sliwa's *Documentos cervantinos* provides an indispensable guide for historical documents relating to

Cervantes's life and family. Gracia imagines the altercation with Segura (or Sigura) as one in which Cervantes defends his own personal honour, leading him to reflect several times in his writing on the difference between an offence (*ofensa*) and an affront (*afrenta*) and the legitimacy of responding with violence to the latter (Gracia, *La conquista de la ironía*, 33–5).

50 Bujanda, "Recent Historiography," 228.

51 In addition to the examples that follow, Preciosa's "grandmother" in *La gitanilla* (*The Little Gypsy Girl*) refers to public shaming: "Three times, for three different offenses, I've found myself on the point of being publicly flogged and humiliated" (30; 119; Tres veces, por tres delitos diferentes, me he visto casi puesta en el asno para ser azotada) – as does the mayor in the episode of the "false captives" of *Persiles y Sigismunda*, who threatens that "these two gentlemen captives are going to take a ride through the streets on [asses]" (*Persiles and Sigismunda*, 3.10.253); han de pasear en [asnos] estas calles estos dos señores cautivos (*Persiles y Sigismunda*, 3.10.533–4).

52 Cervantes, *Persiles y Sigismunda*, 3.7.501–2; *Persiles and Sigismunda*, 3.7.237.

53 Cervantes, *Persiles y Sigismunda*, 3.7.500; *Persiles and Sigismunda*, 3.7.236. Periandro's admonition echoes a piece of exemplary wisdom from Cervantes's novella *La fuerza de la sangre* (*The Power of Blood*): "An ounce of public dishonor wounds more than a bushel of secret disgrace" (*Exemplary Novels*, 202); Más lastima una onza de deshonra pública que una arroba de infamia secreta (*Novelas ejemplares*, 396). Carrera, "The Social Dimension" studies the presence of shame therein.

54 For a discussion of the distinctions between *agravios*, *afrentas*, and *injurias* see Menéndez Pidal, "Del honor," 90; Pérez Cortés, "La ofensa"; and Romero Muñoz's footnote in his edition of *Persiles y Sigismunda* (514n).

55 Cervantes, *Persiles y Sigismunda*, 3.7.502; *Persiles and Sigismunda*, 3.7.237.

56 Cervantes, *Novelas ejemplares*, 287; *Exemplary Novels*, 134.

57 Cervantes, *Novelas ejemplares*, 287–8; *Exemplary Novels*, 135.

58 Cervantes, *Don Quijote*, 2.60.1221; *Don Quixote*, 2.60.851–2.

59 Bernaldo de Quirós, *La picota*, 11–13, 59–60.

60 See Bernaldo de Quirós, who also notes that *picota* and *rollo* were more or less synonymous (*La picota*, 54–5, 58). The Latin terms *arbor infelix*, *arbori suspendere*, and *infelix lignum* all refer to what in the Western world has undoubtedly become the most iconic shame punishment of them all: that of crucifixion. In ancient Roman territories, crucifixion (*supplicium servile*) indexed the social status of its victim, having been reserved for slaves and enemies of the state, while noble citizens were afforded less shameful forms of punishment such as fines, exile, or, at most,

decapitation. The capital punishment of hanging was also regarded as shameful, and the particular posture of hanging (without causing death) even gained an associative connotation of shame, an image that calls to mind Don Quijote's humiliation at being left hanging outside the inn after having his hand tied by Maritornes (Cervantes, *Don Quijote*, 1.43.559–60). For an in-depth study of the iconography of hanging, see Mills, *Suspended Animation*.

61 Bernaldo de Quirós, *La picota*, 89.

62 This revulsion is highlighted by Quevedo's *El Buscón*, in which the protagonist's father is an executioner and a constant source of shame for the young Pablos. See also Stuart, *Defiled Trades*.

63 Rodríguez Marín, *El Loaysa*, 205–7.

64 Cervantes, *Don Quijote*, 1.47.594; *Don Quixote*, 1.47.408.

65 Cervantes, *Don Quijote*, 1.46.588. *Don Quixote*, 1.46.404.

66 Cervantes, *Don Quijote*, 1.48.611–12; *Don Quixote*, 1.48.420–1, translation modified.

67 Cervantes, *Don Quijote*, 1.49.613; *Don Quixote*, 1.49.422.

68 An example of this motif – along with further proof of the differentiation between honour and shame – can be found in an anonymous (though perhaps apocryphal) seventeenth-century paper on the statutes of *limpieza de sangre*: "In Spain there are two classes of nobility. One major, which is Honourableness [*Hidalguía*], and the other minor, which is Cleanliness, which we call Old Christians. And although it is more honourable to have the first class of Honourableness, it is much more shameful [*afrentoso*] to lack the second; because in Spain we esteem a plebeian and clean man much more than an *hidalgo* who is not clean" (quoted in Domínguez Ortiz, *La clase social*, 196).

69 Cervantes, *Don Quijote*, 1.47.590–1; *Don Quixote*, 1.47.405–6.

70 Rawlings, *Spanish Inquisition*, 37.

71 Cervantes, *Don Quijote*, 1.52.644; *Don Quixote*, 1.52.443.

72 Lea, *History of the Inquisition*, 212–13; Rawlings, *Spanish Inquisition*, 37.

73 Additional references throughout the episode offer striking parallels with shaming. For example, when Don Quijote takes off in pursuit of the penitential procession, the narrator makes a point of noting that he "pressed Rocinante with his thighs because he had no spurs" (Cervantes, *Don Quixote*, 1.52.440–1); apretó los muslos a Rocinante, porque espuelas no las tenía (*Don Quijote*, 1.52.640). Historically, chopping the spurs off a disgraced knight's boots was a symbolic act of shaming and degradation (Riquer, *Caballeros andantes españoles*, 166). Trigg examines an example of these practices from *Tirant lo Blanc*, a prominent work in Alonso Quijano's library ("'Shamed Be,'" 81).

74 Cervantes, *Don Quijote*, 1.49.616; *Don Quixote*. 1.49.424.

75 This is the same process that the renegade of "La historia del cautivo" undergoes after returning to Spain: "[he] went to the city of Granada, where, through the mediation of the Holy Inquisition, he would be returned to the blessed fellowship of the church" (Cervantes, *Don Quixote*, 1.41.368); se fue a la ciudad de Granada a reducirse por medio de la Santa Inquisición al gremio santísimo de la Iglesia (*Don Quijote*, 1.41.538–9).

76 Cervantes, *Don Quijote*, 1.49.613; *Don Quixote*, 1.49.421 (emphasis mine).

77 The debility of Don Quijote's self-conscious argument for enchantment has been commented on extensively (Layna Ranz, *La eficacia del fracaso*, 252; Torrente Ballester, *El "Quijote" como juego*, 155).

78 Castro, *Semblanzas*, 363.

79 Cervantes, *Don Quijote*, bk. 2, prologue, 677; *Don Quixote*, bk. 2, prologue, 458.

80 Cervantes, *Don Quijote*, 2.11.782; *Don Quixote*, 2.11.526. Menéndez Pidal speculated that Cervantes's posture against honour retribution stems not from ideology but from genre: "The novel destined for private reading invited condemnatory reflection on bloody vengeance, while the theatre required giving oneself over to feelings of greater sensationalism" ("Del honor," 368).

81 Caro Baroja, "Honour and Shame," 98–9.

82 Taylor, *Honor and Violence*; Horden and Purcell, *Corrupting Sea*, 519–22. It is also worth recalling that in *Fuenteovejuna* Lope gives honour to all, the honour of the masses.

83 Probyn, *Blush*, 53.

84 Domínguez Ortiz cites a fascinating historical case that begins to suggest what this sort of resistance through shame might look like: a Portuguese converso who walked through the streets "with a sanbenito, and with such great ease [*desenfado*] and impudence [*desahogo*], that he caused anger [*ira*] in all those who looked at him" (quoted in Olmos García, "La Inquisición en la época," 86–7).

85 Cervantes, *Don Quijote*, 1.47.597; *Don Quixote*, 1.47.410.

86 Cervantes, *Don Quijote*, 1.52.643; *Don Quixote*, 1.52.443, translation modified.

4. A Mediterranean (Tragi)comedy

1 Cervantes, *Don Quijote*, 2.54.1167–8; *Don Quixote*, 2.54.811.

2 Although estimates of the number of Moriscos expelled have varied over the years, it is generally agreed that approximately three hundred thousand abandoned Spanish lands as a direct result of the edict of expulsion (Vincent, "Geography of the Morisco Expulsion"; Domínguez Ortiz and Vincent, *Historia de los moriscos*, 200).

3 Quoted in García-Arenal and Wiegers, *Mediterranean Diaspora*, 1–2; translation modified.
4 Bunes Ibarra, "Expulsion of the Moriscos," 37–8.
5 To cite a notable yet by no means unique example: no fewer than a half-dozen of the contributors to García-Arenal and Wiegers's volume *The Expulsion of the Moriscos from Spain: A Mediterranean Diaspora*, published as part of a series on Iberian history, mention Cervantes's fictional Ricote.
6 García-Arenal and Wiegers, *Mediterranean Diaspora*, 3.
7 Márquez Villanueva, "El problema morisco," 8–9.
8 Nadeau, in "Critiquing the Elite," provides a lucid analysis of the meal from the perspective of food studies, as well as of the fact, frequently remarked by other critics, that Ricote fails to observe the Muslim prohibition of wine and pork.
9 Cervantes, *Don Quijote*, 2.54.1169; *Don Quixote*, 2.54.812.
10 Observe, for example, that *risa* (laughter) and its variations (*reír, reírse*) are mentioned 130 times in the novel (Rutherford, *Power of the Smile*, 212).
11 Trueblood, "La risa en el *Quijote*," 13.
12 Fajardo also points out important links between the Ricote and Barataria episodes ("Narrative and Agency," 315).
13 Mayans y Siscar, *Vida de Miguel de Cervantes*, 27.
14 Scholars such as Díaz Migoyo ("El *Quijote* muerto de risa") customarily attribute the anecdote to Philip III's biographer Baltasar Porreño; however, it is notably absent in Porreño's *Dichos y hechos del Señor Rey D. Phelipe III el Bueno*, as Fitzmaurice Kelly recognizes (*A Memoir*, 113n).
15 Cervantes, *Don Quijote*, 1.9.118; *Don Quixote*, 1.9.67.
16 López Pinciano, *Philosophia antigua poética*, 3:32. Except for the Latin etymology, the definition of laughter is also conspicuously absent in Covarrubias's entry for *risa*, and, even in Noydens's expanded edition of 1674, he does not attempt to define the concept beyond a few classical anecdotes and behavioural prohibitions (Covarrubias, *Tesoro*, 1597).
17 Eisenberg, *Study of "Don Quixote,"* 109–10. Among the studies whose publication might serve to collectively challenge such an assertion are John J. Allen's "Smiles and Laughter"; Gorfkle's *Discovering the Comic*; Iffland's *De fiestas y aguafiestas* and "Laughter Tamed"; Martín's *Burlesque Sonnet* and "Humor and Violence"; Quint's *Novel of Modern Times*; Paulson's *Aesthetics of Laughter*; Scham's *Lector Ludens*, 150–74; Ugalde's "La risa de don Quijote"; Wood's *Irresponsible Self*; and Zoppi's *Risa, sonrisa, ironía*. Nevertheless, few of these studies have focused on laughter per se, often stressing instead the body, the disruption of the social order, or the carnivalesque in general – elements that perform a consequential role in Sancho's governorship and his return to peasant life but fail to account for his exchange with Ricote.

18 Nevertheless, certain earlier readers had already begun to see beyond the humour of *Don Quijote*. Even in the seventeenth century, French critics had picked up on "a vein of satirical seriousness in the midst of all the comicality" (Rutherford, *Power of the Smile*, 175). John J. Allen also notes several early readers who had already sympathetically identified with the novel's protagonists long before Romanticism ("Smiles and Laughter," 528). Close's *Romantic Approach*, 29n–30n, documents the original writings, many of which remain untranslated, in which Schlegel, Schelling, and their *Romantische* ilk extolled Don Quijote.

19 Russell, "*Don Quixote* as a Funny Book," 324.

20 Close, *Romantic Approach*, 2.

21 Predmore, review, 258. In his now-classic *Don Quixote: Hero or Fool?*, John J. Allen studies at length the textual features responsible for engendering such divisions.

22 Gilman, *Novel According to Cervantes*, 74.

23 Cervantes, *Poesías*, 321.

24 Among them, the analysis by Trueblood, "La risa en el *Quijote*" is the most complete in this regard (see especially 16–21).

25 Martín, "Humor and Violence," 170. Martín herself avoids this trap, recognizing that "Cervantes realized that simple comedy was no longer enough in an age of institutionalized madness, where knights errant and their idealized values were obsolete, and fools (such as the type of idle aristocrats personified by the Duke and Duchess) had taken their place" (167).

26 Russell, "*Don Quixote* as a Funny Book," 323.

27 In critiquing Close, Iffland also acknowledges the difficulty in reconstructing the early modern reception of *Don Quijote* ("Laughter Tamed," 396–7).

28 "[H]ow do you dare reconcile these Heraclituses and Democrituses? Banish, banish from your thoughts the monstrous tragicomedy, which in the law of art is impossible to have! [...] they are made against reason, against nature, and against art" (Cascales, *Tablas poéticas*, 373). Sidney too would vilify the "mongrel tragic-comedy" (*Miscellaneous Works*, 57). The hybrid genre nevertheless had its defenders, such as Ricardo de Turia and his *Apologético de las comedias españolas*.

29 López Pinciano, *Philosophia antigua poética*, 3:17, 34.

30 In addition to the dependence on El Pinciano (a trend salient in Eisenberg's *Study of "Don Quixote"*), even in his more recent *Cervantes and the Comic Mind of His Age*, Close tends to rely inordinately upon dramatic theories of comedy.

31 The "comedy, or tragicomedy, of the modern novel replaces the knowable with the unknowable, transparency with unreliability, and this is surely

in direct proportion to the growth of the characters' fictive inner lives" (Wood, *Irresponsible Self*, 10). This recalls Kundera's thoughtful analysis of the humour of *Don Quijote*: "We are laughing not because someone is being ridiculed, mocked, or even humiliated but because a reality is abruptly revealed as ambiguous, things lose their apparent meaning, the man before us is not what he thought himself to be" (*The Curtain*, 109).

32 As Dopico Black and Layna Ranz recognize in their conciliatory volume *USA Cervantes*, "[d]ismissing the work of the enemy was part of our strategy, an obligation of the good critic. But the quarrel seems to lose steam with each passing day, and reconciliation is an urgent matter of academic commitment" (12).

33 Hobbes, *Elements of Law*, 41.

34 Joubert, *Treatise on Laughter*, 36.

35 "Many philosophers have tried to learn what the reason and cause for laughter is, and none have said anything that can be understood" (Huarte de San Juan, *Examen de ingenios*, 368).

36 Huarte de San Juan, 367.

37 Szameitat et al., "Differentiation of Emotions."

38 Parvulescu, *Notes on a Passion*, 6, 8.

39 Bergson, *Laughter*, 9–11 (italics in the original).

40 Bergson, 39, 56 (italics in the original).

41 Parvulescu, *Notes on a Passion*; Rutherford, *Power of the Smile*. Parvulescu thus proposes that "the 'civilizing of laughter' is simultaneous with the production of the modern smile" (7), a claim that parallels, albeit with different periodization, Jacques Le Goff's question of "whether smiling is not one of the creations of the Middle Ages" ("Laughter in the Middle Ages," 48). These observations further contrast with Bakhtin's notion that the Middle Ages were an epoch of sadness, and the Renaissance one of the liberation of laughter.

42 Relying on Elias's unpublished "Essay on Laughter," Parvulescu's study is one of many that succumb to the conceptual temptations of the civilizing process. In addition to the common objections that Elias's history is too linear and that it devoids medieval peoples of the interiority he grants early moderns, some of these scholars see his influence as unduly stifling the study of emotions in particular, among other complaints (for example, Eustace et al., "Historical Study of Emotions," esp. 1493–4, 1525).

43 Cervantes, *Don Quijote*, 2.31.964; *Don Quixote*, 2.31.660.

44 Cervantes, *Don Quijote*, 2.32.976; *Don Quixote*, 2.32.669.

45 Their muffled laughter also aligns with class-based social prescriptions, as El Pinciano advises that "serious people laugh little, since laughing a lot is for commoners" (*Philosophia antigua poética*, 3:20). More or less the same idea was already present in the work of Plato, who moralized

against laughter as a lower-class practice, and in that of Aristotle, who associated it with his concept of *eutrapelia* and the directive of proper behaviour.

46 To some extent, this common view was informed by genre. Arellano observes, for instance, what he calls an "affective anesthesia" in the comedia that encouraged spectators to laugh at instead of sympathize with the protagonists of a play (*Historia del teatro*, 137).

47 *Oxford English Dictionary*, 2nd ed., s.v. "Schadenfreude."

48 "Before the Enlightenment, Plato and Hobbes's idea that laughter is an expression of feelings of superiority was the only widely circulated understanding of laughter" (Morreall, *Comic Relief*, 6), or what de Sousa calls the "phthonic" dimension of humour (*Rationality of Emotion*, 290–1).

49 Hobbes, *Elements of Law*, 42.

50 Smith, *Joy of Pain*, xi.

51 Lihoreau, *Schadenfreude*, 167, 22, 33, 37, 136.

52 Nabokov, *Lectures on "Don Quixote,"* 51–2. The writer and critic thus reminds us that, particularly in early modernity, reactions such as scorn and sympathy were quite unstable. "Confronted with identical spectacles of suffering," Dickie has observed, even "the same individual might laugh one day and weep the next" (*Cruelty and Laughter*, 11).

53 Don Quijote is, of course, subject to Schadenfreude as well; however, his status as an hidalgo spares him from open derision to a greater extent than his squire, as I will explain in more detail.

54 Sullivan, *Grotesque Purgatory*.

55 See Ruch and Proyer, "Extending the Study of Gelotophobia."

56 Cervantes, *Don Quijote*, 2.30.958–60; *Don Quixote*, 2.30.655–6.

57 Cervantes, *Don Quijote*, 2.32.975; *Don Quixote*, 2.32.668, translation modified.

58 Urbina, *El sin par Sancho Panza*, 13; Bakhtin, *Rabelais and His World*, 142.

59 See especially Durán, "Carnaval, disfraces"; Iffland, *De fiestas y aguafiestas*, 121–41; Redondo, *Otra manera*, 191–203, 453–73; and, for a more sceptical view, Bergman, "Resistance to Carnival."

60 For more general treatments of Sancho Panza see Hendrix, "Comic Types"; Urbina, *El sin par Sancho Panza*; Romero Flores, *Biografía de Sancho Panza*; and Márquez Villanueva, "La génesis."

61 Alonso's "Las prevaricaciones" provides a rigorous philological analysis of some of Sancho's malapropisms, while Hacthoun's "Los mecanismos del humor" focuses on specific rhetorical figures at play in his speech. Joly, on the other hand, suggests an affirmative function of the character's linguistic spontaneity ("Ainsi parlait Sancho Pança"). For the dialogic impertinence and importance of Sancho see Urbina, *El sin par Sancho Panza*,

92–108; and for a more general examination of comical word play in the novel, see Gorfkle, *Discovering the Comic*, 100–24.

62 On Sancho's girth see Cárdenas-Rotunno, "Mirth of Girth"; on his shortness see Urbina, for whom Sancho reflects the chivalric role of the dwarf (*El sin par Sancho Panza*, 70–7).

63 For Close, indeed, the squire only ever pertains to the archetype of "the simpleton-fool" ("Sancho Panza: Wise Fool," 344).

64 On Sancho's gluttony see Barbagallo, "Sancho no es," 54–8.

65 Duclos, "A Squire's Schooling."

66 Molho, "Raíces folklóricas"; Flores, *Sancho Panza*, 172–226. For the related question of Sancho's "asnificación," see Di Stefano, "– Venid, mochachos."

67 On this point see the classic interpretations by Maravall, who viewed Sancho's success as an instantiation of utopia (*Utopía*, 216–21); and Redondo, who approaches Barataria through the lens of the carnivalesque (*Otra manera*, 471–2).

68 Cervantes, *Don Quijote*, 2.45.1085, 1090, 1087; *Don Quixote*, 2.45.749, 752, 750.

69 Riley, *Theory of the Novel*, 89. I examine the different connotations of *admiratio* more closely in chapter 5.

70 Roncero López, "El humor y la risa," 302.

71 Le Goff, "Laughter in the Middle Ages," 50.

72 Castiglione, *Book of the Courtier*, 146.

73 Castiglione, 183–4, 188.

74 Cervantes, *Don Quijote*, 2.53.1161–2; *Don Quixote*, 2.53.806–7. Citing the picaresque buffoon Estebanillo González as an example, Roncero López suggests that the reality of palace life was such that pranks inducing physical harm were actually received rapturously and with little restraint ("El humor y la risa," 318). Schmitz, in "Sancho's Courtly Performance," also studies Sancho in light of early modern conduct manuals.

75 Gracián Dantisco, *Galateo español*, 67.

76 Della Casa, *Galateo*, 42–3. Though following the recent English edition of *Galateo* by M.F. Rusnak, in order to more faithfully render their emotional content I have modified slightly the translations from the Italian in this citation and those that follow.

77 Della Casa, *Galateo*, 43.

78 As with examples highlighted in the previous chapter, they "dissimulated their laughter so that Don Quijote would not become ashamed" (Cervantes, *Don Quixote*, 2.31.664, translation modified); disimularon la risa, porque don Quijote no acabase de correrse (*Don Quijote*, 2.31.969).

79 Cervantes, *Don Quijote*, 2.43.1068; *Don Quixote*, 2.43.736.

80 Cervantes, *Don Quijote*, 2.42.1060; *Don Quixote*, 2.42.730.

81 This is not to say, however, that Sancho leaves the *ínsula* unscathed or that he is blissfully unaware of being the object of practical jokes and laughter. On the contrary, he demonstrates on more than one occasion an ability to see through the prank and lodge a protest (Cervantes, *Don Quijote*, 2.32.985, 2.49.1118, 2.53.1164; *Don Quixote*, 2.32.675, 2.49.773, 2.53.808).

82 Cervantes, *Don Quijote*, 2.49.1120; *Don Quixote*, 2.49.774. This recalls Gracián Dantisco's admonition that "the worst pranks are those that are true" (*Galateo español*, 70; no hay peor burla que la verdadera), as well as El Pinciano's category of "passive laughter" (risa pasiva): "when laughter turns into a joke on the person who intends for someone else to be the one mocked and laughed at" (*Philosophia antigua poética*, 3:73).

83 Cervantes, *Don Quijote*, 2.70.1303; *Don Quixote*, 2.70.914.

84 On the satirical qualities of Barataria see Quint, *Novel of Modern Times*, 136; Murillo, *Critical Introduction*, 200; and Wilson, "Cervantes and the Indies," 372.

85 "Satire can be described as the literary art of diminishing or derogating a subject by making it ridiculous and evoking toward it attitudes of amusement, contempt, scorn, or indignation. It differs from the comic in that comedy evokes laughter mainly as an end in itself, while satire derides; that is, it uses laughter as a weapon, and against a butt that exists outside the work itself" (Abrams and Harpham, *Glossary of Literary Terms*, 353).

86 In addition to critics like Russell and Close, Díaz Migoyo ("El *Quijote* muerto de risa," 17), Hart ("What's Funny about *Don Quixote*?"), and Allen ("Smiles and Laughter," 518) all concur that our laughter at the text has decreased since its first publication and that our sensibilities today prevent our laughing derisively at the misfortunes of the characters. In passing, I would submit that we twenty-first-century individuals are not so evolved as never to laugh at physical violence, as Hart seems to imply ("What's Funny about *Don Quixote*?," 228).

87 However, Cicero does anticipate the theory by discussing similar concepts (*Cicero on Oratory and Orators*, 194). Critchley contextualizes the incongruity theory along with other dominant approaches to humour (*On Humour*, 1–22). Molho, for his part, recognizes a similar function of the "reversible" in Sancho, his ability to pass from the pranked (*burlado*) to the prankster (*burlador*) likewise constituting an essential element of the character's comicality ("Raíces foklóricas," 269–70).

88 Cervantes, *Don Quijote*, 2.72.1318–19; *Don Quixote*, 2.72.925–6. Avellaneda, *El ingenioso hidalgo don Quijote de la Mancha*.

89 Cervantes, *Don Quijote*, 2.32.983; *Don Quixote*, 2.32.674.

90 The latter camp's foremost representative is still Márquez Villanueva, who convincingly dispels the claims of Bataillon (*Erasmo y España*),

who finds Cervantes a more willing adherent of the expulsion policy (Márquez Villanueva, *Personajes*, 232).

91 Cervantes, *Don Quijote*, 2.54.1170; *Don Quixote*, 2.54.813.

92 I defer to Márquez Villanueva, who eloquently explains that "Cervantes did not feel inclined to martyrdom. He knows the terrain he treads on, and, as in the manner of someone who pays tribute, he puts on kid gloves in order to obliquely make himself understood by those who really interest him, those 'discreet' readers that make up his ideal audience" (*Moros, moriscos y turcos*, 228–9).

93 Rancière outlines this theory in *The Politics of Aesthetics*.

94 Márquez Villanueva, *Personajes*, 256. There were, however, other prominent voices of dissent from the political sphere, including the pope and, perhaps most comprehensively, Pedro de Valencia. Hitchcock, in "Expulsion of the Moriscos," surveys the historical landscape of approaches to the Moriscos, and Layna Ranz, for his part, cautions against the tendency to conflate history with fiction in critical treatments of the Ricote episode (*La eficacia del fracaso*, 296–302). Cervantes also treats the Moriscos, often in contrasting ways, in *El coloquio de los perros* (407–8; *The Colloquy of the Dogs*, 721–3) and *Persiles y Sigismunda* (3.11.544–54; *Persiles and Sigismunda*, 3.11.258–62). Armstrong-Roche studies Ricote alongside *Persiles y Sigismunda*'s Jarife, identifying a subtle but powerful critique of the expulsion in the apposite interplay between the classical virtues and fear (*Cervantes' Epic Novel*, 250–64).

95 Cervantes, *Don Quijote*, 2.54.1170–1; *Don Quixote*, 2.54.813.

96 Plata, "Ricote," 268. In a similar vein, see Domínguez ("El laberinto mental"), who productively reads the Ricote episode through the concept of exile.

97 Cervantes, *Don Quijote*, 2.54.1171; *Don Quixote*, 2.54.814.

98 While describing his reading choice, Mann betrays his own approach to Cervantes's novel: "Shipboard reading – it falls into a category generally despised [...] Since I have respect for this enterprise of ours, it is right and proper that I also take heed to the reading that accompanies it. *Don Quixote* is universal; just the right reading for a trip to the end of the world" ("Voyage with Don Quixote," 329–30). On Tieck's translation and the exalted humour of the novel, Mann adds: "It is a beautiful instrument wherewith to render the spacious humour of this style – which is almost impressive enough to make me wonder whether humour after all is not the great essential element of the epic" ("Voyage with Don Quixote," 332).

99 Mann, "Voyage with Don Quixote," 326.

100 Mann, 360.

101 Cervantes, *Don Quijote*, 2.54.1174–5; *Don Quixote*, 2.54.815–16.

102 The annals of history attest to homologous moments of Spaniards weeping at the expulsion of the Moriscos. De la Fuente notes how

it was met with "great pity among all those who saw them depart" (quoted in Domínguez Ortiz and Vincent, *Historia de los moriscos*, 196), while Rojas Casanate reports, in 1613, that "everyone was crying, and there was no heart that wasn't moved by seeing so many homes uprooted and so many victims banished, with the consideration that many were innocent" (quoted in Domínguez Ortiz and Vincent, *Historia de los moriscos*, 189).

103 Castelvetro, "Commentary on Aristotle's *Poetics*," 89.

104 Trueblood, "La risa en el *Quijote*," 16. Trueblood correctly notes that Don Quijote "never laughs mockingly or sarcastically at the expense of his squire" and that "theorists of laughter have paid little attention to [this] laughter of sympathy" (16). He does not, however, apply this class of laughter to that experienced by Sancho with Ricote, instead attributing it to the relief theory.

105 Similarly, Mann ("Voyage with Don Quixote," 344) and Rutherford (*Power of the Smile*) both maintain that Cervantes increasingly venerates in his titular character what was originally but a satirical creation; thus there is an evolution of humour from beginning to end.

106 So asserts Lee in contrasting Sancho's reaction to Ana Félix with his reaction to Ricote (*Anxiety of Sameness*, 206).

107 For an example of the cross-Mediterranean circulation of jocular texts see Marzolph, "Sanitizing Humor."

108 Wood also makes a "laughing at" and "laughing with" distinction and notes Erasmus and Cervantes as exponents of what he calls a "comedy of forgiveness" (*Irresponsible Self*, 3–19).

109 Mann, "Voyage with Don Quixote," 354, 336.

110 Gogol, *Dead Souls*, 141; Freud, *Jokes*, 289.

111 Joubert, *Treatise on Laughter*, 97. These affiliations between laughter and tears also recall *Pedro de Urdemalas*: "[The actor] must scare up the tears of laughter and make them return in a hurry once again to sad weeping" (Cervantes, *Comedias y tragedias*, 897; vv. 2923–6; Ha de sacar con espanto / las lágrimas de la risa / y hacer que vuelvan con prisa / otra vez al triste llanto); and *Persiles y Sigismunda*: "One of the definitions of man says he is a laughing animal, because man alone of all the animals laughs; I maintain it can also be said he is a weeping animal" (*Persiles and Sigismunda*, 2.5.120); Una de las difiniciones del hombre es decir que es animal risible, porque sólo el hombre se ríe y no otro ningún animal; y yo digo que también se puede decir que es animal llorable, animal que llora (*Persiles y Sigismunda*, 2.5.302–3).

112 Quoted in Horden and Purcell, *Corrupting Sea*, 36.

113 See Tueller, "Moriscos Who Stayed Behind."

114 Hitchcock, "Expulsion of the Moriscos," 175.

5. Suspended Admiration

1 Cervantes, *Don Quijote*, bk. 1, prologue, 11; *Don Quixote*, bk. 1, prologue, 4.
2 Cervantes, *Don Quijote*, bk. 1, prologue, 13–14; *Don Quixote*, bk. 1, prologue, 5.
3 "Poets aim either to benefit, or to amuse, or to utter words at once both pleasing and helpful to life [...] He has won every vote who has blended profit and pleasure, at once delighting and instructing the reader" (Horace, *Ars Poetica*, 478–9).
4 Cervantes, *Novelas ejemplares*, 79; *Exemplary Novels*, 4.
5 Quite recently scholars such as Piqueras Flores ("El nacimiento") have begun to challenge the conventional wisdom that Cervantes was the first to *"novelar"* in Spanish.
6 Riley, *Cervantes's Theory of the Novel*, 89, 91.
7 In his otherwise brilliant study on emotion in seventeenth-century French theatre, an overreliance on Cartesian dualism leads Gobert to claim that wonder "is by its nature novel and physiologically unperturbing" and "the only emotion that causes no physiological perturbation" (*Mind-Body Stage*, 63, 64). Early modern understandings of physiognomy easily refute this notion, as I will show with Palomino.
8 Ife also observes the striking frequency of the verb *suspender* in Cervantes's writing, while concurring that it can produce "a state of rapture in which the fiction can bring its full effect to bear on a mind at its most impressionable" (*Reading and Fiction*, 58–9).
9 Barthes, *Preparation of the Novel*, 107. See also Barthes's notion of the "Moment of Truth" (106–7) and Diderot's concept of the *tableau* (*Oeuvres de théâtre*, 338–9).
10 Bakhtin, *Dialogic Imagination*, 243.
11 A conspicuous, if romantically superficial, exception is Cassano's notion of a characteristically Mediterranean "slowness" (*Southern Thought*, 369). See also elhariry and Talbayev, *Critically Mediterranean*, esp. 111–77.
12 I am referring, of course, to the increasing reach of British privateering in the Mediterranean, as well as the queen's other economic inroads to the region, as implied by the international merchant who appears towards the end of the novella. Suggestively, Carroll B. Johnson anoints the novella as "at once the most and least historical" of the collection but claims that critics "have preferred to insist on the anti-historical aspects" ("Catolicismo, familia y fecundidad," 519). Ricapito, in *Between History and Creativity*, 39–68, is one prominent exception.
13 See especially Peers, "Cervantes in England," and Olid Guerrero, "Machiavellian In-Betweenness"; and, for a broader look at Spanish-English relations of the period, Cruz, *Material and Symbolic Circulation*.

14 Currie, *The Unexpected*, 18.

15 Aristotle, *Poetics*, in *Complete Works*, vol. 2, 1450a32; 4975.

16 Maravall, *La cultura del barroco*, 438. In *La española inglesa* these ideas serve as a subtle corrective to the standard premise that romance, a genre with which this particular novella has often been linked (and therefore faulted), draws its dramatic tension from plot instead of characterization (see Frye, *Secular Scripture*, 49–54).

17 Cervantes, *Don Quijote*, 1.47.600; *Don Quixote*, 1.47.412.

18 Bakhtin, *Dialogic Imagination*, 92. Although he refers to the same concept throughout the study, in this case Bakhtin was focusing on the "adventure-time" of the Greek romance.

19 Bakhtin, 84.

20 For how the concepts of tension, intensity, and suspense have been identified with the short story more generally, see Dollerup, "Concepts." McNamer finds, "in the affective play afforded by literature, the potential for conceiving of alternative temporalities – modes of experiencing time that counter the dominance of linear, period-bound 'history'" ("Literariness," 1440n).

21 Currie, *The Unexpected*, 37. Ricoeur discusses discordance and related concepts of narrative temporality in *Time and Narrative* and *Oneself as Another*. For more on time in fictional narrative see Bender and Wellbery, *Chronotypes*, and Morson, *Narrative and Freedom*.

22 Derrida, *Psyche*, 5–6.

23 Currie, *The Unexpected*, 42.

24 Cervantes, *Novelas ejemplares*, 298; *Exemplary Novels*, 142. Consensus among critics is nearly universal that the regal character is indeed none other than Queen Elizabeth I, even if the text never explicitly says as much.

25 Cervantes, *Novelas ejemplares*, 301; *Exemplary Novels*, 144.

26 On this point, see Carroll B. Johnson, "Catolicismo."

27 Cervantes, *Novelas ejemplares*, 302–3; *Exemplary Novels*, 145.

28 Cervantes, 145; 303. For clarity I have maintained the original spelling of "Isabela" instead of the editorial decision to anglicize the name in Grossman's translation.

29 Cervantes, *Novelas ejemplares*, 305; *Exemplary Novels*, 146.

30 The ruse recalls the ending of *El amante liberal*, when Ricardo convinces his crew to adorn their ship and themselves with Turkish and Moorish pageantry as part of an outlandish gag on the Sicilians awaiting their return (Cervantes, *Novelas ejemplares*, 231–2; *Exemplary Novels*, 102–3). Irigoyen-García considers this, along with various historical examples, a case of "imperial Moorishness" that promotes the "cultural coherence

between the two shores of the Mediterranean empire" ("Impersonating the Moor," 355). This would also qualify as the kind of "passing" that Fuchs explores in greater depth and across a number of cultural practices in her book *Passing for Spain*.

31 Although the text refers to them as liberality or generosity (Cervantes, *Novelas ejemplares*, 308–9; *Exemplary* Novels, 148–9), it bears questioning whether Ricaredo's actions can qualify as genuine exemplarity of the sort I discuss because his religious convictions dictate the "generous" sparing of Catholics but not of the Muslim Turks, whom he kills indiscriminately.

32 Cervantes, *Novelas ejemplares*, 311–12; *Exemplary Novels*, 150. I have modified the translation to convey more faithfully the original meaning of the italicized terms.

33 In addition to Riley, other scholars to have studied admiratio in Cervantes include Urbina ("El concepto") and Childers (*Transnational Cervantes*, 44–79), who associates it with "the marvelous real" (lo real maravilloso). Lope expresses his colourful opinion on the matter in the prologue of *Laurel de Apolo*.

34 Descartes, *Passions of the Soul*, 350.

35 Palomino, *El museo pictórico*, 598. Although more laconic, Covarrubias corroborates this by describing *admiración* as "to freeze up and be awestruck [*pasmarse y espantarse*] from some extraordinary effect one sees and whose cause is unknown" (*Tesoro*, 44).

36 Palomino, *El museo pictórico*, 598–9.

37 Covarrubias, *Tesoro*, 594.

38 *Diccionario de autoridades*, 1:508. I have modernized the orthography of all quotations from the *Autoridades* dictionary.

39 *Diccionario de autoridades*, 3:130.

40 *Diccionario de autoridades*, 3:192.

41 Covarrubias, *Tesoro*, 1453.

42 *Diccionario de autoridades*, 3:193.

43 *Diccionario de autoridades*, 3:377.

44 Covarrubias, *Tesoro*, 1496.

45 *Diccionario de autoridades*, 3:377.

46 Additional early modern terms that, according to Covarrubias, maintained a close if not synonymous relationship with those I have already examined included *alboroto*, *alborozo*, *atónito*, *embelesar*, and *espantar*. All of these can also be found, though with somewhat less frequency, in Cervantes's works.

47 See, for instance, Palencia's definition of *ánima* (*Universal vocabulario*, xxi *recto* and *verso*).

48 *Diccionario de autoridades*, 3:193.

49 Barthes, *Camera Lucida*, 26–7.

50 Hutchinson cogently highlights music's utility in this regard, while speculating that such shortcomings in literature owe to the critical resistance to seeing it as precisely a temporal art ("Affective Dimensions," 73–4). See also Martín Moreno, "Música, pasión, razón," and Harré, "Emotion in Music."

51 One must also recall the close relationship between music and rhetoric and that the Greek term *musiké* referred as much to language as it did to the audible tones themselves. See Martín Moreno, "Música, pasión, razón," 321–7.

52 "The adornment of the [traditional Spanish] theatre was an old cloth [...] behind which were the musicians, singing without a guitar some old *romance*" (El adorno del teatro era una manta vieja [...] detrás de la cual estaban los músicos, cantando sin guitarra algún romance antiguo). Cervantes also lauds Navarro because he "brought music, which before was sung behind the cloth, out to the public theatre" (*Comedias y tragedias*, 10–11; sacó la música, que antes cantaba detrás de la manta, al teatro público). We should not forget, however, that Lope increasingly incorporated music in his theatrical productions and wrote the first Spanish opera, *La selva sin amor* (The forest without love) in 1629. For more on Cervantes's engagement with music see Gasta, "Señora" and "Writing to Be Heard"; and Pastor Comín, *Loco, trovador y cortesano*.

53 Granja, "Los actores," 151. On suspension in the comedia see also Heiple, "La suspensión."

54 Dunn, "Gestural Politics," 31.

55 Granja, "Los actores," 155–6.

56 Cervantes, *Novelas ejemplares*, 186; *Exemplary Novels*, 73. Ricardo also reports having momentarily lost his sense of sight in this scene, an effect evocative of the "paroxysm" suffered later by both Ricardo and Mahamut when they believe that Leonisa has died. In his definition for yet another more or less synonymous term of suspension, *pasmo*, Covarrubias describes a similar lack of movement: "*Pasmarse* is to become suspended [*suspenso*], without movement" (*Tesoro*, 1348).

57 Granja, "Los actores," 164.

58 The actor "will feel moved in such a way that, *turbado*, he becomes silent and can scarcely put together a few sentences. The asides that interrupt his speech manifest, only for the spectator, the profound shock [...] The conventionalism of this resource of Baroque theatrical technique [...] determines a faltering speech which, indirectly, turns out to be effectively expressive of the profound agitation that has been produced in the soul" (Orozco Díaz, "Sentido de continuidad," 155–6).

59 As students of the *comedia nueva* are well aware, however, stage directions in early modern Spanish drama tend to be economical, at best, and were

frequently added only by the director or *autor* by way of ad hoc mark-ups or *atajos* after the dramaturge's original manuscript had already been written and passed on to the theatre companies, a reality that requires similarly creative means for reconstructing its mise-en-scène.

60 Quoted in Granja, "Los actores," 168 (italics in the original).

61 Quoted in Granja, 159 (all ellipses in the original).

62 Lope, *La Gatomaquia*, 458, vv. 244–61.

63 Another bodily indication of suspension was the blush, even if the seventeenth-century actress María de Riquelme was apparently the only one capable of voluntarily producing it on stage. In Cervantes's novellas, characters also attend closely to the changing facial complexions of one another, whether this means an increase in colour with the blush or a loss of colour with an event of fear, shock, or surprise. The most explicit example occurs in *Numancia* (in *Comedias y tragedias*, 1015, vv. 169–76).

64 Granja, "Los actores," 164. Fernández and Reina Ruiz, however, in "Metamorfosis dramática," analyse a recent Spanish theatrical reproduction of *La española inglesa*, one that was evidently faithful to some of the emotional effects I have described (see esp. 200).

65 Although my analysis here is more hermeneutic than philological, it is plausible that Cervantes was himself influenced by the mystics, as I have suggested elsewhere with respect to the use of a mystic language in *Persiles y Sigismunda* (Paul Michael Johnson, "Trials of Language").

66 Góngora, *Antología poética*.

67 Río Parra, "*Suspensio Animi*," 404–5.

68 Diego de Jesús, "Apuntamientos," 476.

69 Diego de Jesús, 476. He adds that "this acting without our faculties, this having understanding stopped, shocked [*espantado*], and in bewilderment [*admiración*] Saint [Teresa de Jesús] called *not operating and being suspended* [*suspenso*]; and God told her that it was to not understand even while understanding [*no entender aunque entendiendo*]" (477).

70 Diego de Jesús, 476–7.

71 Saint Teresa of Ávila, *The Life*, 226. This may explain why Teresa employed the term *suspension* as a kind of euphemism for *ecstasy*, as though the latter word connoted a stigma; see Certeau, *Mystic Fable*, 133.

72 Río Parra, "*Suspensio Animi*," 404n.

73 Certeau, *Mystic Fable*, 136.

74 Río Parra, "*Suspensio Animi*," 404n.

75 This is not to say that they are devoid of religious content. Collins shares my assessment of *La española inglesa*, while signalling that it "attests to Cervantes's devotion to Erasmian ideals, the Catholic Church, the concept of a Christian community, and to the power of imaginative literature and imaginary worlds to move, inspire, and uplift humankind"

("Transgression," 71). Conversely, for the historical affinities between the pious and the non-clerical, philosophical dimensions of mysticism see Byrne, *El "Corpus Hermeticum,"* 24–9.

76 Cervantes, *Novelas ejemplares*, 312; *Exemplary Novels*, 151.

77 Cervantes, *Novelas ejemplares*, 317; *Exemplary Novels*, 153, translation modified.

78 Cervantes, *Novelas ejemplares*, 318; *Exemplary Novels*, 154, translation modified (emphasis mine).

79 Cervantes, *Novelas ejemplares*, 319; *Exemplary Novels*, 155.

80 Hutchinson, "Anagnórisis," 345.

81 On the importance of the senses in the novella, especially that of touch, see Ganelin, "Cervantes's Exemplary Sensorium."

82 Shortly after Isabela ingests the poison, the narrator employs yet another acceptation of the word *turbar*: "Isabela's tongue and throat began to swell, her lips turned black, her voice became hoarse, her eyes became turbid [*turbársele los ojos*], and her chest felt constricted" (Cervantes, *Exemplary Novels*, 159, translation modified); a Isabela se le comenzó a hinchar la lengua y la garganta, y a ponérsele denegridos los labios, y a enronquecérsele la voz, turbársele los ojos y apretársele el pecho (*Novelas ejemplares*, 325). It is interesting to note that these physiological effects of poisoning share some of the same traits experienced by someone suddenly caught in emotional suspension.

83 Cervantes, *Novelas ejemplares*, 321; *Exemplary Novels*, 155–6.

84 Cervantes, *Novelas ejemplares*, 324; *Exemplary Novels*, 158.

85 Cervantes, *Novelas ejemplares*, 327; *Exemplary Novels*, 160, translation modified. On the philosophical relationship between passion and action in the seventeenth century see James, *Passion and Action*.

86 Like the English term *temper*, which may be applied to both affectivity (e.g., to temper an outburst) and metalworking (e.g., to temper a sword), the word *templar* enjoys a versatile range of uses, including in painting and music. See *Diccionario de autoridades*, 3:242, and Covarrubias, *Tesoro*, 1465.

87 *Diccionario de autoridades*, 3:242. In this definition of *templar*, the dictionary cites none other than Cervantes's *Persiles y Sigismunda* as an example: "to yell to the sailors to lower the sails, temper them, and secure them" (*Persiles and Sigismunda*, 1.23.101, translation modified); [d]ando voces a los marineros, que amainasen las velas y las templasen y asegurasen (*Persiles y Sigismunda*, 1.23.272).

88 Cervantes, *Novelas ejemplares*, 328; *Exemplary Novels*, 161, translation modified.

89 Covarrubias, *Tesoro*, 44.

90 Spingarn, in his *History of Literary Criticism*, explains in more detail the concept of admiratio, citing Minturno and Dryden as well. On Corneilles see Gobert, *Mind-Body Stage*, 48–83. Admiratio caught on in Spain also, eventually becoming the "fundamental objective of the Golden Age artist" (Arellano, *Historia del teatro*, 97).

91 Herrick, in "Some Neglected Sources," takes issue with the idea that Minturno alone was responsible for popularizing admiratio in early modernity, citing other thinkers whose writings had already begun to explore the possibilities of wonder.

92 Riley, *Cervantes's Theory of the Novel*, 90. "If Cervantes does not specifically connect *admiratio* with the other, the instructional, function of the novel," Riley explains in regards to *Don Quijote*, "they were probably not unconnected in his mind" (90). Spadaccini and Talens (*Through the Shattering Glass*, 120–33) also see the *Novelas ejemplares* as centred more on the reader and an exploration of the self than on the morality of the characters per se. Koch notes that the origin of the term *admiratio* supports this idea through "*ad-miror*," "whose bifurcated etymology includes marveling or wondering at and reflecting or mirroring back" (*Aesthetic Body*, 116).

93 Riley, *Cervantes's Theory of the Novel*, 90.

94 Spingarn, *History of Literary Criticism*, 52.

95 Currie ponders the "question which the theory of narrative has been oddly reluctant to ask: the question of whose surprise we are talking about," concluding that such reluctance owes to an Aristotelian legacy of "a general bracketing of the audience" that has stymied what in his view are necessary efforts "to think about the two activities, of writing and reading, construction and reconstruction, together" (*The Unexpected*, 42–3).

96 Hutchinson, "Anagnórisis," 347.

97 For an overview and bibliography of these fields, see Rolls, "Origins of Aesthetics." For a study of how they have approached the concept of suspense in particular, see Miall, "Emotions."

98 Avilés, "Expanding the Self."

99 Hutchinson, *Economía ética en Cervantes*.

100 Collins, "Transgression," 65; Boruchoff, "Free Will."

101 After Ricardo intervenes to try to betroth Leonisa to Cornelio, his suspension is coextensive with an ethical realization: "And upon saying this he fell silent, as if his tongue were sticking to his palate; but then, before anyone else could speak, he said: 'Lord save me, how difficult tribulations upset one's understanding! I, gentlemen, with the desire I have to do what is right, have not thought carefully about what I said, because it

is not possible for anyone to be generous with what belongs to someone else'" (Cervantes, *Exemplary Novels*, 104). Y en diciendo esto calló, como si al paladar se le hubiera pegado la lengua; pero desde allí a un poco, antes que ninguno hablase, dijo: '¡Válame Dios, y cómo los apretados trabajos turban los entendimientos! Yo, señores, con el deseo que tengo de hacer bien, no he mirado lo que he dicho, porque no es posible que nadie pueda mostrarse liberal de lo ajeno' (*Novelas ejemplares*, 234). Most critics have interpreted this scene ironically, but Avilés rescues its ethical function through the expansive definition of liberality noted earlier ("Expanding the Self").

102 Currie, *The Unexpected*, 37. It bears noting that in the *Nicomachean Ethics* Aristotle establishes that virtue is a choice, but the passions of the soul are not: "we are not called good or bad on the grounds of our passions, but are so called on the ground of our excellences and our vices [...] Again, we feel anger and fear without choice, but the excellences are choices or involve choice" (in *Complete Works*, vol. 2, 1105b29–1106a4; 3754).

103 Cervantes, *Novelas ejemplares*, 335; *Exemplary Novels*, 165. A similar example rehearses the text's fondness for the verb *templar*, while referring to Isabela's determination to enter a convent when she believes that Ricaredo is dead: "almost as if satisfied with her sorrow, and tempering it with the holy, Christian decision she had made" (Cervantes, *Exemplary Novels*, 166); casi como satisfecha de su dolor, templándole con la santa y cristiana resolución que había tomado (*Novelas ejemplares*, 336).

104 Baena, *La grietas de la ejemplaridad*.

105 Fuchs, "Suspended Judgments," 449. By connecting the novellas to Coleridge's concept of the suspension of disbelief, Fuchs explores their precise capacity to induce readerly scepticism: the "paradoxical *Novelas ejemplares* make evident that by the early seventeenth century, particularly in the wake of the expulsion of the Moriscos [...] the kind of moral certainty and mimetic modeling involved in exemplarity were neither available any longer nor especially desirable" ("Suspended Judgments," 449). Nevertheless, we should heed the fact that undecidability has been distinguished as one of the principal characteristics of exempla: "in the Aristotelian tradition, example is not meant to offer certainty but only probability" (Lyons, *Exemplum*, 33).

106 Indeed, sixteenth- and seventeenth-century exempla were often ironic in nature (Lyons, *Exemplum*, 12). See also Hampton, *Writing from History*.

107 Cervantes, *Novelas ejemplares*, 345; *Exemplary Novels*, 171.

108 Nevertheless, critics are divided as to whether the novella manages to fully redeem Clotaldo's illicit and amoral seizure of Isabela at its beginning. If for El Saffar her marriage to Ricaredo constitutes a "restitution of justice" (*Novel to Romance*, 155), then for Clamurro it only "partially

restores the virtuous dimension of Ricaredo's love," because "the criminal circumstances of the girl's arrival in England and incorporation into the family continue to haunt the putatively virtuous character and motives of the son" (*Beneath the Fiction*, 106).

109 Cervantes, *Novelas ejemplares*, 458; *Exemplary Novels*, 242, translation modified. The trope of the "tied tongue" (lengua turbada) is remarkably abundant in the *Novelas ejemplares*, appearing as both a corrective to unethical behaviour, such as at the end of *El amante liberal*, and an impediment to justice or truth, as here.

110 Cervantes, *Novelas ejemplares*, 344; *Exemplary Novels*, 171.

6. Aporias of Love

1 He does so in the dedication of *Don Quijote* of 1615, even if he immediately back-tracks with similar irony: "I must say I regret having said *the worst*, because in the opinion of my friends it is bound to reach the extremes of possible goodness" (Cervantes, *Don Quixote*, 2.679); y digo que me arrepiento de haber dicho *el más malo*, porque según la opinión de mis amigos, ha de llegar al estremo de bondad posible (*Don Quijote*, 2.454).

2 Menéndez y Pelayo chalked the "failure" up to the "senile debility" of Cervantes's old age (quoted in Nerlich, *El "Persiles" descodificado*, 53). For other explanations and means of dispelling the notion that *Persiles y Sigismunda* was a "step backward" from, and an "antidote" to, *Don Quijote* see Gaylord, "Ending and Meaning," 152–3.

3 Wyndham Lewis denounced the work as "a labyrinth-novel twice as large and complicated as *La Galatea*" (quoted in Wilson, *Allegories of Love*, xi).

4 Nelson, *Persistence of Presence*, 195.

5 Martín Morán, "El género del *Persiles*," 173–5. Among the distinct allegorical interpretations are Wilson's *Allegories of Love*, Forcione's *Christian Romance*, and Castillo and Spadaccini's "El antiutopismo." Zimic, in "El *Persiles* como crítica," however, uniquely reads the novel as a parody.

6 Wilson, *Allegories of Love*, xiv. Nerlich is more acerbic when observing that *Persiles y Sigismunda* "has been subjected and continues to be subjected to a reductionism that simply leaves one stupefied" (*El "Persiles" descodificado*, 675).

7 González Echevarría, *Love and the Law*, 221. His assessment echoes the way in which critics like Samuel Lee Wolff had panned the Greek romance for its excessive sentimentalism, "analyzed to death by means of a shallow and distorted 'psychology'" (quoted in Wilson, *Allegories of Love*, 16).

8 González Echevarría, *Love and the Law*, 222.

9 On what are nonetheless the complexities of the word *sentimental* itself, see Erämetsä, *Study of the Word "Sentimental."*

10 For example, Lapesa, *De la edad media*, 258.

11 Armstrong-Roche has fruitfully applied paradoxography to *Persiles y Sigismunda* and noted its "impulse to unsettle facile distinctions": "Through paradox, *Persiles* can be said both to look back to Lucian and Erasmus and to find a novelistic corollary *avant-la-lèttre* [*sic*] for the Russian formalist principle that art estranges or defamiliarizes the known. In *Persiles* we find both urges at work: the urge to familiarize the (apparently) exotic and the urge to alienate the (apparently) unknown" (*Cervantes' Epic Novel*, 18–19).

12 We might thus recall the writings of such sceptics as Francisco Sanches, who asked in his appropriately titled *That Nothing Is Known* of 1581: "What, then, is fixed, when things are so changeable? What is determinate when they are so various? What is certain, when *things* are so uncertain? Nothing, indeed" (229).

13 Sonia Velázquez, "Common Language," 518–19. The "negative consequence" of this difference, Velázquez goes on to explain, was "that these characters were then left unable to represent the world to themselves and themselves to each other." She uses this as a springboard to take a notably different tack to Cervantes's text than the one upon which I expound here: "in the hybrid, polyglot world of the *Persiles*, novelistic astonishment, *asombro*, stems less from the gap separating speaker from community [...] than from a realization that in spite of the world's heterogeneity, and ample room for misunderstandings, and disagreements, communication *does* ultimately take place" ("Common Language," 518–21).

14 On the question of genre I remit the reader to Martín Morán ("El género del *Persiles*"); Nerlich (*El "Persiles" descodificado*, 58–88); and Armstrong-Roche (*Cervantes' Epic Novel*, 167–204), who explicates "the startling incongruity between *Persiles*' overtly epic ambition, title, reference, and diction, and the laborious triumph of love celebrated in its pages" (167).

15 Wilson, *Allegories of Love*, 36, 30. Other differences are noted by the same critic (29–31).

16 It is clear that Cervantes did not merely follow the advice of the anonymous friend from the prologue of *Don Quijote* of 1605: "If you write about love, with the couple of ounces of Tuscan that you know you'll run right into León Hebreo, who will inflate your meters. And if you don't care to travel to foreign lands, right at home you have Fonseca's *Del amor de Dios*, which summarizes everything that you or the most ingenious writer might wish to know about the subject" (Cervantes, *Don Quixote*, 1.7).
   Si tratáredes de amores, con dos onzas que sepáis de la lengua toscana,

toparéis con León Hebreo que os hincha las medidas. Y si no queréis andaros por tierras estrañas, en vuestra casa tenéis a Fonseca, *Del amor de Dios*, donde se cifra todo lo que vos y el más ingenioso acertare a desear en tal materia (*Don Quijote*, 1.17). Hebreo and Fonseca are merely two of an abundance of early modern Spanish figures who, in the tradition of *philographia*, wrote Neoplatonic treatises on love, even if many are now lost, including Cristóbal de Acosta's *Del amor divino, natural y humano*, Carlos Montesa's *Apología en alabanza del amor*, and Francisco de Aldana's *Tratado de amor en modo platónico*. According to Gaylord, Cervantes "clearly means his text to join Renaissance dialogues on love, philosophical and theological" because it explores "many versions and perversions of love" "[u]nsystematically but obsessively" ("Cervantes's Other Fiction," 120).

17 Respectively, Wilson, "'De gracia estraña'"; and Sánchez Jiménez, "Un acercamiento imagológico," 139–40.

18 One of the most recent and fertile ventures in this regard is Armstrong-Roche's proposition of neo-Gothicism (*Cervantes' Epic Novel*, 295–303; "La mirada lucianesca"; "Las paradojas"), which builds on the foundation already laid in his *Cervantes' Epic Novel* that the wanting of Christian charity in the meridional half of *Persiles y Sigismunda* – swapped out for hollow ceremony – tends, in like fashion, to displace the apparently barbarian customs of the Septentrion to the Catholic South. Specific observations of the interpenetration of these spaces include his association of the Barbaric Isle with captivity in Algiers (*Cervantes' Epic Novel*, 52, 263); his analysis of the Feliciana de la Voz episode reveals how similar dynamics are couched in a novel form of irony that allows seemingly innocuous entertainment to be at once morally edifying ("Ironías de la ejemplaridad").

19 Along with a "desire for exoticism," this is how Sánchez Jiménez ("Un acercamiento imagológico," 136n) summarizes the posture of Lozano Renieblas (*El mundo del "Persiles*," 82, 89) regarding the question of Cervantes's motives for choosing the Septentrion as an unknown geographic setting.

20 Pile, "Emotions and Affect," 9. As a solution, Pahl, in "Logic of Emotionality," suggests the term *emotionality*, which avoids simplifying emotions as discrete objects.

21 See Espejo Madrigal, "Fin del amor cortés," 203–4.

22 Fisher, *Vehement Passions*, 18–22.

23 Terdiman, "Can We Read the Book of Love," 472.

24 The romance genre is the largest and most lucrative category of fiction in the United States, earning well over one billion dollars in revenue in 2016 ("Romance Industry Statistics"). For problems in defining and delimiting the genre of sentimental fiction see Cortijo Ocaña, *La evolución genérica,*

7–18. For the influence of sentimental fiction on Cervantes see Cvitanovic, *La novela sentimental española*, 331–58. For general studies on sentimentalism see Deyermond, *Tradiciones*; Gwara and Gerli, *Spanish Sentimental Romance*; and, for a full bibliography, Whinnom, *Critical Bibliography*.

25 Barthes, *Lover's Discourse*, 99.

26 Although I will be focusing on the ineffability of emotions and the resultant inadequacy of poetic language in representing them, a rhetoric of excess is certainly not absent in *Persiles y Sigismunda*, as demonstrated by the following statement: "Auristela felt stunned, felt amazed, felt sadder than sadness itself" (*Persiles and Sigismunda*, 1.20.93, translation modified); quedó suspensa, quedó atónita, quedó más triste que la tristeza misma (*Persiles y Sigismunda*, 1.20.259). According to Luhmann's systems-theory approach to love, such excessiveness is a defining element of the emotion (*Love as Passion*, 67–71).

27 Kermode, *Shakespeare's Language*, 16.

28 To be clear, this risk has not prevented the belated flourishing of political interpretations of *Persiles y Sigismunda* that are too numerous to list.

29 Cortijo Ocaña, *La evolución genérica*, 297–8.

30 Rowland, "Sentimental Fiction," 195–6; also see Braudy, "Form of the Sentimental Novel."

31 Lukács, *Theory of the Novel*, 116.

32 Cortijo Ocaña, *La evolución genérica*, 297–9.

33 Cortijo Ocaña, 3, 300.

34 For Avalle-Arce, the presence of these national characters in the Septentrion brings forth the tension between myth and history (*Nuevos deslindes cervantinos*, 85).

35 Cervantes, *Persiles y Sigismunda*, 2.2.284; *Persiles and Sigismunda*, 2.2.108, translation modified.

36 Cervantes, *Persiles y Sigismunda*, 1.19.253; *Persiles and Sigismunda*, 1.19.19, translation modified.

37 Romero Muñoz, in Cervantes, *Persiles y Sigismunda*, 253n. Romero Muñoz bases this assessment on Corominas's *Diccionario Crítico Etimológico de la Lengua Castellana*.

38 The pelagic nature of the first half, in fact, informs the land-based quality of the second half of the text, with the narrator noting near the beginning of book 3 that "trials and dangers have jurisdiction not only over the sea but over all the land as well" (Cervantes, *Persiles and Sigismunda*, 3.4.213); los peligros no solamente tienen jurisdición en el mar, sino en toda la tierra (*Persiles y Sigismunda*, 3.4.457). Nevertheless, the bipartite structure of the text has long transfixed and confounded critics; see Wilson, *Allegories of Love*, 80–2, for a summary and introduction to the novel solution she proposes in the figure of the androgyne.

39 The Zeno brothers' *Dello scoprimento* is the other treatise that, besides Heliodorus's *Aethiopica*, Magnus's *Gentibus septentrionalibus*, and Tasso's *Discorsi del poema heroico*, is frequently cited as an inspiration for Cervantes.

40 Tasso, *Discorsi del poema heroico*, 48.

41 "In Greek romance the characters are Levantine, the setting is the Mediterranean world, and the normal means of transportation is by shipwreck" (Frye, *Secular Scripture*, 4).

42 Bakhtin, *Dialogic Imagination*, 100–1.

43 Castro described it as "consciously inverisimilar from beginning to end" (*Pensamiento*, 95). For more on the debate see Riley, *Theory of the Novel*, 179–99; Alcalá Galán, *Escritura desatada*, 226–31; Wilson, *Allegories of Love*, 32–4; and Armstrong-Roche, *Cervantes' Epic Novel*, 18–24. Note also the narrator's own words, which promise in book 2 to describe "things [...] that, though they stay within the bounds of truth, will surpass those of the imagination, for the wildest and most ingenious one could scarcely conceive of its events" (Cervantes, *Persiles and Sigismunda*, 1.23.103); cosas que, aunque no pasan de la verdad, sobrepujan a la imaginación, pues apenas pueden caber en la más sutil y dilatada sus acontecimientos (*Persiles y Sigismunda*, 1.23.276).

44 Wittgenstein, *Philosophical Investigations*, 94e, t6e.

45 See John Martin, *Myths of Renaissance Individualism*, 29–30.

46 Alcalá Galán, *Escritura desatada*, 218–19. For her, this makes *Persiles y Sigismunda* "the book of its time that most resembles the human mind in terms of the functioning of the flow of ideas" (*Escritura desatada*, 218–19).

47 Cervantes, *Persiles y Sigismunda*, 2.5.299–300; *Persiles and Sigismunda*, 2.5.118, translation modified.

48 Cervantes, *Persiles y Sigismunda*, 1.6.181; *Persiles and Sigismunda*, 1.6.47.

49 For example, in *Persiles y Sigismunda*, 1.12.206, 1.18.247, 2.7.323, 2.14.378, 2.15.384, 3.4.463, 3.9.526, and 4.14.712. According to Romero Muñoz, these represent variations on a formula also found in Heliodorus (Cervantes, *Persiles y Sigismunda*, 181n). See Cvitanovic for variations on the "antítesis simétrica" (*La novela sentimental española*, 336).

50 As I have shown elsewhere (Paul Michael Johnson, "The Trials of Language"), the rhetorical use of the oxymoron and other figures of speech in *Persiles y Sigismunda* recalls the mystic practice of "turns of phrase or usages that reflect a different practice of language" (Certeau, *Mystic Fable*, 132–3). Certeau further describes a trope as "[a] tour and detour, a turn of phrase, a conversion [...] This process of *deviation* is no longer based, as was the traditional allegory, on an analogy and an order of things. It is exit, semantic exile" (142–3).

51 Cervantes, *Persiles y Sigismunda*, 3.1.429; *Persiles and Sigismunda*, 3.1.197; see also *Persiles y Sigismunda*, 2.3.293 and 4.10.690. For more on the theme,

noted by prominent critics like Casalduero and Forcione, see Nerlich, *El "Persiles" descodificado*, 675–80.

52 In some classical literature the concept of desire was virtually synonymous with that of emotion.

53 Wilson, *Allegories of Love*, 90.

54 Cervantes, *Persiles y Sigismunda*, 4.1.631, 634; *Persiles and Sigismunda*, 4.1.307, 309, translation modified. For Wilson this is the "most subversive" of all the maxims in *Persiles y Sigismunda* as well. For our purposes, the maxims most importantly "stand out as a textbook demonstration of how the sexes are imprisoned in their separate languages, within their own maxims of desire" (Wilson, *Allegories of Love*, 89–90).

55 "It's obvious that one always wants what he lacks and he who doesn't want doesn't lack for anything" (Cervantes, *Persiles and Sigismunda*, 4.1.309); está claro que lo que se desea es lo que falta y, el que no desea, no tiene falta de nada (*Persiles y Sigismunda*, 4.1.635).

56 For a discussion of the cultural and political implications of movement towards and away from the concept of a centre in the novel, see Avilés, "To the Frontier and Back."

57 Hutchinson, *Cervantine Journeys*, 69. Lacan, *Four Fundamental Concepts*.

58 Hutchinson, 25.

59 Employed as early as the works of Sophocles and Aeschylus, the relatively extensive Renaissance topos of ineffability appears in other works by Cervantes as well, often in the lexicalized form of "un no sé qué" (I know not what), of which there are several examples in *Don Quijote*, 1.24.292, 1.28.354, and 2.24.911. For a historical discussion of the trope, see Porqueras Mayo's "El *no sé qué*," and, for its poetic applications, Byrne's *El "Corpus Hermeticum*," 204–12. For a pan-philosophical study of ineffability and a collection of other thinkers' writings on the subject, see Franke, *On What Cannot Be Said*.

60 Cervantes, *Persiles y Sigismunda*, 1.10.201; *Persiles and Sigismunda*, 1.10.58.

61 Luhmann, *Love as Passion*, 70.

62 This formulation of love is consistent with the wonderfully ineffable description of the emotion in the anonymous *L'escole d'amour*: "un ie ne sçay quoy, qui venoit de ie ne sçay où, et qui s'en alloit ie ne sçay comment"; "et par ces termes qui ne nous apprennent rien, ils nous apprennent tout ce que s'en peut sçavoir" (quoted in Luhmann, *Love as Passion*, 65–6).

63 Franke, "Varieties and Valences of Unsayability," 490–1.

64 Cervantes, *Persiles y Sigismunda*, 3.14.574–5; *Persiles and Sigismunda*, 3.14.274, translation modified. Perhaps these sorts of forbearance help to explain what has been called the "strange affectlessness of Cervantes's protagonists" (Wilson, *Allegories of Love*, 137).

65 Cervantes, *Persiles y Sigismunda*, 3.14.576; *Persiles and Sigismunda*, 3.14.275.

66 Additional examples found in *Persiles y Sigismunda*, 2.5.305, 2.5.308, 3.12.562, 4.11.695, and 4.11.697. These tropes, as Romero Muñoz notes, have biblical and Latin precedents, the latter in the form of *vox faucibut haesit* (Cervantes, *Persiles y Sigismunda*, 201n). For an overview of the motif of silence in early modern Spanish literature see Egido, "La poética del silencio."

67 Cervantes, *Persiles y Sigismunda*, 1.4.153; *Persiles and Sigismunda*, 1.4.33, translation modified.

68 Cervantes, *Persiles y Sigismunda*, 1.23.272; *Persiles and Sigismunda*, 1.23.101, translation modified; ellipsis in original.

69 Wilson, *Allegories of Love*, 36.

70 Auerbach, *Mimesis*, 4–5. Here the critic describes the discussion between Goethe and Schiller on these elements and their place in Homeric poetry.

71 Robbins remarks on the receptive impact of this narrative deferral as well: "The entire pilgrimage itself, then, is simply a sustained act of deferral [...] The thwarting of our carefully fuelled expectations of narrative purpose is a *peripateia* that impacts the reader far more than either of the characters" ("Twists and Turns," 17).

72 Luhmann, *Love as Passion*, 70–1.

73 Cervantes, *Persiles y Sigismunda*, 2.5.305, 311; *Persiles and Sigismunda*, 2.5.121, 125.

74 Cervantes, *Persiles y Sigismunda*, 2.6.311–12; *Persiles and Sigismunda*, 2.6.125, translation modified.

75 Cervantes, *Persiles y Sigismunda*, 1.5.170; *Persiles and Sigismunda*, 1.5.40–1.

76 Antonio's scene has further implications for the omnipresent civilized-barbaric motif of the first two parts of the novel, given that the barbarian has, since antiquity, been defined by an inability to speak. For an alternative approach to the novel's relationship to rationalization, see Cascardi, "Reason and Romance."

77 Cervantes, *Persiles y Sigismunda*, 4.11.695; *Persiles and Sigismunda*, 4.11.344.

78 Cervantes, *Persiles y Sigismunda*, 3.19.609–10; *Persiles and Sigismunda*, 3.19.295, translation modified.

79 Cervantes, *Persiles y Sigismunda*, 3.19.610; *Persiles and Sigismunda*, 3.19.295.

80 For example, Daniel Miller (*Materiality*) and Thrift (*Non-representational Theory*). For a cogent critique of non-representational theory, one that my analysis will partly share, see Pile, "Emotions and Affect," esp. 17.

81 Labanyi, "Doing Things," 223.

82 See, for instance, Bearden, who claims that "Cervantine ekphrasis serves as a wedge to pry open Eurocentric concepts of fiction, history, and cultural otherness" ("Painting Counterfeit Canvases," 740); and López Alemany, "*Ut pictura non poesis*," who takes issue with some of Bearden's claims.

83 Ibn Hazm de Córdoba, *El collar de la paloma* (*The Ring of the Dove*).

84 Cervantes, *Persiles y Sigismunda*, 3.17.590–1; *Persiles and Sigismunda*, 3.17.284.

85 Cervantes, *Persiles y Sigismunda*, 3.17.591; *Persiles and Sigismunda*, 3.17.284.

86 Cervantes, *Persiles y Sigismunda*, 2.4.301; *Persiles and Sigismunda*, 2.4.119.

87 Romero Muñoz, in Cervantes, *Persiles y Sigismunda*, 171n.

88 Cervantes, *Persiles y Sigismunda*, 1.5.169; *Persiles and Sigismunda*, 1.5.40.

89 Cervantes, *Persiles y Sigismunda*, 1.5.171; *Persiles and Sigismunda*, 1.5.42.

90 Cervantes, *Persiles y Sigismunda*, 1.15.229; *Persiles and Sigismunda*, 1.15.75. According to Armstrong-Roche, Arnaldo's ignorance of poetry also prevents him from gaining an insight into his love interest of Auristela, which amounts to a "caricature of literary neo-Aristotelianism" (*Cervantes' Epic Novel*, 201).

91 Another example of the failure to interpret the meaning of a character's tears can be found in *Persiles y Sigismunda*, 1.4.154–5; *Persiles and Sigismunda*, 1.4.33.

92 Cervantes, *Persiles y Sigismunda*, 2.2.289; *Persiles and Sigismunda*, 2.2.111, translation modified.

93 She claims that "by just seeing a person's face I can look into his soul and guess his thoughts" (Cervantes, *Persiles and Sigismunda*, 2.10.147); viendo el rostro de una persona, le leo el alma y le adevino los pensamientos (*Persiles y Sigismunda*, 2.10.346).

94 Cervantes, *Persiles y Sigismunda*, 2.19.408; *Persiles and Sigismunda*, 2.19.185.

95 Cervantes, *Persiles y Sigismunda*, 1.23.274; *Persiles and Sigismunda*, 1.23.102.

96 Fisher, *Vehement Passions*, 21.

97 The multiple perspectives opened by the affective aporias here recall what has now become a commonplace, that Cervantes's works are "perspectival," most famously suggested by Spitzer ("Perspectivismo lingüístico"), and updated by Castillo (*(A)wry Views*), who claims that Cervantes's writing is "anamorphic."

98 Cervantes, *Persiles y Sigismunda*, 3.10.526; *Persiles and Sigismunda*, 3.10.250, translation modified.

99 Cervantes, *Persiles y Sigismunda*, 3.14.570–1; *Persiles and Sigismunda*, 3.14.272.

100 Cervantes, *Persiles y Sigismunda*, 3.10.527; *Persiles and Sigismunda*, 3.10.250.
101 Cervantes, *Persiles y Sigismunda*, 2.8.332; *Persiles and Sigismunda*, 2.8.139.
102 Olmos García remarks on Cervantes's "hostile attitude" towards the Inquisition ("La Inquisición en la época," 81), and Castro comments on Cervantes's own relationship to inquisitional censorship (*Obra reunida*, 493–9).
103 Wilson, *Allegories of Love*, 21. Constance Hubbard Rose was the first to propose this interpretation (*Lament of a Sixteenth-Century Exile*, 159).
104 Frye, *Secular Scripture*, 50.
105 Wilson, *Allegories of Love*, xiv.
106 Along these lines and in a twist of characteristically Cervantine self-referentiality, at the beginning of book 2 the narrator remarks that "[i]t seems the author of this story knew more about being in love than being a historian" (Cervantes, *Persiles and Sigismunda*, 2.1.105; [p]arece que el autor desta historia sabía más de enamorado que de historiador; *Persiles y Sigismunda*, 2.1.279), due to his prolixity in describing jealousy.
107 Wilson implicitly recognizes the realism of such a claim when she offers: "Generic transformation is inscribed directly into Cervantes's title where he employs the word *trabajos* (trials, labors, ordeals) as a substitute for Heliodorus's use of *amores* (loves). Love in the late Renaissance, as the *Persiles* makes clear, is becoming harder work for men and women alike" (*Allegories of Love*, 42–3).

Afterword

1 Cervantes, *Persiles y Sigismunda*, 3.10.538; *Persiles and Sigismunda*, 3.10.255.
2 Cervantes, *Persiles y Sigismunda*, 3.11.540; *Persiles and Sigismunda*, 3.11.256.
3 Hutchinson, "Poética de la emoción," 1375.

Bibliography

"About the Romance Genre." Romance Writers of America, 2016. Accessed 10 April 2020. https://www.rwa.org/Online/Resources/About_Romance_Fiction/Online/Romance_Genre/About_Romance_Genre.aspx.

Abrams, M.H., and Geoffrey Galt Harpham. *A Glossary of Literary Terms*. 10th ed. Boston: Wadsworth Cengage, 2005.

Abulafia, David. *The Great Sea: A Human History of the Mediterranean*. Oxford: Oxford University Press, 2011.

Acevedo, Fernando de. "Caso que subcedió en la Ynquisición de Sevilla." *Los Acebedos: Boletín de la Biblioteca de Menéndez Pelayo*. Edited by Mateo Escagedo Salmón, 108–11. Santander, Spain: Sociedad Menéndez Pelayo, 1924.

Adorno, Theodor W. *Aesthetic Theory*. Edited and translated by Robert Hullot-Kentor. Minneapolis: University of Minnesota Press, 1997.

Ahmed, Sara. *The Cultural Politics of Emotion*. Edinburgh: Edinburgh University Press, 2004.

Akbari, Suzanne Conklin. "Introduction: The Persistence of Philology: Language and Connectivity in the Mediterranean." In *A Sea of Languages: Rethinking the Arabic Role in Medieval Literary History*. Edited by Akbari and Karla Mallette, 3–22. Toronto: University of Toronto Press, 2013.

Akbari, Suzanne Conklin, and Karla Mallette, eds. *A Sea of Languages: Rethinking the Arabic Role in Medieval Literary History*. Toronto: University of Toronto Press, 2013.

Alberti, Leon Battista. *On Painting*. Edited and translated by John R. Spencer. New Haven, CT: Yale University Press, 1966. Originally published as *Della pittura*, 1435–6.

Alcalá Galán, Mercedes. *Escritura desatada: Poéticas de la representación en Cervantes*. Alcalá de Henares, Spain: Centro de Estudios Cervantinos, 2009.

Aldrich, Robert. *The Seduction of the Mediterranean: Writing, Art and Homosexual Fantasy*. London: Routledge, 1993.

Alexander, Franz G., and Sheldon T. Selesnick. *The History of Psychiatry: An Evaluation of Psychiatric Thought and Practice from Prehistoric Times to the Present*. New York: Harper & Row, 1966.

Alfonso X, el Sabio. *Las Siete Partidas del rey don Alfonso el Sabio, cotejadas con varios códices antiguos por la Real Academia de la Historia*. 3 vols. Madrid: Imprenta Real, 1807.

Allen, John J. *Don Quijote: Hero or Fool? A Study in Narrative Technique*. 2 vols. Gainesville: University of Florida Press, 1969–79.

– "Smiles and Laughter in *Don Quixote*." *Comparative Literature Studies* 43.4 (2006): 515–31.

– "The Transformation of Satire in *Don Quixote*: 'Dine with Us as an Equal' in Juvenal and Cervantes." In *Ingeniosa Invención: Essays on Golden Age Spanish Literature for Geoffrey L. Stagg in Honor of His Eighty-Fifth Birthday*, edited by Ellen M. Anderson and Amy R. Williamsen, 1–7. Newark, DE: Juan de la Cuesta, 1999.

Allen, Valerie. "Waxing Red: Shame and the Body, Shame and the Soul." In *The Representation of Women's Emotions in Medieval and Early Modern Culture*, edited by Lisa Perfetti, 191–210. Gainesville: University Press of Florida, 2005.

Alonso, Amado. "Las prevaricaciones idiomáticas de Sancho." *Nueva Revista de Filología Hispánica* 2.1 (1948): 1–20.

Amelang, James S. "Braudel and the Cultural History of the Mediterranean: Anthropology and *Les lieux d'histoire*." In *Braudel Revisited: The Mediterranean World, 1600–1800*, edited by Gabriel Piterberg, Teófilo F. Ruiz, and Geoffrey Symcox, 229–45. Toronto and Los Angeles: University of Toronto Press / UCLA Center for Seventeenth- and Eighteenth-Century Studies and the William Andrews Clark Memorial Library, 2010.

– *The Flight of Icarus: Artisan Autobiography in Early Modern Europe*. Stanford, CA: Stanford University Press, 1998.

– "Tracing Lives: The Spanish Inquisition and the Act of Autobiography." In *Controlling Time and Shaping the Self: Developments in Autobiographical Writing Since the Sixteenth Century*, edited by Arianne Baggerman, Rudolf Dekker, and Michael Mascuch, 33–48. Leiden, Netherlands: Brill, 2011.

– "La viuda alegre: Miedo y luto en el llanto ritual." In *Accidentes del alma: Las emociones en la Edad Moderna*, edited by María Tausiet and James S. Amelang, 203–26. Madrid: Abada, 2009.

Anderson, Benedict. *Imagined Communities: Reflections on the Origin and Spread of Nationalism*. Rev. ed. London: Verso, 2006.

Anderson, Kay, and Susan J. Smith. "Editorial: Emotional Geographies." *Transactions of the Institute of British Geographers* 26.1 (2001): 7–10.

Appadurai, Arjun. *Modernity at Large: Cultural Dimensions of Globalization*. Minneapolis: University of Minnesota Press, 2005.

– "Topographies of the Self: Praise and Emotion in Hindu India." In *Language and the Politics of Emotion*, edited by Catherine A. Lutz and Lila Abu-Lughod, 92–112. Cambridge: Cambridge University Press, 1990.

Aquinas, St Thomas. "Treatise on the Passions." *Summa theologica* 1a2ae 22–48. 5 vols. Westminster, MD: Christian Classics, 1981.

Arellano, Ignacio. "Casos de honor en las primeras etapas del teatro de Lope." *Anuario Lope de Vega* 4, 7–31. Barcelona: Milenio / Universitat Autònoma de Barcelona, 1998.

– *Historia del teatro español del siglo XVII.* 5th ed. Madrid: Cátedra, 2012.

– "Las máscaras de Demócrito: En torno a la risa en el Siglo de Oro." In *Demócrito áureo: Los códigos de la risa en el Siglo de Oro*, edited by Ignacio Arellano and Victoriano Roncero, 329–59. Seville, Spain: Renacimiento, 2006.

Ariès, Philippe. *Centuries of Childhood: A Social History of Family Life.* Translated by Robert Baldick. New York: Knopf, 1962.

Arikha, Noga. *Passions and Tempers: A History of the Humours.* New York: HarperCollins, 2007.

Aristotle. *The Complete Works of Aristotle.* Edited by Jonathan Barnes. 2 vols. Princeton, NJ: Princeton University Press, 1984.

Armstrong-Roche, Michael. *Cervantes' Epic Novel: Empire, Religion, and the Dream Life of Heroes in "Persiles."* Toronto: University of Toronto Press, 2009.

– "Ironías de la ejemplaridad, milagros del entretenimiento en el *Persiles* (Feliciana de la Voz, *Persiles* III.2–6.447–484)." In "'Si ya por atrevido no sale con las manos en la cabeza': El legado poético del *Persiles* cuatrocientos años después." Special issue, *eHumanista/Cervantes* 5 (2016): 26–50.

– "La mirada lucianesca en el *Persiles*." *Revista de Occidente* 439 (December 2017): 77–98.

– "Las paradojas de *Persiles y Sigismunda* (con *Don Quijote* y *Viaje del Parnaso*)." In *Cervantes en el Septentrión*, edited by Randi Lise Davenport and Isabel Lozano Renieblas, 17–50. New York: Instituto de Estudios Auriseculares, 2019.

Artiles, Jenaro. "Bibliografía sobre el problema del honor y de la honra en el drama español." In *Filología y crítica hispánica: Homenaje al profesor F. Sánchez Escribano*, edited by Alberto Porqueras Mayo and Carlos Rojas, 235–41. Madrid: Alcalá, 1969.

Attridge, Derek. *The Singularity of Literature.* London: Routledge, 2004.

Auerbach, Erich. *Mimesis: The Representation of Reality in Western Literature.* Translated by Willard R. Trask. 50th anniversary edition. Princeton, NJ: Princeton University Press, 2003.

Avalle-Arce, Juan Bautista. *Nuevos deslindes cervantinos.* Barcelona: Ariel, 1975.

Avellaneda, Alonso Fernández de. *El ingenioso hidalgo don Quijote de la Mancha.* Edited by Fernando García Salinero. Madrid: Castalia, 2005.

Avilés, Luis F. *Avatares de lo invisible: Espacio y subjetividad en los Siglos de Oro*. Madrid / Frankfurt am Main: Iberoamericana/Vervuert, 2017.
– "En el límite de la mirada: El espectador en *Don Quijote*." In *Cervantes y su mundo*, vol. 2, edited by Kurt Reichenberger and Darío Fernández-Morera, 1–22. Kassel, Germany: Reichenberger, 2005.
– "Expanding the Self in a Mediterranean Context: Liberality and Deception in Cervantes's *El amante liberal*." In *In and Of the Mediterranean: Medieval and Early Modern Iberian Studies*, edited by Michelle M. Hamilton and Núria Silleras-Fernández, 233–57. Nashville, TN: Vanderbilt University Press, 2015.
– "To the Frontier and Back: The Centrifugal and the Centripetal in Cervantes' *Persiles y Sigismunda* and Gracián's *El Criticón*." *Symposium* 50.3 (1996): 141–63.
Azorín. "Cervantes y el mar." *ABC*, 6 October 1947.
Baena, Julio, ed. *"Novelas ejemplares": Las grietas de la ejemplaridad*. Newark, DE: Juan de la Cuesta, 2008.
Bakhtin, M.M. *The Dialogic Imagination*. Edited by Michael Holquist. Translated by Caryl Emerson and Michael Holquist. Austin: University of Texas Press, 2008.
– *Rabelais and His World*. Translated by Helene Iswolsky. Bloomington: Indiana University Press, 1984.
Balibar, Étienne. *Politics and the Other Scene*. Translated by Christine Jones, James Swenson, and Chris Turner. London: Verso, 2002.
Barbagallo, Antonio. "Sancho no es, se hace." *Cervantes: Bulletin of the Cervantes Society of America* 15.1 (1995): 46–59.
Barnés Vázquez, Antonio. *"Yo he leído en Virgilio": La tradición clásica en el "Quijote."* Vigo, Spain: Editorial Academia del Hispanismo, 2009.
Barthes, Roland. *Camera Lucida: Reflections on Photography*. Translated by Richard Howard. New York: Hill & Wang, 2010.
– *A Lover's Discourse: Fragments*. New York: Hill & Wang, 1978.
– *The Preparation of the Novel: Lecture Courses and Seminars at the Collège de France (1978–1979 and 1979–1980)*. Translated by Kate Briggs. New York: Columbia University Press, 2011.
Bartra, Roger. *Cultura y melancolía: Las enfermedades del alma en la España del Siglo de Oro*. Barcelona: Anagrama, 2001.
Bass, Laura. *The Drama of the Portrait: Theater and Visual Culture in Early Modern Spain*. University Park: Pennsylvania State University Press, 2008.
Bataillon, Marcel. *Erasmo y España: Estudios sobre la historia espiritual del siglo XVI*. Translated by Antonio Alatorre. Mexico City: Fondo de Cultura Económica, 1966.
Bearden, Elizabeth. "Painting Counterfeit Canvases: American Memory *Lienzos* and European Imaginings of the Barbarian in Cervantes's *Los trabajos de Persiles y Sigismunda*." *PMLA* 121.3 (2006): 735–52.

Bender, John, and David E. Wellbery. *Chronotypes: The Construction of Time.* Stanford, CA: Stanford University Press, 1991.

Benítez Sánchez-Blanco, Rafael. "El Mediterráneo de Cervantes." In *Cervantes Shakespeare 1616–2016: Contexto, Influencia, Relación / Context, Influence, Relation,* edited by José Manuel González, 71–87. Kassel, Germany: Reichenberger, 2017.

Benjamin, Walter. *Illuminations: Essays and Reflections.* Translated by Harry Zohn. New York: Schocken, 1968.

Bennassar, Bartolomé. *The Spanish Character: Attitudes and Mentalities from the Sixteenth to the Nineteenth Century.* Translated by Benjamin Keen. Berkeley: University of California Press, 1979.

Berenson, Bernard. *Lorenzo Lotto: An Essay in Constructive Art Criticism.* Rev. ed. London: George Bell & Sons, 1901.

Bergman, Ted L.L. "Violence, Humor, and Sancho's Resistance to Carnival." *eHumanista/Cervantes* 7 (2019): 24–41.

Bergmann, Emilie L. *Art Inscribed: Essays on Ekphrasis in Spanish Golden Age Poetry.* Cambridge, MA: Harvard University Press, 1979.

Bergson, Henri. *Laughter: An Essay on the Meaning of the Comic.* Translated by Cloudesley Brereton and Fred Rothwell. Copenhagen: Green Integer, 2009.

Bernaldo de Quirós, Constancio. *La picota: Crímenes y castigos en el país castellano en los tiempos medios.* Valladolid, Spain: MAXTOR, 2001.

The Bible: Contemporary English Version (Seek Find: The Bible for All People). New York: G.P. Putnam's Sons, 2006.

Blackmore, Josiah. *Manifest Perdition: Shipwreck Narrative and the Disruption of Empire.* Minneapolis: University of Minnesota Press, 2002.

Bloom, Harold. "Introduction: Don Quixote, Sancho Panza, and Miguel de Cervantes Saavedra." In *Don Quixote,* by Miguel de Cervantes, xxi–xxxv. Translated by Edith Grossman. New York: HarperCollins, 2005.

Blüher, Karl Alfred. *Séneca en España: Investigaciones sobre la recepción de Séneca en España desde el siglo XIII hasta el siglo XVII.* Edited by Juan Conde. Madrid: Gredos, 1983.

Blum, Hester. "The Prospect of Oceanic Studies." *PMLA* 125.3 (2010): 670–7.

Blumenberg, Hans. *Shipwreck with Spectator: Paradigm of a Metaphor for Existence.* Translated by Steven Rendall. Cambridge, MA: MIT Press, 1997.

Boissevain, Jeremy. "Towards a Social Anthropology of the Mediterranean." *Current Anthropology* 20.1 (1979): 81–93.

Bondi, Liz. "Making Connections and Thinking through Emotions: Between Geography and Psychotherapy." *Transactions of the Institute of British Geographers* 30.4 (2005): 433–48.

Boruchoff, David A. "Free Will, the Picaresque, and the Exemplarity of Cervantes's *Novelas ejemplares.*" *MLN* 124.2 (2009): 372–403.

Bourdieu, Pierre. *The Logic of Practice*. Translated by Richard Nice. Stanford, CA: Stanford University Press, 1990.

Bouwsma, William J. *The Waning of the Renaissance: 1550–1640*. New Haven, CT: Yale University Press, 2000.

Bowersock, G.W. "The East-West Orientation of Mediterranean Studies and the Meaning of North and South in Antiquity." In Harris, *Rethinking the Mediterranean*, 167–78.

Brandes, Stanley. "Reflections on Honor and Shame in the Mediterranean." In *Honor and Shame and the Unity of the Mediterranean*, edited by David D. Gilmore, 121–34. Washington, DC: American Anthropological Association, 1987.

Braudel, Fernand. *The Mediterranean and the Mediterranean World in the Age of Philip II*. Translated by Siân Reynolds. 2 vols. Berkeley: University of California Press, 1972.

– *La Méditerrannée et le monde méditerrannéen à l'époque de Philippe II*. Paris: Colin, 1949.

– "Personal Testimony." *Journal of Modern History* 44.4 (1972): 448–67.

Braudy, Leo. "The Form of the Sentimental Novel." *NOVEL: A Forum on Fiction* 7.1 (1973): 5–13.

Brennan, Teresa. *The Transmission of Affect*. Ithaca, NY: Cornell University Press, 2004.

Brewer, Brian. "Jealousy and Usury in 'El celoso extremeño.'" *Cervantes: Bulletin of the Cervantes Society of America* 33.1 (2013): 11–43.

Broodbank, Cyprian. *The Making of the Middle Sea: A History of the Mediterranean from the Beginning to the Emergence of the Classical World*. Oxford: Oxford University Press, 2013.

Broomhall, Susan, ed. *Early Modern Emotions: An Introduction*. London: Routledge, 2017.

Bujanda, Jesús M. de. "Recent Historiography of the Spanish Inquisition (1977–1988): Balance and Perspective." In *Cultural Encounters: The Impact of the Inquisition in Spain and the New World*, edited by Mary Elizabeth Perry and Anne J. Cruz, 221–47. Berkeley: University of California Press, 1991.

Bunes Ibarra, Miguel Ángel de. "The Expulsion of the Moriscos in the Context of Philip III's Mediterranean Policy." In *The Expulsion of the Moriscos from Spain: A Mediterranean Diaspora*, edited by Mercedes García-Arenal and Gerard Wiegers, 37–59. Leiden, Netherlands: Brill, 2014.

Burningham, Bruce R. "Os Manchíadas." In Dopico Black and Layna Ranz, *USA Cervantes*, 251–72.

Byrne, Susan. *El "Corpus Hermeticum" y tres poetas españoles: Francisco de Aldana, fray Luis de León y San Juan de la Cruz; Conexiones léxicas y semánticas entre la filosofía hermética y la poesía española del siglo XVI*. Newark, DE: Juan de la Cuesta, 2007.

– *Law and History in Cervantes' "Don Quixote."* Toronto: University of Toronto Press, 2012.

Cabrera de Córdoba, Luis. *Historia de Felipe II, rey de España.* Edited by José Martínez Millán and Carlos Javier de Carlos Morales. 4 vols. Valladolid, Spain: Junta de Castilla y León / Consejería de Educación y Cultura, 1998. Originally published 1619.

Camacho Morfín, Lilián. "El lenguaje de las emociones en el *Quijote* de 1605." In *"Injerto peregrino de bienes y grandezas admirables": Estudios de literatura y cultura española e hispanoamericana (siglos XVI al XVIII)*, edited by Lillian von der Walde Moheno, 363–74. Mexico City: Universidad Autónoma Metropolitana, 2007.

Campana, Patrizia. "'Et per tal variar natura è bella': Apuntes sobre la *variatio* en el *Quijote.*" *Cervantes: Bulletin of the Cervantes Society of America* 17.1 (1997): 109–21.

Camps, Victoria. *El gobierno de las emociones.* Barcelona: Herder, 2011.

Canavaggio, Jean. "Alonso López Pinciano y la estética literaria de Cervantes en el *Quijote.*" *Anales Cervantinos* 7 (1958): 13–107.

Cárdenas-Rotunno, Anthony J. "The Mirth of Girth: Don Quixote's Stout Squire." *Rocky Mountain Review* 68.1 (2014): 9–31.

Carducho, Vicente. *Diálogos de la pintura: Su defensa, origen, esencia, definición, modos y diferencias.* Madrid, 1663.

Caro Baroja, Julio. "Honour and Shame: A Historical Account of Several Conflicts." In *Honour and Shame: The Values of Mediterranean Society*, edited by J.G. Peristiany, 79–137. Chicago: University of Chicago Press, 1966.

– "Religion, World Views, Social Classes, and Honor during the Sixteenth and Seventeenth Centuries in Spain." In *Honor and Grace in Anthropology*, edited by J.G. Peristiany and Julian Pitt-Rivers, 91–102. Cambridge: Cambridge University Press, 1992.

Carrasco Urgoiti, María Soledad. *Vidas fronterizas en las letras españolas.* Barcelona: Bellaterra, 2005.

Carrera, Elena. "The Emotions in Sixteenth-Century Spanish Spirituality." *Journal of Religious History* 31.3 (2007): 235–52.

– "*Pasión* and *afección* in Teresa of Avila and Francisco de Osuna." *Bulletin of Spanish Studies* 84.2 (2007): 175–91.

– "The Social Dimension of Shame in Cervantes's *La fuerza de la sangre.*" *Perífrasis* 4.7 (2013): 19–36.

Carveth, Donald L. "Psychoanalytic Conceptions of the Passions." In *Freud and the Passions*, edited by John O'Neill, 25–51. University Park: Pennsylvania State University Press, 1996.

Casalduero, Joaquín. *Sentido y forma de "Los trabajos de Persiles y Sigismunda."* Madrid: Gredos, 1975.

Cascales, Francisco. *Tablas poéticas.* Murcia, Spain: Luis Beros, 1617.

Cascardi, Anthony J. *Cervantes, Literature, and the Discourse of Politics*. Toronto: University of Toronto Press, 2012.

– "Reason and Romance: An Essay on Cervantes's *Persiles*." *MLN* 106.2 (1991): 279–93.

Cassano, Franco. *Southern Thought and Other Essays on the Mediterranean*. Edited by Norma Bouchard and Valerio Ferme. New York: Fordham University Press, 2012.

Cassin, Barbara, ed. *Dictionary of Untranslatables: A Philosophical Lexicon*. Translated by Steven Rendall, Christian Hubert, Jeffrey Mehlman, Nathanael Stein, and Michael Syrotinski. Translation edited by Emily Apter, Jacques Lezra, and Michael Wood. Princeton, NJ: Princeton University Press, 2014.

Castanien, Donald G. "Quevedo's Version of Epictetus' *Encheiridion*." *Symposium* 18.1 (1964): 68–78.

Castelvetro, Lodovico. "Commentary on Aristotle's *Poetics*." Translated by Andrew Bongiorno. In *Theories of Comedy*, edited by Paul Lauter, 87–97. Garden City, NY: Anchor Books, 1964.

Castiglione, Baldesar. *The Book of the Courtier*. Translated by Charles S. Singleton. Garden City, NY: Anchor Books, 1959.

– *Il cortegiano*. Edited by Vittorio Cian. Florence: G.C. Sansoni, 1894.

Castillo, David R. *(A)Wry Views: Anamorphosis, Cervantes, and the Early Picaresque*. West Lafayette, IN: Purdue University Press, 2001.

Castillo, David R., and Nicholas Spadaccini. "El antiutopismo en *Los trabajos de Persiles y Sigismunda*: Cervantes y el cervantismo actual." *Cervantes: Bulletin of the Cervantes Society of America* 20.1 (2000): 115–31.

Castro, Américo. *Américo Castro: Obra reunida*. Vol. 1, *El pensamiento de Cervantes y otros estudios cervantinos*, edited by José Miranda. Madrid: Trotta, 2002.

– *Cervantes y los casticismos españoles*. Madrid: Alianza, 1974.

– *De la edad conflictiva: Crisis de la cultura española en el siglo XVII*. 4th ed. Madrid: Taurus, 1976.

– *El pensamiento de Cervantes. Nueva edición ampliada y con notas del autor y de Julio Rodríguez-Puértolas*. Barcelona: Noguer, 1972.

– "El *Quijote*, taller de existencialidad." *Revista de Occidente* 8 (1967): 1–33.

– *Semblanzas y estudios españoles*. Princeton, NJ: Ínsula, 1956.

Catlos, Brian, and Sharon Kinoshita, eds. *Can We Talk Mediterranean? Conversations on an Emerging Field in Medieval and Early Modern Studies*. Basingstoke, UK: Palgrave Macmillan, 2017.

Certeau, Michel de. *The Mystic Fable*. Vol. 1, *The Sixteenth and Seventeenth Centuries*. Translated by Michael B. Smith. Chicago: University of Chicago Press, 1992.

Cervantes, Miguel de. *Comedias y tragedias*. Edited by Luis Gómez Canseco. Madrid: Real Academia Española, 2015.

– *Don Quijote de la Mancha*. Edited by Francisco Rico. 2 vols. Barcelona: Galaxia Gutenberg / Círculo de Lectores / Centro para la Edición de los Clásicos Españoles, 2004.

– *Don Quixote*. Translated by Edith Grossman. New York: HarperCollins, 2005.

– *Exemplary Novels*. Translated by Edith Grossman. Edited by Roberto González Echevarría. New Haven, CT: Yale University Press, 2016.

– *La Galatea*. Edited by Francisco López Estrada and María Teresa López García-Berdoy. 3rd ed. Madrid: Cátedra, 2006.

– *Información de Argel*. Edited by Adrián J. Sáez. Madrid: Cátedra, 2019.

– *Novelas ejemplares*. 2nd ed. Edited by Jorge García López. Barcelona: Crítica, 2010.

– *Obras completas*. Vol. 7, *Obras sueltas de Cervantes*, edited by Real Academia Española. Madrid: Tipografía de la Revista de Archivos, Bibliotecas y Museos, 1923.

– *Poesías*. Edited by Adrián J. Sáez. Madrid: Cátedra, 2016.

– *Los trabajos de Persiles y Sigismunda*. 5th ed. Edited by Carlos Romero Muñoz. Madrid: Cátedra, 2004.

– *The Trials of Persiles and Sigismunda*. Translated by Celia Richmond Weller and Clark A. Colahan. Indianapolis, IN: Hackett, 2009.

– *Vida y hechos del ingenioso hidalgo don Quixote de la Mancha*. 4 vols. London: J. and R. Tonson, 1738.

Chambers, Iain. *Mediterranean Crossings: The Politics of an Interrupted Modernity*. Durham, NC: Duke University Press, 2008.

Chambers, Leland H. "*Harmonia est Discordia Concors*: The Coincidence of Opposites and Unity in Diversity in the *Quijote*." In *Cervantes: Su obra y su mundo; Actas del Primer Congreso Internacional sobre Cervantes*, edited by Manuel Criado de Val, 605–15. Madrid: Edi-6, 1981.

Childers, William. *Transnational Cervantes*. Toronto: University of Toronto Press, 2006.

Christian, William A., Jr. "Provoked Religious Weeping in Early Modern Spain." In *Religion and Emotion: Approaches and Interpretations*, edited by John Corrigan, 33–50. Oxford: Oxford University Press, 2004.

Cicero, Marcus Tullius. *Cicero on Oratory and Orators [De Oratore]*. Edited and translated by J.S. Watson. New York: Harper, 1875.

– *Cicero on the Emotions: Tusculan Disputations 3 and 4*. Translated by Margaret Graver. Chicago: University of Chicago Press, 2002.

Clamurro, William H. *Beneath the Fiction: The Contrary Worlds of Cervantes's "Novelas ejemplares."* New York: Peter Lang, 1997.

Close, Anthony. "La aproximación romántica del *Quijote* desde 1960 hasta ahora." In "La recepción del *Quijote* en su IV Centenario." Special issue, *Ínsula* 700–701 (2005): 31–4.

- *Cervantes and the Comic Mind of His Age*. Oxford: Oxford University Press, 2000.

- "Don Quixote's Love for Dulcinea: A Study of Cervantine Irony." *Bulletin of Hispanic Studies* 50.3 (1973): 237–55.

- *The Romantic Approach to "Don Quixote": A Critical History of the Romantic Tradition in "Quixote" Criticism.* Cambridge: Cambridge University Press, 1977.

- "Sancho Panza: Wise Fool." *Modern Language Review* 68.2 (1973): 344–57.

Coetzee, J.M. *Slow Man*. New York: Viking, 2005.

Cohen, Margaret. *The Novel and the Sea*. Princeton, NJ: Princeton University Press, 2010.

Collins, Marsha S. "Transgression and Transfiguration in Cervantes's *La española inglesa*." *Cervantes: Bulletin of the Cervantes Society of America* 16.1 (1996): 54–73.

Combet, Louis. *Cervantès ou les incertitudes du désir*. Lyon, France: Presses Universitaires de Lyon, 1980.

cooke, miriam. "Mediterranean Thinking: From Netizen to Medizen." *Geographical Review* 89.2 (1999): 290–300.

cooke, miriam, Erdağ Göknar, and Grant Parker, eds. *Mediterranean Passages: Readings from Dido to Derrida*. Chapel Hill: University of North Carolina Press, 2008.

Cortés, Jerónimo. *Phisonomia y varios secretos de naturaleza*. Pamplona, Spain: Carlos de Labàyen, 1611.

Cortijo Ocaña, Antonio. *La evolución genérica de la ficción sentimental de los siglos XV y XVI: Género literario y contexto social*. London: Tamesis, 2001.

Cotarelo y Mori, Emilio. *Bibliografía de las controversias sobre la licitud del teatro en España*. Edited by José Luis Suárez García. Granada, Spain: Universidad de Granada, 1997.

Couderc, Christophe. "El autor ante la edición de sus obras: Los prólogos de las *Partes* de comedia." In *Paratextos en la literatura española, siglos XV–XVIII*, edited by María Soledad Arredondo, Pierre Civil, and Michel Moner, 119–33. Madrid: Casa de Velázquez, 2009.

Covarrubias Horozco, Sebastián de. *Tesoro de la lengua castellana o española*. Edited by Ignacio Arellano and Rafael Zafra. Madrid: Iberoamericana/ Vervuert, 2006. Originally published 1611.

Cowan, Alexander, ed. *Mediterranean Urban Culture, 1400–1700*. Exeter, UK: University of Exeter Press, 2000.

Crespo, Eduardo. "Emotions in Spain." In *The Social Construction of Emotions*, edited by Rom Harré, 209–17. Oxford: Blackwell, 1986.

Critchley, Simon. *On Humour*. London: Routledge, 2002.

Cruz, Anne J., ed. *Material and Symbolic Circulation between Spain and England, 1554–1604*. Aldershot, UK: Ashgate, 2008.

Cummings, Brian, and Freya Sierhuis, eds. *Passions and Subjectivity in Early Modern Culture*. Farnham, UK: Ashgate, 2013.

Currie, Mark. *The Unexpected: Narrative Temporality and the Philosophy of Surprise*. Edinburgh: Edinburgh University Press, 2013.

Curtius, Ernst Robert. *European Literature and the Latin Middle Ages*. Translated by Willard R. Trask. Princeton, NJ: Princeton University Press, 2013.

Cvitanovic, Dinko. *La novela sentimental española*. Madrid: Prensa Española, 1973.

Dainotto, Roberto. "Does Europe Have a South? An Essay on Borders." *The Global South* 5.1 (2011): 37–50.

Dakhlia, Jocelyne. *Lingua franca: Histoire d'une langue métisse en Méditerranée*. Arles, France: Actes Sud, 2008.

Dal Pozzolo, Enrico Maria, and Miguel Falomir, eds. *Lorenzo Lotto: Portraits*. Madrid: Museo Nacional del Prado, 2018.

Damasio, Antonio. *Looking for Spinoza: Joy, Sorrow, and the Feeling Brain*. Orlando, FL: Harcourt, 2003.

Dangler, Jean. *Edging toward Iberia*. Toronto: University of Toronto Press, 2017.

Darnis, Pierre. *Don Quichotte: Éléments sur une satire ménippéenne*. Neuilly, France: Atlande, 2015.

Davis, John H.R. *People of the Mediterranean: An Essay in Comparative Social Anthropology*. London: Routledge and Kegan Paul, 1977.

da Vinci, Leonardo. *Trattato della pittura*. Edited by Rafaelle du Fresne. Parigi, Italy: Giacomo Langlois, 1651.

de Armas, Frederick A. *Ekphrasis in the Age of Cervantes*. Lewisburg, PA: Bucknell University Press, 2005.

– ed. *Writing for the Eyes in the Spanish Golden Age*. Lewisburg, PA: Bucknell University Press, 2004.

Deleuze, Gilles, and Félix Guattari. *What Is Philosophy?* Translated by Hugh Tomlinson and Graham Burchell. New York: Columbia University Press, 1994.

Della Casa, Giovanni. *Galateo: Or, the Rules of Polite Behavior*. Edited and translated by M.F. Rusnak. Chicago: University of Chicago Press, 2013.

– *Il Galateo overo De' costumi*. Edited by Emanuela Scarpa. Modena, Italy: Letteratura italiana Einaudi, 1990. Originally published 1558.

Della Porta, Giambattista. *De humana physiognomonia*. Vico Equense, Italy: Cacchio, 1586.

Delpech, François, ed. *L'imaginaire des espaces aquatiques en Espagne et au Portugal*. Paris: Presses Sorbonne Nouvelle, 2009.

Delumeau, Jean. *La peur en Occident (XIVe–XVIIIe siècles): Une cité assiégée*. Paris: Fayard, 1978.

Derrida, Jacques. *Psyche: Inventions of the Other*. Vol. 1. Edited by Peggy Kamuf and Elizabeth Rottenberg. Stanford, CA: Stanford University Press, 2007.

Descartes, René. *The Passions of the Soul*. In *The Philosophical Writings of Descartes*, translated by John Cottingham, Robert Stoothoff, and Dugald Murdoch, 325–404. Cambridge: Cambridge University Press, 1985.

de Sousa, Ronald. *The Rationality of Emotion*. Cambridge, MA: MIT Press, 1987.

Dewey, John. *Art as Experience*. New York: Perigee, 1980.

Deyermond, Alan. *Tradiciones y puntos de vista en la ficción sentimental*. Mexico City: Universidad Nacional Autónoma de México, 1993.

Díaz Migoyo, Gonzalo. "El *Quijote* muerto de risa." *Cervantes: Bulletin of the Cervantes Society of America* 19.2 (1999): 11–22.

Díaz-Plaja, Guillermo. *En torno a Cervantes*. Pamplona, Spain: Eunsa, 1977.

Díaz-Vera, Javier E. "Reconstructing the Old English Cultural Model for Fear." *Atlantis: Journal of the Spanish Association of Anglo-American Studies* 33.1 (June 2011): 85–103.

Díaz-Vera, Javier E., and Rosario Caballero. "Exploring the Feeling-Emotions Continuum across Cultures: Jealousy in English and Spanish." *Intercultural Pragmatics* 10.2 (2013): 265–94.

Diccionario de autoridades. Edición facsímil. 3 vols. Edited by the Real Academia Española. Madrid: Gredos, 1964. Originally published 1726–39.

Dickie, Simon. *Cruelty and Laughter: Forgotten Comic Literature and the Unsentimental Eighteenth Century*. Chicago: University of Chicago Press, 2011.

Diderot, Denis. *Oeuvres de théâtre, avec un discours sur la poésie dramatique*. Vol. 2. Amsterdam, 1772.

Diego de Jesús Salablanca. "Apuntamientos y advertencias en tres discursos para más fácil inteligencia de las frases místicas y doctrina de las Obras espirituales de nuestro Padre San Juan de la Cruz." In *Obras del Místico Doctor San Juan de la Cruz*, vol. 3, edited by Padre Gerardo de San Juan de la Cruz, 465–502. Toledo, Spain: Viuda é Hijos de J. Peláez, 1912–14.

Di Stefano, Giuseppe. "–Venid, mochachos, y veréis el asno de Sancho Panza ..." *Nueva Revista de Filología Hispánica* 38.2 (1990): 887–99.

Dixon, Thomas. *From Passions to Emotions: The Creation of a Secular Psychological Category*. Cambridge: Cambridge University Press, 2003.

Dollerup, Cay. "The Concepts of 'Tension,' 'Intensity,' and 'Suspense' in Short-Story Theory." *Orbis Litterarum* 25.4 (1970): 314–37.

Domínguez, Julia. "El laberinto mental del exilio en *Don Quijote*: El testimonio del morisco Ricote." *Hispania* 92.2 (2009): 183–92.

Domínguez Ortiz, Antonio. *La clase social de los conversos en Castilla en la Edad Moderna*. Granada, Spain: Universidad de Granada, 1991.

Domínguez Ortiz, Antonio, and Bernard Vincent. *Historia de los moriscos: Vida y tragedia de una minoría*. Madrid: Alianza, 1985.

Doody, Margaret Anne. *The True Story of the Novel*. New Brunswick, NJ: Rutgers University Press, 1996.

Dopico Black, Georgina. "Las lágrimas de Sancho." In Dopico Black and Layna Ranz, *USA Cervantes*, 455–82.

Dopico Black, Georgina, and Francisco Layna Ranz, eds. *USA Cervantes: 39 Cervantistas en Estados Unidos*. Madrid: CSIC/Polifemo, 2009.

Doyle, Laura. "Inter-Imperiality: Dialectics in Postcolonial World History." *Interventions: International Journal of Postcolonial Studies* 16 (2013): 159–96.

Du, Shichuan, Yong Tao, and Aleix M. Martinez. "Compound Facial Expressions of Emotion." *Proceedings of the National Academy of Sciences of the United States of America* 111.15 (2014). E1454–E1462; DOI: 10.1073/pnas.1322355111.

Duclos, G. Cory. "A Squire's Schooling: The Education of Sancho Panza." *Confluencia: Revista Hispánica de Cultura y Literatura* 30.3 (2015): 69–85.

Dunn, Kevin. "'Action, Passion, Motion': The Gestural Politics of Counsel in *The Spanish Tragedy*." *Renaissance Drama* 31 (2002): 27–60.

Durán, Manuel. "El *Quijote* a través del prisma de Mikhail Bakhtine: Carnaval, disfraces, escatología y locura." In *Cervantes and the Renaissance*, edited by Michael D. McGaha, 71–86. Easton, PA: Juan de la Cuesta, 1980.

Dursteler, Eric R. "Language and Identity in the Early Modern Mediterranean." *Mediterranean Identities in the Premodern Era: Entrepôts, Islands, Empires*, edited by John Watkins and Kathryn L. Reyerson, 35–52. Farnham, UK: Ashgate, 2014.

Edgerton, Samuel Y., Jr. *Pictures and Punishment: Art and Criminal Prosecution during the Florentine Renaissance*. Ithaca, NY: Cornell University Press, 1985.

Egginton, William. *The Man Who Invented Fiction: How Cervantes Ushered in the Modern World*. New York: Bloomsbury, 2016.

Egido, Aurora. "La poética del silencio en el Siglo de Oro." In *Fronteras de la poesía en el Barroco*, 93–120. Barcelona: Crítica, 1990.

Egido, Luciano G. *La razón de la sinrazón: Contribución a la lectura del "Quijote."* Madrid: Visor, 2015.

Eisenberg, Daniel. *A Study of "Don Quixote."* Newark, DE: Juan de la Cuesta, 1987.

Ekman, Paul. *Emotion in the Human Face: Guide-Lines for Research and an Integration of Findings*. Oxford: Pergamon, 1972.

elhariry, yasser, and Edwige Tamalẹt Talbayev, eds. *Critically Mediterranean: Temporalities, Aesthetics, and Deployments of a Sea in Crisis*. Cham, Switzerland: Palgrave Macmillan, 2018.

Elias, Norbert. *The Civilizing Process: Sociogenetic and Psychogenetic Investigations*. Rev. ed. Edited by Eric Dunning, Johan Goudsblom, and Stephen Mennell. Translated by Edmund Jephcott. Oxford: Blackwell, 2000.

Eliot, Charles W. *The Harvard Classics*. Vol. 50. New York: Collier, 1910.

El Saffar, Ruth S. *Distance and Control in "Don Quixote": A Study in Narrative Technique*. Chapel Hill: University of North Carolina, Department of Romance Languages, 1975.

– *Novel to Romance: A Study of Cervantes's "Novelas ejemplares."* Baltimore, MD: Johns Hopkins University Press, 1974.

El Saffar, Ruth Anthony, and Diana de Armas Wilson, eds. *Quixotic Desire: Psychoanalytic Perspectives on Cervantes*. Ithaca, NY: Cornell University Press, 1993.

Epalza, Míkel de. "La naturaleza de la lengua franca de Argel y Cervantes." In *Cervantes entre las dos orillas*, edited by María Jesús Rubiera Mata, 85–188. Alicante, Spain: Universidad de Alicante, 2006.

Erämetsä, Erik: *A Study of the Word "Sentimental" and other Linguistic Characteristics of 18th Century Sentimentalism*. Helsinki: Academia Scientiarum Fennica, 1951.

Espejo Madrigal, Ana Isabel. "El *Quijote*: Fin del amor cortés." In *Comentarios a Cervantes: Actas selectas del VIII Congreso Internacional de la Asociación de Cervantistas*, edited by Emilio Martínez Mata and María Fernández Ferreiro, 195–204. Oviedo, Spain: Fundación María Cristina Masaveu Peterson, 2014.

Etreros, Mercedes. *La sátira política en el siglo XVII*. Madrid: Fundación Universitaria Española, 1983.

Ettinghausen, Henry. *Francisco de Quevedo and the Neostoic Movement*. Oxford: Oxford University Press, 1972.

Eustace, Nicole, Eugenia Lean, Julie Livingston, Jan Plamper, William M. Reddy, and Barbara H. Rosenwein. "*AHR* Conversation: The Historical Study of Emotions." *American Historical Review* 117.5 (December 2012): 1487–1531.

Fajardo, Salvador J. "Narrative and Agency: The Ricote Episode (*Don Quijote II*)." *Bulletin of Hispanic Studies* 78.3 (2001): 311–22.

Febvre, Lucien. *Combats pour l'histoire*. 2nd ed. Paris: A. Colin, 1965.

Fernández, Enrique. *Anxieties of Interiority and Dissection in Early Modern Spain*. Toronto: University of Toronto Press, 2015.

Fernández, Esther, and M. Reina Ruiz. "Una 'mesa de trucos' en escena: Metamorfosis dramática de 'La española inglesa.'" *Cervantes: Bulletin of the Cervantes Society of America* 35.2 (2015): 193–213.

Fernandez, James W. "Consciousness and Class in Southern Spain." *American Ethnologist* 10 (1983): 165–73.

Fisher, Philip. *The Vehement Passions*. Princeton, NJ: Princeton University Press, 2002.

Fitzmaurice Kelly, James. *Miguel de Cervantes Saavedra: A Memoir*. London: Oxford University Press, 1913.

Flor, Fernando R. de la. *Era melancólica: Figuras del imaginario barroco*. Barcelona: Universitat de les Illes Balears, 2007.

Flores, R.M. *Sancho Panza through Three Hundred Seventy-Five Years of Continuations, Imitations, and Criticism: 1605–1980*. Newark, DE: Juan de la Cuesta, 1982.

Forcione, Alban K. *Cervantes' Christian Romance: A Study of "Persiles y Sigismunda."* Princeton, NJ: Princeton University Press, 1972.

Foucault, Michel. *Discipline and Punish: The Birth of the Prison*. Translated by Alan Sheridan. New York: Vintage, 1979.

– "Of Other Spaces." *Diacritics* 16.1 (1986): 22–7.

Franco Sánchez, Francisco. "Cervantes y el mar." In *Cervantes entre las dos orillas*, edited by María Jesús Rubiera Mata, 117–88. Alicante, Spain: Universidad de Alicante, 2006.

Franke, William. *On What Cannot Be Said: Apophatic Discourses in Philosophy, Religion, Literature, and the Arts*. Vol. 1, *Classical Formulations*. Vol. 2, *Modern and Contemporary Transformations*. Notre Dame, IN: Notre Dame University Press, 2007.

– "Varieties and Valences of Unsayability." *Philosophy and Literature* 29.2 (2005): 489–97.

Freud, Sigmund. "The Antithetical Meaning of Primal Words." In *Writings on Art and Literature*, 94–100. Stanford, CA: Stanford University Press, 1997.

– *Civilization and Its Discontents*. Edited and translated by James Strachey. New York: Norton, 1961.

– *Jokes and Their Relation to the Unconscious*. Edited and translated by James Strachey. New York: Norton, 1990.

Friedman, Edward H. *Cervantes in the Middle: Realism and Reality in the Spanish Novel from "Lazarillo de Tormes" to "Niebla."* Newark, DE: Juan de la Cuesta, 2006.

Frye, Northrop. *The Secular Scripture: A Study of the Structure of Romance*. Cambridge, MA: Harvard University Press, 1976.

Fuchs, Barbara. "Another Turn for Transnationalism: Empire, Nation, and Imperium in Early Modern Studies." *PMLA* 130.2 (2015): 412–18.

– "Imperium Studies: Theorizing Early Modern Expansion." In *Postcolonial Moves: Medieval through Modern*, edited by Patricia Clare Ingham and Michelle R. Warren, 71–90. New York: Palgrave Macmillan, 2003.

– *Passing for Spain: Cervantes and the Fictions of Identity*. Urbana: University of Illinois Press, 2003.

– "Suspended Judgments: Skepticism and the Pact of Fictionality in Cervantes's Picaresque Novellas." *Modern Language Quarterly* 76.4 (2015): 447–63.

Galt, Anthony H. "Does the Mediterraneanist Dilemma Have Straw Horns?" *American Ethnologist* 12.2 (1985): 369–71.

Ganelin, Charles Victor. "Cervantes's Exemplary Sensorium, or the Skinny on *La española inglesa*." In *Beyond Sight: Engaging the Senses in Iberian Literatures and Cultures, 1200–1750*, edited by Ryan D. Giles and Steven Wagschal, 167–85. Toronto: University of Toronto Press, 2018.

Garcés, María Antonia. *Cervantes in Algiers: A Captive's Tale*. Nashville, TN: Vanderbilt University Press, 2002.

García-Arenal, Mercedes, and Miguel Ángel de Bunes. *Los españoles y el norte de África: Siglos XV–VIII*. Madrid: MAPFRE, 1992.

García-Arenal, Mercedes, and Gerard Wiegers, eds. *The Expulsion of the Moriscos from Spain: A Mediterranean Diaspora*. Leiden, Netherlands: Brill, 2014.

García Valdecasas, Alfonso. *El hidalgo y el honor*. Madrid: Revista de Occidente, 1948.

Garcilaso de la Vega. *Obra poética y textos en prosa*. Edited by Bienvenido Morros. Barcelona: Crítica, 2007.

Garrote Pérez, Francisco. *La naturaleza en el pensamiento de Cervantes*. Salamanca, Spain: Universidad de Salamanca, 1979.

Gasta, Chad M. "'Señora, donde hay música no puede haber cosa mala': Music, Poetry, and Orality in *Don Quijote*." *Hispania* 93.3 (2010): 357–67.

– "Writing to Be Heard: Performing Music in *Don Quixote*." In *Cervantes in Perspective*, edited by Julia Domínguez, 85–107. Madrid: Iberoamericana Vervuert, 2013.

Gaylord, Mary Malcolm. "Cervantes's Other Fiction." In *The Cambridge Companion to Cervantes*, edited by Anthony J. Cascardi, 100–30. Cambridge: Cambridge University Press, 2002.

– "Ending and Meaning in Cervantes' *Persiles y Sigismunda*." *Romanic Review* 74.2 (1983): 152–69.

Geary, Patrick. *The Myth of Nations: The Medieval Origins of Europe*. Princeton, NJ: Princeton University Press, 2002.

Gernert, Folke. *Lecturas del cuerpo: Fisiognomía y literatura en la España áurea*. Salamanca, Spain: Universidad de Salamanca, 2018.

Gerrig, Richard J. *Experiencing Narrative Worlds: On the Psychological Activities of Reading*. New Haven, CT: Yale University Press, 1993.

Gilman, Stephen. *The Novel According to Cervantes*. Berkeley: University of California Press, 1989.

Gilmore, David D., ed. *Honor and Shame and the Unity of the Mediterranean*. Washington, DC: American Anthropological Association, 1987.

– "Honor, Honesty, Shame: Male Status in Contemporary Andalusia." In Gilmore, *Honor and Shame and the Unity of the Mediterranean*, 90–103.

– "Introduction: The Shame of Dishonor." In Gilmore, *Honor and Shame and the Unity of the Mediterranean*, 2–21.

Gil-Osle, Juan Pablo. *Amistades imperfectas: Del Humanismo a la Ilustración con Cervantes*. Madrid: Iberoamericana Vervuert, 2013.

Gil-Sotres, Pedro. "Modelo teórico y observación clínica: Las pasiones del alma en la psicología médica medieval." In *Comprendre et maîtriser la nature au Moyen Age: Mélanges d'histoire des sciences offerts à Guy Beaujouan*, edited by Danielle Jacquart, 181–204. Geneva: Librairie Droz, 1994.

Gitlitz, David. "Inquisition Confessions and *Lazarillo de Tormes*." *Hispanic Review* 68.1 (2000): 53–74.

Gobert, R. Darren. "Behaviorism, Catharsis, and the History of Emotion." *Journal of Dramatic Theory and Criticism* 26.2 (2012): 109–25.

– *The Mind-Body Stage: Passion and Interaction in the Cartesian Theater*. Stanford, CA: Stanford University Press, 2013.

Gogol, Nikolai. *Dead Souls*. Edited by George Gibian. Translated by George Reavey. New York: Norton, 1985.

Goitein, S.D. *A Mediterranean Society: An Abridgment in One Volume*. Edited by Jacob Lassner. Berkeley: University of California Press, 2003.

Góngora, Luis de. *Antología poética*. Edited by Antonio Carreira. Barcelona: Crítica, 2009.

González Echevarría, Roberto. *Love and the Law in Cervantes*. New Haven, CT: Yale University Press, 2005.

Gonzalo Sánchez-Molero, José Luis. *La "Epístola a Mateo Vázquez": Historia de una polémica literaria en torno a Cervantes*. Alcalá de Henares, Spain: Centro de Estudios Cervantinos, 2010.

Gorfkle, Laura J. *Discovering the Comic in "Don Quixote."* Chapel Hill: University of North Carolina, Department of Romance Languages, 1993.

Gracia, Jordi. *Miguel de Cervantes: La conquista de la ironía*. Barcelona: Taurus, 2016.

Gracián, Baltasar. *Oráculo manual y arte de prudencia*. Edited by Miguel Romera-Navarro. Madrid: CSIC, 2003.

Gracián Dantisco, Lucas. *Galateo español*. Edited by Enrique Suárez Figaredo. In *Works of Cervantes*, edited by Fred Jehle. Accessed 19 February 2017. http://users.ipfw.edu/jehle/CERVANTE/othertxts/Suarez_Figaredo_GalateoEspanol.pdf.

Graf, E.C. "From Scipio to Nero to the Self: The Exemplary Politics of Stoicism in Garcilaso de la Vega's Elegies." *PMLA* 116.5 (2001): 1316–33.

Granja, Agustín de la. "Los actores del siglo XVII ante *La vida es sueño*: De la técnica de la turbación a la práctica de la suspensión." *Bulletin of Hispanic Studies* 77.1 (2000): 145–71.

Green, Melanie C., Christopher Chatham, and Marc A. Sestir. "Emotion and Transportation into Fact and Fiction." *Scientific Study of Literature* 2.1 (2012): 37–59.

Green, Otis. "El Ingenioso Hidalgo." *Hispanic Review* 25 (1957): 175–93.

Greenblatt, Stephen. *Renaissance Self-Fashioning: From More to Shakespeare*. Chicago: University of Chicago Press, 2005.

Grove, A.T., and Oliver Rackham. *The Nature of Mediterranean Europe: An Ecological History*. New Haven, CT: Yale University Press, 2001.

Guarracino, Scipione. *Mediterraneo: Immagini, storie e teorie da Omero a Braudel*. Milan: Mondadori, 2007.

Gundersheimer, Werner L. "Renaissance Concepts of Shame and Pocaterra's *Dialoghi Della Vergogna*." *Renaissance Quarterly* 47.1 (1994): 34–56.

Gwara, Joseph J., and E. Michael Gerli, eds. *Studies on the Spanish Sentimental Romance (1450–1550): Redefining a Genre*. London: Tamesis, 1997.

Hacthoun, Augusto. "Los mecanismos del humor en el habla de Sancho Panza." In *Actas del Sexto Congreso Internacional de Hispanistas*, edited by Alan M. Gordon and Evelyn Rugg, 365–7. Toronto: Asociación Internacional de Hispanistas, 1980.

Hamacher, Werner. "95 Theses on Philology." Translated by Catharine Diehl. *Diacritics* 39.1 (2009): 25–44.

Hamblet, Wendy C. *Punishment and Shame: A Philosophical Study*. Lanham, MD: Lexington Books, 2011.

Hamilton, Michelle M., and Núria Silleras-Fernández, eds. *In and Of the Mediterranean: Medieval and Early Modern Iberian Studies*. Nashville, TN: Vanderbilt University Press, 2015.

– Introduction to *In and Of the Mediterranean: Medieval and Early Modern Iberian Studies*. Edited by Hamilton and Silleras-Fernández, ix–xxvii. Nashville, TN: Vanderbilt University Press, 2015.

Hampton, Timothy. *Writing from History: The Rhetoric of Exemplarity in Renaissance Literature*. Ithaca, NY: Cornell University Press, 1990.

Harré, Rom. "Emotion in Music." In *Emotion and the Arts*, edited by Mette Hjort and Sue Laver, 110–18. New York: Oxford University Press, 1997.

Harris, W.V., ed. *Rethinking the Mediterranean*. Oxford: Oxford University Press, 2005.

Hart, Thomas R. "What's Funny about *Don Quixote*?" *Hispanic Research Journal* 10.3 (2009): 227–32.

Heidegger, Martin. *Being and Time: A Translation of Sein und Zeit*. Translated by Joan Stambaugh. Albany: SUNY Press, 1996.

Heiple, Daniel. "La suspensión en la estética de la comedia." In *Estudios sobre el Siglo de Oro en homenaje a Raymond McCurdy*, edited by Ángel González, Tamara Holzapfel, and Alfred Rodríguez, 25–35. Madrid: Cátedra, 1983.

Heliodorus. *The Aethiopica*. Athens: Athenian Society, 1897.

Hendrix, W.S. "Sancho Panza and the Comic Types of the Sixteenth Century." In *Homenaje ofrecido a Ramón Menéndez Pidal*, vol. 2, 485–94. Madrid: Hernando, 1925.

Herrick, Marvin T. "Some Neglected Sources of *Admiratio*." *Modern Language Notes* 62.4 (1947): 222–6.

Hershenzon, Daniel Bernardo. "Traveling Libraries: The Arabic Manuscripts of Muley Zidan and the Escorial Library." *Journal of Early Modern History* 18 (2014): 535–58.

Herzfeld, Michael. "Honour and Shame: Problems in the Comparative Analysis of Moral Systems." *Man* 15.2 (1980): 339–51.

– "The Horns of the Mediterraneanist Dilemma." *American Ethnologist* 11.3 (1984): 439–54.

– "Of Horns and History: The Mediterraneanist Dilemma Again." *American Ethnologist* 12.4 (1985): 778–80.

– "Practical Mediterraneanism: Excuses for Everything, from Epistemology to Eating." In Harris, *Rethinking the Mediterranean*, 45–63.

Hess, Andrew C. *The Forgotten Frontier: A History of the Sixteenth-Century Ibero-African Frontier*. Chicago: University of Chicago Press, 1978.

Hitchcock, Richard. "Cervantes, Ricote, and the Expulsion of the Moriscos." *Bulletin of Spanish Studies* 81.2 (2004): 175–85.

Hobbes, Thomas. *Elements of Law: Natural and Politic*. Edited by Ferdinand Tönnies. London: Routledge, 2013. Originally published 1650.

Hochschild, Arlie Russell. "Emotion Work, Feeling Rules and Social Structure." *American Journal of Sociology* 85 (1979): 551–75.

Horace. *Satires, Epistles, and Ars Poetica*. Translated by H. Rushton Fairclough. Cambridge, MA: Harvard University Press, 2005.

Horden, Peregrine. "Travel Sickness: Medicine and Mobility in the Mediterranean from Antiquity to the Renaissance." In Harris, *Rethinking the Mediterranean*, 179–99.

Horden, Peregrine, and Sharon Kinoshita, eds. *A Companion to Mediterranean History*. Malden, MA: Wiley Blackwell, 2014.

Horden, Peregrine, and Nicholas Purcell. *The Corrupting Sea: A Study of Mediterranean History*. Malden, MA: Blackwell, 2000.

– "The Mediterranean and 'the New Thalassology.'" *American Historical Review* 111.3 (2006): 722–40.

Huarte de San Juan, Juan. *Examen de ingenios para las ciencias*. Edited by Guillermo Serés. Madrid: Cátedra, 1989. Originally published 1575.

Huizinga, Johan. *The Autumn of the Middle Ages*. Translated by Rodney J. Payton and Ulrich Mammitzsch. Chicago: University of Chicago Press, 1996.

Hume, David. *A Treatise of Human Nature: A Critical Edition*. Vol. 1, *Texts*, edited by David Fate Norton and Mary J. Norton. Oxford: Clarendon Press, 2007.

Husain, Adnan A. "Introduction: Approaching Islam and the Religious Cultures of the Medieval and Early Modern Mediterranean." In *A Faithful Sea: The Religious Cultures of the Mediterranean, 1200–1700*, edited by Adnan A. Husain and K.E. Fleming, 1–26. Oxford: Oneworld, 2007.

Husain, Adnan A., and K.E. Fleming, eds. *A Faithful Sea: The Religious Cultures of the Mediterranean, 1200–1700*. Oxford: Oneworld, 2007.

Hutchinson, Steven. "Affective Dimensions in *Don Quijote*." *Cervantes: Bulletin of the Cervantes Society of America* 24.2 (2004 [2005]): 71–91.

– "Afinidades afectivas en *Don Quijote* I." In *El "Quijote" en Buenos Aires: Lecturas cervantinas en el cuarto centenario*, 181–6. Buenos Aires: Instituto de Filología y Literaturas Hispánicas, 2006.

– "Anagnórisis en las novelas de Cervantes (*DQ* I, 42)." In *Edad de Oro Cantabrigense: Actas del VII Congreso de la Asociación Internacional del Siglo de Oro*, edited by Anthony Close, 345–50. Madrid: Iberoamericana, 2006.

– *Cervantine Journeys*. Madison: University of Wisconsin Press, 1992.

– *Economía ética en Cervantes*. Alcalá de Henares, Spain: Centro de Estudios Cervantinos, 2001.

– "Escribir el Mediterráneo: Cervantes entre dos riberas." In Dopico Black and Layna Ranz, *USA Cervantes*, 643–64.

– *Frontier Narratives: Liminal Lives in the Early Modern Mediterranean*. Manchester, UK: Manchester University Press, 2020.

– "Literatura fronteriza mediterránea: Rasgos de un género literario." In *Antes se agotan la mano y la pluma que su historia / Magis deficit manus et calamus quam eius hystoria: Homenaje a Carlos Alvar*, vol. 2, edited by Constance Carta, Sarah Finci, and Dora Mancheva, 1431–50. San Millán de la Cogolla, Spain: Cilengua, 2016.

– "Poética de la emoción: De la risa a la grandeza de Sancho." In *Peregrinamente peregrinos*, edited by Alicia Villar Lecumberri, 1373–84. Madrid: Asociación de Cervantistas, 2004.

– "'Los primeros movimientos no son en mano del hombre': Retórica de la emoción en *Don Quijote*." In *Cervantes en Italia: Actas del X Coloquio Internacional de la Asociación de Cervantistas*, edited by Alicia Villar Lecumberri, 199–206. Palma de Mallorca, Spain: Asociación de Cervantistas, 2001.

Hutchinson, Steven, and Antonio Cortijo Ocaña, eds. "Cervantes y el Mediterráneo / Cervantes and the Mediterranean." Special issue, *eHumanista/Cervantes* 2 (2013). Web.

– "Prólogo." In "Cervantes y el Mediterráneo / Cervantes and the Mediterranean." Special issue, *eHumanista/Cervantes* 2 (2013): i–ix. Web.

Ibn Hazm de Córdoba. *El collar de la paloma*. 3rd ed. Edited by Emilio García Gómez. Madrid: Alianza, 2012.

Ife, B.W. *Reading and Fiction in Golden Age Spain: A Platonist Critique and Some Picaresque Replies*. Cambridge: Cambridge University Press, 1985.

Iffland, James. *De fiestas y aguafiestas: Risa, locura e ideología en Cervantes y Avellaneda*. Madrid: Iberoamericana, 1999.

– "Laughter Tamed." *Cervantes: Bulletin of the Cervantes Society of America* 23.2 (2003): 395–435.

Ignatius of Loyola. *Personal Writings*. Edited and translated by Joseph A. Munitiz and Philip Endean. London: Penguin, 2004.

Infante, Catherine. "Painting and the Memory of Captivity in Cervantes's *Persiles* (II, 10)." *Bulletin of Hispanic Studies* 96.4 (2019): 365–82.

Irigoyen-García, Javier. "'Poco os falta para moros, pues tanto lo parecéis': Impersonating the Moor in the Spanish Mediterranean." *Journal of Spanish Cultural Studies* 12.3 (2011): 355–69.

Isidore of Seville. *The "Etymologies" of Isidore of Seville*. Edited by Stephen A. Barney, W.J. Lewis, J.A. Beach, and Oliver Berghof. Cambridge: Cambridge University Press, 2006.

James, Susan. *Passion and Action: The Emotions in Seventeenth-Century Philosophy*. Oxford: Oxford University Press, 1997.

James, William. *The Principles of Psychology*. Cambridge, MA: Harvard University Press, 1983.

Jáuregui, Juan de. *Diálogo entre la Naturaleza y las dos Artes, Pintura y Escultura, de cuya preeminencia se disputa y juzga*. Seville, Spain: Francisco de Lyra Barreto, 1618.

Jensen, Katherine Ann, and Miriam L. Wallace. "Introduction: Facing Emotions." In "Emotions." Special issue, *PMLA* 130.5 (2015): 1249–68.

Johnson, Carroll B. "Catolicismo, familia y fecundidad: El caso de 'La española inglesa.'" In *Actas del IX Congreso de la Asociación Internacional de Hispanistas*, edited by Sebastian Neumeister, 519–24. Frankfurt: Vervuert, 1989.

– *Madness and Lust: A Psychoanalytical Approach to "Don Quijote."* Berkeley: University of California Press, 1983.

Johnson, Paul Michael. "Don Quijote avergonzado: Trayectoria de un afecto en Cervantes." In *Pictavia aurea: Actas del IX Congreso de la Asociación Internacional "Siglo de Oro,"* edited by Alain Bègue and Emma Herrán Alonso, 477–84. Toulouse, France: Presses Universitaires du Mirail, 2013.

– "The End(lessnes)s of Infamy: Agamben, Enjambment, and Embodiment in a Cervantine Stanza." *MLN* 132.2 (March 2017): 494–506.

– "Estudio introductorio." In *Celos, amor y venganza, o No hay mal que por bien no venga*, by Luis Vélez de Guevara. Edited by William R. Manson and C. George Peale, 11–41. Newark, DE: Juan de la Cuesta, 2018.

– "Feeling Certainty, Performing Sincerity: The Emotional Hermeneutics of Truth in Inquisitorial and Theatrical Practice." In *The Quest for Certainty in Early Modern Europe: From Inquisition to Inquiry, 1550–1700*, edited by Barbara Fuchs and Mercedes García-Arenal, 50–79. Toronto and Los Angeles: University of Toronto Press / UCLA Center for Seventeenth- and Eighteenth-Century Studies and the William Andrews Clark Memorial Library, 2020.

– "Of Fine Arts and Fine Feelings: Mapping Affect across Lessing's *Laocoön*,

Lord Carteret's *Quijote*, and Oldfield's 'Advertencias.'" In "Thinking about Affect in Culture and Art." Special issue, *452°F: Journal of Literary Theory and Comparative Literature* 14 (2016): 121–37.

- "'Salido a la vergüenza': Inquisition, Penality, and a Cervantine View of Mediterranean 'Values.'" In "Cervantes y el Mediterráneo / Cervantes and the Mediterranean." Special issue, *eHumanista/Cervantes* 2 (2013): 340–61.
- "A Soldier's Shame: The Specter of Captivity in 'La historia del cautivo.'" *Cervantes: Bulletin of the Cervantes Society of America* 31.2 (2011): 153–84.
- "Las tecnologías cervantinas del yo: Autoescritura y afectividad en *Don Quijote*." In *Cervantes y sus enemigos*, edited by Eduardo Urbina and Jesús G. Maestro, 245–58. Vol. 9 of *Anuario de Estudios Cervantinos*. Vigo, Spain: Editorial Academia del Hispanismo, 2013.
- "The Trials of Language: Apophasis, Ineffability, and the Mystical Rhetoric of Love in the *Persiles*." In "'Si ya por atrevido no sale con las manos en la cabeza': El legado poético del *Persiles* cuatrocientos años después." Special issue, *eHumanista/Cervantes* 5 (2016): 297–316.

Joly, Monique. "Ainsi parlait Sancho Pança." *Les Langues Néolatines* 69 (1975): 3–37.

Joubert, Laurent. *Treatise on Laughter*. Edited and translated by Gregory David de Rocher. Tuscaloosa: University of Alabama Press, 1980. Originally published as *Traité du ris*, 1579.

Jurado Santos, Agapita. "El ridículo 'Quijote': La vergüenza en España entre el seiscientos y el setecientos." In *Giudizi e predgiudizi: Percezione dell'altro e stereotipi tra Europa e Mediterraneo. Atti del Seminario, Firenze, 10–14 giugno 2008*, vol. 1, edited by Maria Grazia Profeti, 259–78. Florence: Alinea, 2009.

Kagan, Richard L. *Clio and the Crown: The Politics of History in Medieval and Early Modern Spain*. Baltimore, MD: Johns Hopkins University Press, 2009.

Kamen, Henry. *The Spanish Inquisition: A Historical Revision*. 4th ed. New Haven, CT: Yale University Press, 2014.

Keen, Suzanne. "Introduction: Narrative and the Emotions." *Poetics Today* 32.1 (2011): 1–53.

Kermode, Frank. *Shakespeare's Language*. New York: Farrar, Straus & Giroux, 2000.

Kinoshita, Sharon. "Mediterranean Literature." In *A Companion to Mediterranean History*, edited by Peregrine Horden and Sharon Kinoshita, 314–29. Malden, MA: Wiley Blackwell, 2014.

Klein, Julius. *The Mesta: A Study in Spanish Economic History, 1273–1836*. Cambridge, MA: Harvard University Press, 1920.

Koch, Erec R. *The Aesthetic Body: Passion, Sensibility, and Corporeality in Seventeenth-Century France*. Newark: University of Delaware Press, 2008.

Kressel, Gideon M., and Maria Arioti. "Vergogna e genere." *La Ricerca Folklorica* 40 (1999): 105–15.

Kundera, Milan. *The Curtain: An Essay in Seven Parts*. New York: Harper Perennial, 2008.

Labanyi, Jo. "Doing Things: Emotion, Affect, and Materiality." *Journal of Spanish Cultural Studies* 11.3–4 (2010): 223–33.

Lacan, Jacques. *The Four Fundamental Concepts of Psychoanalysis*. Edited by Jacques-Alain Miller. Translated by Alan Sheridan. New York: Norton, 1998.

Laguna, Ana María G. *Cervantes and the Pictorial Imagination: A Study on the Power of Images and Images of Power in Works by Cervantes*. Lewisburg, PA: Bucknell University Press, 2009.

Lapesa, Rafael. *De la edad media a nuestros días*. Madrid: Gredos, 1967.

Larson, Donald R. *The Honor Plays of Lope de Vega*. Cambridge, MA: Harvard University Press, 1977.

Layna Ranz, Francisco. *La eficacia del fracaso: Representaciones culturales en la Segunda Parte del "Quijote."* Madrid: Polifemo, 2005.

Lea, Henry Charles. *A History of the Inquisition of Spain*. Vol. 3. New York: Macmillan, 1907.

Le Brun, Charles. *Méthode pour apprendre à dessiner les passions, proposée dans une conférence sur l'expression générale et particulière*. Hildesheim, Germany: Georg Olms Verlag, 1982. Originally published 1698.

Lee, Christina H. *The Anxiety of Sameness in Early Modern Spain*. Manchester, UK: Manchester University Press, 2016.

Le Goff, Jacques. "Laughter in the Middle Ages." In *A Cultural History of Humour: From Antiquity to the Present Day*, edited by Jan Bremmer and Herman Roodenburg, 40–53. Cambridge: Polity, 1997.

Leys, Ruth. "The Turn to Affect: A Critique." *Critical Inquiry* 37.3 (2011): 434–72.

Lihoreau, Tim. *Schadenfreude: The Little Book of Black Delights*. London: Elliott & Thompson, 2011.

Lipsius, Justus. *On Constancy: "De constantia" Translated by Sir John Stradling (1595)*. Edited by John Sellars. Exeter, UK: Bristol Phoenix, 2006.

Loomba, Ania. "Mediterranean Borderlands and the Global Early Modern." In *Representing Imperial Rivalry in the Early Modern Mediterranean*, edited by Barbara Fuchs and Emily Weissbourd, 13–32. Toronto and Los Angeles: University of Toronto Press / UCLA Center for Seventeenth- and Eighteenth-Century Studies and the William Andrews Clark Memorial Library, 2015.

Lope de Vega. *Arte nuevo de hacer comedias*. 2nd ed. Edited by Enrique García Santo-Tomás. Madrid: Cátedra, 2009. Originally published 1609.

– *Los esclavos libres*. In *Trezena parte de las comedias de Lope de Vega Carpio*, 78–105. Madrid: Viuda de Alonso Martín, 1620.

– *La Gatomaquia*. In *Rimas humanas y divinas del licenciado Tomé de Burguillos y "La Gatomaquia,"* edited by Antonio Carreño, 376–549. Salamanca, Spain: Almar, 2002. Originally published 1634.

– *Laurel de Apolo, con otras rimas*. Madrid: Juan Gonçalez, 1630.

López Alemany, Ignacio. "*Ut pictura non poesis: Los trabajos de Persiles y Sigismunda* and the Construction of Memory." *Cervantes: Bulletin of the Cervantes Society of America* 28.1 (2008): 103–18.

López Pinciano, Alonso. *Philosophia antigua poética*. Edited by Alfredo Carballo Picazo. 3 vols. Madrid: CSIC, 1973. Originally published 1596.

Lorca, Daniel. *Neo-Stoicism and Skepticism in Part One of "Don Quijote": Removing the Authority of a Genre*. Lanham, MD: Lexington Books, 2016.

Lozano Renieblas, Isabel. *Cervantes y el mundo del "Persiles."* Alcalá de Henares, Spain: Centro de Estudios Cervantinos, 1998.

– "'Mar sesgo, viento largo, estrella clara,' o la metáfora de la nave de amor en el *Persiles*." *Anales Cervantinos* 36 (2004): 299–308.

Lucía Megías, José Manuel, dir. *Banco de imágenes del Quijote (1605–1915)*. Centro de Estudios Cervantinos, February 2011. Accessed 8 May 2014. http://qbi2005.windows.cervantesvirtual.com/.

– *Leer el "Quijote" en imágenes: Hacia una teoría de los modelos iconográficos*. Madrid: Calambur, 2006.

Lucian. *Verae Historiae*. In *Lucian*, vol. 1, translated by A.M. Harmon, 247–358. London and Cambridge, MA: William Heinemann and Harvard University Press, 1961.

Luhmann, Niklas. *Love as Passion: The Codification of Intimacy*. Translated by Jeremy Gaines and Doris L. Jones. Stanford, CA: Stanford University Press, 2008.

Lukács, Georg. *The Theory of the Novel*. Translated by Anna Bostock. Cambridge, MA: MIT Press, 1971.

Lynn, Kimberly, and Erin Kathleen Rowe, eds. *The Early Modern Hispanic World: Transnational and Interdisciplinary Approaches*. Cambridge: Cambridge University Press, 2017.

Lyons, John D. *Exemplum: The Rhetoric of Example in Early Modern France and Italy*. Princeton, NJ: Princeton University Press, 1989.

Magnus, Olaus. *Historia de gentibus septentrionalibus*. Rome, 1555.

Maillo-Pozo, Rubén. "Motivos neoestoicos en *El mundo por de dentro*, de Francisco de Quevedo." *Etiópicas* 9 (2013): 353–68.

Maíllo Salgado, Felipe. *El perfume de la amistad: Correspondencia diplomática árabe en archivos españoles (siglos XIII–XVII)*. Madrid: Ministerio de Cultura, 2009.

Malkiel, Yakov. "The Development of *Verecundia* in Ibero-Romance." *Studies in Philology* 41.4 (1944): 501–20.

Mallette, Karla. "Boustrophedon: Towards a Literary Theory of the Mediterranean." In *A Sea of Languages: Rethinking the Arabic Role in Medieval Literary History*, edited by Suzanne Conklin Akbari and Karla Mallette, 254–66. Toronto: University of Toronto Press, 2013.

Mancing, Howard. "Don Quixote's Affective Thoughts." In *The Palgrave Handbook of Affect Studies and Textual Criticism*, edited by Donald R. Wehrs and Thomas Blake, 627–52. Cham, Switzerland: Palgrave Macmillan, 2017.

Mann, Thomas. "Voyage with Don Quixote." In *Essays*, translated by H.T. Lowe-Porter, 325–69. New York: Vintage, 1958. Originally published as "Meerfahrt mit *Don Quijote*," 1934.

Maravall, José Antonio. *La cultura del barroco: Análisis de una estructura histórica*. 2nd ed. Barcelona: Ariel, 1980.

– *Utopía y contrautopía en el "Quijote."* Santiago de Compostela, Spain: Pico Sacro, 1976.

Marculescu, Andreea, and Charles-Louis Morand Métivier, eds. *Affective and Emotional Economies in Medieval and Early Modern Europe*. New York: Palgrave Macmillan, 2018.

Márquez Villanueva, Francisco. "La génesis literaria de Sancho Panza." In *Fuentes literarias cervantinas*, 20–94. Madrid: Gredos, 1973.

– *Moros, moriscos y turcos de Cervantes: Ensayos críticos*. Barcelona: Bellaterra, 2010.

– *Personajes y temas del "Quijote."* Madrid: Taurus, 1975.

– *El problema morisco (Desde otras laderas)*. Madrid: Libertarias, 1998.

Martín, Adrienne Laskier. *Cervantes and the Burlesque Sonnet*. Berkeley: University of California Press, 1991.

– "Humor and Violence in Cervantes." In *The Cambridge Companion to Cervantes*, edited by Anthony J. Cascardi, 160–85. Cambridge: Cambridge University Press, 2002.

Martin, John. "Inventing Sincerity, Refashioning Prudence: The Discovery of the Individual in Renaissance Europe." *American Historical Review* 102 (1997): 1309–42.

– *Myths of Renaissance Individualism*. Basingstoke, UK: Palgrave Macmillan, 2004.

Martínez de Castilla Muñoz, Nuria, and Rodolfo Gil Benumeya Grimau, eds. *De Cervantes y el islam*. Madrid: Sociedad Estatal de Conmemoraciones Culturales, 2006.

Martínez Mata, Emilio. *Cervantes on "Don Quixote."* Translated by Clark Colahan. Bern: Peter Lang, 2010.

Martín Morán, José Manuel. "El género del *Persiles*." *Cervantes: Bulletin of the Cervantes Society of America* 28.2 (2008): 173–93.

Martín Moreno, Antonio. "Música, pasión, razón: La teoría de los afectos en el teatro y la música del Siglo Oro." *Edad de Oro* 22 (2003): 321–60.

Martorell, Joanot, and Martí Joan de Galba. *Tirant lo Blanc i altres escrits de Joanot Martorell*. Edited by Martí de Riquer. Barcelona: Ariel, 1979.

Marzolph, Ulrich. "Sanitizing Humor: Islamic Mediterranean Jocular Tradition in a Comparative Perspective." In *Europa e Islam tra i secoli XIV e XVI / Europe and Islam between 14th and 16th Centuries*, edited by Michele Bernardini, Clara Borrelli, Anna Carbo, and Encarnación Sánchez García, 757–82. Naples, Italy: Istituto Universitario Orientale, 2002.

Massumi, Brian. *Parables for the Virtual: Movement, Affect, Sensation*. Durham, NC: Duke University Press, 2002.

Matar, Nabil. "Introduction: Arab Travelers and Early Modern Europeans." In *In the Lands of the Christians: Arabic Travel Writing in the Seventeenth Century*, edited by Matar, xiii–xlviii. New York: Routledge, 2003.

Matt, Susan J., and Peter N. Stearns, eds. *Doing Emotions History*. Urbana: University of Illinois Press, 2014.

Matvejević, Predrag. *Mediterranean: A Cultural Landscape*. Translated by Michael Henry Heim. Berkeley: University of California Press, 1999.

Mayans y Siscar, Gregorio. *Vida de Miguel de Cervantes Saavedra*. London: J. and R. Tonson, 1737.

McKendrick, Melveena. "Honour/Vengeance in the Spanish 'Comedia': A Case of Mimetic Transference?" *Modern Language Review* 79.2 (1984): 313–35.

– "Writings for the Stage." In *The Cambridge Companion to Cervantes*, edited by Anthony J. Cascardi, 131–59. Cambridge: Cambridge University Press, 2002.

McNamer, Sarah. "The Literariness of Literature and the History of Emotion." In "Emotions." Special issue, *PMLA* 130.5 (2015): 1433–42.

McNeill, W.H. "Fernand Braudel, Historian." *Journal of Modern History* 73 (2001): 133–46.

Mendoza, Diego Hurtado de. *Poemas*. Barcelona: Linkgua, 2012.

Menéndez Pidal, Ramón. "Del honor en el teatro español." In *De Cervantes y Lope de Vega*, 139–66. Madrid: Espasa-Calpe, 1964.

Mentz, Steve. *At the Bottom of Shakespeare's Ocean*. London: Continuum, 2009.

Miall, David S. "Emotions and the Structuring of Narrative Responses." *Poetics Today* 32.2 (Summer 2011): 323–48.

Miller, Daniel. *Materiality*. Durham, NC: Duke University Press, 2005.

Miller, William Ian. "Deep Inner Lives, Individualism, and People of Honour." *History of Political Thought* 16 (1995): 190–207.

Mills, Robert. *Suspended Animation: Pain, Pleasure and Punishment in Medieval Culture*. London: Reaktion, 2005.

Minturno, Antonio Sebastiano. *De poeta*. Munich: Wilhelm Fink Verlag, 1970. Originally published 1559.

Molho, Mauricio. "Raíces folklóricas de Sancho Panza." In *Cervantes: Raíces folklóricas*, 217–336. Madrid: Gredos, 1976.

Montesquieu. *The Spirit of the Laws*. Edited and translated by Anne M. Cohler, Basia Carolyn Miller, and Harold Samuel Stone. Cambridge: Cambridge University Press, 1989.

Morreall, John. *Comic Relief: A Comprehensive Philosophy of Humor*. Malden, MA: Wiley Blackwell, 2009.

Morris, Ian. "Mediterraneanization." *Mediterranean Historical Review* 18.2 (2003): 30–55.

Morros, Bienvenido. "Noticia de Garcilaso de la Vega." In *Obra poética y textos en prosa*, by Garcilaso de la Vega. Edited by Morros. Barcelona: Crítica, 2007.

Morson, Gary Saul. *Narrative and Freedom: The Shadows of Time*. New Haven, CT: Yale University Press, 1994.

Muñoz Sánchez, Juan Ramón. *De amor y literatura: Hacia Cervantes*. Vigo, Spain: Editorial Academia del Hispanismo, 2012.

Murillo, L.A. *A Critical Introduction to Don Quixote*. New York: Peter Lang, 2003.

Nabokov, Vladimir. *Lectures on "Don Quixote."* Edited by Fredson Bowers. San Diego, CA: Harcourt Brace Jovanovich, 1983.

Nadeau, Carolyn. "Critiquing the Elite in the Barataria and 'Ricote' Food Episodes in *Don Quijote II*." *Hispanófila* 146 (2006): 59–75.

Nash, David, and Anne-Marie Kilday. *Cultures of Shame: Exploring Crime and Morality in Britain, 1600–1900*. New York: Palgrave Macmillan, 2010.

Navarro González, Alberto. *El mar en la literatura medieval castellana*. San Cristóbal de La Laguna, Spain: Universidad de La Laguna, 1962.

Nelson, Bradley J. *The Persistence of Presence: Emblem and Ritual in Baroque Spain*. Toronto: University of Toronto Press, 2010.

Nerlich, Michael. *El "Persiles" descodificado, o La "Divina Comedia" de Cervantes*. Translated by Jesús Munárriz. Madrid: Hiperión, 2005.

Ngai, Sianne. *Ugly Feelings*. Cambridge, MA: Harvard University Press, 2005.

Nichols, Wallace J. *Blue Mind: The Surprising Science That Shows How Being Near, In, On, or Under Water Can Make You Happier, Healthier, More Connected, and Better at What You Do*. New York: Little, Brown, 2014.

Nietzsche, Friedrich. *The Gay Science: With a Prelude in Rhymes and an Appendix of Songs*. Translated by Walter Kaufmann. New York: Vintage, 1974.

Noreña, Carlos G. *Juan Luis Vives and the Emotions*. Carbondale: Southern Illinois University Press, 1989.

Nussbaum, Martha C. *Hiding from Humanity: Disgust, Shame, and the Law*. Princeton, NJ: Princeton University Press, 2004.

– *Political Emotions: Why Love Matters for Justice*. Cambridge, MA: Harvard University Press, 2013.

– *Upheavals of Thought: The Intelligence of Emotions*. Cambridge: Cambridge University Press, 2001.

Oatley, Keith. *The Passionate Muse: Exploring Emotion in Stories*. Oxford: Oxford University Press, 2012.

Olid Guerrero, Eduardo. "The Machiavellian In-Betweenness of Cervantes's Elizabeth I." *Cervantes: Bulletin of the Cervantes Society of America* 33.1 (2013): 45–80.

Olmos García, Francisco. "La Inquisición en la época y en la obra de Cervantes." In *Cervantes en su época*, 11–130. Madrid: Ricardo Aguilera, 1970.

O'Neill, John, ed. *Freud and the Passions*. University Park: Pennsylvania State University Press, 1996.

Orobitg, Christine. "El sistema de las emociones: La melancolía en el Siglo de Oro español." In *Accidentes del alma: Las emociones en la Edad Moderna*, 71–98. Madrid: Abada, 2009.

Orozco Díaz, Emilio. "Sentido de continuidad espacial y desbordamiento expresivo en el teatro de Calderón. El soliloquio y el aparte." In *Calderón: Actas del Congreso Internacional sobre Calderón y el Teatro Español del Siglo de Oro*, vol. 1, edited by Luciano García Lorenzo, 125–64. Madrid: CSIC, 1983.

– *El teatro y la teatralidad del barroco*. Barcelona: Planeta, 1969.

Ostle, Robin, ed. *Sensibilities of the Islamic Mediterranean: Self-Expression in a Muslim Culture from Post-Classical Times to the Present Day*. London: I.B. Tauris, 2008.

The Oxford English Dictionary. 2nd ed. Edited by J.A. Simpson and E.S.C. Weiner. 20 vols. Oxford: Clarendon Press, 1989.

Pacheco, Francisco. *Arte de la pintura, su antiguedad y grandezas*. Seville, Spain, 1649.

Pahl, Katrin. "The Logic of Emotionality." In "Emotions." Special issue, *PMLA* 130.5 (2015): 1457–66.

Palencia, Alfonso de. *Universal vocabulario en latín y en romance: Reproducción facsimilar de la edición de Sevilla, 1490*. Madrid: Comisión Permanente de la Asociación de Academias de la Lengua Española, 1967.

Palomino de Castro y Velasco, Antonio. *El museo pictórico y escala óptica*. Madrid: Aguilar, 1947. Originally published 1715–24.

"Para que un alguacil vaya a prender a Miguel de Cervantes." Registro general del sello 9, legajo del mes de septiembre, año 1569. Archivo General de Simancas, Valladolid, Spain.

Parr, James A. *"Don Quijote": An Anatomy of Subversive Discourse*. Newark, DE: Juan de la Cuesta, 1988.

Parvulescu, Anca. *Laughter: Notes on a Passion*. Cambridge, MA: MIT Press, 2010.

Paster, Gail Kern, Katherine Rowe, and Mary Floyd-Wilson, eds. *Reading the Early Modern Passions: Essays in the Cultural History of Emotion*. Philadelphia: University of Pennsylvania Press, 2004.

Pastor Comín, Juan José. *Loco, trovador y cortesano: Bases materiales de la expresión musical en Cervantes*. Vigo, Spain: Editorial Academia del Hispanismo, 2009.

Paulson, Ronald. *Don Quixote in England: The Aesthetics of Laughter*. Baltimore, MD: Johns Hopkins University Press, 1998.

Peers, Edgar Allison. "Cervantes in England." *Bulletin of Spanish Studies* 25 (1947): 226–38.

Penco Valenzuela, Fernando. *Un país llamado Cervantes: El origen judeoconverso del escritor*. Córdoba, Spain: Editorial Almuzara, 2017.

Pennebaker, James W., Bernard Rimé, and Virginia E. Blankenship. "Stereotypes of Emotional Expressiveness of Northerners and Southerners: A Cross-Cultural Test of Montesquieu's Hypotheses." *Journal of Personality and Social Psychology* 70.2 (1996): 372–80.

Percas de Ponseti, Helena. *Cervantes y su concepto del arte: Estudio crítico de algunos aspectos y episodios del "Quijote."* 2 vols. Madrid: Gredos, 1975.

Pérez Cortés, Sergio. "La ofensa, el mentís y el duelo de honor." *Alteridades* 7.13 (1997): 53–60.

Perfetti, Lisa, ed. *The Representation of Women's Emotions in Medieval and Early Modern Culture*. Gainesville: University Press of Florida, 2005.

Peristiany, J.G., ed. *Honour and Shame: The Values of Mediterranean Society*. Chicago: University of Chicago Press, 1966.

Peset, José Luis. *Las melancolías de Sancho: Humores y pasiones entre Huarte y Pinel*. Madrid: Asociación Española de Neuropsiquiatría, 2010.

Picard, Christophe. *Sea of the Caliphs: The Mediterranean in the Medieval Islamic World*. Translated by Nicholas Elliott. Cambridge, MA: Belknap Press of Harvard University Press, 2018.

Pile, Steve. "Emotions and Affect in Recent Human Geography." *Transactions of the Institute of British Geographers* 35.1 (2010): 5–20.

Pina-Cabral, João de. "The Mediterranean as a Category of Regional Comparison: A Critical View." *Current Anthropology* 30 (1989): 399–406.

Pinet, Simone. "Between the Seas: Apolonio and Alexander." In *In and Of the Mediterranean: Medieval and Early Modern Iberian Studies*, edited by Michelle M. Hamilton and Núria Silleras-Fernández, 75–98. Nashville, TN: Vanderbilt University Press, 2015.

Piqueras Flores, Manuel. "El nacimiento de las colecciones de novela corta en español." In *Nuevos enfoques sobre la novela corta barroca*, edited by Mechthild Albert, Ulrike Becker, Rafael Bonilla Cerezo, and Angela Fabris, 77–91. Frankfurt: Peter Lang, 2016.

Piterberg, Gabriel, Teofilo F. Ruiz, and Geoffrey Symcox. Introduction to *Braudel Revisited: The Mediterranean World, 1600–1800*, 3–13. Edited by Piterberg, Ruiz, and Symcox. Toronto and Los Angeles: University of Toronto Press / UCLA Center for Seventeenth- and Eighteenth-Century Studies and the William Andrews Clark Memorial Library, 2010.

Pitt-Rivers, Julian. "Honour and Social Status." In *Honour and Shame: The Values of Mediterranean Society*, edited by J.G. Peristiany, 19–77. Chicago: University of Chicago Press, 1966.

Plamper, Jan. *The History of Emotions: An Introduction*. Oxford: Oxford University Press, 2015.

Plata, Fernando. "Ricote, un español fuera de España: Identidad y espacios de libertad en Cervantes." *Hipogrifo* 3.2 (2015): 263–73.

Plato. *Plato's Symposium*. Translated by Seth Benardete. Chicago: University of Chicago Press, 2001.

Plutarch. *Essays*. Translated by Robin Waterfield. London: Penguin, 1992.

Pocaterra, Annibale. *Due dialogi della vergogna*. Venice, Italy: Domenico Maldura, 1604.

– *Two Dialogues on Shame*. Edited by Werner Gundersheimer and Donald Nathanson. Göttingen, Germany: Jörg Wettlaufer, 2013. Accessed 30 November 2016. http://diglib.hab.de/edoc/ed000237/pocaterra.pdf.

Porqueras Mayo, Alberto. "El *no sé qué* en la literatura española." In *Temas y formas de la literatura española*, 11–59. Madrid: Gredos, 1972.

Pratt, Mary Louise. "Arts of the Contact Zone." *Profession*, 1991, 33–40.

Predmore, Richard L. Review of *The Romantic Approach to "Don Quixote": A Critical History of the Romantic Tradition in "Quixote" Criticism*, by Anthony Close. *Modern Philology* 77.2 (1979): 257–60.

Prinz, Jesse J. *The Emotional Construction of Morals*. Oxford: Oxford University Press, 2007.

– *Gut Reactions: A Perceptual Theory of Emotion*. Oxford: Oxford University Press, 2004.

Probyn, Elspeth. *Blush: Faces of Shame*. Minneapolis: University of Minnesota Press, 2005.

Protevi, John. *Political Affect: Connecting the Social and the Somatic*. Minneapolis: University of Minnesota Press, 2009.

Purcell, Nicholas. "The Boundless Sea of Unlikeness? On Defining the Mediterranean." *Mediterranean Historical Review* 18 (2003): 9–29.

Quevedo, Francisco de. *Bilis negra*. Edited by Antonio Martínez Sarrión. Engravings by Julio Zachrisson. Madrid: Gredos, 2002.

– *El Buscón*. 21st ed. Edited by Domingo Ynduráin. Madrid: Cátedra, 2006.

– *Defensa de Epicuro contra la común opinión*. 2nd. ed. Edited by Eduardo Acosta Méndez. Madrid: Tecnos, 2008. Originally published 1635.

– "Epicteto traducido." In *Obras completas*, 3rd ed., vol. 2, edited by Luis Astrana Marín, 793–828. Madrid: M. Aguilar, 1945. Originally published 1635.

Quinn, Mary. *The Moor and the Novel: Narrating Absence in Early Modern Spain*. Basingstoke, UK: Palgrave Macmillan, 2013.

Quint, David. *Cervantes's Novel of Modern Times: A New Reading of "Don Quijote."* Princeton, NJ: Princeton University Press, 2005.

Raban, Jonathan, ed. *The Oxford Book of the Sea*. Oxford: Oxford University Press, 1992.

Rancière, Jacques. *The Politics of Aesthetics*. Translated by Gabriel Rockhill. London: Continuum, 2008.

– *The Politics of Literature*. Translated by Julie Rose. Cambridge: Polity, 2006.

Rawlings, Helen. *The Spanish Inquisition*. Malden, MA: Blackwell, 2006.

Real Academia Española. *Corpus diacrónico del español*. Accessed 3 July 2019. www.rae.es.

Reddy, William M. *The Navigation of Feeling: A Framework for the History of Emotions*. Cambridge: Cambridge University Press, 2001.

Redondo, Augustin. "En busca del 'Quijote': El problema de los afectos." In *Cuatrocientos años del Ingenioso Hidalgo: Colección de Quijotes de la Biblioteca Cervantina y cuatro estudios*, edited by Blanca López de Mariscal and Judith Farré. Monterrey, 51–65. Mexico: Cátedra Alfonso Reyes, 2004.

– *Otra manera de leer el "Quijote": Historia, tradiciones culturales y literatura*. Madrid: Castalia, 1997.

Reed, Cory A. "Cervantes and the Novelization of Drama: Tradition and Innovation in the *Entremeses*." *Cervantes: Bulletin of the Cervantes Society of America* 11.1 (1991): 61–86.

Reichenberger, Kurt. *Cervantes, ¿un gran satírico? Los enigmas peligrosos del "Quijote" descifrados para el "carísimo lector."* Kassel, Germany: Reichenberger, 2005.

– *Cervantes and the Hermeneutics of Satire*. Kassel, Germany: Reichenberger, 2005.

Rey Hazas, Antonio. *Poética de la libertad y otras claves cervantinas*. Madrid: Ediciones Eneida, 2005.

Ricapito, Joseph V. *Cervantes's "Novelas ejemplares": Between History and Creativity*. West Lafayette, IN: Purdue University Press, 1996.

Ricoeur, Paul. *Oneself as Another*. Translated by Kathleen Blamey. Chicago: University of Chicago Press, 1992.

– *Time and Narrative*. 3 vols. Translated by Kathleen McLaughlin and David Pellauer. Chicago: University of Chicago Press, 1984.

Riley, E.C. *Cervantes's Theory of the Novel*. Newark, DE: Juan de la Cuesta, 1992.

– "The 'Pensamientos Escondidos' and 'Figuras Morales' of Cervantes." In *Homenaje a William L. Fichter: Estudios sobre el teatro antiguo hispánico y otros ensayos*, edited by A. Hutchinson, David Kissoff, and José Amor y Vásquez, 623–31. Madrid: Castalia, 1971.

Río Parra, Elena del. "*Suspensio Animi*, or the Interweaving of Mysticism and Artistic Creation." In *A New Companion to Hispanic Mysticism*, edited by Hilaire Kallendorf, 391–409. Leiden, Netherlands: Brill, 2010.

Ríos, Vicente de los. "Juicio crítico o análisis del *Quijote* (1780)." In *El nacimiento del cervantismo: Cervantes y el "Quijote" en el siglo XVIII*, edited by Antonio Rey Hazas and Juan Ramón Muñoz Sánchez, 271–386. Madrid: Verbum, 2006.

Ripa, Cesare. *Iconologia: or, Moral Emblems*. London: Benj. Motte, 1709.

– *Iconologia ouero Descrittione di diversi Imagini cauate dall'antichità, & di propria inuentione*. Rome: Appresso Lepido Facij, 1603.

Riquer, Martín de. *Aproximación al "Quijote."* Barcelona: Teide, 1970.

– *Caballeros andantes españoles*. Madrid: Espasa-Calpe, 1967.

Robbins, Jeremy. "The Twists and Turns of Life: Cervantes's *Trials of Persiles and Sigismunda*." In *Digressions in European Literature: From Cervantes to Sebald*, edited by Alexis Grohmann and Caragh Wells, 9–20. New York: Palgrave Macmillan, 2011.

Rodríguez Cuadros, Evangelina. *La técnica del actor español, en el Barroco: Hipótesis y documentos*. Madrid: Castalia, 1998.

Rodríguez Marín, Francisco. *El Loaysa de "El celoso extremeño."* Seville, Spain: Francisco de P. Díaz, 1901.

Rogerson, Brewster. "The Art of Painting the Passions." *Journal of the History of Ideas* 14.1 (1953): 68–94.

Rolls, Edmund T. "The Origins of Aesthetics: A Neurobiological Basis for Affective Feelings and Aesthetics." In *The Aesthetic Mind: Philosophy and Psychology*, edited by Elisabeth Schellekens and Peter Goldie, 116–65. New York: Oxford University Press, 2011.

Romero Flores, Hipólito R. *Biografía de Sancho Panza: Filósofo de la sensatez*. Barcelona: Aedos, 1952.

Roncero López, Victoriano. "El humor y la risa en las preceptivas de los Siglos de Oro." In *Demócrito áureo: Los códigos de la risa en el Siglo de Oro*, edited by Ignacio Arellano and Victoriano Roncero, 285–328. Seville, Spain: Renacimiento, 2006.

Rose, Constance Hubbard. *Alonso Núñez de Reinoso: The Lament of a Sixteenth-Century Exile*. Rutherford, NJ: Farleigh Dickinson University Press, 1971.

Rosenwein, Barbara H. *Emotional Communities in the Early Middle Ages*. Ithaca, NY: Cornell University Press, 2006.

Rowland, Ann Wierda. "Sentimental Fiction." In *The Cambridge Companion to Fiction in the Romantic Period*, edited by Richard Maxwell and Katie Trumpener, 191–206. Cambridge: Cambridge University Press, 2008.

Ruch, Willibald, and René T. Proyer. "Extending the Study of Gelotophobia: On Gelotophiles and Katagelasticists." *Humor: International Journal of Humor Research* 22.1–2 (2009): 183–212.

Rupp, Stephen. *Heroic Forms: Cervantes and the Literature of War*. Toronto: University of Toronto Press, 2014.

Russell, P.E. "*Don Quixote* as a Funny Book." *Modern Language Review* 64.2 (1969): 312–26.

Rutherford, John. *The Power of the Smile: Humour in Spanish Culture*. London: Francis Boutle Publishers, 2012.

Sabuco de Nantes Barrera, Oliva. *New Philosophy of Human Nature, Neither Known to Nor Attained by the Great Ancient Philosophers, Which Will Improve Human Life and Health*. Edited and Translated by Mary Ellen Waithe, María Colomer Vintró, and C. Ángel Zorita. Urbana: University of Illinois Press, 2007.

– *Nueva filosofía de la naturaleza del hombre y otros escritos.* Edited by Atilano Martínez Tomé. Madrid: Editora Nacional, 1981. Originally published 1587.

Said, Edward. *Orientalism.* London: Penguin Books, 2003.

Salazar, Eugenio de. *Textos náuticos: Navegación del alma por el discurso de todas las edades del hombre (1600); Carta al licenciado Miranda de Ron (1574).* Edited by José Ramón Carriazo Ruiz and Antonio Sánchez Jiménez. New York: IDEA, 2018.

Salillas, Rafael. *Un gran inspirador de Cervantes: El doctor Juan Huarte y su "Examen de ingenios."* Madrid: Librería general de Victoriano Suárez, 1905.

Sanches, Francisco. *That Nothing Is Known (Quod nihil scitur).* Edited by Elaine Limbrick and Douglas F.S. Thompson. Cambridge: Cambridge University Press, 1988.

Sánchez Jiménez, Antonio. "Cervantes y los pueblos del norte: Un acercamiento imagológico." *Atalanta* 6.1 (2018): 129–48.

Santa Cruz, Alonso de. *Sobre la melancolía: Diagnóstico y curación de los afectos melancólicos.* Edited by Juan Antonio Paniagua and Raúl Lavalle. Pamplona, Spain: Universidad de Navarra, 2005. Originally published ca. 1569.

Santos, Francisco. *Las tarascas de Madrid, y tribunal espantoso.* Valencia, Spain: Francisco Antonio de Burgos, 1694.

Santos de la Morena, Blanca. "El tema musulmán en la literatura de Cervantes: Turcos y renegados desde la intratextualidad." *Castilla: Estudios de Literatura* 7 (2016): 686–713.

Sbarbi, José María. *Diccionario de refranes, adagios, proverbios, modismos, locuciones y frases proverbiales de la lengua española.* 2 vols. Edited by Manuel José García. Madrid: Los sucesores de Hernando, 1922.

Scham, Michael. *Lector Ludens: The Representation of Games and Play in Cervantes.* Toronto: University of Toronto Press, 2014.

Schmauser, Caroline, and Walter Monika, eds. *¿"¡Bon compaño, jura Di!"? El encuentro de moros, judíos y cristianos en la obra cervantina.* Madrid: Iberoamericana; Frankfurt: Vervuert, 1998.

Schmidt, Rachel. *Critical Images: The Canonization of "Don Quixote" through Illustrated Editions of the Eighteenth Century.* Montreal: McGill-Queen's University Press, 1999.

Schmitz, Ryan. "Cervantes's Language of the Heart in the *Novelas ejemplares* and *Don Quijote*." *Cervantes: Bulletin of the Cervantes Society of America* 32.2 (2012): 171–95.

– "Sancho's Courtly Performance: *Discreción* and the Art of Conversation in the Ducal Palace Episodes of *Don Quijote II*." *MLN* 128.2 (2013): 445–55.

Scholberg, Kenneth R. *Sátira e invectiva en la España medieval.* Madrid: Gredos, 1971.

Schwartz, Lía. "Justo Lipsio en Quevedo: Neoestoicismo, política y sátira." In *Encuentros en Flandes,* edited by Werner Thomas and Robert A. Verdonk,

227–74. Leuven, Belgium: Leuven University Press / Presses Universitaires de Louvain, 2000.

Schwartz Lerner, Lía. *Metáfora y sátira en la obra de Quevedo*. Madrid: Taurus, 1983.

Sedgwick, Eve Kosofsky, and Adam Frank. "Shame in the Cybernetic Fold: Reading Silvan Tomkins." In *Touching Feeling: Affect, Pedagogy, Performativity*, 93–121. Durham, NC: Duke University Press, 2003.

Sère, Bénédicte, and Jörg Wettlaufer, eds. *Shame between Punishment and Penance / La honte entre peine et pénitance*. Florence: Sismel / Edizioni del Galluzzo, 2013.

Serrano Poncela, Segundo. "Estratos afectivos en Quevedo." In *El secreto de Melibea y otros ensayos*, 37–54. Madrid: Taurus, 1959.

Shuger, Dale. *Don Quixote in the Archives: Madness and Literature in Early Modern Spain*. Edinburgh: Edinburgh University Press, 2012.

Sidney, Philip. *The Miscellaneous Works of Sir Philip Sidney*. Edited by William Gray. Oxford: D.A. Talboys, 1829.

Sliwa, Krzysztof. *Documentos cervantinos: Nueva recopilación; lista e índices*. New York: Peter Lang, 2000.

Smith, Adam. *The Theory of Moral Sentiments*. New York: Prometheus, 2000.

Smith, Richard H. *The Joy of Pain: Schadenfreude and the Dark Side of Human Nature*. Oxford: Oxford University Press, 2013.

Socorro, Manuel. *El mar en la vida y las obras de Cervantes*. Santa Cruz de Tenerife, Spain: Goya, 1952.

Solomon, Robert C. *In Defense of Sentimentality*. Oxford: Oxford University Press, 2004.

Sommi, Leone de'. *Quattro dialoghi in materia di rappresentazioni sceniche*. Edited by Ferruccio Marotti. Milan: Il Polifilo, 1968.

Sosa, Antonio de. *Topografía e historia general de Argel*. Edited by Ignacio Bauer y Landauer. Madrid: Sociedad de Bibliófilos Españoles, 1929. Originally published under the name of its editor, Diego de Haedo, 1612.

Soufas, Teresa Scott. *Melancholy and the Secular Mind in Spanish Golden Age Literature*. Columbia: University of Missouri Press, 1990.

Spadaccini, Nicholas, and Jenaro Talens. *Through the Shattering Glass: Cervantes and the Self-Made World*. Minneapolis: University of Minnesota Press, 1993.

Spingarn, Joel Elias. *A History of Literary Criticism in the Renaissance*. New York: Macmillan, 1899.

Spinoza, Benedict de. *Ethics*. Translated by Edwin Curley. London: Penguin, 1996.

Spitzer, Leo. "Perspectivismo lingüístico en el *Quijote*." In *Lingüística e historia literaria*, 161–255. Madrid: Gredos, 1955.

Stearns, Peter N., and Carol Z. Stearns. "Emotionology: Clarifying the History of Emotions and Emotional Standards." *American Historical Review* 90 (1985): 813–36.

Steinberg, Philip E. "Of Other Seas: Metaphors and Materialities in Maritime Regions." *Atlantic Studies* 10.2 (2013): 156–69.

Storrs, Christopher. *The Resilience of the Spanish Monarchy, 1665–1700*. Oxford: Oxford University Press, 2006.

Strachan, John. "The Colonial Cosmology of Fernand Braudel." In *The French Colonial Mind*, edited by Martin Thomas, 72–95. Vol. 1 of *Mental Maps of Empire and Colonial Encounters*. Lincoln: University of Nebraska Press, 2011.

Stuart, Kathy. *Defiled Trades and Social Outcasts: Honor and Ritual Pollution in Early Modern Germany*. Cambridge: Cambridge University Press, 1999.

Subirats, Eduardo. *Américo Castro y la revisión de la memoria (El Islam en España)*. Madrid: Libertarias, 2003.

Subrahmanyam, Sanjay. "Connected Histories: Notes towards a Reconfiguration of Early Modern Eurasia." *Modern Asian Studies* 31.3 (1997): 735–62.

– "Holding the World in Balance: The Connected Histories of the Iberian Overseas Empires, 1500–1640." *American Historical Review* 112.5 (2007): 1359–85.

Sullivan, Henry W. *Grotesque Purgatory: A Study of Cervantes's "Don Quixote,"* Part II. University Park: Penn State University Press, 1996.

Syverson-Stork, Jill. *Theatrical Aspects of the Novel: A Study of "Don Quixote."* Valencia, Spain: Albatros Hispanófila, 1986.

Szameitat, Diana P., Kai Alter, André J. Szameitat, Chris J. Darwin, Dirk Wildgruber, Susanne Dietrich, and Annette Sterr. "Differentiation of Emotions in Laughter at the Behavioral Level." *Emotion* 9.3 (2009): 397–405.

Szpiech, Ryan. "The Convivencia Wars: Decoding Historiography's Polemic with Philology." In *A Sea of Languages: Rethinking the Arabic Role in Medieval Literary History*, edited by Suzanne Conklin Akbari and Karla Mallette, 135–61. Toronto: University of Toronto Press, 2013.

Tabak, Faruk. *The Waning of the Mediterranean, 1550–1870: A Geohistorical Approach*. Baltimore, MD: Johns Hopkins University Press, 2008.

Tasso, Torquato. *Discorsi del poema heroico*. Naples, Italy: Paolo Venturini, 1594.

Tausiet, María. "Agua en los ojos: El 'don de lágrimas' en la España moderna." In *Accidentes del alma: Las emociones en la Edad Moderna*, edited by María Tausiet and James S. Amelang, 167–202. Madrid: Abada, 2009.

Tausiet, María, and James S. Amelang, eds. *Accidentes del alma: Las emociones en la Edad Moderna*. Madrid: Abada, 2009.

Taylor, Bruce. "The Enemy Within and Without: An Anatomy of Fear on the Spanish Mediterranean Littoral." In *Fear in Early Modern Society*, edited by William G. Naphy and Penny Roberts, 78–99. Manchester, UK: Manchester University Press, 1997.

Taylor, Scott K. *Honor and Violence in Golden Age Spain*. New Haven, CT: Yale University Press, 2008.

Terdiman, Richard. "Can We Read the Book of Love?" *PMLA* 126.2 (2011): 472–82.

Teresa of Ávila, Saint. *The Life of Saint Teresa of Avila by Herself*. Translated by J.M. Cohen. Harmondsworth, UK: Penguin, 1987.

Thrift, Nigel. *Non-representational Theory: Space, Politics, Affect*. London: Routledge, 2008.

Tolan, John. "Forging New Paradigms: Toward a History of Islamo-Christian Civilization." In *A Sea of Languages: Rethinking the Arabic Role in Medieval Literary History*, edited by Suzanne Conklin Akbari and Karla Mallette, 62–70. Toronto: University of Toronto Press, 2013.

Tomkins, Silvan S. *Affect Imagery Consciousness: The Complete Edition*. New York: Springer, 2008.

– "The Varieties of Shame and Its Magnification." In *Exploring Affect: The Selected Writings of Silvan S. Tomkins*, edited by E. Virginia Demos, 397–410. Cambridge: Cambridge University Press, 1995.

Torrente Ballester, Gonzalo. *El "Quijote" como juego*. Madrid: Guadarrama, 1975.

Torres, Bénédicte. *Cuerpo y gesto en "El Quijote" de Cervantes*. Alcalá de Henares, Spain: Centro de Estudios Cervantinos, 2002.

Trías, Eugenio. *Tratado de la pasión*. Barcelona: Random House Mondadori, 2006.

Trigg, Stephanie. "'Shamed Be ... ': Historicizing Shame in Medieval and Early Modern Courtly Ritual." *Exemplaria: A Journal of Theory in Medieval and Renaissance Studies* 19.1 (2007): 67–89.

Trueblood, Alan S. "La risa en el *Quijote* y la risa de don Quijote." *Cervantes: Bulletin of the Cervantes Society of America* 4.1 (1984): 3–23.

Tueller, James B. "The Moriscos Who Stayed Behind or Returned: Post-1609." In *The Expulsion of the Moriscos from Spain: A Mediterranean Diaspora*, edited by Mercedes García-Arenal and Gerard Wiegers, 197–215. Leiden, Netherlands: Brill, 2014.

Turia, Ricardo de. *Apologético de las comedias españolas*. In *Preceptiva dramática española del renacimiento y el barroco*, edited by Federico Sánchez Escribano and Alberto Porqueras Mayo, 176–81. Madrid: Gredos, 1972. Originally published 1616.

Ugalde, Victoriano. "La risa de don Quijote." *Anales Cervantinos* 15 (1976): 157–70.

Urbina, Eduardo. "El concepto de *admiratio* y lo grotesco en el *Quijote*." *Cervantes: Bulletin of the Cervantes Society of America* 9.1 (1989): 17–33.

– dir. and ed. "Iconografía textual del *Quijote*." Co-edited by Fernando González Moreno. Proyecto Cervantes, Texas A&M University, 12 August

2013. Accessed 8 May 2014. http://cervantes.tamu.edu/V2/iconography/index.html.

– *El sin par Sancho Panza: Parodia y creación*. Barcelona: Anthropos, 1991.

Urbina, Eduardo, and Jesús G. Maestro, eds. *"Don Quixote" Illustrated: Textual Images and Visual Readings / Iconografía del "Quijote."* Pontevedra, Spain: Mirabel / Cátedra Cervantes, 2005.

Valensi, Lucette. "The Problem of Unbelief in Braudel's *Mediterranean.*" In *Braudel Revisited: The Mediterranean World, 1600–1800*, edited by Gabriel Piterberg, Teófilo F. Ruiz, and Geoffrey Symcox, 17–34. Toronto and Los Angeles: University of Toronto Press / UCLA Center for Seventeenth- and Eighteenth-Century Studies and the William Andrews Clark Memorial Library, 2010.

Velázquez, Andrés. *Libro de la melancholia*. Seville, Spain: Hernando Diaz, 1585.

Velázquez, Sonia. "'Pero, ¿quién eres tú?': The Radical Politics of a Common Language in *Los trabajos de Persiles y Sigismunda.*" In "'Si ya por atrevido no sale con las manos en la cabeza': El legado poético del *Persiles* cuatrocientos años después." Special issue, *eHumanista/Cervantes* 5 (2016): 518–33.

Verdon, Jean. *Travel in the Middle Ages*. Notre Dame, IN: University of Notre Dame Press, 2003.

Vincent, Bernard. "The Geography of the Morisco Expulsion: A Quantitative Study." In *The Expulsion of the Moriscos from Spain: A Mediterranean Diaspora*, edited by Mercedes García-Arenal and Gerard Wiegers, 19–36. Leiden, Netherlands: Brill, 2014.

Vives, Juan Luis. *The Passions of the Soul: The Third Book of "De Anima et Vita."* Edited by Carlos G. Noreña. Lewiston, NY: Edwin Mellen Press, 1990.

Wagschal, Steven. *The Literature of Jealousy in the Age of Cervantes*. Columbia: University of Missouri Press, 2006.

Wardropper, Bruce W. "*Don Quixote*: Story or History?" In *Cervantes' "Don Quixote": A Casebook*, edited by Roberto González Echevarría, 141–61. Oxford: Oxford University Press, 2005.

Warren, Michelle R., ed. "Philology and the Mirage of Time." Special issue, *postmedieval: A Journal of Medieval Cultural Studies* 5.4 (2014).

Watkins, John, and Kathryn L. Reyerson, eds. *Mediterranean Identities in the Premodern Era: Entrepôts, Islands, Empires*. Farnham, UK: Ashgate, 2014.

Whinnom, Keith. *The Spanish Sentimental Romance, 1440–1550: A Critical Bibliography*. London: Grant & Cutler, 1983.

Wikan, Unni. "Shame and Honour: A Contestable Pair." *Man* 19.4 (1984): 635–52.

Williams, Raymond. *Marxism and Literature*. Oxford: Oxford University Press, 1997.

Willis, Ika. "Philology, or the Art of Befriending the Text." *postmedieval: A Journal of Medieval Cultural Studies* 5.4 (2014): 486–501.

Wilson, Diana de Armas. *Allegories of Love: Cervantes's "Persiles and Sigismunda."* Princeton, NJ: Princeton University Press, 1991.
– "Cervantes and the Indies." *Philosophy and Literature* 24 (2000): 364–76.
– "'De gracia estraña': Cervantes, Ercilla y el Nuevo Mundo." In *En un lugar de la Mancha: Estudios cervantinos en honor de Manuel Durán*, edited by Georgina Dopico Black and Roberto González Echevarría, 37–55. Salamanca, Spain: Almar, 1999.
– "'Unreason's Reason': Cervantes at the Frontiers of Difference." *Philosophy and Literature* 16 (1992): 49–67.
Wimsatt, W.K., and Monroe Beardsley. "The Affective Fallacy." *Sewanee Review* 57.1 (1949): 31–55.
Wittgenstein, Ludwig. *Philosophical Investigations*. Translated by G.E.M. Anscombe. Oxford: Basil Blackwell, 1986.
Wood, James. *The Irresponsible Self: On Laughter and the Novel*. New York: Farrar, Straus & Giroux, 2004.
Zeno, Nicolò, Antonio Zeno, Caterino Zeno, and Niccolò Zeno. *Dello scoprimento dell'isole Frislanda, Eslanda, Engrovelanda, et Icaria*. Venice: F. Marcolini, 1558.
Zimic, Stanislav. "El *Persiles* como crítica de la novela bizantina." *Acta Neophilologica* 3 (1970): 49–64.
Zoppi, Federica. *Risa, sonrisa, ironía en el "Quijote": Burlas de acción y burlas de palabra*. Vigo, Spain: Editorial Academia del Hispanismo, 2016.

Index

Abulafia, David, 197–8n3, 211n43

Acevedo, Fernando de, 67–8, 218n1

admiratio/admiración, 56, 115, 134–5, 137, 143–4, 151, 157–9, 235nn33, 35, 239nn90, 91, 92; physiognomy of, 135, 144, 233n7. *See also* wonder

adversity, 42, 62, 161, 163, 193–4

adynaton, 178, 187

Aeschylus, 246n59

aesthetics, 145; characterological, 39; emotional, 60; empirical, 159; of humour, 119; literary, 13, 104; neuro-, 159; of penality, 85; politics and, 43, 49, 170–1, 191, 193; of the unexpected, 136–8. *See also* literature; music; painting

affect, 25–6. *See also* emotion(s); history of emotion(s); *and specific emotions*

affective fallacy, 7

"affective false consciousness," 168–9, 243n20

affective turn, 7, 26, 198n4, 198–9n14

affectivity. *See* Cervantine affectivity

Affektenlehre, 146

agelastoi, 126

Ahmed, Sara, 22, 23, 32, 43

Alberti, Leon Battista, 10, 173, 217n111

Alcalá Galán, Mercedes, 60, 173, 245n46

Alfonso X, *Siete Partidas*, 81, 221n48

Algiers, 16, 18, 204n68, 218n120, 243n18

Aljamía, 37

Allen, John J., 203n52, 226nn18, 21

alterity. *See* difference

El amante liberal (*The Generous Lover*) (Cervantes), 17, 40–1, 148, *149*, 160, 212n53, 234–5n30, 235n31, 241n109

amor studentium. *See* epistemophilia

les Amours, 169

anagnorisis, 137, 152, 154, 159, 162

anaphora, 182, 184, 187

Anderson, Benedict, 31

anonymity, 85, 162

apatheia, 9

apophatic discourse, 182

aporia(s), 173–6, 187, 248n97

aposiopesis, 179, 187

apostrophe, 40, 184–5, 187

Appadurai, Arjun, 59, 217n106

Aquinas, Thomas, 12, 20, 202n42

Arabian Nights, 42

Arabic, 37, 211n40

area studies, 31, 47

Arellano, Ignacio, 228n46

Ariès, Philippe, 9

71, 94, 96, 193, 223n68. *See also*
blood purity; Catholic Church
chronotopes, 61, 135, 137–8, 234n18
Cicero, 12, 112, 116, 230n87; *Tusculan
Disputations*, 202n42
"civilizing process," 8, 9, 77, 110,
227n42
Clamurro, William H., 240–1n108
Close, Anthony, 105, 106, 107, 108,
124, 226n27, 230n86
Coleridge, Samuel Taylor, 106, 240n105
Collins, Marsha S., 160, 237–8n75
El coloquio de los perros (*Colloquy of the
Dogs*) (Cervantes), 161, 231n94
Combet, Louis, 205n72
comedia, 12, 21, 60, 147, 148, 228n46;
honour in, 70, 74, 219n8; stage
directions and, 236–7n59;
suspension in, 236n53; textual
form of, 206n81. *See also* spectacle;
theatre
comedy, 99–127; definition of, 107;
"of forgiveness," 232n108. *See also*
humour; laughter; tragicomedy
conduct manuals. *See* behaviour
manuals
confusión/confuso, 72, 133, 134, 144,
145, 156–7
connectivity, 29, 30, 32, 43, 59
contact zones, 15, 69
conversos, 32, 69, 96, 188, 193, 194,
224n84. *See also* Jews
convivencia, 62, 208n4
cooke, miriam, 47
Corneille, Pierre, 158
Correas, Gonzalo, 9, 200n22
corsairs. *See* piracy
Cortijo Ocaña, Antonio, 17, 170,
243–4n24
Counter-reformation, 8, 166, 187
court (royal), 157; humour and,
111–12, 114, 115–18; parody of,

119, 125; rise of, 8, 9; treatises on,
115–16
courtly love, 14–15, 168–9, 203n51
Covarrubias, Sebastián de, 80,
144, 157, 197n1, 220n37, 225n16,
235nn35, 46, 236n56
criminality, 68–9, 221n46
Critchley, Simon, 230n87
crying, 10, 123, 126, 140, 183, 185,
200–1n28, 207n91, 231–2n102,
232n111. *See also* tears
Currie, Mark, 137, 138, 159, 160,
239n95
Curtius, Ernst Robert, 46

Dangler, Jean, 209n13
da Vinci, Leonardo, 201n35
de Armas, Frederick, 22
deferral, 166, 175, 187, 189, 247n71.
See also temporality
Deleuze, Gilles, 54
Della Casa, Giovanni, 102, 117, 119;
Galateo, 117, 229n76
Democritus, 126, 226n28
Derrida, Jacques, 138, 152, 187
Descartes, René, 12, 53, 108–9, 143
desire, 8, 14, 108, 134, 145, 155,
157, 166, 174–6, 180, 246n52; lack
(*manque*) and, 175
de' Sommi, Leone, 201–2n39
de Sousa, Ronald, 228n48
despair, 150, 156
deviation, 58–9, 174
Dewey, John, 20, 131, 205n73
Díaz Migoyo, Gonzalo, 225n14,
230n86
Diccionario de autoridades, 144, 155–6,
238n87
Dickie, Simon, 228n52
Diderot, Denis, 135, 233n9
Diego de Jesús Salablanca, 151–2,
237n69

Toronto Iberic

1 Anthony J. Cascardi, *Cervantes, Literature, and the Discourse of Politics*
2 Jessica A. Boon, *The Mystical Science of the Soul: Medieval Cognition in Bernardino de Laredo's Recollection Method*
3 Susan Byrne, *Law and History in Cervantes' "Don Quixote"*
4 Mary E. Barnard and Frederick A. de Armas (eds.), *Objects of Culture in the Literature of Imperial Spain*
5 Nil Santiáñez, *Topographies of Fascism: Habitus, Space, and Writing in Twentieth-Century Spain*
6 Nelson R. Orringer, *Lorca in Tune with Falla: Literary and Musical Interludes*
7 Ana M. Gómez-Bravo, *Textual Agency: Writing Culture and Social Networks in Fifteenth-Century Spain*
8 Javier Irigoyen-García, *The Spanish Arcadia: Sheep Herding, Pastoral Discourse, and Ethnicity in Early Modern Spain*
9 Stephanie Sieburth, *Survival Songs: Conchita Piquer's "Coplas" and Franco's Regime of Terror*
10 Christine Arkinstall, *Spanish Female Writers and the Freethinking Press, 1879–1926*
11 Margaret E. Boyle, *Unruly Women: Performance, Penitence, and Punishment in Early Modern Spain*
12 Evelina Gužauskytė, *Christopher Columbus's Naming in the* diarios *of the Four Voyages (1492–1504): A Discourse of Negotiation*

Milton Keynes UK
Ingram Content Group UK Ltd.
UKHW011255210424
441408UK00003B/76/J